MW01196336

This book is a labor of love—for the Scriptures, for readers, for learning, for teaching, and for God himself. The author takes up each topic in a wise, thorough, probing, and reverent manner. Readers will gain fresh insight into the history of New Testament times, the convictions of the biblical writers, and the implications of the age-old yet ever new Christian message for today. Readers will also glimpse the work of major New Testament scholars as their research has unfolded over recent decades. This is an excellent intermediate survey for college students, as well as for laypersons eager to move to new levels of biblical understanding.

Robert W. Yarbrough

Julius Scott's *New Testament Themes* is in fact a theology of the New Testament helpfully pitched at the level of the college student and general reader rather than the professional theologian and affords a detailed but readily readable and comprehensible topical exposition of New Testament teaching. Among its particular features I single out its careful treatment of the church's relation with and responsibility to society. Clearly and simply presented, it should attract a wide audience among Christians wanting a systematic guide to the main theological themes in the New Testament.

I. Howard Marshall

This book crowns the author's 50 years of Christian ministry. Evident here, as throughout his career, are Dr. Scott's love for the Triune God (see chapter 12); his passion for Holy Scripture (as a young pastor, he read through the Bible seven times in two years); his devotion to students under his care (the present work developed in the college classroom); and his conviction that Scripture must change people's lives (see chapters 5-7). As a friend of the author for more than 50 years, I know that he has sought both to *hear* and to *do* the Word; and that his obedient life has deepened his theological understanding (see Colossians 1:10).

Knox Chamblin

To

Three Special Persons
Who Took the Course,
"New Testament Literature and Interpretation"
With Me While They Were Students at
Wheaton College

MARY ELEANOR SCOTT SMITH
JULIA WYMOND SCOTT FOX
JAMES JULIUS SCOTT[3]

Love,
Daddy

To

GREGORY M. SMITH
RICK L. FOX
DESTINY J. SCOTT

Who bring marital joy to our children

Love,
Julius

And to grandchildren

ANNA, LILLY, JULIA, LEAH, and GRAYSON SMITH
and
REBECCA, HANNAH, and CALEB FOX

Who have given us reason to have confidence
in the rising generation

Love,
Papa and Grandmama

New Testament Theology

A new study of the thematic structure of the New Testament

J. Julius Scott, Jr.

MENTOR

New Testament work and citation are based on *Greek-English New Testament* . Stuttgart: Deutsche Bibelgesellschaft, 1981. The Greek text is that of Nestle-Aland, *Novum Testamentum Graece*, the 26th revised edition, 1979.

Unless otherwise stated Scripture quotations are from the Revised Standard Version, copyright 1952 [2nd edition, 1971] by the Division of Christian Education of the National Council of the Churches of Christ in the United States of America. Used by permission. All rights reserved.

LIST OF ABBREVIATIONS

cf.	Confer (compare)
ff.	Following
ESV	English Standard Version
KJV	King James Version
n.b.	Nota bene (note)
NIV	New International Version
NASB	New American Standard Bible
NRSV	New Revised Standard Version
RSV	Revised Standard Version

Copyright © J. Julius Scott, Jr. 2008

ISBN 978-1- 84550-256- 0

Published in 2008
in the
Mentor Imprint
by
Christian Focus Publications Ltd.,
Geanies House, Fearn, Ross-shire,
IV20 1TW, Scotland, UK

www.christianfocus.com

Cover design by Moose77.com
Printed and bound by WS Bookwell, Finland

Contents

Preface

I taught "New Testament Survey" at the undergraduate level from 1970-2000 in three different institutions. At the Wheaton (IL) College Graduate School "New Testament Theology" was my beloved responsibility from 1977-2000. I looked in vain for a survey of New Testament teachings somewhere between the elementary level and that of a specialized, technical New Testament theology. Such an intermediate study would serve as a capstone for the beginning survey course, and the initial assignment to help classes of graduate students to attain approximately the same level. Relatively early I began preparing outlines and then annotating them to fulfill these functions.

The initial draft of the present manuscript was completed during a 1993-1994 sabbatical leave, spent with my wife, Florence and our son's dog, Sydney. We lived in a remote cabin, out from Otto, in Macon County, North Carolina, in the beautiful southern Appalachian Mountains. That location provided an ideal setting for reflecting on the material I have studied and taught for decades.

Since that time my *New Testament Theology* has been duplicated several times for use in my classes at Wheaton College. Corrections and additions preceded each new duplication. During the spring of 1999 the entire manuscript was carefully and professionally edited by Carol Freeze Berry, then of the Distance Learning Department of Wheaton College. Since retiring in 2000 I have continued to "tweak" the content and form of the manuscript.

Use of this material in the classroom confirmed my conviction of the need for such a work and that *New Testament Theology* can get the job done. A number of teachers, pastors, and laypersons beyond the walls of Wheaton College and the shores of the U.S.A. have used *New Testament Theology*. A complete translation exists in the Bulgarian language and is being duplicated for use in that country. (By means of which I am not completely sure, this *New*

Testament Theology found its way into Bulgaria from Romania!).
Parts of the manuscript have been translated into Spanish for use in
student work.

I send out this little book on a big subject with the prayer that it
may be useful and helpful to twenty-first century pilgrims as they
strive to make progress in the way of the cross, toward the celestial
city.

Black Mountain, North Carolina
Summer 2007

Acknowledgements

The opportunity to acknowledge and thank friends and associates for their help and encouragement is one of the pleasures of completing a manuscript like this. There are many who deserve note and expressions of appreciation. Most must go unnamed; some cannot.

Julius and Laverne, Mamma and Daddy, knew little of formal Biblical studies but taught eloquently by living out Biblical teachings before their children. I am also fortunate to have a very supportive extended family. Their continuing interest has been of more help and encouragement than they can know. My brother, David W. Scott, of Atlanta, Georgia has been of immense help in assisting me to view things through the eyes of an informed layperson and has made important, appropriate suggestions. My sister and brother-in-law, Mary and Jack Ward of Atlanta, Georgia and my sister-in-law, Mary Elizabeth Swayze of Ridgeland, Mississippi, have been particularly faithful in asking about the progress of this project, encouraging the writer, and/or in praying for me as I worked on this manuscript. My late uncle, Clifford B. Schonert, a retired farmer of Bow Island, Alberta, Canada, read the manuscript in an earlier edition and shared it with friends there. His positive reaction and reports encouraged me by confirming the potential usefulness of this survey.

I have had three mentors. Professor William Childs Robinson of Columbia Theological Seminary, Decatur, GA, introduced me to a form of New Testament theology as he directed attention to the Biblical and historical meaning of important New Testament words. Dr. John R. Richardson, a godly pastor for whom I worked as student assistant, gave constant examples of the importance of careful scholarly work as the background for pulpit work. Dr. Richardson contributed greatly to my life in another area when he presided at the ceremony which united me in marriage to his daughter. Space would fail me to even try to express my gratitude for the influence of my doctoral supervisor, Professor F. F. Bruce, then Rylands

Professor of Biblical Criticism and Exegesis at the University of Manchester, England. His learning was unquestioned, as were his personal devotion and piety by all who knew him. His teaching and friendship, both in person and through his writings, continue to shape profoundly my thought and life. Robert A. Kraft is another from whose tutelage I benefited at the University of Manchester, 1961-63; our friendship has continued since he joined the faculty of the University of Pennsylvania.

The major direct impetus and influence behind the structure and content of this book are the students I have taught formally and informally, in classrooms, churches, and elsewhere for more than four decades. I wish I could thank each one personally and by name. There are, however, three who, although they have sat in my classrooms, I also taught in other ways and settings; their names are listed in first section of the dedication page.

Certain individuals have been of direct assistance, both in general and specifically, in the making of this book. At times I have turned to them for general advice and for precise answers. Professor Walter A. Elwell, with whom I taught for almost thirty years. The results of innumerable talks and discussions dot almost every chapter. In 1970 Professor Gordon D. Fee was a teaching colleague. He continues to be a friend. During our times together I have learned much and from him received support and encouragement.

Dr. Robert Yarbrough, now of Trinity Evangelical Divinity School, Deerfield, IL, is a former student and colleague, always a close friend. He has generously shared observations and insights about New Testament Theology so that both I as the teacher and the students who enrolled in my courses after him are much the richer. Robert D. Carlson, a supportive friend, an unusual Christian layman with a profound knowledge of the Greek New Testament, has frequently shared his insights. He has read the entire manuscript several times and contributed both in content and in correcting spelling and other technical mistakes.

Additional help and encouragement has come from other fiends, Dr. J. Knox Chamblin, retired Professor of New Testament at Reformed Theological Seminary, Dr. John N. Akers, former teaching colleague, now long time Special Assistant to Dr. Billy Graham, and Wheaton colleagues. Professors C Hassell Bullock and Gene Green, as well as Mr. Larry Fuhrer of Naperville, IL.

Since I my initial classes in "New Testament Theology" at Wheaton College Graduate School I have used *A Theology of the New Testament*[1] by George E. Ladd as primary textbook. Working with and through that volume for more than a decade and a half has placed me in his debt far more than I can adequately document. Also, I regard Rudolf Bultmann, Oscar Cullmann, C. H. Dodd, and Joachim Jeremias as the "giants" of creative New Testament studies in mid-twentieth century. I am indebted to each in different ways. I also learned from such scholars as A. M. Hunter, Ethelbert Stauffer, G. E. Kümmel, Leonhardt Goppelt, Earl E. Ellis, Leon Morris, Donald Guthrie, and I. Howard Marshall. The same could be said of many others whose legacy has also come primarily in written form. I appreciate the support and insights gleaned from those with whom I share basic commitments and outlook; at the same time I have often learned much from those with whom I disagree.

Most of the work on this book was completed while I was on sabbatical leave during the 1993-94 academic year graciously made available by Wheaton College. While writing in North Carolina I was exposed to the influence of an unusually gifted preacher, Rev. Tom Schmitt, then pastor of the Emmanuel Presbyterian Church of Franklin, NC. Tom has a high respect for and loyalty to the Biblical text. His expository method depends heavily upon Biblical concepts and teachings. Within this framework he explains the meaning of the text and then applies it pointedly and meaningfully to the needs of his congregation in the modern world. From this younger man, I, the elder professor, was spiritually blessed and learned much about the text and its contemporary application. He gave me fresh assurance of the importance and relevance of what I try to do in this book. The same is true of my present pastor, Rev. Dr. Richard White, of the Montreat Presbyterian Church, EPC, Montreat, NC.

[1] Rev. ed. (Grand Rapids, MI: Eerdmans, 1993).

Most influential and helpful has been an elect lady with broad theological training, both informal and formal. She, while studying for her MA in theology, was a students in several of my classes, including "New Testament Theology." She is a person with both profound spiritual and common sense. I have discussed virtually every issue in the book with her, she has made perceptive criticisms and suggestions, and given solid advice. Florence has been my first and major proofreader and editor. Nevertheless, her influence upon me did not begin during her graduate studies or with this project. Florence, is my constant colleague, collaborator, advisor, wife, and best friend. The day we moved into our sabbatical mountain retreat we celebrated the thirty-fifth anniversary of our marriage. It's her book too!

I have sought to keep footnotes and other non-biblical references to a minimum. I realize that some people are intimidated by the presence of even a few footnotes; to them I offer a word of advice, ignore them! The content of the book does not require reading them.

Introduction

In this book we assume readers have or are in process of obtaining some basic awareness of the New Testament, its structure, and contents. Such a 'survey-level' may involve an awareness of the overall sweep of the latter part of Biblical history, of major people and events, of the general content of each New Testament book, and how the books and other parts fit into the whole. Here we focus upon the major themes of the New Testament. This includes an introduction to the relationship between the various parts and how they join together to convey essential points of Biblical teaching.

Another element in Biblical studies involves some familiarity with the principles and procedures for understanding and interpreting the Bible, a book from another time and place, and applying it to the contemporary world and life in it. We will have to assume and utilize some of this data without much discussion of it. For those interested there is a variety of good introductory works on this subject.[1]

The Whole Counsel of God

The importance of this step is reflected by Paul as he spoke to the elder-overseers of the church of Ephesus who had come to meet him at the port of Miletus (Acts 20:17-38). Paul knew that in a very short time he would leave these people and that the separation would

[1] Hermeneutics is the name given this field of study; see R. C. Sproul, *Knowing Scripture* (Downers Grove, IL: InterVarsity Press, 1977); Gordon D. Fee and Douglas Stuart, *How to Read the Bible for All Its Worth*, 3rd ed. (Grand Rapids, MI: Zondervan, 2002); Henry A. Virkler, *Hermeneutics: Principles and Processes of Biblical Interpretation* (Grand Rapids, MI: Baker, 1981); Dan McCartney and Charles Clayton, *Let the Reader Understand: A Guide to Interpreting and Applying the Bible* (Phillipsburg, NJ: Presbyterian and Reformed, 1994); and Gerald Bray, *Biblical Interpretation: Past and Present* (Downers Grove, IL: InterVarsity, 1996). Knowledge of and careful use of responsible hermeneutical procedures can be of great help to the Bible reader. However, theories and techniques cannot replace the work of God's Spirit working along with his word.

be permanent – he and they, in this life, would see each other no more. During his third missionary journey, Paul had spent more than three years in Ephesus preaching, teaching, admonishing, caring. Hence, these were individuals in whom he had invested much: time, spiritual and physical labour, emotional energy, and prayer. And, he loved them; loved also those for whom they were responsible. What should he do? What must he say? It was necessary for him to encourage and provide a review of his work and teaching. Paul knew his words must challenge and provide help to those who must both grow in the faith and live in a hostile world. He also realized the necessity of providing a basis for Ephesian officers and all Christians to resist the 'fierce wolves' (Acts 20:29) he knew would come to ravage the flock.

Quickly Paul reviewed his time with them: he had, at his own expense, lived in Ephesus and both publicly and privately testified 'of repentance to God and of faith in our Lord Jesus Christ' (Acts 20:21). He admonished the elders to gently tend the Christian community committed to their care. Paul warned that some of the coming false teachers and other disruptive influences would arise even from the group before him. He commended them to God. They prayed, wept, and parted.

Two phrases in Paul's brief parting words (Acts 20:18-35) reveal much about his ministry to the church in Ephesus. He said 'I did not shrink from declaring to you anything that was profitable,... teaching you...' (vs. 20). Later he clarified this, 'I did not shrink from declaring to you the whole counsel of God' (vs. 27).

Paul did not have the luxury of picking and choosing what in the Christian message might be popular or appealing, what might meet those needs of which his hearers were aware at that moment, or might be uplifting and thrilling. Paul knew, as he expressed in his letter which bears the name of the Ephesian church, that they were 'not contending against flesh and blood, but against the principalities, against the powers, against the world rulers of this present darkness, and against the spiritual hosts of wickedness in heavenly places' (Eph 6:12).

Persons in such circumstances needed, not 'sound bites' of the gospel, but the whole thing. Now he could only remind them of the full scope of his teaching, of 'the whole counsel of God', with the hope and confidence that this reminder would lead to remembrance and review; that they would be able to live consistent Christian lives founded on the totality of God's revelation, and having done all, to stand. He commended the Ephesian elders to the grace of God. They wept and prayed together. They parted.

What was the content of that 'whole counsel of God'? We can discern some of its details from the words of Paul recorded in Acts and in his epistles. His Ephesian letter gives hints of what he must have covered. It begins with reference to God's determination and choice 'before the foundation of the world' (1:4). Human persons are 'dead in trespasses and sin' (2:1), but God's grace and salvation through faith was revealed and made available through Jesus Christ; it is to result in 'good works, which God prepared beforehand, that we should walk in them' (2:8-10). In Ephesians Paul insists that in Christ the barrier between Jews and Gentiles has been broken down (2:11–3:13). He calls his readers to know and love Christ, admonishes them 'to lead a life worthy' of their calling from God (4:1), 'no longer as the heathen[2] do' (4:17). He gives both general and specific instruction for so doing and for maintaining the relationships within the Christian community. Paul speaks of the officers of the church and its nature as the bride of Christ (5:23). He calls for Christians of all social, economic, and other levels to 'Be subject to one another out of reverence for Christ' (5:21). All believers must be watchful and prepared because they live in a hostile environment and are engaged in a spiritual battle (6:10-18). In Ephesians Paul speaks also of the presence and work of the Holy Spirit, the present seal for the day of redemption (4:30) and the future promised inheritance (1:14). Hence, in this epistle 'the whole counsel of God' covers the person and work of God from eternity past into eternity future, from before creation to beyond the end of life, the world, and history as we now know them.

In short, 'the whole counsel of God' appears to contain an

---

[2] The RSV and many other modern translations say 'no longer as the Gentiles do.' The Greek word can be translated either 'Gentiles' or 'heathen.'

overview of the main content and topics of information about God, his work, and his will. We should also assume that, as a part of 'the whole counsel', Paul and other Christian leaders built upon this foundation a superstructure containing far more than a 'general survey' of the things concerning God.

Contemporary Christians are in equal need of 'the whole counsel of God'. But this book deals with only a part of the Christian Scriptures, the New Testament, which is only the last one third of the whole Bible. This leads to some important questions. Can we really seek the whole counsel of God by limiting ourselves only to themes of the New Testament? Certainly not! Then why should I write and you read this book? There are three parts to the answer. First, the New Testament is a part of the whole; I hope readers will seek an understanding of Old Testament themes as well, but an introduction to New Testament themes can be a good start. Second, although I cannot give a complete survey of the Old Testament, in dealing with New Testament themes we have to make frequent reference to the Old Testament; this book cannot ignore what precedes the New Testament in the Old. Third, the New Testament portrays the climax and the coming end of the drama of God's revelation and work begun in the Old Testament. Here we find the major themes most fully developed and brought to their conclusion.[3]

Were this a formal work on New Testament theology there are numerous technical questions with which we would have to deal.

---

[3]There are some helpful books which seek to present New Testament themes by concentrating on their Old Testament phase and then their full development in the New Testament. Particularly helpful to me are two by my teacher and mentor, the late Professor F. F. Bruce, *The New Testament Development of Old Testament Themes* (Grand Rapids, MI: Eerdmans, 1968) and *The Time is Fulfilled: Five Aspects of the Fulfillment of the Old Testament in the New* (Grand Rapids, MI: Eerdmans, 1978). Another British scholar, C. H. Dodd, wrote an excellent little pamphlet on the subject, *The Old Testament in the New* (Philadelphia: Fortress, 1952). Another brief, but fairly technical book on the subject by Professor Dodd is *According to the Scriptures: The Sub-Structure of New Testament Theology* (Digswell Place, England: James Nisset and Co., 1952). I have not used this as my primary approach because I have little to add to what these men have already ably said.

Most of the details of such matters we must leave to others.[4] We provide a brief description of three issues in the appendix to this introduction.

Nevertheless, the 'Introduction' is the place where a writer maps out his or her program and assumptions. Consequently, there are a number of items upon which we must touch to help orient the reader and help her or him to see from where this writer is coming.

Theology and Theologies

The word 'theology' scares a lot of people. It shouldn't because, coming from two words meaning 'God' and 'word', its definition is 'words about God' or simply 'teachings about God'. A more traditional explanation is that theology is the science (organized study) of God, the universe, and particularly human beings in it, and their relationship. Many contemporary scholars suggest other definitions; for example, that the primary concern of theology should be the quest for universal ethical principles or the individual's search for meaning or true selfhood. We'll use the traditional definition as a working hypothesis.

Theology as a field of study is divided into at least four sub-divisions: *historical theology* – the study of what has been believed in the successive periods of the history of the church; *practical theology* – the investigation of both the theory and methods for practising, proclaiming, and teaching the faith; and *systematic* and *Biblical theology*. These last two require more explanation. The systematic theologian consciously and openly seeks some pattern for organizing material other than that found or implied in the Bible, such as one adapted from philosophy or the social sciences. The Biblical theologian seeks for one that in some way arises from the Scriptures and seeks to interpret it within its original historical-cultural setting. We will look briefly at the issue of 'Biblical Theology and

---

[4]Gerhard Hasel, *The New Testament Theology: Basic Issues in the Current Debate* (Grand Rapids, MI: Eerdmans, 1978); George Eldon Ladd, *A Theology of the New Testament* (Grand Rapids MI: Eerdmans, 1993), 20-28; and Donald Guthrie, *New Testament Theology* (Downers Grove, IL: InterVarsity Press, 1981), 21-74.

History' in the appendix to this introduction.

Some Biblical theologians like to claim they are avoiding forcing the Biblical data into an artificial outline or system. Nevertheless, we must acknowledge that to some extent any organization used will be one imported to the New Testament.

The Nature of the Bible and Its Message

These debates lead to the question of the nature of the Bible and how it presents its message. This is not the place to discuss the options and issues that surround this subject. Rather, we here state in general terms the assumptions upon which this book proceeds. The Bible is the inspired word of God. 'Inspiration,' when related to the Bible, is from the Greek word which means literally 'God-breathed.'[5] This is in sharp contrast to the modern usage in which we may speak of an athlete or actor giving an 'inspired' performance or the 'inspiration' of an artist. In such instances 'inspiration' means the coming together of natural talent and training in a special circumstance which produces something beyond normal expectation; nevertheless, it is still a purely human activity. The inspiration of Scripture means that the message originates with God and he is active in its communication. But there is also a human dimension; the original writers were human beings. They used natural writing materials, human languages, and reflect the times and cultures of their own days and surroundings. Indeed their own personalities shine through the finished product.

How do the divine and human elements work together? They work together in a way far more intimate than would be involved if the writers were merely human typewriters or stenographers taking dictation. God selected the men[6] whose backgrounds and personalities would express that which he desired; he 'breathed' (2 Tim 3:16) his message into them, and remained active in the writing process, superintended the project (2 Peter 1:21 says 'being carried by the Holy Spirit') to assure its authority and accuracy.

---

[5]*Theopneustos*, as in 2 Timothy 3:16, usually translated 'inspiration'; it might also be translated something like 'God-spirited.'

[6]Some manuscripts say 'holy men of God' (2 Pet 1:21).

But, it might be observed that the Bible does not look like a theology book, or, for the most part, even a book about morals and ethics. How does this 'word about God' come through in it? *The Bible is not so much concerned to reveal concepts, principles, and rules as to reveal a person, God.* It does so primarily by showing him at work and in relation to the universe and human beings. There are a couple of important assumptions at work: first, that God does what he does because of who he is; we come to know him by seeing him in action. Second, the moral and spiritual principles of the universe are simply reflections or extensions of God's nature. A thing is true or false, good or bad, because of God's attitude toward it. The person who desires to live pleasingly before God must first know him and then conform her/his will, attitudes, and actions to accord with the person of God. The Bible, then, is God's record of his own presentation of himself and his works. But there is more. The Bible also shows varying human reactions to God and the consequences of those reactions. In addition it provides interpretations of God and his will; it shows how God's will was applied and worked out in specific situations and circumstances.

But for at least two reasons this is more than simply an academic exercise. First, Christians are convinced that the activity of the Holy Spirit continues his work with the Scriptures as he guides the interpretation and application of them in succeeding generations of believers.[7] Second, Biblical studies has a practical as well as a theoretical side. A major task of the contemporary interpreter is, in dependence upon the Holy Spirit, to identify those moral and spiritual principles inherent in the nature of God, which were applied to individuals and situations in the historical and cultural situation of Biblical times. Since the Bible's words about God are for all times and places, the Biblical student must also seek to apply these same moral and spiritual principles, appropriately, to the situations of modern times, cultures, and places as well.

---

[7]Of course this does not mean that each and every interpretation of Scripture by one claiming the guidance of the Holy Spirit is automatically correct. Individuals and the Church must be aware of the proper ways for 'handling accurately the word of truth' (2 Tim 2:15, NASB).

The ultimate purpose of the Bible is to reveal God and to call humans into relationship with him. The careful study of the Bible involved in theology, Biblical history and other forms, misses its own mark if it does not bring one to know God better and into a proper relationship with him.

Organization and Structure

Traditional books on New Testament theology are usually organized along the lines of either the analytic or the thematic (synthetic) approach. The former investigates the various units (such as the Synoptic Gospels, the writings of John, those of Paul, and other divisions) to determine the teachings and emphases of each. Synthetic structure looks for common themes and the distinct way they are dealt with throughout the New Testament.

For this brief survey we will focus more upon the 'whole counsel of God' than its parts and the variety within its presentation in the New Testament. It seems to me that either consciously or subconsciously, there were in the minds of the New Testament writers a set of basic questions with which they dealt in one way or another. These questions arise naturally to many readers of the New Testament and the New Testament documents provide answers for them. The questions are:

1) Who is Jesus?
2) What Must I Do to be Saved?
3) How Should the Christian Live?
4) What is the Church?
5) What is the Church's Relation to Society?
6) How Shall it End? and
7) What Does the New Testament Teach us About God?

The first two questions actually appear in the New Testament. The question of the identity of Jesus is raised in a number of settings. For example, after he calmed a storm the disciples 'said to one another, "Who then is this, that even wind and sea obey him?" ' (Mark 4:41); in response to some claims by Jesus, the Jews queried, 'Who do you claim to be?' (John 8:53). On another occasion Jesus himself asked, 'Who do you say that I am?' (Mark 8:29). The wording of our second question is that of the jailor of Philippi (Acts 16:31). The other questions are implied, inherent questions whose answers call for the types of things the writers seek to clarify for their readers. The answers for the questions may be expressed in different ways in different situations. However put, these answers comprise the basic message of the New Testament, the central New Testament themes, and the foundational elements of New Testament teaching.

Essentially by organizing the discussion around these questions we have adopted something of a thematic (synthetic) structure[8] but have not followed that method consistently. Rather we have looked to the New Testament itself for help in determining structure. In dealing with some of the usually implied questions and answers the structure of our presentation shows concern for historical development and for the distinctive aspects of individual groupings of writings (an analytic approach). Our consideration of Jesus takes this form. Other theme-answers seem to be best presented within an outline which brings together the sum total of the relevant data from each of the various parts of the New Testament but with some attention to the identity and uniqueness of the particular parts from which the themes arise. Such themes as the Christian life and the church fit this pattern. The chapter on 'The End' shows a combination of both methods in which the focus is first upon the parts, then the whole picture. The 'word study method,' which identifies important terms and focuses on their shades of meaning and relation to similar

---

[8]The thematic or synthetic approach is less often used in studies of New Testament theology than the analytic structure. Donald Guthrie, in his massive study *New Testament Theology* (Downers Grove, IL: InterVarsity Press, 1981), uses a more-or-less synthetic approach. George Ladd, whose organization is analytic, notes that A. M. Hunter 'expressed the desire that all future textbooks in New Testament theology be written from the synthetic rather than the analytic point of view' (George E. Ladd, *The Message of the New Testament* (1944), 121, cited by Ladd in *A Theology of the New Testament*, 28). See also I. Howard Marshall, *New Testament Theology. Many Witnesses, One Gospel* (Downers Grove, IL: InterVarsity, 2004) and Frank Thielman, *Theology of the New Testament: A Canonical and Synthetic Approach* (Grand Rapids: Zondervan, 2005).

terms, has been both much used and maligned by others. It has its place and is evident throughout our study.

The first chapter introduces 'auxiliary' areas of New Testament studies which, I hope, will be particularly influential. It mentions some of the essential features of the world and cultures in which the New Testament writers and their readers lived. Much of the content of the New Testament is shaped to address meaningfully the issues and needs of that particular time and those societies. New Testament studies, I am convinced, must pay careful attention to the issues of the original setting of the New Testament for they are the setting for the piece of literature we are studying.[9] It is only as we familiarize ourselves with their world that we may learn the basic principles, the theological truths, upon which the writers operated. We may then seek to apply those same truths to the different conditions in our world. In short, we must ask what these Biblical teachings meant to them, the original recipients, before asking what they mean to and for us.

There are yet two other features of organization which I must explain. Why I have chosen to deal with the New Testament's teachings about God last rather than first. The New Testament writers begin by assuming the existence of God and of some knowledge of him on the basis of Old Testament revelation. The distinctive elements in their presentation of God are contained in and permeate their writings as a whole. There is a sense that as we look at each of the New Testament themes we are also seeing at least their implied contribution to the whole of the New Testament's portrayal of God. Hence, it seems appropriate to let our focus upon God serve as the grand climax of what we say about his self-revelation and work in the successive parts of the New Testament teachings which we summarize.

Secondly, why does the table of contents show no study of the Holy Spirit? Some will argue for the need for specific attention upon

---

[9]It is not a coincidence that the initial draft of this study was made immediately after I completed *Customs and Controversies: Intertestamental Jewish Backgrounds of Christianity* (Grand Rapids, MI: Baker, 1995). In the second and subsequent printings (2000 ff), the title of the book changed to *Jewish Backgrounds of the New Testament*.

the person and work of the Holy Spirit in our time. I agree but have attempted to deal with Him in a way similar to that in which He is presented in Scripture itself. The Holy Spirit is the one person of the Godhead whose work is not to call attention to Himself. Jesus said of the Spirit, 'He will not speak on his own, but will speak whatever he hears, and he will declare to you the things that are to come. He will glorify me, because he will take what is mine and declare it to you' (John 16:13-15). For this reason I have dealt with the specific parts of the work of the Holy Spirit and his nature in appropriate chapters. Thus we see his work in salvation, in the Christian life, in the church, and in our discussion of God.

Some will raise eyebrows at my failure to make more use of contemporary critical methodologies and tools. At times the influence of these will be detected in my background. There is, of course, much help and many insights that could be derived from a more obvious and consistent use of them. There are also dangers and even those most devoted to critical methodologies and studies are frequently in disagreement about much associated with their practice and conclusions. Keeping in mind the audience I envision, I have chosen to focus primarily upon the surface meaning of the text.

Greek, but Not All

Greek was the language in which the New Testament was written. The derogatory phrase, 'It's all Greek to me,' has scared many away from anything that even uses the name of the feared language. It doesn't need to be that way. Even if New Testament Greek is an unfamiliar world to you, please don't be intimidated. I'll try to help you.

As is true in all languages, Greek carries some fine points of meaning that are difficult if not impossible to translate into other languages. It does not seem unreasonable to assume that 'intermediate-level' Bible students could be open to exploration of some fine points of meaning which can be conveyed only with reference to the language in which the New Testament was originally written. And so I will occasionally refer to Greek to clarify more precisely what the writer intended (our use of Greek may also encourage some readers to seek to learn more of the language). When I must use a Greek word I will transliterate it into English letters, and indicate its meaning. I will try to explain simply the implications of Greek grammatical constructions to which I refer.

Let's now mention two or three of the more important features of the Greek language that differ from English. English verb tenses primarily indicate time – past, present, or future. In the Greek tenses time, if present at all, is of only secondary significance. Greek verb tenses primarily denote the kind of action the writer has in mind. Some tenses indicate action that is continuing, going on as he or she writes or speaks. Some tenses envision action which was in process, reached its conclusion, and now its results continue. Finally, one Greek tense, the aorist, views action as a whole; the action may occur over a long period of time, but the writer or speaker views it at a glance, in its entirety.

Another feature of Greek is that the construction of a conditional sentence indicates the degree of certainty with which the writer or speaker expects the condition to be fulfilled. Also, questions may be asked in a way that shows whether a positive or negative answer is expected.

One more note about Greek. The Greek word usually translated *Christ* means *anointed*. In the ancient Hebrew world a leader (priest, king, or prophet) was inducted or inaugurated into office by being anointed. Usually this meant that in the proper ceremonial setting oil was poured on the person's head. In some cases one was *anointed* by the Spirit of the Lord (The Holy Spirit) coming upon him. In either case after being anointed the individual was an *anointed one*, a recognized leader. In the Hebrew language the word for *anoint* is the one from which comes the word *Messiah*.

In the world of the Greek New Testament *Christso* usually meant *Messiah*, a title, in those parts where the Jewish influence is strong. In parts written to or about the Gentile world *Christso* was usually a proper name, Christ, Jesus Christ, or Christ Jesus. The context of the passage helps determine whether *Christso* should be translated *Messiah* or *Christ*. When a definite article appears before the word it should usually be translated *the Messiah*. *The Christ* probably means *the Messiah*. Some of the newer translations, such as the *New Revised Standard Version* and *Today's New International Version,* frequently, but not always, translate *the Christ* as *the Messiah*.

In the New Testament world *the Messiah* was understood in a number of different ways. The title always referred to *The Greatest Leader*. Most often it was thought to refer to the coming great king from David's family, the one who would bring the Hebrew nation back to her position of power, wealth, and prominence. There were numerous other ideas about the person and work of Messiah. In his teachings Jesus sought to correct and redefine the meaning of the title and to present himself as *The Messiah*, as he understood the title.

There are other distinctive features of the Greek language that are helpful to know as we study the New Testament. Hence, I'll introduce other features as needed.

A Personal Word Before We Continue

As I come to the close of this work (writers usually write introductions last – we're an odd lot!) I must state some personal goals and intentions and confess some failures. First, as does every writer, I have come to this study with a complex set of experiences, commitments, opinions, and predispositions. I have done my best to set these aside and let the New Testament text speak its own message. Of course I have failed; no one can erase all that has gone before. But I have tried. Some who have known me may be tempted to say, 'Oh, I didn't know he thought that!' There's a good chance I didn't before I began this work. I hope and pray that I will continue to grow and to change when the better understandings of the text through the guidance of the Spirit so indicate.

Second, I openly acknowledge again that I have not presented 'the whole counsel of God', even all of that part contained in the New Testament. My aim and objectives are limited in scope; there are areas and issues I have omitted. I have striven for simplicity and brevity. I have sought to provide an introduction to the second step of Biblical study, that toward attaining understanding of the entirety of God's counsel. Hopefully this effort will both assist and lead to continuing understanding and growth.

As I look back over these pages I am reminded of the words of A. M. Hunter in the preface to one of his books.

> I have no hope of pleasing the pundits who will give my little book a superior smile and reach for Bultmann or Stauffer. But it may help the hard-working parson who wants to keep up to date theologically, and the theological student in our church colleges may value a short and simple Introduction to a very big subject. Is not this one of the things that Divinity professors like myself are for?[10]

I have no desire or even thought of replacing Professor Hunter's 'little book'. It is my hope and prayer that mine may some day, somewhere, give the kind of help to a pilgrim in progress as his gave to me.

Third, I realize I have written as a labour of both conviction and love. I am convinced, primarily by my own experience, that today's Christians desperately need much greater awareness of 'the whole counsel of God'. Too often, even those who have been in the faith for many years have only bits and pieces. We all need the whole counsel, the whole platform of Christianity, to serve as a firm foundation upon which to meet the challenges of daily life and the onslaughts of the enemy.

The writing of this book has been a labour of love. Love, first of all, for Jesus Christ, the subject of the New Testament, love and gratitude for salvation by grace which God made available through him, love for the life into which Christians have been called, love for the church, and love for God's word. I do not claim neutrality. This book is by a committed Christian primarily for other Christians and those who want to know more about the New Testament.

Finally, anyone speaking or writing from such a stance as mine, recognizing human limitations and frailties, cannot help but ask her

---

[10]A. M. Hunter, *Introducing New Testament Theology* (London: SCM, 1957), 8.

or himself, 'Have I got it right? Am I presenting the truth?' I have done my best to do so. Where I have not, I pray that God will prevent damage. I pray that through this brief survey of 'the whole counsel of God' as revealed in the New Testament, unbelievers will be confronted with Jesus who loves them, my fellow believers will be informed and strengthened, and, above all, that God will be glorified.

Added Notes: Some Related Introductory Issues

Technical Biblical theologians confront a number of important issues. One category of such asks about matters related to the author, the audience, place and time of writing, sources of information, literary forms, purpose, point of view, and similar concerns of each literary unit under consideration. A second asks such questions as: Is it possible to write a theology of the New Testament? Is there sufficient information? Are New Testament teachings primarily characterized by unity or diversity? Are they authoritative and normative for all times and places or do they merely describe the beliefs of certain peoples in particular times and places?

Finally, there are at least three matters which have to do more with one's presuppositions and basic assumptions. These include (1) Biblical Theology and History, (2) Ideas about the Nature of Religion, and (3) Supernaturalism and Naturalism. These lie more properly within the realm of studies with more philosophical-theological orientations than Biblical studies but they have significant impact upon such studies. What follows is a very brief introduction to these three.

Biblical Theology and History

History is very important to the Biblical theologian. There is, however, disagreement about the nature of history in general and about what Biblical history relates. Some theologians may assume that it reports the actual events, thoughts, people, and institutions of the time and place of which the author writes. Others believe that some history, Biblical history in particular, is really a presentation of the situations, conditions, and concerns of the writer and his audience in their own setting. Thus, it is suggested, the writer used his account of the past as a framework within which to relate and wrestle with the issues of his own day or to present his own ideas. This record may or may not accurately relate what actually happened. The author, these students believe, selected, organized, and emphasized the purported record of the past to reflect his own day; the author even may have invented persons, events, statements, and situations. All this is of little consequence because the purpose of history, according to this perspective, is not to describe that which was in the writer's past but in the present. Finally, history may be looked upon as having virtually no concern for past events, institutions, ideas, and the like, but rather with the experiences of the writer and those about him through which he came into experiences of meaningful existence or true being, authentic selfhood. This view, stimulated by contemporary relativistic philosophical outlooks, denies that any truth can be absolute and eternal;[11] it assumes only that history has relevance which has value for the individual in the present.

These differences of opinion about Biblical history affect the assumptions and methodologies used in studying it. Some, usually the more 'liberal' in their orientations, argue that the Bible is 'just another human book' which must be studied with the same assumptions and tools used in the investigation of any other book. More traditional Biblical students argue that the presence of the divine activity in the production, nature, and message of the Bible require that it be handled in special ways.

These debates are closely related to the two differing sets of presuppositions which underlie the conflicts between Biblical and theological scholars. To these we must now turn.

Ideas About the Nature of Religion
There are at least three major differences of opinions about the nature of religion itself, especially of Christianity. The traditional view assumes that Christianity *primarily* involves God's actions and

---

[11]One such example is Existentialism which asserts that each person must find what is true and worthwhile for him or herself at a particular time and place and thereby become an authentic individual.

human response. Human sin brought separation from God, guilt, and affected adversely the essential make-up or nature of persons and their environment, leaving them helpless. Therefore God, out of love for his created beings, took the initiative and provided the way of salvation through Jesus Christ, making possible forgiveness from sin, a new nature, and a right relationship and fellowship with himself. Humans are to respond by accepting this provision by faith.

The so-called 'old Liberal' (or 'Modernist') view held that Christianity *primarily* involves human efforts for self-improvement or development. All people are basically good but need to extend further and use the moral and spiritual faculties already present to enable them to attain complete God-likeness. The Bible provides the principles, ideals, guidelines, and examples humans needed to improve themselves. Much contemporary non-evangelical Christianity, as that exemplified above in our reference to Bultmann (1884-1974), believed religion primarily involves human attainment of existential self-awareness, of true selfhood. He said Christianity is the 'conceptual presentation of man's existence as an existence determined by God.'[12] Scripture affirms the possibility of experiences of authentic being, tells of others who have sought and found it, and calls us to the type of freedom, decision, and experiences which lead to it.

Postmodernism

By the end of the twentieth and beginning of the twenty-first centuries a new outlook, *Postmodernism*, had supplanted Existentialism as the philosophical *mode-of-the-day* in many circles. Its newness and widespread influence requires a bit more explanation than the description given previous *schools of thought*.

Postmodernism is committed to absolute relativism and so rejects any notion of objective or universal truth. Furthermore, it operates with a pluralism that entertains the possibility that many "truths" may be correct, even if they are contradictory. As might be expected,

---

[12]R. Bultmann (1925), 'The Problem of Theological Exegesis of the New Testament,' reprinted in *The Beginnings of Dialectic Theology*, James M. Robinson, ed., (Richmond, VA: Knox, 1968), 236-37.

such an approach is hard to define or describe. It can affect virtually all academic areas. Although suspicious of it, some liberal or conservative theological groups[13] are attracted[14] to parts of Postmodernism.

At first glance it is evident that Postmodernism differs from Existentialism in that it focuses upon the community rather than the individual for responses to significant questions and issues. Often it looks to the process of developing interpersonal relations between diverse members of a group for significant guidance in confronting concerns.[15]

There is no specific Postmodern view of the Bible or statement of theology. Christianity is *one* of many paradigms of the human-divine relationship. Biblical authority is usually viewed as relative at best. It is one of the sources for opinions brought to the discussion. The Bible must be interpreted like any other document (with approaches such as structuralism and deconstructionism). Postmodernism lays special concern for the protection of the rights of the disadvantaged and oppressed of society. It acknowledges no ultimate (absolute) moral or ethical standards.

Supernaturalism and Naturalism
Closely related to disagreements about the nature of history, which we previously noted, are those regarding the existence and nature of God (or gods), spiritual beings, and the possibility of supernatural occurrences within human experience. Until about the eighteenth century there was general agreement that divine or spiritual beings or forces could and did intervene in history. Since then, with the

---

[13]Cf, Millard J. Erickson, *Postmodermizing the Faith. Evangelical Responses to the Challenge of Postmodernism* (Grand Rapids: Baker, 1998).

[14]Steven Connor, ed. *The Cambridge Companion to Postmodernism* (Cambridge/New York, The Cambridge University Press, 2004).

[15]The 2006 General Assembly of the APresbyterian Church in the United States of America@ adopted an amended report on APeace, Unity, and Purity of the Church.@ The initial pages describe the process used by the Task Force which drew up the report. It illustrates how a group with different backgrounds and views might work within a Postmodern framework.

birth of the intellectual movement called 'The Enlightenment', has come an increase in the notion that whatever occurs does so on the basis of natural forces inherent within the universe – that supernatural occurrences cannot and do not happen. Thus, those holding anti-supernaturalistic or naturalistic presuppositions assume that divine revelation, miracles, resurrections, divine judgments, supernatural conversions, and the end of history and the world are impossible and are outdated ways of thinking. Religion is rather to be understood and described as a perfectly natural part of the experience of some societies and individuals; it conforms to the same patterns of origin, development, and change present in other intellectual, philosophical, sociological, psychological, or artistic phenomena. It is to be studied 'scientifically,' that is objectively, with human reason and scientific methods, and without assuming or admitting the possibility of supernatural occurrences.

What does all this mean in the study of Biblical theology? Liberal scholars assume that Biblical history is simply the record of natural, human experiences. The claims that divine revelations and miracles happened are to be disregarded or explained in modern, scientific terms which show them to be natural occurrences. Once shorn of these, the Biblical record may be studied as descriptions of the teachings and actions of great religious thinkers of the past, persons whose concerns for moral goodness, justice, and love should be a pattern for all generations. Some believed the New Testament describes religion as the human spirit becoming conscious of itself through dialectical conflicts[16] or as a pure spiritual-ethical phenomenon which resulted from the influence of religious personality and its development within the Christian community.[17] The 'History of Religions School'[18] suggested that Christianity grew naturalistically, following an evolutionary pattern, in which later forms of religious thought and life developed (by borrowing and adaptation) from those

---

[16]E.g., F. C. Baur (1792–1860).

[17]E.g., Albrecht Ritschl (1822–1889) and Adolf Harnack (1851–1930).

[18]E.g., Richard Reitzenstein (1861–1931), Wilhelm Bousset (1865–1920), and Wilhelm Wrede (1859–1906).

of earlier periods or from other contemporary religions. For this group Biblical theology is concerned solely to describe religion within its environment at particular points in its history.

In the twentieth century existential outlooks deprecate history in an objective sense. Rudolf Bultmann and his followers regard the New Testament as a record of the early church's attainment of selfhood through Jesus. This record is in imprecise, unscientific language which includes interpreted (even 'created') history in the literary form 'myth,' the language and forms which were borrowed from Jewish apocalyptic literature and Gnosticism. The real goal of Christianity is the search for personal meaningfulness, self-identity, authentic being of the sort experienced by the early Christians. This can be accomplished only by cutting through the mythological form of the Biblical language ('demythologizing') to encounter the writers' experiences of personhood.

Chapter 1

The Conceptual Setting of the New Testament

Four Phases of the Worldview of Biblical Writers

'Worldview' refers to a way of looking at the universe. It has to do with what one thinks about the nature of reality, why things happen, why they are the way they are, and what the real goals and proper outlook on life are. The Bible does not clearly describe a worldview, yet the writers assume one. It is implied in the way they address, describe, and evaluate their subjects. Not all writers necessarily have precisely the same worldview, but broad parameters of a general Biblical worldview emerge from an overall examination of Scripture.

In Genesis, the Bible begins with the account of God creating the heavens and the earth. It ends in Revelation with the prediction of the second coming of Jesus, the kingdoms of this world becoming the kingdoms of our God and of his Christ, and with the description of the new heaven and the new earth. Between these is the account of human fall into sin and its consequences. The major themes of the Bible are concerned with the phase of 'Redemption' or 'Reconciliation.' Let's note briefly four phases of the biblical worldview.

Phase I: Creation is a doctrine with two important implications. First, it asserts the existence and activity of the transcendent sovereignty of God even before 'the beginning'. Both the Old Testament and the New Testament writers never argue for but proceed with the conviction of his existence. The writer of the Epistle to the Hebrews lays down the 'lowest common denominator', the essential presupposition of Christianity: 'Without faith it is impossible to please him. For whoever would draw near to God must believe that he exists and that he rewards those who seek him' (Heb 11:6). It is useless to seek a non-existent God or one who is unreachable or unknowable – a being who will not reward the search of those who seek him. From these 'givens' spring the rest of the essential affirmations of Christianity – the self-revelation of this knowable

God, his activities in creation, providence, and redemption.

Second, the Biblical doctrine of creation asserts that the world came into being as a result of the will, power, and action, of God. The writer of Hebrews treats the fact of God's creating out of nothing as an article of faith, 'By faith we understand that the world was created by the word of God, so that what is seen was made out of things which do not appear' (11:2). Such a statement implies that the universe or matter is not eternal as is claimed by some forms of philosophical dualism. It also stands against pantheism in the assertion that the created order is separate or distinct from God, that nature is not divine. Biblical references to creation also clearly indicate that the universe is not independent of God.

In the New Testament, as in the Old, creation is a fundamental teaching within the whole counsel of God. The fact of creation by God has widespread implications for other parts of basic Christian doctrine. An essential part of the worldview of Biblical writers is that people occupy a special place in God's creative work. God's sovereign rule rests upon his nature, but also upon his right as Creator to control that which he has made. The New Testament writers are at one with the Old Testament in asserting that the human race came from a single original pair, Adam and Eve. This, they assume, is a fact with wide theological significance. It includes the assumptions:

(1) that human beings, like the rest of the universe, were made by God and therefore are dependent upon him;

(2) but they also were a distinct part of his creative work;

(3) that humankind have a unique nature and pattern, 'the image and likeness of God' (cf. Gen 1:2-27; Jas 3:9);

(4) that the descent of all people from an originally created single couple is the basis for the Biblical view of the biological unity of all peoples;[1]

(5) and that it is also the foundation for the conviction of the spiritual unity of all humankind (cf. Rom 5:14; 1 Cor 15:22, 45-49; 1 Tim 2:13-14). Creator–created is the initial part of the God-to-human relationship.

---

[1]'He made from one every nation of men to live on all the face of the earth' (Acts 17:26).

The newly created universe, its inhabitants, and life in it were without defect. Genesis 1:31 says that 'God saw everything that he had made, and behold, it was very good.' Although we do not fully understand all implications of the word 'good', it certainly includes the fact that the universe was originally morally good, made according to a plan, with order and purpose, with its parts functioning together harmoniously. Biblical writers assume it was created to function under the control of God, the King, who would continue to be intimately involved in it. By implication the Biblical doctrine of creation affirms the sacredness of the material, that it is not inherently evil, and that the believer may in fact sing, 'This is my Father's world!'

Phase II: The Fall affirms that humanity now experiences the universe, in the oft repeated phrase, 'not as God made it but as sin marred it.' The disobedience of Adam and Eve, described in Genesis 3, was a violation of God's law and, therefore, rebellion against his sovereign rule. The Bible calls this violation *sin* and depicts those acts of the first people as the reason for the break in the relationship between God and human beings and as the source of evil and corruption in the world.

This original disobedience, this spiritual treason against the rightful Ruler of the universe, had far reaching consequences. All parties – God, humanity, and nature – were affected.

God takes sin seriously and by it his moral nature was and is affronted. This is well illustrated in Jeremiah 23:22, where, in marking the difference between the true and the false prophet, God says, 'If they had stood in my counsel, then they would have proclaimed my words to my people, and they would have turned them away from their evil ways, and from the evil of their doing.' In other words, those who have stood in God's presence (counsel), who have some understanding of his nature, know his abhorrence of sin. In the New Testament, Paul reflects the same truth when he says sin is to 'come short of the glory of God' (Rom 3:23).

In the Biblical view of things sin is far more than mere acts. Because of the spiritual as well as the biological unity of the human race our moral characters, dispositions, and status were changed. All descendants of Adam and Eve bear the sinful nature, responsibility, and guilt incurred by our first parents.[2] People not only commit sins but *are* sinners. Along with Adam and Eve all their descendants lost the innocence and real freedom enjoyed before the Fall. We now bear culpability, liability to punishment, and we are helpless to alter our situation.

As the result of the Fall, the universe has become apparently evil, purposeless, disharmonious. Genesis 3:16-18 alludes to pain and natural evils as a part of the curse of sin. In the New Testament Paul asserts that 'creation was subjected to futility' (Rom 8:20). The word translated here 'futility' (*mataiotes*) carries such meanings as 'emptiness', 'purposelessness', 'frustration', 'transitoriness'. The word seems to refer generally to the sin, evil, disharmony, depravity, apparent meaninglessness, and the rest of the 'dark side' of the universe, especially of humans and their experiences. Unlike many modern viewpoints, Paul indicates this condition came *after* creation was complete. It is not inherent in the way the universe was made; rather it is the result of alienation from God, caused by human beings rejecting God's person and right to rule his intelligent and rational creatures.

We may further clarify the situation by noting that just as a disruption of significant human relationships can affect all areas of life, so the Biblical writers assume the breaking of the spiritual-religious relationship between God and humanity – the ultimate relationship – is behind all problems arising in all other relationships. Psychological problems come from conflicts within the individual; sociological and political disruptions spring from disharmony between individuals and groups. Environmental disorders stem from improper relationships between humanity and nature and even between the various parts of nature itself. All these are results of the loss of the necessary harmony and purpose possible only when God's rightful place and role in the universe are acknowledged. We must return to this matter in a couple of different ways in chapter 3, as we ask the question, 'What must I do to be saved?'

---

[2]'Sin came into the world through one man and death through sin, and so death spread to all men because all men sinned' (Rom 5:12).

In addition, in some way, not fully explained in the Bible, human disobedience made possible an invasion of the world, a takeover by an evil hostile power, the Kingdom of Satan. Satan, the spiritual adversary of God, has and does work through the original sin to multiply its effects and further his ends which are in opposition to God.

As a result of the Fall, any solution for the ills of nature, society, and individuals lies beyond natural processes or human abilities. It is possible only because of God's grace; in his redemptive work he is restoring all things to the condition in which they will fulfill his original intention.

Phase III: Regeneration, Reconciliation, and Restoration are essentially synonymous with human history and involve God's actions to reclaim and restore his rebellious and spoiled creation. Biblical writers assume that God continues to be active in history, that this activity is related to his creative purpose – to exercise his sovereign rule over his creation, especially his creatures. Thus, God's activity in history is *redemptive* and centred in Jesus Christ through whom God has done something decisive. This supernatural redemption involves all of the universe, all parts of the make-up of individuals and societies, and all aspects of life. Nevertheless, although accomplished, redemption is not yet consummated.

Phase IV: The final phase of the Biblical worldview, is that of *Consummation* ('the age to come'). This looks forward to the completion of the reversal of those conditions caused by the Fall. It involves the expectation of the restoration of the fellowship, harmony, and purpose between those elements alienated by the Fall and the ultimate goal and result of God's work, forgiveness and reconciliation.

The goal of history will be realized, the Rule (Kingdom) of God will be re-established in its fullest form. God's purpose will eventually be worked out. His sovereignty will be established over all and over all of history. Humankind is not caught in an endless, meaningless cycle – history is going somewhere, toward God's goal.

The New Testament writers assert that from Christ's earthly sojourn until the final consummation, the universe, especially humanity, now exists in a state of tension between promise and fulfilment. Yet, the consummation is not just a hope; it, with the finalization of God's victory, is a certainty.

> This is my Father's world, O let me ne'er forget;
> that 'though the wrong seems oft so strong, God is the ruler yet.
> This is my Father's world, the battle is not done;
> Jesus who died, shall be satisfied, and heaven and earth be one.[3]

Dualism

Among the various ways in which the Biblical writers depict the present spiritual situation, they frequently assume some form of a dualistic structure.[4] They may work with several different kinds of dualism; we will note two of these.

Cosmic Dualism focuses upon both the existence of and struggle between two great forces in the universe, good and evil, God and Satan. This is portrayed in various ways – war between nations, strange beasts attacking God's people, conflicts between angels and demons, and more. In one way or another Biblical writers show humanity caught up in a struggle that involves not only its own realm and experience but also one that is beyond the world of time and space. This spiritual warfare explains much of what is going on in the world.

Temporal Dualism is also an important part of the conceptual framework of the Biblical writers. It has to do with the third phase of the worldview of Biblical writers, the phase of redemption. It assumes that this phase, and all of human history, is divided into two great 'Ages.' The first, when seen from the New Testament perspective, is the 'Former Age'. During this initial age God's work is seen as primarily *indirect* and through *symbol*. It was a time of preparation and predictive for something expected in the future. God's revelation of himself and demonstration of how he deals with

---

[3]From Maltbie D. Babcock, 'This is My Father's World,' *Thoughts for Every Day Living* (Copyright, 1901 by Charles Scribner's Sons; 1929 by Katharine T. Babcock).

[4]Some philosophical systems assume a dualism between equally powerful and enduring forces. Biblical writers, on the other hand, assert that, because of God's superior power, evil will be defeated and eliminated.

people was presented primarily in the history and experience of the Nation Israel.

The 'Final or the Last Age' is expected as a result of God's *direct* intervention into human history. This marks the passage from one 'age to another' and results in a radical *change* in the way God deals with humanity. It brings the culmination of God's struggle against hostile forces. In this age God deals *directly* with the *reality*, with the fact, results, and consequences of sin. God's divine and holy justice is satisfied in conjunction with his offering love, mercy and forgiveness. God defeats the power of evil and reasserts his right to rule, his sovereignty over the entire universe. The Old Testament and Intertestamental Jews looked forward to the coming of the Final Age. In the first century AD apocryphal book of 4 Ezra (2 Esdras) the writer asks, 'What will be the dividing of the times? Or when will be the end of the first age and the beginning of the age that follows?' (6:7). Christians assume the crisis point in history, the beginning of the Final Age, took place in the ministry of Jesus, who 'appeared once for all at the end of the age' (Heb 9:26) and, consequently, institutions and practices of the first age (such as the sacrificial system and the first covenant) are 'obsolete ... [and] ready to vanish away' (Heb 8:13). Yet, New Testament Christians also look forward to the Consummation, to the conclusion of God's work; the New Testament Christian lives 'between the times', between the arrival of the Final Age and the completion of God's work.

The Literary Setting of the New Testament

Obviously, the New Testament is written material; that is, it is a literary document. Wise reader-interpreters of literature are aware of the particular type of material with which they deal. They then seek to understand it in ways that are appropriate to its nature. Narrative must be viewed differently than poetry; legal or instructional writing must not be construed in the same way as 'wisdom' literature such as the Book of Job or Proverbs; epistles should be handled differently than the apocalyptic form in which Mark 13 and the Book of Revelation are written. The key word is 'appropriate'. The New Testament reader must ask such questions as:

'What is a written Gospel? How should I interpret it?'

'What are the implications of the fact that at least twenty of the twenty-seven New Testament books are 'epistles' or 'letters'?'

'What should be the consequences for interpretation that 'Hebrews' calls itself a 'word of exhortation' (13:22)?'

'Acts certainly appears to be history, but is not a complete account of the early church; what is its purpose? How should the contemporary church seek to learn from it?'

'The Book of Revelation is certainly different! Why? How is it to be understood and applied in our world?'

The New Testament writings can be grouped together in various ways. The most obvious are those by different authors, Paul, Luke, John and, according to ancient tradition, Peter (Mark and 1 and 2 Peter). There are also other groupings. Matthew, Mark and Luke all look at the ministry of Jesus with the same general outline, with many of the same accounts, and very similar emphases. They are often considered as a single unit, called the 'Synoptic Gospels'; the word 'synoptic' means 'to look at together'. Although no one would assume they come from the same writer, Matthew, Hebrews, and James all have a 'Jewish' emphasis that is distinct from others, say, that of Luke–Acts.

The serious reader of the New Testament must take into account the various literary forms and relationships within and between New Testament books.

Historical Setting of the New Testament

The New Testament arises from a distinct time and place. Its events and teachings took place in the Roman Empire in the first century AD. They reflect the history, ideas, and customs of that world. Hence, it is a historical document.

It is also more than a historical document. Its history is a special kind and has a distinct purpose. Awareness of both parts of this historical setting is necessary equipment for the New Testament student.

The World of the New Testament

The world of the New Testament was a complex society. This is reflected in the three languages of the sign affixed to the cross detailing the charge against Jesus – Hebrew, Latin, and Greek (John 19:20).

The ministry of Jesus and at least the earlier parts of the life of the first church took place in the Land of Israel, hence in a predominately Jewish setting. That Jewish setting was, however, different from the Hebrew culture of the Old Testament. The destruction of the Jewish state, including Jerusalem and its temple, by the Babylonians in 586 BC had widespread results. From that time forward, the majority of the Jews at every period of time lived in the diaspora or dispersion, outside the boundaries of the Land of Israel. In the fourth century BC, Alexander the Great spread Hellenistic (Greek) culture throughout the world. This had a profound effect on the Jews, and later the early Christians. The New Testament reader should be prepared to deal with non-Old Testament differences, including the presence of such groups as Pharisees and Sadducees, institutions as the Sanhedrin and synagogues, and many ideas and beliefs including those regarding the particular role of God's people, the Kingdom of God, and the Messiah.

The world of the New Testament was also that of Greece and Rome. Herod the Great, the king under whom Jesus was born, was a Roman vassal. Jesus was executed under a Roman governor. The early missionaries proclaimed their message in Roman society and were subject to Roman law. That society had been strongly influenced by Greek culture and thought. The early Christians had to wrestle with issues arising out of the ways and beliefs of these two great non-Jewish powers and influences. The New Testament, we must remember, was written in the common Greek (Koine) of the day.

As stated previously, the conscientious interpreter seeks to understand the Scriptures in their original historical and cultural setting before seeking to apply their message to our own.

Salvation in history

In speaking to the Hebrews Samuel reminded them of key events in their history and referred to them as 'the saving deeds of the LORD' (1 Sam 12:7). Similarly, Micah calls upon his hearers to 'remember ... that you may know the saving acts of the LORD' (6:5). Clearly, the writers see God at work in a special way within a particular part of the general history of the world. This history-within-history has been called 'Salvation or Saving History', 'The History of Salvation,' or 'Holy History'. It designates those particular events, or better that stream of history, within all of human history, in which God reveals himself, provides salvation, calls persons to himself, lives in favourable relationship with those who respond to his call, and in concrete situations demonstrates how he deals with his creation.

In the Old Testament, Salvation History is virtually synonymous with the history of the Hebrews it records. It is also roughly parallel to the first of the two ages mentioned above. Christian history in the New Testament is also a part of Salvation History. It depicts the 'change of the times', the coming of the Final Age through the life and ministry of Jesus. It is also present in the extension of his ministry (the 'greater works' of which he spoke in John 14:12) as the early church reported the facts about Jesus, as the apostles gave the authoritative interpretation of those facts, and as the Holy Spirit worked with the Old Testament Scriptures and the preaching and teaching of the church to bring converts into the community and to direct their corporate and individual lives.

The divine component of the New Testament is at least twofold. First, it records a particular time of God at work in the world; it is an account of a part, a climactic part, of Salvation History. It is a book about God's own doings, his activities for and through human beings. Second, as we noted in the previous chapter, its origin and writing also lie in God's activities. It is God's book, a part of the one he authored!

Chapter 2

Who is Jesus? – The Synoptic Gospels

Information about Jesus is found in all parts of the New Testament – Gospels, Acts, Epistles, and Revelation. In a general way the Gospels may be viewed as presentations of the basic facts and the rest of the New Testament as interpretations and applications of the person and work of Christ. This is true only in a general sense, for the authors of the Gospels present interpretations of Jesus which are reflected in their choice of material, emphases, organization, purposes, and intended audiences. The term 'gospel' implies that these documents are far from 'neutral' presentations. The Greek word, *euangelion*, of which 'gospel' is a translation, was used in the ancient world to refer to 'good news', or 'the message from a king'. In the Greek translation of the Old Testament it describes the announcement of a coming time of deliverance, restoration, comfort, justice, divine favor, and salvation as a result of the arrival of the reign of God in history (e.g., Isa 40:9-19; 52:7-10; 61:1-4). The Gospel of John, reflecting the purpose of all the Gospels, states plainly that its intention is to bring the reader to faith that 'Jesus is the Messiah, the Son of God' which will bring 'life in his name' (20:30-31).

Throughout the centuries scholars have wrestled with the fact of the similarities and diversities in the presentations of Jesus in the New Testament. In some cases their efforts have proceeded from humanistic, antisupernaturalistic biases and have been detrimental to the basic teachings of traditional Christianity. These, in my opinion, are a hindrance to finding a proper answer to our question, 'Who is Jesus?' Other scholars, at times using similar methods but without naturalistic biases, have made positive contributions to a better understanding of the nature of the evidence (its literary form and purpose), our understanding of the data, and the interpretation of it.

In some way each Gospel implies there was something unique about the origin of Jesus. Matthew and Luke affirm he was born to a woman who had not had sexual relations with a man (the virgin birth). Mark introduces his writing as 'the good news (gospel) of Jesus Christ the Son of God'. John equates Jesus with the 'Word' (*logos*), who existed before and took part in the creation of the world. Other New Testament writers assume and hint at an existence and activity of Jesus 'before the foundations of the world' (Eph 1:4; Col 1:17; 1 Pet 1:20). Thus the reader is prepared to expect to find in Jesus someone whose person, work, and significance will be well beyond the ordinary.

In this chapter, we will consider the contents of the Synoptic[1] Gospels; in subsequent chapters we will look at the content of the Gospel of John and of the rest of the New Testament.

The Identity of Jesus

Matthew, Mark, and Luke leave little doubt about the initial impression made by Jesus upon those with whom he came in contact. In Mark (but usually also in the other two Synoptics) there is reference to his teaching with authority (1:22), authority over evil spirits (1:27; 3:15), authority to forgive sins (2:10), and his ability to give authority over spiritual powers to his disciples (6:7). Luke tells of a centurion who, even at a distance, recognized Jesus' authority (7:8) while Matthew says Jesus based his right to commission his followers 'to make disciples of all nations' on the fact that 'all authority in heaven and on earth' has been given him (28:18-19).

When messengers from John the Baptist came to Jesus to enquire about his identity, he called attention to certain works he was doing and to the way he preached (Matt 11:2-6; Luke 7:18-35). On the basis of Isaiah (29:18-19; 35:5-6; and 61:1) these were precisely the types of activities which should have been expected with the

---

[1]The word 'synoptic' means 'to look together,' or 'to view from the same point of view. Matthew, Mark, and Luke are called the 'Synoptic' Gospels because they 'look together' at Jesus from a common point of view. This includes their use of the same general outline and include much of the same material.

arrival of the Day of the Lord and the Messiah. Elsewhere Jesus affirmed that his works testified on his behalf (John 5:3; 10:11; 14:11; cf. Acts 2:22). The first line of evidence for determining 'Who is Jesus?' is to be found in looking at his actions and listening to what he said. This appears to be precisely the approach taken by the Synoptic Gospels.

Mark may serve as an example for how the Synoptic writers go about presenting Jesus. He seems to begin his portrayal by providing a sample of Jesus' activities, his teachings, and of differing reactions to him. The reader is thus provided data for confronting the implied question, 'Who is Jesus?' (cf. Mark 4:41). A climax comes in 8:27-30 when Jesus himself asks, 'Who do you say that I am?' and Peter's answer, 'The Messiah.' When understood against the background of the day, Peter's statement (or 'confession,' as it is often called) identifies Jesus as God's Anointed, the long-sought leader *par excellence* who brought the time of deliverance and salvation.

The prevalent belief in Jesus' time assumed the Messiah would mainly conduct an earthly ministry as a political-military king, whose primary (if not exclusive) concern would be for the Hebrew people. Peter and his contemporaries doubtlessly expected that rescuing Israel from her enemies (cf. Luke 2:74), the Romans, would be high on the Messiah's agenda. Jesus accepted the Messianic designation but immediately linked the concept with that of the Son of man who would suffer.

The exact background and meaning of 'Son of man' is debated. However, its use in the Old Testament (Dan 7:13-14), Inter-testamental literature (e.g., 1 Enoch 45-71), and elsewhere, makes clear that in responding to Peter Jesus has in mind an apocalyptic, heavenly, spiritual person whose concern was not for the Hebrews alone but would receive dominion and glory and kingship, that all peoples, nations, and languages should serve him. His dominion is an everlasting dominion that shall not pass away, and his kingdom is one that shall never be destroyed (Dan 7:14). Such a statement has affinities with the enthronement scene of the Messiah in Psalm 110.

'Son of man' is Jesus' favorite self-designation in all the Gospels. It may mean little more than 'I, myself.' It may carry special connotations as well. In Mark, for an instance, 'Son of man' is used in three distinct settings: (1) he is present and active on earth with authority (Mark 2:10, 27), (2) he is the redeemer who is to suffer (Mark 8:31; 9:12, 31; 10:31, 33-34, 45; 14:21, 41; note also 9:9), and (3) he is coming again as judge and ruler (Mark 8:38: 13:26; 14:62). Matthew and Luke use the term in a similar manner. The union of Messiah and Son of man may have called for a shift in the disciples' thinking, but not an impossible one.

Note that of the three settings in which 'Son of man' occurs in Mark, it does so most often in that of suffering and death. This is tantamount to equating it with the role and experience of the Suffering Servant of Isaiah. It was this suggestion, that the Messiah-Son of man would suffer, which was most difficult for Jesus' intimate associates to understand, much less to accept. By so doing Jesus introduced quite a different element into the various Messianic concepts with which they were familiar.

The 'Servant' of Isaiah (42:1-4; 49:1-9a; 50:4-11; 52:13–53:13) was the chosen and the delight of God but was rejected, tortured, and killed by humans. Nevertheless, he makes possible the forgiveness of sins and re-establishes the covenant between God and humans. There was a wide variety of opinions about the identity of the Servant but hardly, if ever, was he identified as the Messiah. The idea of a 'suffering Messiah' was incomprehensible to most Jews of the time; little wonder that Peter 'began to rebuke' Jesus when his Master alluded to it (Mark 8:32).

Jesus' response to Peter was nothing less than a redefinition of Messiahship. Following Peter's confession Jesus reiterated time and again that he, as the Son of man, would be rejected, suffer, be killed, but rise again (Mark 8:31; 9:31; 10:33-34). Along with this new conception of Messiahship went a redefinition of discipleship as well. Not only the Messiah but also the disciples must take up their 'cross' (8:33), be servants of all instead of the greatest (9:34; 10:44).

Beginning with Jesus' dramatic entrance into Jerusalem the Gospel writers show him consciously casting himself into the role of Messiah. He entered into conflict with Jewish leaders, discoursed about 'last things', placed himself in the center of sacred history by reinterpreting the Passover. Then, he went out to die. But he rose from the dead! And, Luke says, that 'While he blessed them, he parted from them' (24:51). This is the final act that the Synoptic writers ask the reader to consider in answering the question, 'Who is Jesus?'

The Bearer of the Kingdom of God

Mark 1:14-15 says Jesus introduced his message by 'proclaiming the good news of God, and saying, "The time is fulfilled, and the kingdom of God has come near; repent and believe in the good news."' To first-century Jewish ears this statement was filled with 'loaded terms'. We have already noted that 'good news' refers to the announcement of the time during which God would work in a new and different way to make salvation available. The word 'time' is a translation of the Greek word *kairos* which indicates a particular point in time, a crisis moment, which changes all that follows. 'Has come near' translates a particularly difficult word which means 'to draw near' or 'approach.' Mark's use of the perfect tense here is significant, because it indicates that action which has been in process, has reached its conclusion, but with continuing results. Perhaps a better translation might be 'has just arrived' or 'is already here'. With these words Jesus did nothing less than announce that the Final Age, expected as a part of the temporal dualism described in the previous chapter, had arrived! What had previously been viewed as the 'Future Age' was now the 'Present Age'.

It was the 'Kingdom of God' that Jesus proclaimed had 'just arrived'. There is a sense in which the Kingdom of God has always been present. Yet, in the person and ministry of Jesus it assumed a new dimension. In the Synoptic Gospels this new dimension of the Kingdom of God is the principal theme and purpose of Jesus' activity and teaching.

First-century Jewish notions about the 'Kingdom of God' were often confused and contradictory. There were, however, some basic ideas associated with it which appear to have been widely recognized. Some of these Jesus accepted, others he rejected or modified. In any case it must be understood that the concepts of 'Messiah' and 'Kingdom of God' were closely related. As Messiah,

Jesus was intent on announcing the presence of the kingdom, to clarify its nature, and to actively implement it. With his ministry the Kingdom arrived; he was bearer of the Kingdom of God.

The Kingdom of God in Pre-Christian Jewish Thought

In the ancient Hebrew, Aramaic and Greek languages the words for 'kingdom' do not primarily refer to a geographical area but to 'lordship,' 'rule,' 'reign,' or 'sovereignty'. In general, 'Kingdom of God' designates God's sphere of influence or control; it is present wherever His sovereignty is acknowledged. 'Sovereignty' or 'Rule of God' might be a better translation. The phrase 'Kingdom of God' occurs frequently in the New Testament. Matthew, with four exceptions (12:28; 19:24: 21:31, 43; and in some texts of 6:33), speaks of the 'Kingdom of Heaven', including places where in parallel contexts in Mark and Luke the phrase 'Kingdom of God' occurs. It is likely that in the Gospels 'Kingdom of God' and 'Kingdom of Heaven' are synonyms.

The concept, although not necessarily the phrase 'Kingdom of God', has a long background in the Hebrew Scriptures, and in the Jewish thought of the first century AD. The basic assumptions of the Biblical world recognized that God alone is the king who has the absolute right and ability to rule all things in heaven and earth. Without his rule and control the universe is thrown into disorder and confusion. This, as we noted in surveying the Biblical worldview, is precisely what the Biblical writers assume occurred as a result of human sin. This rejection of God's right to rule and violation of his kingly commands constituted spiritual treason. It also opened the way for the influence and activity of another spiritual power, one hostile to God, his adversary.

The Bible assumes that even before the creation of the material universe, God's authority was contested by this spiritual force (being) called 'Satan' (which means 'adversary'). When human beings rebelled against God, they passed from God's control (God's kingdom or sphere of influence) to rule by Satan (Satan's sphere of influence or kingdom). From this point of view Satan's kingdom is both real and present, not confined to some 'other world' but is in this world and world order. Because of human sin and rebellion against God, the presence and influence of Satan has invaded the souls, bodies, and environment of humankind. Thus, the Kingdom of Satan is operating in the exact territory in which the Kingdom of God should operate – in the material world and especially within the hearts, lives, souls, society, and in the experience of people. Before God reasserts the influence of his kingdom in the material world and humanity, he must first drive out the occupying force, the Kingdom of Satan. Thus, a conflict between the two is inevitable. It is precisely this conflict, the 'cosmic struggle', to which we alluded in our survey of the conceptual setting of the New Testament writers.

The concept of 'Kingdom' held a special place in the thought and history of the nation Israel. Israel rightly believed that through the covenant which God had made with Abraham (Gen 12–17) she enjoyed a unique, special relationship with God. Furthermore, Israel, as 'the people of God', was forced to live in a hostile environment, one dominated by the Kingdom of Satan. She understood that political, military, and social forces which oppressed her were really instruments of the Kingdom of Satan. Through them Satan sought to strike God by attacking his people, Israel.

Quite logically, the Hebrews came to believe that the coming of God's Kingdom would bring an end to control of the material world by Satan. This would produce favorable results for themselves as God's people. Their individual, social, environmental, and other problems would be solved; Israel would become dominant in the political sphere and be recognized as the greatest of all nations.

In the Old Testament the Hebrew kings were viewed as representatives of God, the Great King. Consequently the 'Kingdom of God' was often described in metaphors drawn from descriptions of the Hebrew kingship. It is recorded in 2 Samuel 7 that God made promises of an everlasting kingdom to David, and the Kingdom of God was frequently expected to come into being through the Davidic family. In the Jewish mind the expectation of the Kingdom of God and the kingdom of David and his family were often inseparable. The Davidic kings were considered God's vice regents, representative of the heavenly King. The Psalms and prophets frequently speak of the coming agent of God, the one through whom the kingdom would be established in an ultimate sense, as the Son of David (see Pss 2, 45, 110; Isa 9:6-7; Jer 23:5-6).

Exactly what would happen when the Kingdom of God arrived was debated. It was expected to bring an immediate and radical change; but there was no agreement as to which areas would be most affected. Some felt that the Kingdom of God would bring a change in the world of nature, a *cosmic renewal*. Natural evils, agricultural pests, and physical disease would be eliminated. Prosperity would be greatly increased. The *social order* is another area expected to be changed when the Kingdom of God arrived. Peace would be established between people; justice would prevail; God's purposes in history would be realized. Some expected that the *spiritual* disposition of people and nations would be so reordered in the kingdom that all would properly serve, obey, and worship God. The revelation of God's will would be either reinterpreted or reissued in such a form that all people would have little difficulty in conforming to it.

During the tumultuous and often dark days of Hebrew history from about the eighth century BC through the New Testament period, 'God's People' were increasingly attacked, harassed, and subdued by foreign nations. Not surprisingly, the majority of the people in Jesus' day expected the Kingdom of God to deal with the political situation. *National deliverance* would bring freedom from Rome and the restoration of the political power and prestige of the Hebrew nation. Kingdom expectations might combine some other emphasis with the political. The prayer of Zechariah, the father of John the Baptist, brings together both military and religious-spiritual concerns and doubtlessly reflects the hope of many. He asked that through the fulfillment of God's promise Israel would

> be saved from our enemies and from the hand of all who hate us... that we, being rescued from the hand of our enemies might serve him without fear, in holiness and righteousness...' (Luke 1:71-75)

The 'coming of the Kingdom of God' and related ideas, as we have said, refer generally to God's reassertion of his right to rule over the universe and includes his bringing humankind under his authority. Some writers refer to the coming of the Kingdom as the initial thrust of God's decisive invasion into the territory occupied by the Kingdom of Satan. Other ancient writers use it to refer to the final victory and assumption of complete control by God. Nevertheless, it must be clear that whatever was expected, many first century Jews understood that the Kingdom of God and the *Final Age* and/or the *Messianic Age* were closely bound together. Either God himself or the Messiah (or a number of 'Messianic Figures or Personages'), as his agent or representative, would come to bring the Kingdom of God to earth. The appearance of the Messiah was expected to be clear proof that 'the right time' ('the Day of the Lord,' 'the Final Age') had come and that the Kingdom of God was either near or had actually arrived.

The Kingdom of God in the Ministry of Jesus

Jesus carried on his ministry through the presence of his person, what he did, and what he said. The Synoptic Gospels portray the major emphasis of Jesus' ministry as bringing in the Kingdom of God, clarifying its nature, and implementing the Reign of God on earth.

The fact of the Kingdom is deeply embedded in the opening phases of the ministry of Jesus – his birth, the ministry of John the Baptist, and Jesus' baptism and temptation. Matthew's birth account begins with his genealogy and establishes Jesus' lineage from the kingly line of David's family (Matt 1:1-17). The wise men came asking, 'Where is he who has been born *king* of the Jews?' (Matt 2:2). In Luke the angel promises Mary, '. . . the Lord God will give to him the *throne of his father David*, and he will *reign* over the house of Jacob forever; and of his *kingdom* there will be no end' (Luke 1:32-33; cf. 2 Sam 7:12-16, 26). His birth took place in 'the city of David' (Luke 2:4), the location predicted by Micah where the Messiah would be born (Matt 2:4-6; Mic 5:2). The devout Simeon associated the new born babe with the kingly position of the glory of Israel (Luke 2:32) and the prophetess Anna spoke of him to those 'looking for the redemption of Jerusalem' (Luke 2:38).

John the Baptist, who filled the role of forerunner who was to prepare the way for the coming Messianic king (cf. Mal 4:5-6; Isa 40:3-5), announced the soon coming of the kingdom (Matt 3:2) and identified Jesus as 'The Coming One', a synonym for 'Messiah' (Matt 3:11). And then, somewhat reluctantly, John baptized Jesus (Matt 3:13-16).

The significance of John's baptism was not lost on the Jewish leaders, who rejected it (Mark 11:31 = Matt 21:25 and Luke 20:4-5; Luke 7:29-30). By it one (1) prepared for the coming Messiah, (2) sought cleansing outside the structure of both the religious ceremonies and the ethnic boundaries of Israel, and (3) looked for forgiveness as a matter of repentance, an inner attitude and relationship with God. Jesus' baptism identified him with the 'program' of John, but the implications of Jesus' ministry were markedly different.

The baptism of Jesus must be viewed in the context of certain Old Testament passages to which they allude. Many Jews would have recognized not only these statements but also the whole Old Testament context in which they occur. The coming of the Holy Spirit was equivalent to Jesus' anointing, his coronation or inauguration as the Servant of the Lord foreseen in Isaiah 42:1 and 61:1. The voice also designated Jesus as 'beloved son', an allusion to Psalm 2:7 and associates Jesus with the kingly family of David. The declaration that God 'delights' in him or 'is well pleased' with Jesus further identifies him with what is said of the Servant in Isaiah 42:1; he is the one who would accomplish his mission through suffering (Isa 52:13–53:13). Thus, at his baptism Jesus assumed his office, that of the Messianic king who reigns and the servant who suffers.

These two themes, reigning and suffering, run parallel through his ministry. He himself said that he was 'hard pressed,' 'constrained,' 'preoccupied or absorbed' with the 'baptism' with which he was 'to be baptized' (Luke 12:50). It is not unreasonable to assume that the language used here, of a coming 'baptism' of death (cf. Mark 10:38-39; Matt 20:22-23), is a reflection of Jesus' understanding of the commission given him at his baptism, a commission which included death. His whole ministry was limited by and directed toward that 'date with death' which by his resurrection would resolve into a broader, unlimited horizon for himself and his followers.

No sooner was his coronation complete than the king was 'led' or 'driven' into the wilderness by the Spirit (Mark 1:12; Matt 4:1; Luke 4:1), there to face the foe. For this initial encounter he relied entirely on spiritual resources; his physical strength was depleted by hunger. Satan proposed that he alter the terms of his commission, that he accept only one of the current models expected of the Messiah – the Mosaic prophet who would provide bread in the wilderness, the apocalyptic Son of man who would come floating down to earth, or the earthly king who would rule all the nations of the world. The tempter also suggested that he accomplish his goals, not through suffering, but by miraculous display or negotiation with the enemy. He who had been present before the foundations of the world, when the design of redemption had been set forth, knew full well the implications of any compromise. He fought with 'the sword of the Spirit, which is the word of God' (Eph 6:17) and then 'angels came and ministered to him' (Matt 4:11). He now had won the first battle; there would be others. Luke says the devil departed only 'until an opportune time' (Luke 4:13).

We have already seen that Mark depicts that Jesus began his Galilean ministry with the announcement of the arrival of the crisis moment (*kairos*), the right time, that the Kingdom of God had just arrived. In Luke the opening announcement is made in the synagogue of Nazareth. There Jesus identified his presence with the deliverance and healing which Isaiah (61:1-2a) had said would come in 'the acceptable year of the Lord' (Luke 4:16-21). The rejoicing of Jesus' townspeople (4:22) was cut short when he went on to imply that just as God had been graciously disposed to non-Jews in the past, so too the 'Year of the Lord', the Messianic age, would include his favor for Gentiles as well as Israelites.

And so, this phase of his public ministry began in controversy. But the conflict was broader than ethnic or national pride. This was but a symptom. The Galilean ministry was war! The Kingdom of God had invaded the territory of the Kingdom of Satan. Jesus, through his person, actions, and words, was spearheading the attack.

He explained the situation as he countered those who explained his power over demons by virtue of his being possessed by a demon who outranked the others.

> How can Satan cast out Satan? If a kingdom is divided against itself, that kingdom cannot stand. And if a house is divided against itself, that house will not be able to stand. And if Satan has risen up against himself and is divided, he cannot stand, but is coming to an end. But no one can enter a strong man's house and plunder his goods, unless he first binds the strong man; then indeed he may plunder his house (Mark 3:23-27).

Jesus had entered the house of the Satan, the strong man. As the stronger man, Jesus was subduing him and reclaiming for God those whom Satan had stolen away from their rightful Sovereign. The other two Synoptics add that Jesus' power over demons is confirmation of the arrival of the Kingdom of God (Matt 12:28; Luke 11:20) and that God is winning!

Who is Jesus? The bearer of the Kingdom. The assumption behind Jesus' mighty acts is that since Satan was being defeated, sins could be forgiven. Human beings can, therefore, again place themselves under the rule of God. Note the implications of the imperfect tense in Luke 10:18; as 'the Seventy' were casting out demons, Jesus says he '*was seeing* Satan falling like lightning from heaven'. The disciples, as representatives of Jesus, participate in the overthrow of the Satanic dominion as they proclaim his presence and kingdom!

This leads us to look more closely at the most dramatic part of the deeds of Jesus, the miracles. We noted above that they help identify him. They attracted attention and helped draw the crowds that flocked to listen to his message. But, the miracles were not 'magic shows', they were more than simple deeds of kindness to the sick and needy. We must remember that Jesus, as the representative and bearer of God's Reign, was at war. The miracles were a part of his weapons of warfare against the Kingdom of Satan. This becomes clear by focusing upon the various 'types' or categories of miracles. Best known are the miracles of physical healing, but in his day, Jesus' acts of exorcisms, casting out evil spirits, seem to have caught more attention. There were also his nature miracles such as stilling the storm, multiplying loaves and fishes, and causing a fig tree to wither. Finally, there is a group of special New Testament miracles including the virgin birth, raising the dead, as well as his own resurrection. Each of these show Jesus reclaiming for God an area that had come under the influence of Satan. Jesus healed bodies that had been made ill or deformed by the power of evil, he forced evil spirits to abandon persons upon whom they had established a special claim. God's sovereignty extends to the realm of nature and here too Jesus was in command. The 'last enemy', says Paul, is death (1 Cor 15:26); resurrections and Jesus' own resurrection destroyed the Devil's 'trump card' and demonstrated the impotence of his kingdom in the face of God's Kingdom. 1 John 3:8 says, 'The reason the Son of God appeared was to destroy the works of the devil.' The miracles show him doing it!

The miracles reveal another aspect of the Kingdom, which although invisible, is real. They provide proof by visible signs of the reality of Jesus' invisible, spiritual activities and authority. The healed and walking, former paralytic was proof 'that the Son of man has authority on earth to forgive sins' (Mark 2:10).

The miracles demonstrate some important facts about both the nature of the Kingdom of God and the person and work of Jesus, its representative. By way of summary we may note that they (1) display the presence and the kingly control (authority and power) of Jesus and the Kingdom of God; (2) unlike most earthly kingdoms of the day, that which Jesus brought was compassionate.[2] Jesus had genuine, active compassion and concern for those entrapped by the Kingdom of Satan and its influences. Finally, (3) the miracles attest and vindicate the person of Jesus, the bearer of the Kingdom (cf. Acts 2:22).

The socio-political-religious environment of the Land of Israel in the first century was, as we have noted, rife with many types of expectations about the coming kingdom. In such a setting Jesus knew

[2]Mark 6:34 = Matt 9:36; Mark 8:2 = Matt 15:32; Matt 14:14; Luke 7:12-13; cf. 15:20.

well that his miracles could be misunderstood. Consequently, perhaps this is the place to note a puzzling and controversial phenomenon of Jesus' ministry called, by modern scholars, 'The Messianic Secret.' The phrase refers to Jesus' commands to healed persons, disciples, and others not to report some miraculous works, and to some aspects of his private ministry and activities. In Mark, for an example, he commanded demons not to make him known (1:25, 34; 3:12). A healed leper (1:43-44) and other persons he restored to health (7:36; 8:26) were instructed to tell no one about what he had done for them. At one point in his ministry (7:24; 9:30) Jesus embarks upon an apparent policy of deliberate concealment. Mark reports that Jesus repeatedly withdrew to teach his disciples, sometimes only the inner group, privately (4:10, 33; 7:17; 9:28, 30-31; 13:3; 14:13ff.). Secrecy is again specifically ordered after Peter's confession (8:30) and the transfiguration (9:9), although in the latter case a silence is to be maintained only until after his resurrection.

What is behind these commands? Did he want to keep secret the fact of his Messiahship or was he denying that he was the Messiah? Was he using reverse psychology, knowing that such instructions would result in even more intense proclamation of his deeds and teachings? Perhaps he wanted more time to adequately prepare his followers for a future, public disclosure of his identity. Maybe silence was ordered to minimize confrontation with leaders which was intense enough as it was. Liberal scholarship of the nineteenth century suggested these secrecy commands were invented by the disciples to explain why they claimed he was the Messiah although the multitudes knew that Jesus himself did not publicly make the claim.

A much better explanation takes into account the fact and implications of the varied expectations about the Kingdom of God and the Messiah. For an example, John 6:15 relates that, following the feeding of the five thousand, when Jesus perceived that the crowd was 'about to come and take him by force to make him king', he withdrew. This incident suggests that in the highly charged atmosphere of his day Jesus did not want his Messiahship known until the term had been clarified by his teaching, and especially until after his death and resurrection when his explanation could take on fuller meaning.

The spiritual conflict took material form in Jesus' conflict with scribes, Pharisees, chief priests, and other representatives of the established Judaism of his day. He did not shrink from such confrontations; at times, especially toward the end of his ministry, he even initiated them. By such encounters Jesus demonstrated that the Kingdom is not a nationalistic-political body nor is it to be identified with a particular ethnic group. It is not characterized by ceremonial or legalistic religious observances. The leaders recognized themselves as the implied wicked tenants of the vineyard (Mark 12:1-12). By rejecting these usurpers of authority over God's people, Jesus, in the name of God reasserted God's prerogatives and reign.

As Jesus called followers, he taught that entrance into the Kingdom came only through a commitment to himself. 'Follow me,' he said time and again. To do so meant taking his 'yoke' (Matt 11:29) and bearing the cross (Mark 8:34). Yet, it was only through such a personal relationship and dedication that disciples could find 'rest for your souls' (Matt 11:29).

And, it was 'disciples' that Jesus called. The word means a 'learner' or 'student', and there is always a teaching-learning relationship between Jesus and his followers. In the ancient world the student seldom went to a particular place; rather he associated himself with the teacher, followed, and learned as the teacher taught on the road, in the house, on the job, or wherever they were. Students were also 'servants' of sorts. They assisted the teacher in his work (most rabbis supported themselves with trades or occupations), they served in the details of daily life (which might include washing his feet, preparing his meals, or other menial tasks). To be a disciple entailed making a thorough commitment to the person of the teacher. That is what Jesus demanded.

As he called disciples, Jesus enrolled citizenry in the Kingdom of God. His selection of twelve special persons is important, for they were to be the foundation and the leaders of the new community he gathered. It is the number that is significant, even more than the particular individuals he chose. As Old Testament Israel had been built upon twelve 'founding fathers', so too would be the new Israel, the new people of God. These special disciples, *apostles* (those called, commissioned, and sent out as official representative-spokesmen, Matt 10:2-4; Mark 3:16-19; Luke 6:13-19; Acts 1:13) as they were later called, took their place alongside the fathers and prophets of the Old Testament as the leaders and channels through whom God spoke and directed the citizens of his kingdom.

The events near Caesarea Philippi mark the climax of the first phase of Jesus' ministry. By that time he had taught and attempted to demonstrate that the Kingdom, Messiahship, and discipleship were other than commonly understood. His words and actions in days to follow built on that event. He came, he said, 'not to be served but to serve [to be a servant] and to give his life a ransom for [instead of] the many' (Mark 10:45). He was doing nothing less than turning topsy turvy the notions of the day by declaring that the kingdom is not of this world, the Messiah is a divider of people and even of families, masters are servants, strength comes through weakness, life is gained through death, and glory and honor are the results of bearing the cross. Such are some of the things he sought to establish, but that does not mean his followers accepted or even comprehended what he said.

The cross! It was the cross that was a major stumbling block. In the ancient world crucifixion was the most degrading, socially repugnant form of death by torture. The gibbet itself (and it could take numerous forms), the victim and anyone associated with a crucified person fell under a cloud of shame and scandal. In the Jewish world it was even worse, for the holy Scriptures themselves pronounce a curse on anyone executed by any method involving elevating the body (Deut 21:23). Yet, Jesus had prescribed it for the disciples (Mark 8:34) and at least three times predicted such a fate for himself (Mark 8:31; 9:31; 10:33-34). Furthermore, Jesus insisted that 'it is enough for a disciple to be like his lord' (Matt 10:24-25). Some might be willing to die for a kingdom, but death by crucifixion in the Kingdom of God? Inconceivable!!!

Against such a background as this we must look at the transfiguration of Jesus. Predicting it he had said that 'there are some standing here who will not taste death before they see the kingdom of God' (Luke 9:27). In the transfiguration, if but for a moment, the invisible majesty and glory of the Kingdom became visible. Here Jesus shines out amidst the Law (Moses) and the Prophets (Elijah). For those who saw and those who later heard, there should no longer be doubt. Here on the mount was confirmation. Here was a demonstration of the fact, the spiritual nature of Jesus' Messiahship and the reality of the Kingdom of God he proclaimed. But even there, in the brightness of the moment, was that dark cloud, the cloud of death. Luke suggests the transfiguration was the prelude to Jesus' death; the heavenly visitors 'spoke of his departure which he was to accomplish in Jerusalem' (9:31). The word 'departure' in Greek is *exodos*, from whence comes 'Exodus', and probably implies that deliverance would once again come through the death of the Passover lamb, *the* Passover Lamb (cf. 1 Cor 5:7-8).

In his teaching Jesus never discussed the Kingdom of God in all of its aspects at one time. Rather, his accustomed manner was to announce, define, and teach about it little by little and frequently indirectly. Perhaps his most direct statements are in Luke 17:20-21: 'The kingdom of God is not coming with signs to be observed; nor will they say, "Lo, here it is!" or "There!" for behold, the kingdom of God is in the midst of you.' Just how difficult this was for his followers to comprehend is illustrated two chapters later where, describing Jesus' approach to Jerusalem, Luke notes those with him 'supposed that the kingdom of God was to appear immediately' (19:11).

The implied theme of Jesus' teaching is that the Kingdom is the Kingly rule of God, the sphere of his sovereignty. In Jesus that sovereign rule is present. In his ministry God was reassuming control over the world and especially over his people; God was reclaiming his right to rule the universe and of receiving honor from his creation.

To go further, Jesus' role as 'Messiah' is inseparably bound to the Kingdom. He brings the Kingdom, explains his own person and ministry against the background of Old Testament promises and expectations which include the Kingdom. The Kingdom is centered in Jesus the Messiah himself, the revelation, agent, and embodiment of God, for Jesus is Lord! It is through a personal relationship with the Messiah-Jesus that one acknowledges and enters the Kingdom;

it is Jesus who brings God's subjects back to Him. With the arrival of Jesus the Final Age, the Kingdom Age, had begun.

The general descriptions of the Kingdom of God in Jesus' teaching display its contrasting features. It is spiritual and heavenly, but has earthly and materialistic aspects. It is both present and future. The Kingdom is universal (= worldwide), yet selective, involving, not the masses, but a select group, a 'Remnant', the 'Chosen', who enter by heeding his call and so acknowledge the Kingdom's presence and Jesus as the Messiah-Lord. The Kingdom demands individual response and commitment but also involves life in a community, the 'New People of God', the church; it is based upon a personal relationship with God through Jesus, yet it is a corporate body with an organization.

Jesus' parables are closely related to the Kingdom of God and one of his principal forms for teaching about it. Over a third of them are directly associated with some such phrase as 'the Kingdom of God is like . . .' (e.g., Matt 13:31, 33, 44, 45, 47, 52; 20:1; Luke 13:18; cf. Mark 4:26, 30). Many of the parables without direct reference to the Kingdom of God reflect some feature of it. In fact, most of them explain one or more aspects of the Kingdom or the ways his contemporaries were responding to it. It does not come with dramatic apocalyptic or military display but, like crops growing or dough rising, the kingdom starts small and grows slowly, silently, but surely. Like treasure hidden in a field or a pearl of great price, the Kingdom is worth giving up everything to obtain. But all do not see this. The varied responses to kingdom preaching are determined by the spiritual states of the hearers, even as the produce of seed broadcast over a field is determined by the condition of the soil upon which it falls. As the landholder will punish the tenants who refused to give him fruits from his vineyard, so the King will deal with those who refuse to acknowledge his place in his kingdom. In addition to such direct teachings about the Kingdom, parables give illustrations of some patterns in God's dealing with humans, provide insights into Jesus' own person and his work as God's Messiah, and they extend the call to enter the Kingdom.

Jesus' teaching about the time of the arrival of the kingdom is complex. In Mark he speaks of the kingdom as having already 'drawn near' (1:15) and that it 'will come with power' (9:1). Later, the same Gospel records his report that the kingdom 'will come with clouds of heaven' (14:62). The exact time sequence intended in such statements is not always clear. However, we must elaborate upon at least two distinct temporal elements of Jesus' Kingdom teaching – that it is both present (visible) and future (unseen), and it is both in history and beyond it. Jesus told his disciples that 'it is in the midst of you', or 'is within you' (Luke 17:21); his miracles, especially his casting out demons, demonstrated the presence of the Kingdom (Matt 12:28; Luke 11:20). The kingdom is a forceful present reality (Matt 11:12) but with its secrets (Matt 13:11). Jesus proclaimed the kingdom as a present reality.

At the same time, it is coming in the future both in and beyond history. Jesus' followers are to pray, 'Let (or may) your Kingdom come; let (or may) your will happen upon earth even as it does in heaven' (Matt 6:10; cf. Luke 11:2). In parables the householder (Matt 24:43-44), doorkeeper (Mark 13:34), servants (Mark 13:43-44; Matt 24:46-50), and virgins (Matt 25:1-13) await a future appearance. Disciples are warned that since no one knows the 'day or hour' they are to 'take heed, watch!' (Mark 13:32-37). It is with reference to the future that Jesus said, 'Fear not, little flock, for it is your Father's good pleasure to give you the kingdom' (Luke 12:32). The so-called 'Apocalyptic or Olivet Discourse' (Mark 13; Matt 24–25; Luke 21) looks for some future 'end'. Evoking the imagery of the expected 'Messianic Banquet' Jesus speaks of sitting 'at table with Abraham, Isaac, and Jacob' (Matt 8:11) and drinking 'in the kingdom of God' (Mark 14:25). Clearly, he believed the enemy was subdued but not yet eliminated; he anticipated something more, the future victory, establishment, and dominance of the Kingdom of God. Although it has almost become a cliche, the statement that, for Jesus, the Kingdom is 'Here and now, but not yet present and consummated,' well summarizes this part of his teaching.

Jesus asserts that in the Kingdom of God there is a special relationship between King and subjects. The relationship with Jesus, through which one enters the Kingdom, also establishes a relationship with God. Of course such persons are ruled and controlled by God, the King and Judge. Yet they will stand before that Judge with sins forgiven, guilt removed, as 'new creatures', reconciled to and by God. Still more, the special relationship between the King and the subjects of the Kingdom was initiated by, based on, and characterized by love. God, as the King who forgives debtors in the parable of Luke 7:41-47, thus shows his love through forgiveness.

The Kingdom of God also sets forth new standards for living. The basis for life and conduct in the Kingdom is love for God and neighbor – love which itself is a response to God's prior love (Mark 12:30-31; Matt 22:37-40; Luke 10:27). This matter will be a major concern as we ask 'How must Christians live?'

Princes and princesses in earthly kingdoms have a special relationship with the sovereign and unique privileges. So it is with those in the Kingdom of God. All citizens in the kingdom are children of the King; God is their Father! They pray, 'Our Father who is in heaven' (Matt 6); it is the Father who delights to give the Kingdom to his children (Luke 12:32). Even more, Jesus both addressed God and taught his disciples to refer to God as 'Abba' (Mark 14:36; Rom 8:15; Gal 4:6). Such was the Aramaic term used by the little children in the home to refer, lovingly, to their devoted male parent. Awareness of this relationship explains Jesus' frequent withdrawals for prayer.

For humans this relationship with the divine Father should assure the provision for an innate need, a caring, loving father. Such an image is easy for me; my father was the epitome of love, care, and tenderness. For others it is more difficult, for in this life there are those for whom the word 'father' evokes images of an absent entity who avoids his responsibilities, or, even worse, of a selfish, heartless, demanding, abusive, tyrant. For all who through Scripture come to understand the implications of the term 'Abba', there is no more wonderful privilege than to call the Creator of the Rolling Spheres, the Mighty Sovereign of Heaven and Earth, the King of Kings and Lord of Lords – Potentate of Time and Eternity, the King in the Kingdom of God, 'Abba,' 'Daddy!' It reflects a level of intimacy seldom, if ever, known in the Judaism contemporary with Jesus.

The supreme events through which the Kingdom of God is displayed and implemented are those of Jesus' last week in Jerusalem. He enters Jerusalem in the splendor of a king. It was an act the Messiah was expected to do (Ps 24:7-10); the cries of the crowds, using Psalm 118:26, confirm they have in mind the Messianic panoply reflected in the whole of that Psalm. But Jesus is in charge; he directs the drama. The details better fit the entry of the smitten-shepherd King of Zechariah 9:9 (cf. 12:1, 6-7) than the processions of the Gentile rulers who 'lord it over' their subjects (Mark 10:42). Instead of an army, he led a mob of peasants. Instead of brandishing swords, they waved palm branches. A donkey, the beast of the poor and servants, substituted for the accustomed prancing white horse of conquerors. He attacked, not the Roman fortress, the Castle of Antonia, which towered above the northwest corner of the temple area, but the abuses in the temple court itself.

As he cleansed the Temple, Jesus challenged the right of the priestly rulers to use it for their own purposes. He claimed authority to direct the affairs of his Father's house, which included turning it from an ethnic, nationalistic symbol to a place of prayer 'for all the nations' (or 'Gentiles,' Mark 11:17).

In the days immediately following, the King confronted pretenders to his throne as Jesus consciously heightened controversy with Jewish Leaders. Jesus' parable of the Tenants and the Vineyard is one such occasion (Mark 12:1-12; Matt 21:33-46; Luke 20:9-19). Most of his hearers would have known that the vineyard parable of Isaiah 5:1-7 bespoke judgment upon the nation. Jesus' use of the same figure was clearly directed against the leaders.

At the Last Supper Jesus pointedly placed himself at the center of Salvation History. The Passover commemorated direct divine actions to liberate slaves, provide guidance, and give protection and sustenance for the trip to the Promised Land; it remembered God's establishing Israel as a nation and giving them the Law, instructions for life within the covenant community. All this, Jesus rendered obsolete as he claimed to be the new divine intervention, savior-liberator, guide, lawgiver, and judge. Moses and God's mighty acts of the past are now of secondary importance, 'Do this in remembrance of me!' Little did the disciples realize that they were sitting at the King's banquet table, partaking of the solemn festive meal before the decisive battle with his foe.

As we move through the records of Jesus' Passion, his agony in the garden, trial, and execution, we cannot escape the conclusion that here the lordly victim is in control. It was not something done to him, but that which he did. When asked if he were the Messiah, his affirmative answer (Mark 14:61-62) included his own definition of the term which combined it with the heavenly ruler of Psalm 110:1 and the Son of man of Daniel 7:13. In the end even his executioners announced publicly that he was 'The King of the Jews'. The forces of evil, through the unlikely coalition of Jewish priests and pagan rulers, did their worst 'in order that the Scriptures might be fulfilled' that, as he himself said, 'Everything written about me in the law of Moses and the prophets and the psalms must be fulfilled' (Luke 24:44). In the grand design of the Kingdom of God, the King must die!

The passion of Jesus cannot be understood apart from his work as bearer of the Kingdom of God. The cross and resurrection, (and the two must never be separated), did not bring in the kingdom; rather, they constitute its decisive battle and victory, the kingdom coming 'with power' (cf. Mark 9:1; Rom 1:3). Jesus knew that his Father willed the cross. The method for his ministry as servant required that 'The Son of man must suffer ...' (Mark 8:31 = Matt 16:21 and Luke 9:22; Luke 17:21; 24:26; Acts 17:3; 26:23). And so, to fulfill God's purpose, the coming of the Son of man was 'to serve ... give life ... as a ransom ...' (Mark 10:45).

The whole of Jesus' ministry had a way of reversing conventional, earthly thinking. In that same way, the death of King Jesus was the victory. The resurrection vindicated his claims and marked his enthronement and personal exaltation which indicate and lead to the final victory of the Kingdom of God.

A. M. Hunter, in his way of stating the profound simply and the complex briefly, summed up the relation between Jesus and the Kingdom of God this way:

In simple terms, the career of Jesus as the Servant Messiah, from Jordan to Calvary, is the Kingdom of God, God acting in his royal power, God visiting and redeeming his people. For the Kingdom of God is no earthly empire to be set up by a political coup d'etat. It is a Kingdom in which God rules redeemingly through the ministry of Jesus; not something added to the ministry, but the ministry itself. The suffering and sacrifice of Jesus, the Servant Son of man, so far from being only a prelude to the triumph, are the triumph itself, a triumph which the resurrection ... clarif[ies] and reveal[s].[3]

---

[3]A. M. Hunter, *Introducing New Testament Theology*, 23-24.

Chapter 3

Who is Jesus? – The Gospel of John

The phrase 'Kingdom of God' occurs in the fourth Gospel only in John 3:3, 5. At that point 'new birth' which results in 'life' or 'eternal life' replaces inclusion in the Kingdom as the usual way of speaking of a right relationship with God. In our seeking to understand the kind of life John has in mind, it is again to Professor Hunter that we turn for help.

> If we ask what he [John] means by 'life' the answer is: the life which is life indeed, life lived in fellowship with God through Christ its mediator, life freed from the slavery of sin, life whose finest trait is love, life that can never die.[1]

Our concern in this chapter is with 'Who is Jesus?' rather than the full meaning of life in this Gospel. However, in John part of the answer to our question is that Jesus is 'life' (14:6; cf. 5:26) and the one through whom eternal life is made available to humans (3:15-16, 36; 5:40; 10:10; 20:31). This is but a part of a much broader picture.

In the Synoptics the Kingdom of God is the primary theme for presenting the ministry of Jesus. In John the primary theme for introducing Jesus is his person as the incarnate (= 'in flesh') God-man who reveals the Father and accomplishes the work assigned by the Father. The humanity of Jesus, that he was in fact 'in flesh', is emphasized even more in 1 John 4:2: 'Every spirit which confesses that Jesus Christ has come in the flesh is of God.' Whereas in the Synoptics one was identified with the Kingdom through a commitment to Jesus, in John one is asked to 'believe' in Jesus in order that he or she may be 'in him'.

---

[1]A. M. Hunter, *Introducing the New Testament*, 3d ed.; 178.

The Synoptic presentation stresses the horizontal, temporal, the earthly tensions in the ministry of Jesus. That is, with his coming the Final Age arrived. John reflects an interplay of more of the variety of the different tensions within the conceptual setting of the New Testament. He also alludes to several dualistic structures: light and darkness, above and below, spirit and matter (or of earth), life and death, here and now versus the future, among others. Jesus is the resolver of all tensions. We will mention only a couple as illustrations of the way John speaks of Jesus in such contexts.

In Jesus, the cosmic, vertical tension melts since, while on earth, he can say, 'You are from below, I am from above; you are of this world, I am not of this world' (8:23). In his ministry he bridges that gap so that even after his return to heaven his disciples are both to 'abide in him' (15:4) and are one with each other (17:11). As he is 'lifted up' (on the cross) he 'will draw all men'[2] to himself (12:32).

In John the temporal tension is reflected in Jesus' keen awareness that he was to work within a prescribed time-frame (cf. 7:6, 8). He had come to do the Father's will (5:30), works (10:32, 37), to speak his words (12:50), and to 'be lifted up' (3:14; 8:23; 12:32), but all at the proper time. He spoke of 'his hour'. There were times that it had not yet come or was coming (2:4; 4:23; 5:25, 28; 7:30; 8:20). Later, he announces that it had come or is present (12:23; cf. vs. 27; 13:1; 17:1).

John's portrait of Jesus has many dimensions. We will look at some which will contribute to answering our question about his identity.

Jesus, the Incarnate, Divine Word

The prologue of this Gospel (1:1-14) is a unique 'essay' which presents Jesus as the 'Word' (*logos*). 'Word,' with the special meaning it has here, has a complex background in both Hebrew and Greek thought. Scholars have spread gallons of ink in attempting

---

[2]Greek, *helkuō*. In addition to 'draw', other possible translations include 'drag,' 'pull,' 'haul,' and 'attract.' The word always implies resistance. For an example, note John's use of the word in 21:6, because of the great number of fish, the disciples were not able to haul (*helkisai*) in the net.

to define the relationship between this background and its use by John. We will focus on two facts: (1) a general summary of its meaning, and (2) what is being said here about Jesus.

For the Greeks, especially Stoic philosophy, *logos* described the impersonal force through which the universe came into being. It also provided the unifying, rational principle which gives it unity and meaning.

In the Jewish world, *logos* was the translation for the Hebrew term *dābār* which denotes the avenue through which the personal God created the universe, spoke through the prophets, and revealed himself and his message to humans. This special term for *logos* can be closely associated with 'wisdom', when it is personified, as in Proverbs 8–9, which also speaks of God's creative and governing activities. In Intertestamental Jewish writings *logos* and wisdom are virtually synonymous.[3] The Intertestamental Jewish writer, Philo, who had been strongly influenced by Greek thought, uses *logos* in referring to an even more intimate self-expression and communication of God. In the post-New Testament Rabbinic writings, the Aramaic *mē'mrā* ('word'), as a translation for *logos*, can stand for the divine name.

John's use has affinities with all of these, but is distinctively Christian. The Word is not only in intimate proximity 'with God' but 'is God'. (The lack of an article before the word 'God' does not mean simply 'a god' or 'a divine being,' as some sects claim, but sets up a grammatical equation in which 'Word' and 'God' are of the same quality or kind.) The key to John's meaning is found in verses 14 and 18 where the word 'became flesh' and thereby 'he has made him [God] known'.

The *Logos* is the self-revelation of him who existed before creation and through whom 'all things were made' (vs. 3), life originated, and is 'the light of men' (vs. 4). Yet, when he, the true light, entered the world, he was neither generally recognized nor received (vss. 9-11). Those who did receive him, by God's own actions, 'became children of God' (vss. 12-13).

---

[3]Sirach 4:11-19; 14:20-27; 24:1-34; 51:13-30; Wis of Sol, esp. 6:12–11:1.

Thus, the 'bottom line' for an acceptable, favorable relationship with God in John is the same as in the Synoptics. There citizens in the Kingdom of God call him 'Father . . . Abba', in John they are called 'children of God'. But explaining this further, John introduces a term not used in those writings. Jesus is the one through whom God conveys 'grace upon grace', 'grace and truth' (vss. 16-17); grace, the unearned, undeserved gift of God's favor and acceptance. This leads to another fact about the identity of Jesus.

Jesus, the Essence and Expression of the Love of God

In his first epistle John makes the startling statement, 'God is love' (1 John 4:8). Apart from God's revelation of himself in Jesus, this might reduce God to an impersonal force, similar to the virtues of the greater pagan world. In Jesus the God-who-is-love is personal; he has become flesh and is knowable through human, sensory experiences (John 1:14; 1 John 1:1-3). The word used to equate God and love is not one of the more common nouns for 'love' (*philia*, which means 'kindly disposed or devoted', 'the love for friends one has chosen') or another word for love (*eros*) which denotes desire, (usually sexual) pleasure, joy, romantic love, love for one considered worthy. John uses a rare term for love (*agapē*) which involves love for the unworthy (1 John 4:10; Rom 5:8) and moves to creative action.

In the Synoptics God's love was implied, he is the forgiving King who through Jesus invites people into his Kingdom. John makes clear that human redemption, salvation, finds its motivation and implementation in the nature of God. In Jesus 'God so loved the world that he gave . . .' (3:16); the self-revealing God becomes also the self-giving God. Hence, Jesus says to his disciples, 'Greater love has no man than this, that a man lay down his life for his friends. You are my friends if you do what I command you' (15:13-14). This declaration of love comes beneath the shadow of the cross, the ultimate demonstration of love that is intensely personal.

Who is Jesus? He is the fleshly embodiment of God, who is love. He is the God, who is love, at work. He reveals that this kind of love expresses itself in grace; it is love for the unlovable, the unworthy, the hostile, and the resisting. In Jesus the work of this kind of love is evident in giving, rescuing, and abiding with those who respond to it.

Jesus, the 'Son' with a Unique Relation with the Father

Jesus refers to or addresses 'the Father' over a hundred times in the Fourth Gospel. Jesus himself uses the phrase 'the Son,' applying it to himself, about fifteen times and John referred to him as 'Son' in a special sense in other contexts (e.g., 1:14, 18). Jesus affirmed, 'I and the Father are one' (10:30). The implication of this claim is, 'I am the Son of God' (10:36). The title 'Son of God' is applied to him another six times (1:49; 3:18; 5:25; 11:4, 27; 20:26). Jesus' claim of divinity was clearly understood by his enemies who once sought to stone him because 'you being a man, make yourself God' (10:33; cf. 19:7).

We must give some explanation of the phrase sometimes translated 'only begotten' in reference to Jesus' sonship. Since 'to beget' means 'to become the father of', this translation has often led to misunderstanding. The Greek word is *monogenēs*. Elsewhere in the New Testament it means 'only' (Luke 7:12; 8:42; 9:38; Heb 11:17). It is used of the relationship between Jesus and the Father (John 1:14, 18; 3:16, 18; and 1 John 4:9). The Greek verb 'to beget,' 'to become the father of' comes from the root-word *gennaō*, with two '*n*s'. The root of *monogenēs* is *genēs*, with one 'n', which means 'race', 'stock', 'class' or 'kind'. The prefix *mono*- means 'one'. Hence, *monogenēs* does not refer to 'origin' but to 'being', 'type', or 'nature'; the basic idea is 'unique', or 'one of a kind'.[4] Jesus has a relation with the Father that is like none other.

The sheer weight of the numbers given above indicate that the relationship between Father and Son is a major concern of John. In John 14:28 Jesus says 'the Father is greater than I', and from this statement some have concluded that Jesus is an inferior being to

---

[4] 1 Clement (ca. AD 95, one of the 'Apostolic Fathers'), referring to an ancient legend, describes the phoenix bird as *monogenēs*, 'one of a kind,' because of the legend that it lived for 500 years and after its death it returned to life.

God the Father. However, earlier Jesus had made the affirmation, 'I and the Father are one' (10:30). On the basis of this Gospel the distinction of traditional theology seems justified, that as far as actual nature or being is concerned, the Father and Son are equal and divine; however within their role and function as to the work of God, the Son has voluntarily subordinated himself to the Father.

The identity of the two is seen in such statements as 'the Father is in me and I am in the Father ... the Father is with me' (10:38; 14:10-11, 20; 16:32); 'he who has seen me has seen the Father' (14:9). The Son lives because of the Father (5:26; 6:57). Furthermore, to know Jesus is to know the Father also (8:19; 14:7); 'to honor the Son is to honor the Father' (5:23), and to hate Jesus is to hate the Father (15:23-24). The Father and Son know each other (10:15) and the Son does what the Father does (5:19). The Son is in the bosom of the Father (1:18), came from, or was sent by, the Father (1:14; 5:36-37; 6:57; 8:18; 12:49; 13:3; 16:27-28; 20:21), and is going to the Father (13:1; 14:12, 28; 16:10, 28; 20:17).

Even in their work Father and Son are not completely separate. Both the Father and Son are working simultaneously (5:17). Jesus says he is 'the true vine,... [the] Father is the vinedresser' (15:1). The Father raises the dead and the Son gives life (5:21).

The Father sent the Son (11:42; 17:8, 18; 20:21), loves the Son (3:35; 5:20; 10:17; 15:9), and set his seal upon him (6:27). Jesus said, 'It is my Father who glorifies me, of whom you say that he is your God' (8:54; cf. 17:5). The Father bears witness to the Son (5:36-37; 8:18) and has given all things (13:3) into his hand, including judgment (5:22). The Father gives both commands (12:49) and authority (8:28) to the Son. When arrested in Gethsemane Jesus boldly accepts the cup his Father had given him to drink (18:11).

For his part, Jesus, the Son, obeys (12:50; 14:31) and honors his Father (8:49). An essential part of his task is to reveal the Father (John:18; 6:46; 10:32, 37-38; 15:15; 16:15, 25; cf. 8:27), to bear witness to and make the Father known (1:18; 5:37). In so doing he says, 'No one has seen the Father except him who is from God' (6:46); 'I speak of what I have seen with my Father' (8:38). 'The

Son can do nothing of his own accord, but only what he sees the Father doing' (5:19). In John's Gospel Jesus both speaks of praying to his Father and is portrayed doing so (11:41; 12:27-28; 15:26; 16:26; 17:1, 5, 11, 21, 24-25). The Son provides access to the Father. Of this we will speak more presently.

Jesus is the Son with a unique relation to the Father. Both are the one God, there is also a distinction between them. Jesus, the Son, is God, with God, and the Son of God. Clearly we are dealing here with both a unity and distinction of being that is beyond human comprehension.

Jesus, Revealed in 'Signs'

The most common Greek word for 'miracle' (*thauma*; Latin *miraculum*) is not used in the Gospels, and only twice in the whole of the New Testament (2 Cor 11:14; Rev 17:6). The supernatural acts of Jesus are designated by other Greek words which say something about their effect on observers. *Dunamis* means 'power' and indicates that those present were aware of the force which made the act possible. *Teras*, 'wonder,' calls attention to the reactions of those who saw the deed. These words reflect the awe of the witnesses and their awareness of both the power behind the deeds and their remarkable results. John's Gospel uses none of these, but another term, *sēmeion*, 'sign.' A sign points towards something, but what?

Of the seven miracles related by John five are specifically called 'signs': turning water into wine (2:1-11), healing an official's son (4:46-54), feeding the five thousand (6:5-14, 26), giving sight to the man born blind (9:1-41), and the raising of Lazarus from the dead (11:47; 12:18). In 6:2 John says the crowds came to Jesus because they saw the 'signs which he did on those who were diseased'. On five occasions Jesus' mighty deeds are mentioned in general as 'signs' (2:33; 3:2; 7:31; 17:27; 20:30). There were also occasions when 'signs' were requested to validate either Jesus' person, claims, or teachings (2:18; 6:30).

Sometimes in John the signs are accompanied by teaching sections which draw spiritual parallels to and from them. As examples, the feeding of the multitude is followed by his discourse on 'the bread

of life'. In connection with the healing of the blind man Jesus discusses
spiritual sight. He declares himself to be the resurrection and the life
just before raising Lazarus from the dead.

Several passages, scattered throughout the Gospel, help us
understand what John has in mind in using the word 'sign'. At a
Passover feast 'many believed in his name when they saw the signs
which he did' (2:23). Nicodemus sought an audience with Jesus
because, he said, 'We know that you are a teacher come from God;
for no one can do these signs that you do, unless God is with him'
(3:2). People who believed on him defended their conversion saying,
'When the Christ [Messiah] appears, will he do more signs than this
man has done?' (7:31). The Gospel concludes, affirming that 'Jesus
did many other signs ... which are not written in this book' but says
those which have been recorded are intended to lead the reader to
'believe that Jesus is the Christ [Messiah], the Son of God, and that
believing you may have life in his name' (20:30-31).

In John's Gospel these supernatural acts have a specific purpose,
they point to something and they help answer the question, 'Who is
Jesus?' The 'signs' point to the uniqueness and power of Jesus and
his relation to God. They validate his person; specifically they show
him to be both the Messiah and the Son of God. In addition they
provide a forum and framework with which to present expansion of
this truth and additional spiritual teachings and challenge.

The '*I Am*s' of Jesus in John

John's report about Jesus also includes some graphic figures of
speech through which Jesus presented himself and carried on his
work. A number of these are called the 'I Am' sayings because
Jesus directly says, 'I am' thus and so. Commentators often refer to
seven such statements. These traditional 'I Am's' include Jesus' claim
to be (1) the bread of life (6:35-51), (2) the light of the world (8:12),
(3) the door of the sheep (or sheepfold) (10:7-9), (4) the good
shepherd (10:11, 14), (5) the resurrection and the life (11:25), (6)
the way, the truth, and the life (14:6), and (7) the true vine (15:1).
There are other claims by Jesus using similar grammatical
constructions: (1) I am he (i.e. the Messiah, 4:27), (2) I have come

in my Father's name (5:43), (3) I am from him (= God, 7:28-29), (4) I am from above . . . not of this world (8:23), (5) I am before Abraham was (8:58), (6) I am the Son of God (10:36), and (7) I have not yet gone up (20:17).

Each of these statements could be the subject of detailed comments and studies. Here we are interested in the total force of these 'I am' statements when seen at the same time. This should convey something of the impact of what Jesus claimed about himself. These statements contribute important data for the answer to our question about Jesus' identity.

Jesus, The Messianic Son of Man

We have reached the point in our survey at which some repetition is inevitable. Yet, there are two further topics about Jesus which must be singled out. The first has to do with his person and role, the second with what he accomplished.

In most English translations of John, such as the RSV, the term 'Messiah' occurs only twice. Andrew told his brother, 'We have found the Messiah' (John 1:41) and the Samaritan woman affirms her expectation in the coming of Messiah (4:25). This is deceiving because, of course, as John explains in 1:41, 'Christ' means 'Messiah' – while 'Messiah' is from the Hebrew term and 'Christ' from the Greek, both mean 'The Anointed One'. The word 'Christ' is used nineteen times in this Gospel. In three of these John the Baptist denies that he is the Christ-Messiah. The majority of the rest report the perplexity of Jesus' contemporaries; the Samaritan woman asked, 'This one can't be the Christ, can he?' (John 4:29). At one point the Jews pled, 'If you are the Christ, tell us plainly' (10:24). However, four times John records the affirmation that Jesus is the Christ-Messiah – by Andrew (1:41), Martha, the sister of Lazarus (11:27), by Jesus himself (17:3), and as John states that his reason for writing was to bring the reader to faith that 'Jesus is the Christ, the Son of God' (20:31).

John is acutely aware of the presence of wrong notions about the Messiah and other figures expected to appear during the Final Age. He relates how John the Baptist specifically denied being 'the

Messiah', 'Elijah', or 'the Prophet [like Moses]' (1:20-21). John
mentions several occasions in which the possibility was raised that
Jesus was the Messianic Prophet, the Second Moses (on the basis
of Deuteronomy 18:15-19). In 7:40-52 'the Prophet' and 'the
Messiah' are equated.[5] It was the obvious parallel between Moses
providing food in the wilderness and Jesus feeding five thousand in
a remote area that prompted the people to conclude, 'This is indeed
the prophet who is to come into the world!' (6:14). This occasioned
Jesus' withdrawal to thwart the attempt to 'take him by force to
make him king' (6:15).

In the previous chapter we commented on the meaning of the
term 'Messiah'. In all three Synoptic Gospels Peter's confession,
that Jesus is the Christ (Messiah), is a major turning point. John,
although perhaps more obliquely, is just as concerned to present
Jesus as 'God's Anointed One,' 'The Leader *Par Excellence*,' the
long-awaited deliverer for whom Israel yearned. Just as the other
Gospel writers, John shows Jesus handling the term and concept
'delicately' and redefining it against the popular view of the day. The
other Gospels redefine it by linking it with the Son of man and suffering
servant figures of the Old Testament. John does this too; he focuses
on suffering as he devotes a larger percentage of his writing to the
final days, death, and resurrection of Jesus. As we shall see, he too
identifies Jesus as the Son of man. Unlike the others, John equates
'Messiah' with 'Son of God' (11:27; 20:31).

'Son of man' is one of the more frequently recurring designations
of Jesus in the Fourth Gospel. The Son of man descended from
heaven and is in touch with heaven through angels (1:51; 3:13; 6:6);
he will be 'lifted up' (3:14; 8:28; 12:34), gives eternal life (6:27),
and is the object of faith (9:35). Even while on earth Jesus, as Son
of man, was glorified (12:23; 13:31). God 'has given him authority
to execute judgment' (5:27). The ideas and roles of the Son of man
found in the Synoptic Gospels are here too. However, John
emphasizes in an even greater way the heavenly origin of the Son of

---

[5]The oldest known Greek manuscript of John (P[66], AD ±200) has the
definite article before the word 'prophet' in verse 52. Hence it reads, 'The
Prophet is not to arise from Galilee.'

man. Thus he reveals God and his saving work. In himself Jesus combines the themes of the Son of man both being 'lifted up' to die and his coming glorification.

Jesus, 'The Way' to God and to Life

In one of the best known passages of the Fourth Gospel, Jesus clearly states that access to the Father comes only through the Son.

> Jesus said to him, 'I am the way, and the truth, and the life; no one comes to the Father, but by me. If you had known me, you would have known my Father also; henceforth you know him and have seen him.... He who has seen me has seen the Father' (14:6-9).

Also, in 8:30, Jesus says that while sin blocks access to the Father, freedom from it comes through the Son.

There is a 'universality' of this access to God through Jesus in the Gospel of John. 'Power[6] to become children of God' is for 'all who receive him' (1:12). Eternal life is for 'whoever believes' in Jesus (3:15-16, 18, 36). 'This is the will of my Father,' he says, 'that every one who sees the Son and believes in him should have everlasting life' (6:40). As Greeks came desiring to see Jesus, he alluded to his coming death; then, stressing that any one, by implication including Gentiles, may come, says,

> He who loves his life loses it, and he who hates his life in this world will keep it for eternal life. If any one serves me, he must follow me; and where I am, there shall my servant be also; if any one serves me, the Father will honor him (12:25-26).

Jesus is 'the Christ [Messiah], the Son of God' through whom those believing in him 'may have life in his name' (20:31).

Yet, there is more; a limiting factor is also at work in attaining access to God. This is clear in statements in the sixth chapter. It is only those who have 'heard and learned from the Father' (6:45), only those whom the Father gives, who will come to Jesus (vs. 37). 'No one,' says Jesus, 'can come to me unless the Father who sent

---

[6]'Authority' is a better translation.

me draws him' (6:44-45; cf. 14:6; note that the Greek word implies 'draws in spite of resistance' [Explanation: The gist of this statement and footnote have been put on page 68.]), 'no one can come to me unless it is granted him by the Father' (6:65). This element of compulsion, drawing, is present also in 12:32: 'When I am lifted up from the earth, I will draw all men to myself.' The security of those who come to Jesus lies in the power of the Father, for, Jesus says, 'My Father, who has given them to me, is greater than all, and no one is able to snatch them out of the Father's hand' (10:29).

There is one element of access to the Father still to be noted. Disciples are instructed that they are to pray to the Father but to do so in Jesus' name (14:13; 15:16; 16:23).

In John 14:6 Jesus also says he is 'the life'. Of the concept of life in John we have already spoken. Jesus both is life and gives life (1:4; 5:21, 26, 40; 6:53; 8:12; 20:31). His provision for life is also part of his discourses on the Good Shepherd, the Resurrection and Life, and the bread of life. At times it is not clear whether the gift of life is physical or spiritual. Each of the sixteen times John records the phrase 'eternal life', 'the life of (or into) the ages,' it is clearly associated with spiritual life, that life of which we earlier quoted Hunter as describing as 'life that can never die'.

Summary: John's Answer to the Question, 'Who is Jesus?'

In the Gospel of John, Jesus is the one whose self-disclosure reveals the person and will of God and accomplishes the work of God. Jesus is the Son of God who came from and returns to the Father. He is the pre-existent *Logos,* the divine Son of the Father, yet he 'became flesh'. He was so truly human that even from the cross he made provision for Mary, his mother (19:26). Jesus is the Messiah-Mosaic Prophet-Son of man who is 'lifted up' to suffer, redeem, and bring people back to God. Jesus is the one in whom people are to believe in order to obtain eternal life. The hated Samaritans affirmed of him, 'this is indeed the Savior of the world' (4:42).

Throughout his earthly life Jesus said that the Scriptures (5:39) and the works that were done in his Father's name (10:25) bore witness to him. He predicted that after his departure 'the Counselor (the Paraclete), 'whom,' he said, 'I shall send to you from the Father, even the Spirit of truth, who proceeds from the Father, he will bear witness to me' (15:26).

After the resurrection of Jesus his disciples moved into a new dimension of their understanding of who Jesus is. The fact of the resurrection enabled them to view events and teachings he gave earlier in a new light (2:17, 22; 12:16). As it all began to come together, as he saw the risen Jesus, a previous doubter among their number summed up and answered the question of Jesus' identity personally, 'My Lord and my God!' (20:28).

Chapter 4

Who is Jesus? – The Rest of the New Testament

We would not be far wrong to say that the Gospels present the person and work of Jesus and the rest of the New Testament is concerned with the interpretation and the implications of his person and ministry. Indeed, very little is added to the facts of his pre-resurrection life in these writings. The only statement in the New Testament quoted from Jesus that is not found in the Gospels is, 'It is more blessed to give than to receive' (Acts 20:35). The letters of Paul make brief allusions to the life of Jesus here and there but only in 1 Corinthians 15:3-7 are there significant additions to what we learn of Jesus in the Gospels. Here we are told of post-resurrection appearances of Jesus 'to more than five hundred brethren at one time, most of whom are still alive, though some have died' and 'to James' (meaning, James the relative of Jesus, not the apostle). Both the writer of Hebrews and Peter make some references to the sufferings of Jesus, and 2 Peter makes reference to his transfiguration (1:16-18).

We will attempt to collect data about the identity of Jesus by (1) listing some important names and titles applied to Jesus, (2) looking at statements arising from some important passages in Acts and the epistles of Paul, (3) making some observations on Jesus in Hebrews, James, 1 and 2 Peter, Jude, and, finally (4) note some aspects of Jesus shown in the Book of Revelation.

Names and Titles

Vincent Taylor, in *The Names of Jesus*, gives brief studies of some forty two or more names and titles of Jesus.[1] The main reason for such an approach is exemplified by Professor Oscar Cullmann in his book *The Christology of the New Testament*.[2] He attempts

---

[1]Vincent Taylor, *The Names of Jesus*, Macmillan, 1953).
[2]Oscar Cullman (1959), *The Christology of the New Testament*, SCM Press.

to give answers to the question 'Who is Jesus?' by using what he called 'Functional Christology'. In the early centuries of the church this term was used by some outside mainstream orthodoxy to mean that Jesus was really not divine, but only functioned in that role. This is not at all Cullmann's assumption. Rather, he focuses attention on certain names and titles which, he believes, reveal the functions or roles of Christ. These, he believes, tell us something of what he *did*; the assumption is that Jesus did what he did because of who he was. Thus the names and titles provide clues to the individuality and nature of Jesus as well as give interpretation of his significance.

Many of the names and titles have either explicit or implicit backgrounds in the Old Testament, Intertestamental Judaism, and/ or the Greco-Roman world. Nevertheless, and this is most important, the names and titles, although they reflect their broader background, have been *adapted* in view of the life and ministry of Jesus.

Here we will list less than half the number of the names and titles as did Taylor. We cannot dig as deeply into their significance as did Cullmann. Among the more important ways with which New Testament writers speak of the man of Nazareth are (1) Jesus ('The LORD is Savior'), (2) Christ; The Christ; Jesus Christ; Christ Jesus; the Lord Jesus Christ; Our Lord Jesus Christ; Jesus Christ our Lord; Our Savior, Christ Jesus, (3) The Lord, (4) The Son of God; The Son; His Son; The Only Begotten Son, (5) Servant/Child (*pais*, a term which usually associates Jesus with the Servant of God of Isaiah), (6) The Holy One, (7) The Righteous/Just One (*ho Dikaios*), (8) Author/Pioneer/etc. (*Archēgos*), (9) Savior, (10) Prophet, The Prophet, The Prophet Like Moses, (11) The Mediator, (12) The High Priest, (13) The Image of God, (14) The Radiance of the Divine Glory, (15) The Power and the Wisdom of God, (16) The Last or Second Adam, (17) The Crucified One, (18) The Reconciler, and (19) Son of man.

We have already commented on the significance of some of the names and titles in previous chapters. We will look at others as we continue our study of 'Who is Jesus?'

Who is Jesus in Acts and the Epistles of Paul?

The major emphasis outside the Gospels is summarized in Acts 2:36: 'It is this Jesus whom you nailed to the cross, that God has made *Lord* and *Messiah*.' 'Messiah', as we have discussed above, is a distinctively Jewish title, but we must remember that as it is used by the early Christians, they do so believing that 'Jesus is the Messiah'. Hence, their meaning is different from that of their Jewish contemporaries. For the Christians, the Messiah is a not a coming force or person, he is an individual who had come, lived among people; one whom they knew and to whom they bore witness.

Outside the Jewish world it held little meaning. Hence, in Gentile areas 'Jesus the Messiah (the Christ)' became 'Jesus Christ'; 'Christ' ceased being a title and became a personal name. This appears to be what happened in Antioch when Jesus' followers became known as 'Christ's Ones', or 'Christians' (Acts 11:26).

'Lord' (*kurios*) has a wide range of possible meanings. It might be equivalent to such English terms as 'mister,' 'sir,' 'master,' 'your honor,' 'your excellency,' 'your majesty,' or 'God.' Only the context can determine the shade of meaning intended. Liberal theology frequently claims that Jesus was called 'Lord', in a superhuman sense, only after the resurrection and only after Christianity entered the Gentile world. That the lordship of Jesus was better understood after the resurrection there is no doubt. However, there are clear indications that even during his earthly life he was called or referred to as 'Lord' in a more than human sense.[3] The Aramaic phrase *maran atha* ('Our Lord is coming') or *marana tha* ('Our Lord, Come!') shows that the earliest Jewish church prayed to Jesus as 'Lord'.[4] The circumstances hardly

---

[3]Special uses of 'Lord' by others as they refer to Jesus: Matt 8:25; 14:30; 20:30ff.; Mark 9:24; special uses of the term by Jesus about himself: Luke 6:46 (= Matt 7:21); Mark 2:28 (= Matt 12:8; Luke 6:5); Mark 5:19; 11:3; cf. Mark 12:35-36 (= Luke 20:42-44; Matt 22:40-46) along with quotation of Ps. 110.

[4]*Mar* is the Aramaic word for 'lord' (1 Cor 16:22; Rev 22:20; Didache 10:6).As an example, in these references *Mar* is the first syllable of a well known Aramaic phrase which can be read in one of two different ways: Maran atha (2d person indicative) a statement of faith, "Our Lord Comes" or "Our Lord Will Come" or Marana tha (imperative) , a prayer, "Our Lord, Come!"

allow understanding the address of the dying Stephen's prayer, 'Lord Jesus, receive my spirit' (Acts 7:59), as meaning something like, 'Mr. Jesus . . .'

'Lord' was the term used most often by the early Christians. They did so with the full conviction that Jesus was the long-sought Messiah, the one who had been raised from the dead, ascended into heaven, and is even now at the right hand of the Father. One of the earliest Christian confessions was 'Jesus is Lord!' More about this title when we comment on Philippians 2.

The next title for Jesus appears as Peter, addressing Jews in Jerusalem and their leaders, also described Jesus as the one 'whom you nailed to the cross'. Jesus is 'the crucified one!' We have already commented on the shame this title bore in the Gentile world and the scandal it was for Jews – a crucified Messiah was a cursed Messiah (cf. Deut 21:22-23). It is this very problem that Paul addresses in Galatians 3:10-14: Jesus' curse was really our curse; the curse of the law (sin is a result of breaking God's law) fell upon him so that we might escape out from under it, and that the blessing of the Messiah might come upon us.

In summarizing the 'good news', the 'gospel', Paul affirms that through Jesus' death and resurrection, sins can be forgiven, according to the Scriptures (1 Cor 15:1-8). He mixes both historical facts – 'Christ died,' 'he was buried,' ' and 'he was raised on the third day' – with interpretation: this was 'for (or with reference to) our sins' and the Christ-event was 'according to the Scriptures'. This is what God had planned long ago and revealed in the Old Testament. This was God's way of dealing with sin, of making salvation possible. It is to be accepted by faith.

Third, the early church affirms that only through Jesus can human beings be accepted by God. There are numerous names and titles which highlight one or another aspect of this fact. For example, he is the 'Savior' since it is by him that people may be 'saved' (Acts 16:31). He is our 'Reconciler' because through him we who were enemies may be turned into friends and allies of God (2 Cor 5:15-21).

In Philippians 2:6-11 Paul's rhetoric, possibly as he quotes from an ancient Christian hymn, soars as he sets forth, as an example of humility, the suffering and now exaltation of Jesus as Lord of heaven and earth. Jesus was in the 'form of God', and 'did not count equality with God a thing to be grasped' (presumably, because he already had it). He 'emptied himself.' For centuries theologians have debated the question, 'Of what did Jesus empty himself?' Jesus himself probably gives us the answer when he prayed, 'Father, glorify me in your own presence with the glory which I had with you before the world was made' (John 17:5). He took 'the form of a servant', but even such spiritual beings as angels are servants. Jesus was actually born 'in the likeness of men ... [and] found in human form,' definitely, as Hebrews 2:7 says, 'lower than the angels.' He 'became obedient unto death', and, death is, to say the least, humbling. His was even death by crucifixion, the worst of all forms of death!

But now, the dramatic turning point!

> God has highly exalted him and bestowed on him the name which is above every name, that at the name of Jesus every knee should bow, in heaven and on earth and under the earth, and every tongue confess that Jesus Christ is Lord, to the glory of God the Father (vss. 9-11).

Who is Jesus? He is the exalted 'Lord' before whom all must bow!

Paul gives glimpses of Jesus from another perspective. As creator, sustainer, and ruler of the material and spiritual universe, he is 'The Cosmic Christ.' The elements of the text in Colossians 1:15-17 are instructive.

> He is the image of the invisible God,
> the first-born of all creation;
> for in him all things were created, in heaven and on earth, visible and invisible, whether thrones or dominions or principalities or authorities – all things were created through him and for him.
> He is before all things, and in him all things hold together.

In the same vein, Paul says, through 'one Lord Jesus Christ ... are all things and through [him] we exist' (1 Cor 8:6). In 1 Corinthians 1:24, Christ is 'the power of God and the wisdom of God'. This, then, provides the setting for 1 Corinthians 2:6-10:

Among the mature we do impart wisdom, although it is not a wisdom of this age or of the rulers of this age, who are doomed to pass away. But we impart a secret and hidden wisdom of God, which God decreed before the ages for our glorification. None of the rulers of this age understood this; for if they had, they would not have crucified the Lord of glory. But, as it is written, 'What no eye has seen, nor ear heard, nor the heart of man conceived, what God has prepared for those who love him,' God has revealed to us through the Spirit. For the Spirit searches everything, even the depths of God.

In Romans 8:19-22 Paul informs us that by his death Christ redeems the cosmic order.

Much more could, of course, be said of Paul's presentation of Jesus. It will be, especially in the next chapter, when we look at his role as the provider of salvation. Perhaps the best summary is found in 1 Timothy 2:5 where he who is uniquely the Son of God is 'the Mediator' between God and human beings.

Who is Jesus in Hebrews and the Epistles of James, Peter, and Jude?
In addition to frequent references to Jesus, Christ, or Jesus Christ, Hebrews refers to Jesus with such names and titles as (1) Lord (1:10; 2:3; 12:6 [?]) and the Lord, Jesus Christ (13:20); (2) Son (1:2, 5, 8:3:6; 5:5, 8; 7:28); (3) Son of God (4:14; 6:6; 10:29); (4) God (1:8); (5) first-born (1:6); (6) Author/Pioneer/etc.;[5] (7) Priest or High Priest (2:17; 3:1; 4:14, 15; 9:11; 10:21); (8) Apostle (or 'messenger,' 3:1). He is (9) likened to or, by implication, identified as the second Moses (3:2 [8:5ff.]) and Joshua (4:8). Jesus is compared to (10) Melchizedek (5:6, 10; 6:20; 7:1). He is (11) The Coming One (10:37); (12) The Righteous (or Just) One (10:38), (13) The Perfecter (or 'finisher,' 12:2); (14) Mediator of a New Covenant (12:24); and (15) The Great Shepherd of the Sheep (13:20). The phrase 'The Day' (10:25) may also refer to Jesus.

---

[5]*Archēgos*, Heb 2:10; 12:2. See J. Julius Scott, Jr., '*Archēgos* in the Salvation History of the Epistle to the Hebrews,' *Journal of the Evangelical Theological Society*, 29/1 (March, 1986), 47-54.

Three facets of the evidence about Jesus in Hebrews must be singled out for special note. First, the opening statement:

> In many and various ways God spoke of old to our fathers by the prophets; but in these last days he has spoken to us by a Son, whom he appointed the heir of all things, through whom also he created the world. He reflects the glory of God and bears the very stamp of his nature, upholding the universe by his word of power. When he had made purification for sins, he sat down at the right hand of the Majesty on high, having become as much superior to angels as the name he has obtained is more excellent than theirs (Heb 1:1-4).

The initial phrase contrasts God's revelation in the Old Testament, through the patriarchs and prophets, to that now available ('in these last days,' that is, 'in this, the Final Age') through Jesus, the Son. Again he is designated as the 'Cosmic Christ' – as heir, creator, and sustainer of 'all things'. The cosmic Lord is also the one who has made available cleansing from sin. His present position is that of highest power and greatest glory.

Verse 3 makes a profound statement about Jesus but one difficult to convey in English. The key word is translated in the RSV as 'reflects'.[6] It refers to that light which shines out from the source of light, the actual embodiment of light itself. (Hence, some of the early church fathers spoke of Jesus as 'Light of Lights'.) It is 'the Glory' of which Jesus is the 'out shining'. The words 'of God' in most English translations, which make the passage read 'the glory of God', are not found in the Greek. 'The Glory' was a common Jewish way of speaking about God without using the word God or one of his names. The later Rabbis actually had a special word, 'the Shekinah,' which they used to describe the clouds, brightness, and other forms in which God revealed himself in glory. Hence, Jesus is described as the actual embodiment, the outward-radiant manifestation of 'The Glory'; that is, the 'out shining' of God himself. In Hebrew circles

---

[6]*Apaugasma*, 'effulgence' in the KJV and 'radiance' in the NASB and NIV.

there could hardly be a more pointed and graphic way of affirming the full deity of Jesus.

The fourth verse of our passage refers to Jesus as being 'better' or 'superior' to angels. The idea of 'better' is expressed thirteen times in this little book of as many chapters. Three references set the tone for the rest: through Jesus a 'better hope is introduced, through which we draw near to God' (7:19); Jesus is a 'surety of a better covenant' (7:11); and 'Christ has obtained a ministry which is as much more excellent [better] than the old as the covenant he mediates is better, since it is enacted on better promises' (8:6). The point of the author is twofold. First, Jesus is better than Old Testament means of revelation, leadership, and worship – angels, Moses, Joshua, priesthood, sacrifices, and other ceremonies. He is the actual embodiment of all of which these spoke and toward which they pointed. Second, Hebrews assumes that the Final Age has been brought by Christ. In him, because Jesus 'appeared once for all at the end of the age' (9:26), believers have 'obtained [a better] salvation' (1:14), 'better rest' (3:18), 'tasted the power of the age to come' (6:5). Consequently, because of Jesus the old is 'obsolete and growing old and is ready to vanish away' (8:13). Jesus is the bearer of the Final Age and all that it entails!

Of particular concern in Hebrews is Jesus' role as High Priest (after the order of Melchizedek (3:1; 4:13–10:39). An understanding of the fact and implications of this is a mark of Christian maturity (6:12–7:3). We cannot here go into detail about Jesus as High Priest. Suffice to say that in this role Jesus has revealed God, offered sacrifice and completed other parts of the Levitical cremony, rules over God's people, has made atonement[7] and provided forgiveness for sins and thus opened the way 'once-and-for-all'.

The finality of God's redemptive work in Jesus, is established by one little Greek word, *ephapax*, meaning once-and-for-all.

---

[7]Strictly speaking 'atonement' is not a Biblical word; its lone occurrence in the KJV in Romans 5:11 should be translated 'reconciliation'. 'Atonement' is an Anglo-Saxon term meaning 'making at one' or referring to the process of bringing estranged parties together.

Why is there no longer new revelation from God? The purpose of revelation is to make God and his will known. This has been done finally and completely as humans are confronted with and brought to know and understand God in the life and ministry of Jesus. Why are there no longer daily sacrifices and temple-centered observances? Because Jesus offered himself and entered into the Holy Place *once-and-for-all* (7:27; 9:12); outside of his death there is no longer any other sacrifice for sin (10:18, 26); believers need no other sanctifying work, for it has been provided *once-and-for-all* 'through the offering of the body of Jesus' (10:10). No more needs to be done, no more can be done, for Jesus is the completed word and work of God. His kingdom is forever (1:8); in Christ believers receive a kingdom 'that cannot be shaken' (12:28).

Sometimes the Epistle of James has been assessed as essentially a Jewish document. Well, James (2:5) asks, 'Has not God chosen those who are poor in the world to be rich in faith and heirs of the Kingdom which he has promised to those who love him?' The rest of the New Testament assumes that the kingdom is offered through Jesus, and its heirs are those who come into it through him. This statement may, then, be an allusion to Jesus as the bearer of the Kingdom of God.

Otherwise, James answers our question, 'Who is Jesus?' with only five brief references to him. But in those the epistle shows itself to be thoroughly Christian. He is 'The Lord, Jesus Christ' (1:1), 'our Lord, Jesus Christ' (2:1). His is the 'good name' (RSV says, 'honorable name') by which Christians are called (2:7). Although the name 'Jesus' is not mentioned in the immediate setting, he is certainly the one to whom James refers as 'The Righteous' (or The Just One) who has suffered and died (5:6), the coming Lord (5:7), and the Judge who is standing at the doors (5:9).

James' most powerful statement about Jesus is almost buried in English translations of 2:1, 'our Lord Jesus Christ, the Lord of glory.' As in Hebrews 1:3 the phrase 'the Lord', as a modifier of 'the glory', is not in the original. A perfectly legitimate translation would read 'our Lord, Jesus Christ, the Glory'. In this case, as in the

Hebrews passage, 'the Glory' becomes a typically Jewish way of saying 'God'. If this verse is so understood, the other references to James in this epistle make an even more powerful statement about the divine nature of Jesus.

In 1 Peter, Jesus is the Lord of Christians and the church (1:3; 2:3; 3:12); believers are specifically instructed to 'reverence Christ as Lord' (3:15). Although certainly not as clear as in John's Gospel, 1:20 implies the pre-existence of Jesus: [he] 'was destined before the foundation of the world but was made manifest at the end of the times for your sake.' He is the 'living stone, rejected by men but in God's sight chosen and precious' (2:4). His suffering is an example for Christians who suffer (2:21-23); but his suffering is the basis for our righteousness which should lead to lives of holiness (2:24; 3:17-18; 4:1-3, 13-16). The hope of believers is established 'through the resurrection of Jesus Christ from the dead' (1:3-4). Jesus is the 'Shepherd and Guardian' of the souls of those who belong to him (2:25; 5:4). Believers are called to the 'eternal glory in Christ, he himself will establish and strengthen' (5:10).

In 2 Peter, again, Jesus is the Christian's Lord (1:2, 11, 16; 2:9, 11, 20; 3:2, 8-10, 15, 18). He is the Savior (1:11; 2:20; 3:3, 18; cf. 3:15). The epistle's greeting expresses the wish, 'May grace and peace be multiplied to you in the knowledge of God and of Jesus our Lord' (1:2). This implies a close relationship, if not the actual identity, of God and Jesus. The reference to 'knowledge' here and elsewhere (1:8; 2:20; 3:18; cf. 1:16ff) and to the 'corruption that is in the world' (1:4) have led some interpreters to assume the epistle reflects an incipient Gnosticism (which regarded everything material as evil). It is more likely that Peter turns the Gnostics' vocabulary back upon themselves. Although, like the Gnostics, Peter does see the material world as temporal (3:8-10), he does not view the material world as completely useless and to be rejected. God has revealed himself in it through both the written and the incarnate word (1:16-21); Christ's saving and preserving work takes place in the material world and Christians are to live appropriately in it.

Conduct and perseverance in the world (1:3-10) are based upon the 'kingdom theology'; 'so there will be richly provided for you an entrance into the eternal Kingdom of our Lord and Savior Jesus Christ' (1:11). The end of the material order will come with the return of Jesus. The book holds that he who was the earthly Jesus is also the Son, the Savior, Lord, and in control in heaven and earth, in time and eternity.

Jesus is called Master (*despotēs*) and Lord in Jude (4, 21). Through him comes God's mercy which leads to eternal life (21). In Jude's majestic benediction, Jesus is the Lord through whom God saves, preserves, and glorifies. To him it ascribes glory, majesty, dominion, and authority for all eternity (25).

Who is Jesus in the Book of Revelation?

It is Jesus Christ who is the object of revelation[8] in this book (1:1). Were this fact better appreciated, interpretations of it would proceed much differently than is customary. The tone is set in the first chapter where Jesus is presented as 'the faithful witness, the first-born of the dead, and the ruler of kings on earth ... who loves us and has freed us from our sins by his blood' (1:5). He is the Alpha and the Omega ... who was and who is to come, the Almighty (1:8; cf. 21:6; 22:13). He is 'like a son of man' in the middle of the lampstands, awesome in his appearance, majestic in his clothing (1:13-16; cf. 14:14). He is 'the first and the last, and the living one; [who] died, and ... [is] alive for evermore, and ... [possesses] the keys of Death and Hades' (1:12-18; cf. 20:13-14). With authority he addresses the churches.

There are over twenty-five references to 'the Lamb' in Revelation. Usually a lamb symbolizes meekness and submission, the victim at sacrifices, and is both the sacrifice and the meal for the observance of Passover. Although the fact and concept of sacrifice is never totally absent from any context in which the Lamb appears in Revelation, John's Apocalypse expands these images.

The Lamb first appears in chapter five with the breaking of the seals on the scroll. At first 'no one was found worthy to open the scroll or to look into it' (5:4). Upon realizing this the prophet wept. He was comforted with the assurance that 'the Lion of the tribe of

---

[8] *apokalupsis,* 'a revealing of the hidden.'

Judah, the Root of David, has conquered, so that he can open the scroll' (5:5). That Lion and Root was none other than a Lamb, 'as though it had been slain' (5:6), whom the hosts of heaven and earth honor and worship (5:8, 13). The Lamb proceeds to open the seven seals (6:1–9:21, note esp. 6:1; 8:1).

Hints as to the identity of the Lamb include his having been slain (5:6; 12:21; 13:8), his close relation with God (5:13; 7:9-10, 17; 14:4, 10; 21:22; 22:1, 3), his being called 'Lord of lords and King of kings' (17:14), and the mention of 'the twelve apostles of the Lamb' (21:14). Although after the first chapter and until 22:16 Jesus does not appear by name as an actor in the book, there can be little doubt that 'The Lamb' is none other than Jesus himself. In the latter passage he also identifies himself as 'the root and offspring of David, the bright and morning star.' It is he, Jesus, the Lamb, who plays the central role in Salvation History.

The Lamb is the Savior, leader-ruler of his people (7:14, 17; 14:4; 19:11), and the warrior who conquers and through whom his followers have conquered (12:11; 14:1; 17:14). He is the object of honor and worship (5:8, 12-13; 7:9-10; 15:3). Those whose names are not written in his 'book of life' (13:8) face the judgment and wrath of the Lamb (6:16; 14:10; 19:11). When the end comes, the Lamb receives his Bride (19:7; 21:9) and dines with the Blessed at his marriage supper (19:9). 'The Lord God Almighty and the Lamb' are central in the new heaven and the new earth (21:22; 22:1). In a statement reflective of Hebrews 1:3 and James 2:1, where the Son is 'the Glory', Revelation 21:23 says of the celestial city that it 'has no need of sun or moon to shine upon it, for the glory of God is its light, and its lamp is the Lamb.'

We have hardly exhausted the Christological names, titles, roles, and deeds in Revelation. In addition to what has been said, he is entitled the Messiah (11:15; 12:10; 20:4-6), the Son of God (2:18), 'the Amen, the faithful and true witness, the beginning of God's creation' (3:14). Jesus is also called 'Faithful and True' (19:11), and 'the Word of God' (19:13).

Early in our quest to determine 'Who is Jesus?' we saw him as the bearer of the Kingdom of God. Now, the reader of Revelation also recognizes him as the King in that Kingdom. As the eschatological drama enters its final acts, heavenly voices cry, 'The kingdom of this world has become the Kingdom of our Lord and of his Christ, and he shall reign for ever and ever' (11:15). As the end draws nearer and the consummation of Christ's victory dawns, the words ring out, 'Now the salvation and the power and the Kingdom of our God and the authority of his Christ have come, for the accuser of our brethren has been thrown down' (12:10). And then, 'Hallelujah! For the Lord our God the Almighty reigns' (19:6). In the end, in the heavenly city, 'There shall no more be anything accursed, but the throne of God and of the Lamb shall be in it, and his servants shall worship him' (22:3).

Who is Jesus? – A Summary

It is not with the carefully crafted, precise statements so much adored by the theologian that the New Testament presents Jesus. It does not employ the abstract metaphysical propositions of western philosophical thought. One does not come to know a person in that way. The New Testament invites the reader to come, see, hear, feel, contemplate, and make a personal response. And yet, information about an individual can be a valuable prologue to becoming acquainted with the person of that individual. Modern personal information and recommendation forms usually enquire about the background and nature of the subject, something of his or her activities, and the relation with and reactions of others.

What can we say about the background and nature of this person, Jesus of Nazareth, who is called 'The Christ'? The New Testament says he is the virgin-born, unique Son of God, the Logos who is God in flesh. He was a teacher who acted and taught with distinct authority. It claims that Jesus was the suffering, dying, rising Servant, Son of man, Messiah. In him were met 'the hopes and fears of all the years', especially for God's people. In Jesus, God did his work. He is commended further as one who did not stay dead! He arose; God raised him up. And, he ascended into heaven and now sits as Lord at the right hand of God. But that's not all, he is also coming again, as king.

What about his activities, accomplishments, and the caliber of his work? Well, he inaugurated the 'Final Age', brought to earth the Kingdom of God in a special way. He reveals the person and will of God; he was and remains the mediator between God and human beings. This involved a unique display of divine love and infinite, amazing grace! For he accomplished God's will and he made provision for salvation within Salvation History at the cost of his life, which he willingly gave. Because his death and resurrection dealt with human sin and the estrangement and guilt it caused, he dealt effectively, efficiently, and completely with both the objective and the interpersonal, relational aspects of the God-human relationship. He does not leave work incomplete, along with the Father he sends the Holy Spirit and works through 'his own' to continue and expand the establishment of the Kingdom of God and his own Lordship. He has planned for and anticipates the completion of his work, at the consummation.

What can we say about the reactions to Jesus? We must admit he was the center of controversy. While Jesus enjoyed great popularity, he also faced severe opposition. There was much perplexity about Jesus' person. Individuals who came into contact with him made different assessments of him. The majority of the crowds who flocked to him thought him to be a prophet, a good man, a teacher, a doer of supernatural 'signs'. Others, including some from the leadership of the nation and religious structure, saw Jesus as one who led people astray (a dangerous man), maybe a demon-possessed individual. Even some members of his own family feared he was insane. Those who knew him best, convinced that he was the Messiah, the Son of God, committed themselves to him completely.

The divinely inspired writers of our primary sources of information about Jesus, the Gospels, present the evidence, indicate their convictions, and invite readers to make their own assessments of Jesus. The rest of the New Testament expands and interprets. History confirms that each person must make her or his own decision and act accordingly on their answer to the question, 'Who is Jesus?'

Chapter 5

What Must I Do to be Saved?

The Need For Salvation

This question, regarding the 'how' of salvation, presupposes another one, 'saved from what?' The traditional, theological answer is, 'From sin and its consequences.' True, but much more needs to be said. The Old Testament portrays sin as essentially disobedience against God, as rebellion against his government and law. The emphasis is on positive refusal of humans to conform to God's will or to obey his laws, on their committing overt acts rather than upon their omissions of right attitudes or action. This positive rebellion and refusal of people may take different forms: deviation from the clearly marked path (= the Law), rebellion against the rightful, righteous ruler, or doing what is intrinsically evil. In any case, the Old Testament emphasizes that sin leaves the individual or community guilty before the divine Judge.

The New Testament view of sin is somewhat more complex. The writers use at least fifteen Greek words to spotlight differing aspects of sin. A few brief statements may help illustrate this point. Jesus indicates that sin is not to believe in him (John 16:9). Paul, in Romans, says sinners 'fall short of the glory of God' (that is, the perfect standard which is God's very nature, 3:23) and that 'whatever does not proceed from faith is sin' (14:23). In 1 John 3:4, 'sin is lawlessness'; in 5:17, 'wrongdoing' (wickedness, moral inconsistency, injustice). When viewed as a whole, sin, in the New Testament, is missing the mark (failing to conform to God's nature and will), a deviation from the standard, or a depraved condition which results in a whole lifestyle as well as individual attitudes and actions. It consists of both a state of being and acts of rebellion or disobedience against God.

The Synoptic Gospels assume that sin is closely linked to the presence and activity of the Kingdom of Satan. John lays it to Satan himself (John 13:27; 1 John 3:8-10). James, speaking of individual acts of sin, recognizes the inner, subjective influence as the individual is 'tempted by one's own desire, being lured and enticed by it' (1:14). Paul alone deals more precisely with the origin of sin. He connects it with the fall of Adam and Eve as described in Genesis 3 (Rom 5:12ff.; 1 Cor 15:21ff., 45; 2 Cor 11:3, and 1 Tim 2:13ff).

Much contemporary theology tends to minimize or deny the effects of sin upon God. Yet, the basic New Testament assumption is that God is holy and just, and that 'the wrath of God is revealed ... against all ungodliness and wickedness' (Rom 1:18). The entire elaborate scheme of God's provision of salvation in which Christ came 'to serve and to give his life a ransom for many' (Mark 10:45) and died 'for our sins' (1 Cor 15:3) demonstrates that the results of sin include both its offence to God as well as leaving humans in desperate need. Paul has this in mind when he says that God put Christ Jesus forward to show or prove 'that he himself is righteous and that he justifies the one who has faith in Jesus' (Rom 3:26); that maintaining God's personal nature as 'righteous' requires that satisfaction for sin be made before he can pronounce the guilty person 'innocent' or 'justified'.

It is the effects of sin upon humanity about which we are better informed. At the outset we noted the distinction between people *being* sinners, i.e. that they have sinful natures, and that they are *doing* or *committing* sinful acts or omissions. This appears to be Jesus' point when he says that all kinds of evil come 'from within, from the human heart' (Mark 7:21-22). 'Heart' here is a metaphor for 'the governing disposition' of the person. Paul reflects on the same, 'By one man's disobedience the many were made sinners' (Rom 5:19). The assumption of Biblical writers as a whole is that humankind is corrupt and depraved as a result of their refusal to recognize and honor God. This is precisely Paul's point in Romans 1:18-32, that sinful deeds, habits, attitudes, and lifestyles come from humanity's prior rejection of God. Furthermore, the New Testament writers as a whole assume that whether they speak of the sinful nature (originating in the acts of Adam as representative of the race), or acts by the individual, one is responsible for one's own sin and will bear its consequences.

The New Testament considers results of sinful natures and deeds from a number of points of view. From the legal perspective, the sinner is guilty, 'condemned already' (John 3:18). Using the language of social status the sinner is said to be in bondage (Rom 8:21; Gal 4:8; Heb 2:14), a 'captive' (Luke 4:18, quoting Isa 61:1), and a 'slave' (John 8:34). In political-military terms as well as the language of interpersonal relationships, sin makes people enemies with God and alienates them from him and even from one another.

In surveying the worldview of Biblical writers we noted that Paul, in Romans 1:21 and 8:10, speaks of sin as bringing the mental state of persons and the condition of the natural order into a situation he describes with a special Greek word, *mataiotēs*. We noted that this word speaks of emptiness, futility, transitoriness, purposelessness, and frustration – a state assumed to be inherent in the universe by many contemporary thinkers, but, by Biblical writers, rather the result of sin. This point is very important. Within the succession of passing generations the effects of sin often show themselves with different emphases. To illustrate, here in the first quarter of the twenty-first century, many thoughtful persons view life with anger, hostility, and restless rebellion in the face of what they perceive as their own helplessness and disgust at their inability to make a difference in the world. The social world has indeed changed since the middle of the twentieth century. The breakdown of moral standards and traditional institutions such as the family, coupled with economic instability, and the increase of violence are real, and often engender a loss of hope. The result can be emotional and spiritual trauma rendering the person powerless to make lasting commitments, begin careers or families, or develop the maturity needed to function in the greater world.[1] It is important to understand that these social, moral, political, and cultural evils are not inherent in the universe. Nor do they accurately

---

[1]See the helpful analysis by William Mahedy and Janet Bernardi, *A Generation Alone: Xers Making a Place in the World* (Downers Grove, IL: InterVarsity, 1994).

reflect the true value of the individual. The Biblical writers correctly recognize the nature of the universe as corrupted and distorted by sin. They also realize two additional facts, that (1) this is not the way things were made, intended to be, nor always will be and (2) God's saving work is directed specifically at both the cause and the symptoms of the perceptions of emptiness, frustrations, and aloneness.

Finally, the New Testament depicts humanity helpless to do anything about its sin and its sinful condition. Paul insists that the best of human efforts at keeping even the God-given Old Testament law cannot bring innocence or freedom from sin (Rom 3:20; Gal 2:16; 3:11). In fact, sin brings 'death'. 'Death' may, of course, refer to the cessation of human life, 'the last enemy to be destroyed' (1 Cor 15:26). Of even greater consequence is spiritual death, death 'through trespasses and sins' (Eph 2:1; cf. vs. 5) which leaves one incapable of earning acceptance with or even responding to God.

Were the question of this chapter 'What *can* I do to be saved?', the answer, because of sin and its consequences, would be, 'Nothing!' In Romans 1:18–3:20 Paul shows the wrath and judgment of God upon sin. He declares that sin has left people and the world helpless, and that all people, Jews and Gentiles alike, are at an equal disadvantage because of sin. Even 'before the foundation of the world' God determined to make hope and salvation available through Jesus Christ (Eph 1:3-14). In Romans 3:21-30 he uses a number of figures of speech to show that God's justice is vindicated and human helplessness is overcome through God's actions in Jesus.

The Ministry of Jesus Christ: The Provision of Salvation

'God's actions' – these words return us to 'grace', a concept to which we have already made reference. We define grace as 'the unearned, undeserved gift of God's favor and acceptance'. Grace is a Biblical affirmation to which we will return time and again. We must seek to expand both our understanding of it and its implications; it is one of those features which make Christianity unique. Here we should add that the grace of God is evident in God's taking the initiative to provide salvation – just as he called Abraham,[2] so too he draws sinners to himself.

In the New Testament 'grace' is 'God's actions *in Jesus*.' In Jesus, God's work of grace reaches its climax; in him grace is made known in its fullest sense. All of Jesus' earthly ministry is involved in God's gracious provision of salvation, for God's grace attracts and calls through him. In fact, the answer to the question, 'Who is Jesus?' is an exposition of grace. However, it was Jesus himself who focused attention upon one particular aspect of his ministry, the cross, when he said, 'When I am lifted up from the earth, I will draw all men to myself' (John 12:32). The ransom paid by Jesus on the cross is God's great act of grace.

The Gospels show that throughout his ministry Jesus was keenly aware of the fact of his coming death. It was an essential part of his total ministry, that part of his understanding in which his ministry was linked with Old Testament motifs of suffering on behalf of another. Although the Gospels provide considerable information about Jesus' suffering, death, and resurrection, they give little explanation of why his death was necessary or what its significance was.

Before his birth an angel told Joseph, 'He shall save his people from their sins' (Matt 1:21). Certainly his work as 'Bearer of the Kingdom of God' was intimately involved in his work of providing salvation. The assumption of the Synoptic writers is that all human future destiny is dependent upon present response to Jesus. The power of the Kingdom of God, which will be fully realized in the future, was present in Jesus. Jesus confronted people with his person and the demand that they make a decision for or against the rule of God. A decision for Jesus was a decision for the Kingdom and involved both the forgiveness of sins and inclusion in the Kingdom's future aspects.[3]

There are, however, a few comments in the Gospels that show that Jesus himself began the process of interpreting his death and resurrection as God's work to do something about sin, the ultimate barrier between God and his creation.

---

[2]Note that Joshua 24:2, 14-15 says that Abraham was a worshipper 'of other gods' when God called him.

[3]Cf. Ladd (1993), *A Theology of the New Testament*, 181.

The *Synoptic Gospels* record that as Jesus taught about greatness in the Kingdom of God he said, 'The Son of man also came not to be served but to serve, and to give his life as a ransom for many' (Mark 10:45; Matt 20:28; cf. Luke 18:27). This verse brings together the phrase *Son of man* and the function of the Suffering Servant in an unexpected combination. The words 'to serve, and to give his life' are powerfully reflective of Isaiah 53. As we noted earlier, the imagery of the Servant in Isaiah was an important part of the background against which Jesus and his followers explained the significance of his death. The linkage between this statement by Jesus and Isaiah 53:10-11 is especially important.

> It was the will of the LORD to crush him with pain.
> When you make his life an offering for sin,
> he shall see his offspring, and shall prolong his days;
> through him the will of the LORD shall prosper.
> Out of his anguish he shall see light;
> he shall find satisfaction through his knowledge.
> The righteous one, my servant, shall make many righteous,
> and he shall bear their iniquities.[4]

Both the Mark and Isaiah passages emphasize the giving up of life. In both passages this death is the price paid for the benefit of others. The New Testament context introduces the word *ransom*, one of many terms we will meet which describe the effects of the death of Christ. A ransom is the price that is paid to obtain the possession of something or to gain the freedom for someone. Jesus means that his life is the price paid 'for many'.

Behind the preposition 'for' in Mark 10:45 stands the Greek word *anti*, which means 'in the place of' or as a 'substitute for'. Some early church writers speculated about the one to whom the ransom was paid; to God? to the Devil? to some other party? Such conjectures miss the force of Jesus' statement. His life was given up

---

[4]Quoted here from the NRSV, partly because, unlike the RSV, this version contains the addition to verse 11 found in the Dead Sea Scrolls, 'he shall see light.' This is probably a reference to the resurrection of the one whose life was made 'an offering for sin'.

as a substitute for others, so that their lives need not be forfeited. The Isaiah passage is helpful, it shows that suffering and death were endured to bear iniquity, sin. In the death of Jesus he was *the* Suffering Servant giving himself up for humans' sin, 'to make many righteous,' that is, to make them acceptable before a righteous God. Salvation is available for many because of God's gracious gift through the suffering, death, and resurrection of Christ.

The New Testament *Johannine literature* is more specific about the significance of the death of Christ. God's act of giving reveals his love, provisions, forgiveness, and salvation which is eternal life (John 3:16). In John 12:32 (cf. 6:44), a passage quoted just above, Jesus implies that his being 'lifted up' (crucifixion) is God's way of bridging the gap between himself and sinful humanity. John, in his first epistle, makes one of the boldest statements about the entire ministry of Christ, including his death: 'The reason the Son of God appeared was to destroy the works of the devil' (1 John 3:8).

Yet another interpretation of the death of Jesus comes again from his own lips at the Last Supper, as he distributed bread and wine. To get the maximum impact we must combine statements from several places in the New Testament.

> I have earnestly desired to eat this passover with you before I suffer (Luke 22:15).... This is my blood of the [new] covenant which is poured out for many (Mark 14:24; Matt 26:28) ... for the forgiveness of sins (Matt 26:28 only).... This is my body, which is given for you. Do this in remembrance of me (Luke 22:19).... I say to you, I shall not drink again of the fruit of the vine until that day when I drink it new in the kingdom of God (Mark 14:25; Matt 26:29).... For as often as you eat this bread and drink the cup, you proclaim the Lord's death until he comes (1 Cor 11:26).

Here we have an encapsulation of Salvation History as it is focused upon Jesus, especially upon his death and resurrection as the provision for salvation. 'Blood ... poured out' is, first of all, a giving up of life, for as Leviticus, in discussing Old Testament sacrifice, explains:

The life of the flesh is in the blood; and I have given it for you upon
the altar to make atonement for your souls; for it is the blood that
makes atonement, by reason of the life (Lev 17:11; cf. vs. 14).

Jesus' death was a 'blood atonement'. Also, Jesus' sacrificial blood
ratified the new covenant. In Matthew's version of Jesus' words at
his last meal with his disciples before his crucifixion he says explicitly
that his blood is to be poured out specifically 'for the forgiveness of
sins', to make salvation possible (Matt 26:26-29).

Thus far we have said little about the covenant, but in Mark's
record of the Last Supper the word is used when Jesus said, 'This
is my blood of the covenant.'[5] Throughout the Bible *covenant*, a
special non-negotiable agreement in which one party lays down all
conditions, and makes all the promises, is the framework within
which God offers a right relationship with himself. Originally it was
offered to Abraham and his descendants. At the core of the covenant
God said to Abraham, 'I will be your God and you will be my people
... through you shall all the nations of the earth be blessed.' Here is
grace, pure and simple. The holy God who has been offended by
human sin is saying to the offender, 'I will be yours' and 'I want you
to be mine. I want to use you as a channel of blessing for others.'
This motif, 'I will be yours ... you will be mine,' in one form or
another, runs through the Bible, uniting the phases of Salvation History.
We meet it last in Revelation 21, in the vision of the new heaven and
new earth, as the voice from the throne says, 'the dwelling of God is
with men ... and they shall be his people' (vs. 3); 'He who conquers
shall have this heritage, and I will be his God and he shall be my son'
(vs. 7).

God sealed the covenant with Abraham with blood – in a special
ceremony (Gen 15), in circumcision (Gen 17), and in the blood of
sacrifices. When the covenant was re-established at Mount Sinai,
'Moses took the blood and threw it upon the people, and said,
"Behold the blood of the covenant which the LORD has made with
you"' (Ex 24:8). Now, once again, in an upper room as the covenant

---

[5]Some ancient manuscripts add the word 'new,' hence, ' . . . my blood of
the new covenant.'

was about to be renewed, there is reference to the blood which seals it!

Explanation of the significance of the Supper requires all three tenses of the English verb. It looks to the past as a remembrance, a memorial, of the person, ministry, and especially of the death of Jesus through which salvation was made available. It is also a fellowship with him who is spiritually present with later participants, just as he was physically present with the original ones, to whom he spoke of eating 'with you'. In addition the Lord's Supper has a future aspect; it proclaims 'the Lord's death until he comes'. Then he shall again partake with his own 'new in the Kingdom of God'.

The death of Jesus is the re-ratification of the divine expression of grace set forth first in the covenant given in the Old Testament. His death is the central focus of Jesus' own ministry. Because it results in the forgiveness of sins, his death foreshadows the consummation, the final act of the drama of Salvation History. When the Kingdom comes in its fullest extent, those for whom his blood was poured out will again gather to partake of the benefits of his salvation *with him*.

The Proclamation of the Early Church: The Exposition of Salvation

Acts

The question of this chapter is that of the Philippian jailor in Acts 16:30 (cf. Rom 1:16). An earthquake at midnight, coupled with the probable consequences to himself if his prisoners had fled, doubtlessly raised the jailor's fears for his personal safety. 'Salvation' in the ancient world had a variety of meanings. In the Greco-Roman world at large it was sometimes used of deliverance from dangerous and threatening situations or circumstances; to obtain a position of well-being, safety, acceptance, peace, and security. It might refer to rescue from a storm at sea, the dangers of battle, severe disease, and the like. The Gentiles also sought salvation from the fear of death, purposelessness, the nameless insecurities of life, and the unseen powers – as Shakespeare called them, 'the slings and arrows of outrageous fortune.'[6] In addition, the Jews were concerned for salvation from the penalty of breaking God's Law.

Paul turned the jailer's question into an entirely spiritual one. In the Christian sense 'salvation' is to be delivered from sin, its guilt and punishment, from the separation and enmity it brings between God and a person, and all that that entails. Paul's answer, 'Believe in the Lord Jesus, and you will be saved, you and your household,' is rooted in the New Testament affirmation that salvation is God's answer to the needs and longings of people through the revelation of himself and his love, by the provision for making forgiveness of sins possible through the death and resurrection of Jesus Christ.

Paul says, 'believe.' From the same Greek root are both the noun and verb forms of the words *believe, faith, trust,* and *commit.* In the contemporary world *faith* can mean little more than *awareness, hope, inner resolve,* or *determination.* In the Biblical sense it involves (1) intellectual content (knowledge), awareness of what one believes in, (2) an act of will, a volitional response, in which one acts on the knowledge, and, in the case of relationships, (3) an emotional commitment or involvement such as love or affection, loyalty, or some other appropriate, subjective response.

The object of faith is essential. Is what or who is believed real and reliable, and does it have sufficient resources and strength to do what is expected? Is the one who is believed willing and able to respond as the believer anticipates? In the Christian sense the object of faith is God. It involves knowledge of him as he is; that is, as God has revealed himself, not as we may think, wish, or assume him to be. Faith must be based on what God expects and on the basis upon which he will accept, forgive, and renew.

God offers salvation on the basis of grace, a gift offered because of what God himself has done. To seek it on any other basis or grounds – for example, by my own efforts or goodness, or trying to contribute to what he has already completed – is an insult to him

---

[6]William Shakespear, *Hamlet*, Act 3, Scene 1, Line 58.

and really a lack of faith or trust in God and his promises. This is what Jesus had in mind when, calling himself 'the door of the sheepfold', he says, 'Truly, truly, I say to you, he who does not enter the sheepfold by the door but climbs in by another way, that man is a thief and a robber' (John 10:1).

When Paul says, 'Believe in the Lord Jesus Christ,' he means that, in Jesus, God has already done all that is necessary for salvation. The next verse reports, 'They spoke the word of the Lord to him and to all that were in his house' (Acts 16:32). Surely this means that Paul and Silas explained what salvation is, why it is needed, what God had done in Jesus to make it possible, and what they meant by *believe*. In other words, they laid the intellectual foundation for salvation. The jailor and his household responded.

Faith is living as if that which has been promised is a reality. If I told one of my children I had deposited a thousand dollars in her or his checking account, their faith in me would be expressed as that son or daughter began to live and act as if he or she were in fact a thousand dollars richer, simply because she or he trusts me. In the New Testament, faith is a complete trust and confidence in the unseen because of one's assurance of the reliability of God, the one making the promises. Hence, Hebrews 11:1 says, 'Faith is the assurance of things hoped for, the conviction of things not seen.'

Earlier in Acts we see the first Christians presenting salvation in different forms other than that used by Paul with the Philippian jailor. At Pentecost, Peter first explained who Jesus was and what he did, then he called for response (Acts 2:38-39). Before the Jewish officials he boldly asserted that God had worked through Jesus, that his death and resurrection were crucial, and that salvation is not available elsewhere or on other bases.

> By the name of Jesus Christ of Nazareth, whom you crucified, whom God raised from the dead.... This is the stone which was rejected by you builders, but which has become the head of the corner. And there is salvation in no one else, for there is no other name under heaven given among men by which we must be saved (Acts 4:10-12).

One of the most helpful results of modern Biblical scholarship has been the identification of 'the *kērugma*.' This word means *proclamation*, or *preaching*. Contemporary students refer to it as the *content* of the *evangelistic* preaching of the early Christians, that is, what they proclaimed when they were seeking to win converts.

To identify the content of the *kērugma* we study the evangelistic sermons in Acts. By outlining these sermons we are able to identify the major points of each. As we compare the outlines certain common elements or points appear. Furthermore, in the New Testament epistles, all of which were written to Christians, we find this same basic message either assumed or summarized. Not all points are in all speeches in Acts and the epistles; the common points do not necessarily always appear in the same sequence. Nevertheless, we learn what was the basic core of information the early Christian preachers gave in answering the question, 'What must I do to be saved?'

There are numerous reconstructions of the *kērugma*. One of the better known is that of the British scholar, C. H. Dodd;[7] the following is a version similar to his.

1. The age of fulfillment predicted in the Old Testament has dawned, the promises have been fulfilled, the Messiah has come.

2. This has taken place in Jesus of Nazareth.

   a. He was descended from the seed of David.
   b. He went about teaching, doing good, and executing mighty works by the power of God through which God indicated His approval of Him.
   c. He was crucified in accordance with the purpose of God.
   d. He was raised by the power of God.

3. The Church is witness to these things.

---

[7]C. H. Dodd (1944), *The Apostolic Preaching and its Development* (London: Hodder and Stoughton).

4. He has been exalted into heaven at the right hand of God where He reigns as the Messianic head of the New Israel with the title 'Lord.'

5. The Holy Spirit in the Church is now the seal of Christ's present power and glory.

6. Jesus will come again for judgment and the restoration of all things.

7. Therefore all who hear should repent and be baptized for the remission of sins.

The first Christians, then, believed that God had intervened in history, that the Final Age had arrived, and that this had taken place in the person and ministry of Jesus.

The Epistles of Paul

Paul's letters frequently refer to salvation by grace through faith and elaborate on it. In 1 Corinthians 15:3-5 he summarizes 'the gospel' which, he insists, was not original with him, but he received it from those who were his predecessors in the faith: 'Christ died for our sins, according to the Scriptures, that he was buried, and the third day he rose again from the dead, according to the Scriptures, and he appeared...' Here is a statement of certain historical facts – Christ died, was buried, arose, and was seen alive. There is also theological interpretation – that this was 'for our sins' and that it happened 'according to the Scriptures'. Both a report of what happened and its meaning and significance are essential components of the gospel.

Of the many sections of Paul's letters which summarize the nature of salvation, we will look briefly at four.

Romans 1-4

First is Romans, chapters one through four. In Romans 1:16-17, Paul says the gospel is a demonstration of 'the power' and the 'righteousness of God'. Its purpose is 'for salvation', it is received 'through faith', and it is available on a non-discriminatory basis 'to the Jew first and also to the Greek'. Also, although he does not say so directly in these verses, by speaking of 'the power of God' Paul implies that salvation comes at God's initiative. This becomes evident throughout the first eleven chapters of this letter. The statements in these two verses introduce the major themes of Romans.

From 1:18 to 3:20 Paul goes to great lengths to demonstrate the all-pervasive results of sin, which leaves its victim subject to the wrath of God (1:18; 2:5, 8; 3:5). He depicts Jew and Gentile alike as equally disadvantaged before God, the impartial Judge. But, he insists, that is not the end. The section can be summarized in the following verses:

> The wrath of God is revealed from heaven against all ungodliness and wickedness of men who by their wickedness suppress the truth (Rom 1:18).

> Do you not know that God's kindness is meant to lead you to repentance?... God shows no partiality. All who have sinned without the law will also perish without the law, and all who have sinned under the law will be judged by the law (Rom 2:4, 11-12).

> None is righteous, no, not one; . . . No human being will be justified in his sight by works of the law, since through the law comes knowledge of sin . . . all have sinned and fall short of the glory of God (Rom 3:10, 20, 23).

Paul then moves to the solution of the human problem in 3:24–4:25. The argument is summed up in 3:24-27.

> They are justified by his grace as a gift, through the redemption which is in Christ Jesus, whom God put forward as an expiation by his blood, to be received by faith. This was to show God's righteousness, because in his divine forbearance he had passed over former sins; it was to prove at the present time that he himself is righteous and that he justifies him who has faith in Jesus. Then what becomes of our boasting? It is excluded. On what principle? On the principle of works? No, but on the principle of faith.

Paul explains the reason for God's work through Christ when he says this was 'to prove at the present time that he himself is righteous and that he justifies him who has faith in Jesus.' The words *just, justification, right, righteous, righteousness,* all come from the same root; they are essentially legal terms, conveying such ideas as *fair, innocent, legally perfect.* The first issue is God's righteousness which must be maintained; that is, he must judge in harmony with his own perfect nature, which is righteous, just, absolutely fair. Were God to pronounce as innocent, just, or righteous one he knew to be guilty, God would be an unjust, unrighteous judge. If the sinner is to be forgiven, the just demands of God's nature and laws must be met. Here we move to the second point: God justifies, pronounces innocent, by means of faith in Jesus. When a person accepts for herself or himself Jesus' death and resurrection as the satisfaction of God's demands, God then pronounces that one 'not guilty' because the penalty has been paid. God can accept the sinner on the basis of Jesus' sacrifice which satisfies the demands for justice. (Note Romans 6:23: 'For the wages of sin is death, but the free gift of God is eternal life in Christ Jesus our Lord.')

Paul states clearly that God's salvation is 'by his grace as a gift' (3:24). He then uses terms from various areas of life to look at what Jesus accomplished from different points of view. We will discuss these and similar terms in more detail later. Here we simply note that *justify* (vs. 24) is a legal term that deals with law and justice. *Redemption* (vs. 25) is from the world of commerce, and speaks of the paying of a price to regain control of that which one previously owned. *Propitiation* designates the sacrifice offered to turn away the wrath of an offended deity. Through such words Paul clarifies that, in Jesus, God has done all that is necessary for human salvation. Where then is the basis for human boasting? There is none! Salvation is all God's doing; humans receive it solely as a gift, a gift of grace (Eph 2:8-9)!

Grace is received by faith. Hence, Paul, in Romans 4, illustrates what faith is by pointing to the experience of Abraham. Abraham was not saved by circumcision or by observing the Jewish law. The Scriptures (Gen 15:6) say, 'Abraham believed God, and it was reckoned [imputed] to him as righteousness' (Rom 4:3). This was before he was circumcised and centuries prior to God's giving the Law through Moses. Abraham simply trusted God, that somehow God would make possible righteousness and acceptability possible.

Ephesians 1–2

In Ephesians 1–2 Paul stresses that salvation comes by God's choice and plan established 'before the foundation of the world' (1:4; cf. vss. 5, 9-14). This has been realized through Jesus Christ, in whom believers 'have redemption through his blood, the forgiveness of our trespasses, according to the riches of his grace' (1:7). The Holy Spirit is the guarantee, the down payment, of our future inheritance (1:14) which awaits the conclusion of God's plan in Christ (1:18-23).

God's initiative and provision of salvation are necessary because humans are helpless, 'dead through trespasses and sins' (2:1, 5). Yet God, 'rich in mercy, out of the great love with which he loved us' has made us alive in Christ and made glory available 'in the coming ages' (2:4-7).

> For by grace you have been saved through faith; and this is not your own doing, it is the gift of God – not because of works, lest any man should boast. For we are his workmanship, created in Christ Jesus for good works, which God prepared beforehand, that we should walk in them (Eph 2:8-10).

The phrase 'this is not your own doing' has caused considerable discussion. To what does it refer, salvation or faith? The most likely answer is, 'Both! Everything involved is God's doing, God's gift.'

But then Paul, having excluded human effort in the provision of salvation, introduces 'good works'. Here they are the result, not the cause, of salvation. In Romans Paul asserted that 'God shows no partiality ... there is no distinction' between unbelieving Jews and Gentiles (2:11, 3:22), 'for all have sinned' (2:23). Now, in Ephesians 2:11-21, he insists that such human distinctions no longer count among believers. 'In Christ Jesus ... [he] has made us both one ... [creating] in himself one new man in place of two ... [reconciling] us both to God in one body through the cross' (2:13-15).

In Ephesians, we meet again themes which became familiar in Romans. Salvation is God's work through Christ; his death is central in providing it. Grace, faith, gift of God, not of works, no grounds for boasting, and God's impartiality in dealing with people continue as key words and concepts.

2 Corinthians 5:17-21

The idea of reconciliation, noted in Ephesians 2:16, is the major focus in 2 Corinthians 5:17-21. The term essentially means 'to change enemies into friends'. Reconciled sinners become 'a new creation' and move into a peaceful, harmonious relation with God in Christ. This is the work of God 'who through Christ reconciled us to himself ... in Christ God was reconciling the world to himself, not counting their trespasses against them' (5:18-19). Clearly it is God who reconciles, but who is reconciled? The New Testament speaks only of human beings, never God, as being reconciled. Hence, it is often argued that reconciliation is always directed toward humans, that God does not to need to be reconciled. However, Leon Morris notes that it

> is difficult to harmonize this with the general New Testament position. That which set up the barrier was the demand of God's holiness for uprightness in man. Man, left to himself, is content to let bygones be bygones. He is not particularly worried by his sin. Certainly he feels no hostility to God on account of his sin. The barrier arises because God demands holiness in man. Therefore when the process of reconciliation has been effected it is impossible to say it is completely man-ward, and not God-ward in any sense. There must be a change from God's side if all that is involved in such expressions as 'the wrath of God' is no longer exercised toward man.[8]

---

[8]Leon Morris (1982), 'Reconciliation,' *New Bible Dictionary*, 2nd ed., IVP, 1012-13.

Morris' statement implies the same principle for reconciliation as that stated by Paul in Romans 3. As God is both Just and Justifier, so he is also the Reconciler of those who have offended him and is also himself reconciled to them.

Galatians 1–3

The final Pauline passage for our study is Galatians 1–3. Here he confronts the problem of the relation of the Jewish Law and Christian salvation. There were those who answered the question, 'What must I do to be saved?' by referring to God's choice of the nation Israel and his giving the Law to his people. This Old Testament Law was, after all, of divine origin. Is it not reasonable to assume that it plays a major role in salvation? A complicating factor arose when Gentiles began to believe in Jesus. Was their believing in Jesus for salvation enough? Did they not also have to observe the Jewish Law and observe rituals and ceremonies? Some even seem to have demanded that Gentiles actually become Jews in order to become Christians. They would need to become converts or proselytes to Judaism, that is, naturalized Jews. This would include being circumcised, keeping the Jewish Law, and living as Jews.

To this Paul vigorously objected. Such demands meant that racial, cultural, or nationalistic elements contribute to salvation. Insistence upon observing any part of the Jewish Law meant that human efforts are necessary for salvation. Such, says Paul, is not Christianity but 'another' or a 'different gospel' (Gal 1:6-9); those who proclaim such are 'accursed' (Gal 1:8-9). There is no place for human contribution in salvation, even observance of the Old Testament Law.

> A man is not justified by works of the law but through faith in Jesus Christ, even we have believed in Christ Jesus, in order to be justified by faith in Christ, and not by works of the law, because by works of the law shall no one be justified (Gal 2:16).

To attempt to do so is an affront to God's gracious gift and a rejection of the saving significance of the death of Christ. Citing himself as an example, he says, 'I do not nullify the grace of God; for if justification were through the law, then Christ died to no purpose' (2:21).

As in Romans, here in Galatians Paul cites the example of Abraham, who was saved by faith. In the face of those who claim one must be a Jew, a descendant of Abraham, to be a Christian, Paul says that all who come to God by faith are Abraham's children. Human, external factors, including racial, socio-cultural, and gender differences, play no part in salvation and the standing of believers before God.

> There is neither Jew nor Greek, there is neither slave nor free, there is neither male nor female; for you are all one in Christ Jesus. And if you are Christ's, then you are Abraham's offspring, heirs according to promise (Gal 3:28-29).

Paul's view of Israel, circumcision, and the Mosaic Law in Christianity was not equally evident to all. The issue of whether salvation was by Law, by grace, or both was the major issue of the Apostolic church.

The Law versus Grace Controversy
The ascension of Jesus left the early church with some unclarified issues about the Christian faith. These included details relating to the nature of Christianity's concept of salvation, Christianity's code of morals and conduct, and the relationship between Judaism and Christianity. In the Old Testament, as in the ministry of Jesus, we see the content of theology revealed within history. Now we observe how these and other issues were clarified within the experience of the church and on the plain of history.[9]

The expansion of early Christianity carried the faith far and wide into geographical areas with considerable racial diversity. As a result, persons of differing social, cultural, and racial backgrounds were incorporated into the church. This, of course, ran counter to the convictions of many Jews, including some Jewish Christians.

Jewish traditions, both Biblical and those which had grown up during the Intertestamental period, led many to assume that since Israel is 'God's people' any individuals wishing to become a part of

---

[9]See J. Julius Scott, Jr. 'The Church's Progress to the Council of Jerusalem' *Bulletin for Biblical Research* 7 (1997), 1-20.

'The Chosen People' must do so by first becoming members of the Jewish nation; Jewish national, cultural, and religious affairs could not be separated. Fierce loyalty to the nation, determination to maintain her uniqueness, and to protect her special status were expressed in many forms. Many Jews refrained from all unnecessary contact with non-Jews; the laws and traditions relating to clean–unclean encouraged this. Even the suggestion that God might be disposed to express kindness to some non-Jews outside the framework of Israel could evoke strong resistance. This might even reach the point of violence, as it did in the case of Jesus (Luke 4:24-29) and Paul (Acts 22:21-22).

Cultural differences that existed within Judaism emerged within Jewish Christianity in Jerusalem. Acts 6:1 records discord raised by the believing Hellenists. These were Jews who held to their traditional religion but had adapted many cultural features from the Greeks. The object of their murmuring was 'the Hebrews', Jewish Christians who maintained the traditional Hebraic culture. Stephen's defense in Acts 7 shows some of the distinctive emphases of Jewish Christians who viewed the new faith through glasses colored by Hellenism. Their more 'open' approach to non-Jews seems to have played an important part in the Christian missionary enterprise, the beginnings of which are described in the following chapters of Acts.[10]

Acts 8 recounts early conversions among the Samaritans and of an Ethiopian. Both groups had traditional associations with Jews. The legitimacy of including Samaritans in the church was recognized only after a 'high level' investigating team (Peter and John) witnessed concrete evidence of divine approval in the form of the coming of the Holy Spirit upon the Samaritans (Acts 8:14-17). Philip contacted the Ethiopian only when directed to do so by 'an angel of the Lord' (8:26). The preaching of Philip (8:40) and Peter (9:32-43) brought the gospel to Jews living along the sea coast. This was a racially mixed area; Jews living there faced the constant threat of ceremonial uncleanliness, and their more strict countrymen in places like

---

[10]See J. Julius Scott, Jr., 'Stephen's Speech and the World Mission of the People of God,' *Journal of the Evangelical Theological Society*, 21/2 (June 1978), 131-41.

Jerusalem questioned their faithfulness to the Jewish way of life. The healing of Aeneas (9:33-34) and the raising of Tabitha/Dorcas from the dead (9:36-42) showed God's presence and validated the work of Christians in that area.

The conversion of Cornelius (Acts 10:1–11:18) marked an important new step, a step initiated by God, within the church. Although Cornelius was an exceptionally good Gentile, a 'God-fearer' (a non-Jew who observed some Jewish practices and who was permitted some contact with Jews), he was not circumcised. The coming of the Holy Spirit upon him and his associates during the preaching of Peter forced recognition 'that God shows no partiality, but in every nation any one who fears him and does what is right is acceptable to him' (10:34-35). Still, this development was called into question by the Jerusalem Church (11:1-18).[11] The preaching to Greeks in Antioch, a step initiated by the Christians themselves, brought even more non-Jews to faith and again prompted the Jerusalem Church to action – it sent Barnabas to the area (11:19-26). Paul's first missionary journey resulted in large numbers of Gentiles coming into the church (Acts 13–14).

At first, the underlying causes of the Jewish Christians' hesitancy in the face of the racial and cultural expansion of Christianity are not clear. Early questions centered around such matters as the validity of the conversion of the Samaritans, clean/unclean foods, persons with whom to associate, eating companions, and circumcision. These were but symptoms of the real issue. Galatians 2 shows that in Antioch questions about associations between Jewish and Gentile Christians, especially their eating together (2:11-14), quickly moved from comments about living 'like a Gentile' or 'like a Jew' (vs. 14) to the issue of justification by faith (2:16-21). It was also in Antioch that, as Paul and Barnabas reported the conversion of Gentiles, other problems surfaced. Acts recounts that 'some men came down from Judea and were teaching the brethren, "Unless you are circumcised

---

[11]J. Julius Scott, Jr.,'The Cornelius Incident in the Light of its Jewish Setting,' *Journal of the Evangelical Theological Society*, 34/4 (December 1991), 475-484.

according to the custom of Moses, you cannot be saved'" (15:1). Later, in Jerusalem a similar demand was made, 'It is necessary to circumcise them, and to charge them to keep the law of Moses' (15:5). Thus the real issue surfaced; it was 'What must the Gentiles do to be saved?'

Within such a question lay other matters, all related to the broad issue of the relationship of Israel and Christianity. These involved the nature of Christian 'salvation;' (1) on what basis is it available? and (2) who are proper candidates for salvation? The demand for circumcising Gentile converts assumed that Christianity and Judaism are inseparable and that one must become a Jew in order to become a Christian. It also assumed that God's grace was not given on the basis of faith alone, but that socio-nationalistic relationships, ceremonies, and human, materialistic factors in general play a part in obtaining salvation. Refusal of table fellowship with Gentile believers or insistence upon circumcising them as precondition for salvation implied a rejection of justification by faith alone.

The new faith had reached an impasse. It could go no further until the issue, 'How is a person made acceptable before God?' was resolved. We may define the options, viewed in the broadest scope, as those of law or grace. In the early church, one group held to law (loosely defined) and answered, 'God's favor is earned by human effort (or at least involves some sort of a human contribution) such as joining (belonging to) the right group, performing good works (deeds) which merit or deserve God's favor and salvation, and/or through observing ceremonies and rituals, such as those of the Jewish Law. The other side, grace, insisted that God's favor is neither earned nor merited by human beings, it is a free *gift*, given at God's initiative. Grace means that all that needs to be done in order to make a person acceptable before God has already been accomplished in the life, death, and resurrection of Jesus. This grace is received by faith alone.

The Book of Acts alludes to as many as three conferences in Jerusalem at which the matters may have been discussed and action

---

[12]This is not merely a meaningless debate among scholars. One's conclusion affects the way one reconstructs the history of the Apostolic Age which, in turn, has important theological implications. As mentioned earlier, history and theology are intimately related.

taken; Galatians 1 and 2 speak of two such meetings. There is a major problem relating to the date of the writing of Galatians and to the relation of Paul's post-conversion visits to Jersualem described in Galatians with those related in the 9th, 11th, and 15th chapters of Acts.[12] Here we will focus upon Acts 15, the Council of Jerusalem, which, I believe, followed the two meetings described in Galatians and where final clarification was achieved.

In understanding this account, we must take seriously the statement of verse 7, 'after there had been much debate.' We do not have the complete minutes of the meeting. At best we have only a summary statement of the conclusions reached and an indication of the type of thinking that led to them.

Furthermore, it is evident that the type of solution sought was not the will of the majority nor what seemed to be the best judgment or the most workable to human minds, but to determine the will of God. This they did by looking at the past experience of the church to see how God had worked in matters relating to the salvation of non-Jews. Peter cited Cornelius as a 'precedent case' which shows that God accepts uncircumcised persons (vs. 7-11). Barnabas and Paul related their experience on the mission field in Gentile areas which confirmed God's acceptance of those from outside the Jewish structure who believe (vs. 12). James, the relative of Jesus, turned to the *Scripture*. Quoting Amos 9:11-12, he cited evidence that God has always intended to accept Gentiles (vs. 12-18). Although Acts reports these statements by leaders, it also stresses the *role of the Holy Spirit* throughout the deliberations (vs. 8, 28).

The decision focuses upon two factors. First, that salvation is 'through the grace of the Lord Jesus (vs. 11) ... through faith ...' (vs. 9). This means that there can be no distinction between racial and cultural groups before God; there can be no legal nor ceremonial requirements through which an individual must attempt to earn or merit God's favor. What must I do to be saved? Believe on the Lord Jesus Christ, believe that in him all that is necessary has already been accomplished. Start living accordingly. A secondary issue dealt with practical implications of this decision for moral and ethical conduct and the living of life from day to day. We must look closely at this in our next chapter, 'How Shall Believers Live?'

The implications of the clarifications achieved in the Law versus Grace controversy are far reaching. They provide a Christian understanding of the nature of religion in general. There are *false religions* which worship the wrong god or gods; these are pagan and idolatrous. There are also false religions which seek to obtain the favor of the right God in the wrong way. These attempt to make human contribution a necessary ingredient for obtaining divine approval; in the broadest sense of the term, these are legalistic religions. The sole *true religion* understands salvation as God's grace, a gift, to be received by faith.

The experience of the church throughout her history demonstrates the need to constantly proclaim grace. It is humbling to seek God's favor solely on the basis of his grace; the human way is to do it oneself, or at least to contribute. But, that is not God's way and in this matter it is his way that counts!

A second implication of the decisions of the Jerusalem Council is that Christianity is not bound to any one national, racial, nor cultural group. There can be no requirements for inclusion in the fellowship of Christians (= the church) which God has not made for salvation. Specifically, this means that national, racial, and cultural restrictions have no place within the church. As Peter learned in the house of Cornelius, 'God shows no partiality' (Acts 10:36).

Third, although we must look at this issue in more depth later, the Acts 15 Council of Jerusalem rejected either alternative of the ever recurring problem of the extremes of legalism on the one hand, and on the other, the assumption of absolute freedom that rejects all restrictions or guidelines for Christian conduct. Christianity is a religion of grace but with moral and ethical implications for those who have received God's grace. Paul's great statement of 'salvation by grace through faith' in Ephesians 2:8-9 is followed by the affirmation that we are 'created in Christ Jesus for good works' (vs. 10); likewise the Council demonstrates that there are indeed implications for the lives and attitudes of those who have been saved by grace.

The Vocabulary of Salvation: Some Terms used by New Testament Writers to Describe Various Aspects of the Effects of the Work of Christ

We have already met a number of specialized terms in our look at the New Testament's teaching about salvation. We must now seek to collect these and add others. We will also include in this survey mention of some of the more important issues of controversy associated with the study of salvation-words in the New Testament.

The basic terms, of course, are *salvation* (*sōtēria*), grace (*charis*), and faith (*pistis*). We need not repeat definitions of these given above. One issue, however, requires comment because it affects the way we look at each of these terms: Are salvation and related matters primarily objective or subjective? Is there a real, objective, barrier (sin) outside us or is the spiritual difficulty a part of our psyche, our subjective feelings of guilt, disposition, or environment? Is God in any way the object of his work of salvation? Is his nature – justice or any other part of his being – affected by human sin so that he too is involved in the salvation obtained by Jesus? To put it another way, are grace, salvation, and faith ways of speaking about spiritual realities which exist and take place both externally, outside the individual, and also internally within a person? The implication here is that both are involved. This is contrary to the views of some traditional theologians who concentrate upon the objective implications of the work of Christ as well as many contemporary theologians who believe these terms represent only something which takes place within the individual.

Traditional interpretation has stressed the objective nature of salvation; that sin is a real barrier that must be forgiven and removed. God's holiness and justice must be satisfied and human beings must be made new. Liberal theology emphasizes that God is always forgiving and loving and needs no atoning work to make it possible for him to forgive and accept. It frequently looks only at the subjective side of salvation and calls for humans to change their inner disposition and/or attitudes.

A number of the following terms can be interpreted as describing primarily either an objective or subjective change or experience.

The New Testament reader is amiss if either the objective (outward, toward God) or the subjective (inward, a change in the person) is ignored. However, the statement quoted above from Leon Morris, dealing with reconciliation, could be extended to other terms as well. The terms must be considered in their total New Testament context. They also have histories of application in the greater world which cannot be ignored.

We will attempt to group the figures of speech about the work of Christ in providing salvation within a number of different categories. It is significant that the New Testament writers, realizing the magnitude of the subject of salvation, attempt to reveal its many facets by drawing terms and word-pictures from various aspects of life and experience. An appreciation of the work of Christ and the salvation he provides requires its contemplation from more than one point of view.

The facet of human experience that is common to all is that of *physical birth, growth and development*. The New Testament writers use a number of terms from this area as they describe what happens to the person who turns to God through Christ. They speak of *new birth (gennēthēnai anōthen)*, a phrase which means *born again, born from above*, or *regeneration (palingenesia)*. The concept behind these words is the truth that in salvation God starts all over with the individual. God remakes the individual so that he or she is given a new nature and becomes a new being. This is the heart of Jesus' words to Nicodemus in John 3. The Pharisee had difficulty because he could imagine no concept of birth which takes place outside a material and physical framework. Jesus made clear, 'That which is born of the flesh is flesh, and that which is born of the Spirit is spirit' (John 3:6). Jesus indicated that he was speaking of spiritual birth.

In a normal person birth is followed by growth and development. The individual who has experienced the new birth is expected to grow and New Testament writers frequently give the admonition to *grow* or *grow up (auxanō, auxēsis)*. The goal is *maturity* or *full development (teleioō, teleios, teleiēsis)*; the Greek words are also sometimes translated *perfect*. There are stages of spiritual development just as there are in physical development. The Christian is expected to pass through these. But, more on that in the next chapter.

Another term often taken to be a 'growth word' is *sanctification* (*hagios, hagiasmos*). Here again we will defer major discussion to our consideration of Christian life. However, we must make a few comments here. The basic meaning of the term is *to set apart for and dedicate to God, to make holy, consecrated, be hallowed*. In the Bible it may denote either a ceremonial state or moral fitness.

There is a controversy regarding the nature of Christian growth and development in general and sanctification in particular. It involves such questions as: (1) Is sanctification the result of an instantaneous experience or a prolonged process? (2) Is sanctification ever completed in this life (so that an individual can be completely morally and spiritually perfect) or is it completed only after death? (3) Is sanctification entirely the work of God (so that the believer is passive) or does it involve the effort and activity of the believer? In any case, the goal is that believers will become holy, completely separated for and to God, and 'be perfect' (*teleioi*), 'fully developed,' and 'complete, lacking nothing' (Jas 1:4), 'without blemish before the presence of his glory' (Jude 24).

We have already noted some terms which come from the law court (of either civil or religious Law). *Righteous* or *righteousness* (*dikaios, dikaiosunē*) may be used in at least three different ways: to speak of (1) the standard of perfection based on the character of God, thus reflecting the very nature of God – hence, God is righteous; (2) God's administration of justice, his absolute fairness; God is legally perfect in his being, therefore he is completely fair in passing judgment; and (3) the status of the sinner who is pronounced 'not guilty' by God – she or he becomes *righteous, just, innocent*, or *upright*.

Justification, justify, to make or declare righteous, is the act of making innocent or of declaring the sinner 'not guilty', and making the person righteous or legally acceptable before God. *The Good News Bible* translates the term, 'God's way of putting men right with Himself.' That certainly captures the idea.

There are a couple of terms that come from the world of *commerce*. The simplest is *bought,* or *bought with a price* (*agorazō*). We are all familiar with the process of purchasing or buying something. In so doing we obtain possession by the payment of a price. The New Testament says that through Jesus sinners have been 'bought' by God.

A less common word is *impute, imputation* or *reckon* (*logizomai*). It is essentially a book-keeping term and means *to put to one's account, to credit, to count it a fact.* Just as money may be credited (imputed) to my account without cash actually changing hands, so the believing sinner may be credited with the righteousness, the innocence, even the holiness, of Christ.

Our fourth category of words were quite familiar in the first century world; less so in ours. They are drawn from experiences of *captivity* and *bondage. Ransom* (*lutron*) means the price paid to purchase freedom. Prisoners in war or persons who were kidnap victims might be released by the payment of a ransom.

We saw above that Jesus used the term to refer to his own ministry (Mark 10:45). As we also noted, the term has its limitations, especially when the question is asked, 'To whom was the ransom paid?' *Ransom* normally focuses attention upon the price. In Jesus' mind the emphasis was probably upon the power or force needed to gain freedom for many. *Ransom* is a useful term to remind us that our freedom has been purchased by someone who gave up himself for us.

To *redeem* or *redemption* (*apolutrōsis*) conveys ideas very similar to *ransom.* It denotes the act of salvation or deliverance but not just this alone; it stresses the fact that freedom was obtained by the payment of a price. (*Ransom* emphasizes the price or means of obtaining freedom; *redemption* focuses upon the fact that freedom has been purchased.)

Another element of redemption is evident in the English prefix *re-* that calls attention to the fact that salvation restores something. To redeem is to regain possession of or to buy back through the payment of a price. It acknowledges that God is our rightful owner, yet he has paid a price to regain control over us.

The elements of ceremony and sacrifice in the Old Testament should prepare even moderns who never witnessed the slaying of a sacrificial animal for the use of the language of the *religious cult* in describing what Jesus accomplished.[13] The New Testament writers employ several words which are translated *sacrifice* (e.g., *thusia, peri hamartias, holokautōma*). These may refer to either the act or victim of sacrifice in general, to the specific purpose of a particular sacrifice, or to the way it was offered. Nevertheless, in all cases the stress is upon the object that is given up to obtain that which one wants or desires to obtain or to communicate. In reference to sin, the sacrifice always involved the death of the victim, thus proclaiming the seriousness of sin and the cost of forgiveness.

The idea of Christ as a sacrifice appears throughout Hebrews. Direct statements are few. Hebrews 9:26 says: 'He has appeared once for all at the end of the age to put away sin by the sacrifice of himself', and 10:12: 'When Christ had offered for all time a single sacrifice for sins, he sat down at the right hand of God.' Paul admonished the Ephesians: 'Walk in love, as Christ loved us and gave himself up for us, a fragrant offering and sacrifice to God' (5:2).

In quoting Romans 3:25 above, we used the word *propitiation*. This is also the translation of such versions as the KJV, NASB, and ESV. Others, including the NIV and NRSV, render the word *a sacrifice of atonement*. Some, such as the RSV, use *expiation*. The problem is that the Greek words found here and elsewhere (*hilaskō, hilasmos, hilastērion*) refer to a particular kind of offering, one presented in pagan religions to appease the wrath of an offended deity. From this two issues arise: (1) most English speaking persons today have no idea of this special meaning of *propitiation*; (2) many moderns object to the idea of the Christian God being angry or wrathful. Hence they prefer such a term as *expiation* which simply refers to the forgiveness of sins without specific reference to the means or especially to the wrath of the one who forgives. This substitutes a subjective view of the work of Christ in a passage that clearly stresses the objective.

---

[13]The word *cult* need not carry negative connotatons. We use it here to mean *formal religious worship* or *ritual*.

In the sections of Romans leading up to the occurrence of our word, Paul speaks five times of God's wrath in response to sin (1:18, twice in 2:5, 8; 3:5) and once of his fury (2:8). Although he would certainly reject any notion of the Christian God as a capricious being who 'flies off the handle' at any minor infraction of his will, Paul emphasizes that sin is against God, an affront to his nature, and evokes strongly negative reactions from him. Furthermore, the depth of Christ's sacrifice is seen in his enduring and turning his wrath aside so the believers may escape it.

Substitution and *vicarious atonement* represent New Testament ideas rather than specific terms. These concepts may be conveyed in a number of different ways, most often through prepositions (such as *anti, peri, huper*), all of which may indicate one thing or person taking the place of another and/or acting for another. *Substitution* carries the connotation of replacement. Jesus says he came 'to give his life as a ransom *for* (*anti*, 'instead of,' as a replacement for 'for') many' (Mark 10:45). Paul probably has some idea of substitution in mind when he says, 'Christ redeemed us from (or out from) the curse of the law, having become a curse for (*huper*) us' (Gal 3:13). *Vicarious* denotes the idea of *for the benefit* or *on behalf of.*

The New Testament also uses vocabulary associated with *personal relationships* to describe the results of the salvation provided by Christ. We spoke of *reconciliation* (*katallassō, katallagē*) in our look at 2 Corinthians 5:17-21. In both ancient and modern worlds where loneliness, isolation, and hostility are frequent experiences, reconciliation speaks with special poignancy. It affirms that God, the Great Reconciler, breaks through barriers, sets the lonely in families, and, as we said above, turns enemies into friends. He first does this through Christ as he reconciles 'to himself all things, whether on earth or in heaven, making peace by the blood of his cross' (Col 1:20). In Christ he also heals divisions between redeemed people to establish for himself a great body drawn from all peoples, nations, and languages. Indeed, the church might well be called *The Reconciled*, reconciled both to God and to each other.

Redeeming, reconciling, and making friends are closely associated activities. Hence, it is not surprising that Jesus referred to his disciples as *friends* (*philoi*, John 15:13-15). Fellow Christians are also *friends* (Acts 4:23; 3 John 15).

Humanly speaking, the closest of all personal relationships should exist in families. Through the work of Christ believers are brought into the *family of God*. Paul speaks of the believer's 'adoption' (*huiothesia*) by God (Rom 8:23; Gal 4:5). John uses the language of real, natural children when he says that those who receive him (Jesus) become '*children* (*tekna*) of God', that is, his sons and daughters (John 1:12-13) in the fullest sense. The likening of the relation of Christ with the church to marriage and the church as the bride of Christ (Eph 5:22-33) also implies a family relationship.

Paul too can use this word in referring to the relation between God and Christians. In 2 Corinthians 6:18 he applies to Christians God's words spoken earlier about David's family (2 Sam 7:14)[14] to Christians, 'I will be a father to you, and you shall be my sons and daughters, says the Lord Almighty.' One could hardly think of more intimate terms than Paul uses in Romans 8:14-17:

> For all who are led by the Spirit of God are sons of God. For you did not receive the spirit of slavery to fall back into fear, but you have received the spirit of sonship. When we cry, 'Abba! Father!' it is the Spirit himself bearing witness with our spirit that we are children (*tekna*) of God, and if children, then heirs (*klēronomo*i), heirs of God and fellow heirs with Christ, provided we suffer with him in order that we may also be glorified with him.

In fact, while Paul uses some form of the word *justifies* over twenty times, he uses words designating a family relationship with God through Christ almost as much, and in more of his writings. The description of Christians as God's children is found also in Hebrews (2:10), James (2:5), and 1 John (3:1-2; 3:10; 5:1).

Finally, the cross and resurrection establish something of a mystical element between Jesus and the believer. Jesus said, 'Abide in me, and I in you. As the branch cannot bear fruit by itself, unless it abides in the vine, neither can you, unless you abide in me' (John 15:4).

---

[14]Similar statements are made of Israel as a whole, Isa 43:6; Hos 10:1.

The phrase *in Christ* or *in him* is common in the letters of Paul. Paul affirms a mystical union when he speaks of dying and rising with Christ in Romans 6:2-11. His great statement in Galatians 2:20 might be seen in the same light.

> I have been crucified with Christ; it is no longer I who live, but Christ lives in me; and the life I now live in the flesh I live by faith in the Son of God, who loved me and gave himself for me.

The Work of the Holy Spirit: The Application of Salvation

Thus far we have said little about the Holy Spirit. By way of definition, in general terms, it is helpful to think of the Holy Spirit as the unseen, but real, person, presence, power, and activity of God. The term *Holy Spirit* speaks of his divine nature, for God is both holy and spirit. The Holy Spirit is distinct from both Father and Son. Of course this brings us to the subject of God as 'Trinity', a subject at which we will look in some detail in answering the question, 'What does the New Testament Tell us About God?' Later we will note some of the aspects of the work of the Holy Spirit in connection with the Christian life and then those of the church. Nevertheless, here we must say a bit more about the Spirit and his activity in the divine work of salvation.

As a part of the Godhead, the Holy Spirit is divine (fully God). Jesus likens the Spirit to wind which, although invisible, can be heard and felt, whose power and results are readily evident. Yet, the Holy Spirit is a personal being with such personal qualities as self-consciousness, the ability to speak, go and come, be grieved, and more. The Bible depicts the Holy Spirit as present and active in the world from creation onward (Gen 1:2).[15] His person and work come into plainer focus in the New Testament.

The Holy Spirit came upon Mary at the conception of Jesus (Matt 1:20; Luke 1:35) and on Jesus at his baptism (Mark 1:10; Matt 3:16; Luke 3:22; John 1:32-34). The Spirit was active

---

[15]The NRSV translation, *a wind from God* may be technically correct (the same Hebrew word can be translated *wind, breath, or spirit*) but is hardly adequate. Most other English translations render the phrase, *the Spirit of God* (e.g., KJV, RSV, NIV).

throughout the ministry of Jesus. As that ministry drew to a close, Jesus promised that he and the Father would send the Spirit (here called the *Paraclete*) upon his disciples after his departure (John 14:16, 26; 15:26; 16:7; cf. 1 John 2:1).

In Acts, the coming of the Holy Spirit is evidence of the presence of the Final Age (2:15ff.). The presence and activity of the Holy Spirit, often accompanied by signs that could be detected with the senses, led and validated the actions of the community of believers and their witness to Jesus as they moved into new areas and cultures (8:14-17; 10:46; 13:2-4; 16:6 cf. 8:39; 15:12). He is the seal and guarantee (down payment) of the believer's future inheritance in the Kingdom of God (Eph 1:13-14). It is also evident from the New Testament that the Holy Spirit has a major role in salvation.

This role is that of the *Agent of Salvation*. He bears witness to Jesus (John 15:26). He applies to believers the salvation which the Father has planned and ordained and which the Son carried out. Jesus said,

> When he [the Holy Spirit-Paraclete] comes, he will convince the world concerning sin and righteousness and judgment: concerning sin, because they do not believe in me; concerning righteousness, because I go to the Father, and you will see me no more; concerning judgment, because the ruler of this world is judged (John 16:8-11).

The work of the Spirit in salvation may be summarized under a number of headings. His work in *convicting and calling*, in addition to the words from John 16 just quoted, is noted in 2 Thessalonians 2:13-14:

> God chose you as the first fruits for salvation through sanctification by the Spirit and through belief in the truth. For this purpose he called you through our proclamation of the good news, so that you may obtain the glory of our Lord Jesus Christ.

His general work in the *application of salvation* is evident in Jesus' words to his disciples, 'He [the Holy Spirit] will glorify me, because he will take what is mine and declare it to you' (John 16:14). To Nicodemus he said, 'That which is born of the flesh is flesh, and that which is born of the Spirit is spirit' (John 3:6). Paul asserts the same truth, 'For the law of the Spirit of life in Christ Jesus has set you free from the law of sin and of death' (Rom 8:2).

Rebirth and renewal are the work of the Holy Spirit.

> You were washed, you were sanctified, you were justified in the name of the Lord Jesus Christ and in the Spirit of our God (1 Cor 6:11).

> When the goodness and loving kindness of God our Savior appeared, he saved us, not because of any works of righteousness that we had done, but according to his mercy, through the water of rebirth and renewal by the Holy Spirit. This Spirit he poured out on us richly through Jesus Christ our Savior, so that, having been justified by his grace, we might become heirs according to the hope of eternal life (Titus 3:4-7).

The Holy Spirit *makes Christians*. Without the presence and work of the Holy Spirit it is impossible for anyone to be saved. Jesus made this clear to Nicodemus when he insisted, 'What is born of the Spirit is spirit.... You must be born from above.' Paul says, 'God's love has been poured into your hearts through the Holy Spirit which has been given to us' (Rom 5:5) and 'Anyone who does not have the Spirit of Christ does not belong to him' (Rom 8:9).

In both Romans 5:15 and Galatians 4:6 adoption is connected to the work of the Spirit. Assurance of salvation comes through the 'Spirit bearing witness with our spirit that we are children of God' (Rom 8:16). It is no more possible to be a Christian without the person and work of the Holy Spirit than to be a human being without birth parents.

Conclusion

What Must I Do to Be Saved?
Humans do nothing to be saved; it is a gift. Yet, it is not free, it cost God in Christ a terrible price. But that price has been paid. Solely

on the basis of God's grace, because of his love, salvation is now available.

God's gift of salvation must be received by faith. Faith involves awareness and acceptance of what Christ has done as sufficient and applicable for the individual. That person must respond in love and gratitude. He or she then starts living with the confidence that he or she is a forgiven sinner, a new person in Christ, a child of the King within the Kingdom of God!

What Should Be the Result of Salvation Upon the Individual's View of Self?

We began this chapter with observations about sin and its effects. Such could and should leave us with an understanding of our wickedness, depravity, guilt, and helplessness. It is appropriate that we end with some comments about the implications of salvation, of God's provision of salvation, especially through the death and resurrection of Jesus, for our new self-understanding. The *atonement words*, for an example, not only indicate the many-faceted work of Christ, they also say something about human beings. They imply the awfulness of the sin which encompasses us. Sin is so common, we are so accustomed to it, that we need new perspectives from which to view it and ourselves as sinners. The glory, the perfection of God, is, as we have noted, one such vantage point. The scope of what Christ did for us is another.

The results of the atonement should also be the basis for a new self-image for believers. They are loved! They have been bought with a price – God regarded us as worth saving, even at the cost of his Son. The result is not only that we are forgiven, justified, reconciled, and the rest, we are also *accepted*. The saved sinner is not only accepted but becomes a member of a community, the Kingdom of God, and even is a part of the court of the King. There is more; the redeemed person actually becomes a member of the family of God: 'see what love the Father has given us, that we should be called children of God; and that is what we are' (1 John 3:1; cf. John 1:12; Rom 8:14-21; Gal 3:26). Children of the King, both by adoption and by new birth. The believer is no longer alone!

In an age of uncertainty about the value of the individual person, the implications of the twin Biblical teachings of creation and redemption need constant reaffirmation – we have been made by God in his image; we have been saved by him at an awful cost. In *Prince Caspian*, C. S. Lewis expresses it well as he has Aslan, the Christ-figure lion, say to the children, as a representative of redeemed humanity, 'You come of Lord Adam and the Lady Eve.... And that is both honor enough to erect the head of the poorest beggar, and shame enough to bow the shoulders of the greatest emperor on earth. Be content.'[16]

How should such a person live? The Christian is both an individual and part of a community, the church. Throughout Christian history there has been the temptation to place either the individualistic or the communal parts of the Christian life above the other. They are equal parts of the same life and lifestyle of the believer. The next two chapters look at the individualistic part of the Christian life and they will be followed by two chapters considering the communal part. Of course, it is important to note that we are separating the parts only for the purpose of close examination; they are part of the same whole!

---

[16]C. S. Lewis (1951), *Prince Caspian*, Collier Books, 211-12.

Chapter 6

How Should Believers Live?
(The Importance of Growth)

The Christian life is the new life of the believer, made available by the Triune God.[1] It has been ordered and planned by God the Father, purchased by God the Son, Jesus Christ, and is applied, sealed, and directed by God the Holy Spirit. It is the life of Christ, or life 'in Christ'. It is lived in the world by those who in their nature, goals, and conduct are different from the world because they are not of the world. It is life in the church, of which Christ is the Head, by those who are sanctified, filled, dominated, controlled, guided, chastened, and empowered by the Holy Spirit. A Christian should live in a manner appropriate for one in a personal relationship with God through Jesus Christ. The Christian's values, attitudes, and

---

[1]Gordon D. Fee, in *God's Empowering Presence: The Holy Spirit in the Letters of Paul* (Peabody, MA: Hendrickson, 1994), 28-29, lists passages in the Pauline epistles in which all three members of the Godhead are mentioned in connection with salvation: Rom 5:1-5; 8:3-4, 9-11, 15-17; 15:16, 18-19, 30; 1 Cor 1:4-7; 2:4-5; 6:11, 19-20; 12:16-18; 2 Cor 1:21-23; 3:16-18; 13:13; Gal 3:1-4; 4:4-7; Eph 1:3, 13-14, 17-20; 2:17-22; 3:16-19; 4:4-6; 5:18-19; Phil 1:19-20; 3:3; Col 3:16; 2 Thess 2:13-14; Titus 3:5-7.In evaluating this list one should note that Fee argues that in the writings of Paul the adjective *spiritual* (*pneumatikos*) should be capitalized for it 'functions primarily as an adjective for the Spirit, referring to *that which belongs to, or pertains to the Spirit*' (italics his). This word is almost entirely Pauline, occurring 24 times in his writings 1) as a **masculine substantive** a) referring to *people:* 1 Cor 2:15; Gal 6:1; b) as a **neuter plural substantive**: Rom 15:27; 1 Cor 2:13; 9:11; 12:1; 14:1; c) as a **neuter plural substantive** referring to *demonic spirits;* 2) as an **adjective** a) referring to *people*: 1 Cor 3:1; 14:37; b) and as an **adjective** modifying *impersonal nouns:* Rom 1:11; 7:14; 1 Cor 2:13; 10:3, 4 (twice); 1 Cor 44 (twice), 46 (twice); Eph 1:3; 5:19; Col 1:9; 3:16.Elsewhere in the New Testament the adjective occurs only twice in 1 Pet 2:5. The adverb *spiritually* (*pneumatikōs*) occurs only in 1 Cor 2:14 ('in a manner consistent with the [divine] Spirit') and Rev 11:8 ('in a spiritual [allegorical] way').

actions should reflect positively upon the name of the God whom she or he bears.

Although there are differences in detail and emphases, all of the New Testament is concerned with the believer's life and development. In all parts the distinguishing mark of this new life is that the possessor is associated with Jesus. In the Gospels this often involved following him physically. His followers were the 'little flock' (Luke 12:23) of which he was the shepherd (John 10:11). But Jesus knew also of 'other sheep,... not of this fold; I must bring them also, so ... there shall be one flock, one shepherd' (John 10:16). These, doubtlessly, are those of whom Jesus said, 'who believe in me through their [his apostles'/disciples'] word' (John 17:20). For these who come into association with Jesus after his physical body had ascended into heaven, their relationship with him is spiritual, described so often by Paul as being 'in Christ' or 'in him'.

The characteristics of the Christian life found in the New Testament arise out of the historical situations in which the writers and original readers found themselves. The epistles in particular were addressed to real people, in real places, facing real situations and problems. As the writers respond they speak of first one, then another, feature of the Christian life. The writers' goal is to inform their readers of the Christian life as a whole and of various aspects of it. They also seek to encourage efforts for development in this life. We can best understand this life by seeking to identify the assumptions upon which the writers build and apply as they teach, admonish, correct, warn, and encourage the believers whom they address.

To seek to answer the question, 'How should believers live?' by looking separately at each literary section or author would require an investigation too long and detailed for our purpose here or would run the risk of missing the whole because of preoccupation with the parts. Hence, we will seek the answer for this question in general, looking at particular parts and issues to illustrate or note applications of the basic principles of this new life assumed by Jesus and his commissioned, apostolic representatives.

Characteristics of the Christian Life

The Christian life is that which follows the new birth. It involves a balanced development of the whole person. Its example is Jesus (Luke 2:52) who increased in wisdom (intellectually), stature (physically), in favor with God (spiritually), and in favor with man (socially).

The Christian life is one of relationships. Its present relationships include those with God, other believers, one's self, and with the world.

The Christian life is one of potential in which a person both experiences and expects the realities of the Final Age now and at the future consummation. Its goal is the restoration of the divine image (Rom 8:29; Col 3:9-10), of God's purposes (Rom 8:28; Eph 1:5-11; 3:11; 2 Tim 1:9) and, eventually, glorification (Rom 2:7-10; 5:2; 8:18; Col 3:4; 1 Thess 2:12; 2 Thess 2:14; 1 Pet 5:1, 10).

The Christian life is one in which sin is forgiven, its dominance broken, and guilt removed. The disharmony caused by the disintegration of the individual begins to yield to a new center for integration; the same potentiality exists for the universe as well. Speaking of Christ Paul says,

> He is before all things, and in him all things hold together. He is the head of the body, the church; he is the beginning, the first-born from the dead, that in everything he might be pre-eminent (Col 1:17-18).

The Christian life is one with commitment, purpose and meaning. It is lived in Christ, under the sovereignty of God, the Lordship of Christ (Phil 2:11), and is dominated by the Spirit of God (Gal 5:25). Its purpose is 'to live for the praise of his glory' (Eph 1:12).

The Christian life is one with concerns, commitments, and activities which, because they reflect those of God, are different from those of the world in general. One in relation with God in Christ has one's mind set on things above, where Christ is (Col 3:1-4). Such a person's life is characterized by love for God and one's neighbor (Mark 12:28-31). The characteristics of a Christian include those listed in the Beatitudes – who is poor in spirit, who mourns, who is meek, who hungers and thirsts for righteousness, who is merciful, who is pure in heart, who is a peacemaker, who is persecuted for righteousness, and when reviled reviles not in return (Matt 5:3-11). This person loves justice, righteousness, and steadfast love (mercy),[2] 'strives for peace ... and holiness' (Heb 12:14), and is not a 'respecter of persons', he or she is impartial.[3] The judge in Matthew 25:35-39 expects his own to have fed the hungry, given drink to the thirsty, welcomed the stranger, clothed the naked, visited the sick and imprisoned; James 1:26-27 insists that a religious person controls one's tongue, visits orphans and widows, and keeps oneself unstained from the world.

The Christian life, however, is life in tension. The new believer is but a 'babe in Christ' and often still closely aligned with the things of his or her former life. In growing and adapting in this new life, there is the real and sometimes frustrating struggle of living both under the sovereignty of God and still facing genuine human choices and responsibilities.

Christians live in this world as 'foreigners,' 'sojourners' (Phil 3:20; Heb 11:8-9). Often the Christian must face a hostile environment (1 Pet 4:4; cf. 2 Thess 2:3-10). For, as the Christian lives between the arrival of the Kingdom of God in the ministry of Christ and the future consummation, she or he lives as alien and pilgrim, who is 'in the world but not of it' (John 15:18-25; 17:14-16).

---

[2]Cf. Isaiah 61:8; Amos 5:24; Hosea 6:5; Matthew 23:23.

[3]In the New Testament, certain relationships are specifically mentioned as those in which there is to be no discrimination among Christians because God is not a respecter of persons: (1) the relationships between Christian masters and slaves (Eph 6:9), (2) church administration (1 Tim 5:21), and (3) the esteem and treatment toward the poor within the Church (Jas 2:1, 9). The principle was so sufficiently grounded within Christian thought that it was cited as a basis for conduct by at least three second-century Christian writers (in the 'Apostolic Fathers:' The First Epistle of Clement 1:3; The Epistle of [Pseudo] Barnabas 4:12; and the Epistle of Polycarp 6:1).

Spiritual Growth and Development

Growth and development are the natural, expected results of birth in all forms of life. So too should they be present in spiritual re-birth. Spiritual growth must be distinguished but never separated from regeneration, the new birth. Sometimes both physical and spiritual birth are not followed by development. In such cases there may be genuine life, but an abnormal situation.

Growth is both commanded and expected by Paul and other writers of the New Testament epistles. Paul says of the Corinthians:

> I, brethren, could not address you as spiritual men, but as men of the flesh, as babes in Christ. I fed you with milk, not solid food; for you were not ready for it; and even yet you are not ready, for you are still of the flesh. For while there is jealousy and strife among you, are you not of the flesh, and behaving like ordinary men? (1 Cor 3:1-3)

The Book of Hebrews both enjoins growth and gives examples of immaturity.

> For though by this time you ought to be teachers, you need some one to teach you again the first principles of God's word. You need milk, not solid food; for every one who lives on milk is unskilled in the word of righteousness, for he is a child. But solid food is for the mature, for those who have their faculties trained by practice to distinguish good from evil. Therefore let us leave the elementary doctrine of Christ and go on to maturity, not laying again a foundation of repentance from dead works and of faith toward God, with instruction about ablutions, the laying on of hands, the resurrection of the dead, and eternal judgment. And this we will do if God permits (Heb 5:11-6:3).

Peter uses the same metaphor as he instructs his readers: 'Like newborn babes, long for the pure spiritual milk, that by it you may grow up to salvation' (1 Pet 2:2).

Stages of Growth: Immaturity and Maturity

Scripture often describes spiritual growth with language that is similar to that denoting the stages of human development. 1 John 2:12-14 is a particularly illuminating passage, for it not only implies the need for spiritual growth but also clearly enumerates some of the stages of that growth. When we supplement the list of 1 John 2 with terms used elsewhere, there emerges an interesting array of words referring to the various stages of spiritual maturation. These include: (1) babe (*brephos*), (2) child (*pais*, a broad, general term which can also mean 'slave' or 'servant'), (3) infant (*nēpios*), (4) child (*teknon*, of either gender, in relation to parents), (5) little child (*teknion*, diminutive of *teknon*), (6) young man (*neanias*, between 24 and 40 years old), (7) father (*patēr*), (8) elder (*presbuteros*), and (9) perfect, complete, mature, full grown, grown up (*teleios*). Other terms which recognize distinctions within spiritual development include (1) old man versus new man, (2) the man of flesh (fleshly) versus the man of spirit (spiritual), and (3) worldly versus spiritual.

We must stress that these stages are not clearly defined in the New Testament. Throughout Christian history there have been and are differences both in the interpretation of the Biblical data related to Christian growth and in the way individual Christians experience it. The important thing to remember is that the need to make progress is acknowledged by all. Problems arise concerning the how, the means, and the timing of spiritual growth.

It is legitimate to raise the issue of uniformity in the Christian life: to what extent must/do all Christians have the same experiences, pass through precisely the same stages, exhibit the same evidence of conversions and growth? Much anxiety and grief have resulted from judgments based upon the expectation, even the demands, for such uniformity. There are undeniable differences between individuals in the rate and experiences of physical, social, and intellectual development. Is it not reasonable to assume the same for spiritual growth? Both the New Testament and Christian experience seem to indicate as much.

Immaturity and maturity, both humanly and spiritually speaking, can be recognized but are difficult to describe. The steps which lie between the two are hard to calculate. One way is to focus upon individual traits which may indicate one or the other extremes of immaturity or maturity. We are justified in beginning with an examination of the negative; what the Christian should not be and do, because this helps us to better understand what we should be and do.

It is interesting to note that there is little difference between the New Testament lists describing the attitudes and lives of non-Christians and of worldly, immature Christians. As 1 Peter 4:2-3 says,

> live for the rest of the time in the flesh no longer by human passions but by the will of God. Let the time that is past suffice for doing what the Gentiles like to do, living in licentiousness, passions, drunkenness, revels, carousing, and lawless idolatry.

Paul's lists of characteristics of the 'old nature', the unbeliever, and those of the immature Christian are also frighteningly similar. The 'works of flesh' of Galatians 5:19-21, the description of living 'as the Gentiles do' in Ephesians 4:17-32, the list of 'what is earthly' of Colossians 3:5-11, and the repulsive portrayal of the corruption which comes from denying God in Romans 1:21-32, although different in details, contain all too similar strands. And even so, the lists are not complete.

We may, perhaps, draw from such passages something of a generalized description of features which, at one time or another, may be evidence of spiritual immaturity. Such a person is deficient in knowledge of the facts and implications of the person and nature of God, of the work of Christ, and of the teachings of God's authorized spokespersons. Ignorance, lack of understanding, callousness and hardness of heart pull one away from God and keep the believer immature. The 'manner of life' of both the unbeliever and the immature Christian may be sensual, lustful in every sense of the word – sexual, yes, but also preoccupied with the inordinate pursuit of earthly pleasures and other things, activities, and attitudes which feed material and non-material desires. But there are less evident features as well, such as evil desire, gossip, enmity, jealously, envy, covetousness, slander, foul talk, and lying. Sorcery and other forms of the occult and idolatry may, unfortunately, be found among immature believers. Fleshly Christians promote strife, disunity, engage in dissension, have a party spirit, are 'respecters of persons' (that is, they discriminate between persons for insignificant reasons), and are slanderers. Insolence, haughtiness, conceit, and boastfulness may be characteristics of such persons. The item most often occurring in the lists we are examining is *anger*.

The immature are prone to imbalance. This may take many forms. Gnostics and ascetics reject all concern for the material world, thinking it to be inherently evil (a failure to adequately recognize that the material was created and is being redeemed by God). A frequent evidence of imbalance is unduly emphasizing certain parts of the Christian life and teachings above or to the exclusion of others. Excessive emphasis upon the intellectual, on the one hand, or the emotional aspects of the Christian life, on the other hand, are common. A Christian may find himself or herself depending upon human effort, or, conversely, fatalistically doing nothing and depending entirely upon direct interventions of God in all matters. 'Fleshly' or 'worldly' believing persons may show their immaturity and imbalance through preoccupation with externals (ceremonies, laws, rites, customs) rather than the things of the Spirit. Most problems can be traced back to a failure to grasp the fact of God's grace and human responsibility in response to it.

The epistles also show aspects of the new nature and of the mature Christian. Galatians 5:22-23 lists the 'fruit of the Spirit' as love, joy, peace, patience, kindness, goodness, faithfulness, gentleness, and self-control (which must certainly mean 'control of self' or 'self-discipline'). It is also instructive to note the things for which Paul and others pray to be evident in the lives the Christians to whom they write (e.g., Eph 1:16-19; Phil 1:8-11; Col 1:9-14). They want to see in their associates love and intellectual development, including factual and experiential knowledge of the things of God, understanding and wisdom, and discernment. They are concerned as well that believers have proper self-evaluation, patience, steadfastness, and unity.

Hebrews 5:14, says 'the mature ... have their faculties trained by practice to distinguish good from evil.' Romans 5:2-5 describes the Christian life as a combination of hope and certain, specific qualities:

> we rejoice in our hope of sharing the glory of God. More than that, we rejoice in our sufferings, knowing that suffering produces endurance, and endurance produces character, and character produces hope, and hope does not disappoint us, because God's love has been poured into our hearts through the Holy Spirit which has been given to us.

No list can be exhaustive, but the following summary is helpful in evaluating our own spiritual status and in helping others in 'going on to maturity'. A well developed spiritual life knows and reflects the love of God. It has endurance, is free from anxiety, thankful, is both at peace with God and has the peace of God, and is able to discern right from wrong, good from evil, and the best from the good. The Christian's mind should be set on that which is honorable, just, pure, lovely, gracious, excellent, worthy of praise, on things above (Phil 4:4-9).

What can we say about the traits of the immature and the mature Christian life? The wording of Paul's statement in Ephesians 4:17, 'You must no longer live as the Gentiles (= heathen) do,' is similar to that of Peter in the passage quoted above. Both apostles assume that the lifestyle of the immature believer is similar to that of the non-Christian. Both writers insist that there is a genuine difference between the attitudes, priorities, and conduct of God's people and those of the world. The words of God to Israel, explaining the reason for certain purity laws, applies as well to New Testament Christians, 'I am the LORD your God who have separated you from the peoples' (Lev 20:24). The Good News Bible translation of Galatians 5:25, pointedly expresses the major feature of the mature Christian: 'The Spirit has given us life, he must also control our lives.' Instead of being dominated by the concerns and allure of the fleshly, the material, Paul admonishes the Colossians, 'If then you have been raised with Christ, seek the things that are above, where Christ is, seated at the right hand of God. Set your minds on things that are above, not on things that are on earth. For you have died, and your life is hid with Christ in God' (3:1-3).

Before leaving our consideration of the stages of growth, we stress again that growth requires conscious effort. Christians are called to be disciples. A disciple is a learner. Learning is hard work, requiring concentration, patience, practice, and experience. Also, Christian growth, like human development, takes time; people require different amounts of time for growth, but all need time. Full maturity cannot and will not be acquired overnight. Patience is part of the fruit of the Spirit (Gal 5:22; cf. Col 3:12). Patience is necessary both in facing the challenges and difficulties of life, and in looking forward to the hope that awaits us as God's redeemed ones.

How should believers live? As those in a personal relationship with God through Jesus Christ. They should live as growing, developing persons in this new life into which they have entered.

Means of Growth

The development of the human organism requires food, exercise, instruction, practice, and experience, in a caring, loving, nurturing atmosphere. At the beginning of this section we quoted 1 Corinthians 3 and Hebrews 5: 'I fed you with milk, not solid food; for you were not ready for it' (1 Cor 3:2); 'You need milk, not solid food; for every one who lives on milk is unskilled in the word of righteousness, for he is a child. But solid food is for the mature' (Heb 5:12-14). 1 Peter 2:2 says, 'Long for the pure spiritual milk, that by it you may grow;' but Hebrews 6:1 admonishes, 'Let us leave the elementary doctrines of Christ and go on to maturity.' The normal Christian outgrows a 'milk diet'.

The Source and Strength for Growth

The New Testament indicates that growth comes through a combination of activities and use of resources. It also assumes that it is accomplished through the work of both the individual and God. Such commands as 'grow,' 'seek,' 'put to death,' and 'put on' indicate that the believing person is to exert conscious effort in the growth process. Such injunctions are like the words of the parent, 'Come,' encouraging the little one to take the first step, for walking requires effort; 'Eat your beans,' for a balanced diet is necessary for healthy growth, and no one can chew and swallow for another; or 'Study your math,' because, again, learning is something in which the growing person must be intimately, laboriously involved. This is behind Paul's words in Philippians 2:12: 'Work out your own salvation with fear and trembling.' The 'out-working', the development of salvation, requires human effort. It is as if the apostle were saying, 'God has given you new life in Christ. Now live, use, and develop it!'

But the verse division at the end of this statement is (as is often the case) unfortunate. Grammatically it falls in mid-sentence. We might paraphrase Paul's words,

> With due reverence and awe and a nervous anxiousness to do right, continue exerting the effort necessary for fully developing your own salvation, for God is the Energizer within you, both causing you to want to and to put forth the power to fulfill what pleases him.

God is at work in Christian development! Earlier in the same epistle, Paul expresses confidence that God 'who began a good work in you will bring it to completion (or 'bring to its goal' or 'to full maturity') at the day of Jesus Christ' (Phil 1:6). The infant is completely passive at birth; growth and development requires the effort of both parent and child.

As we will see later, it is the Holy Spirit who has the special charge for the divine part in Christian growth. But the will and concern of the one God – Father, Son and Holy Spirit – is that salvation reaches its completion in mature Christians.

Food for Growth

From the passages quoted above it is clear we are dealing with different spiritual diets for different levels of Christian development. 'Milk' is for babes, the immature, and 'solid food' for the more advanced. The proper 'food' for the Christian is that which is *appropriate* to the individual's level of maturity and that which is necessary for continuing growth and development. Note the twofold requirement; that which will sustain the person at his or her present level, and also that which will stimulate growth. For a while the human infant needs and can take only milk. Then there comes the time when milk must be supplemented with strained foods, then, gradually, more and more solid, adult-type, foods. Every parent knows that changes in diet are difficult for both parent and child. Babies, when fed something new and more advanced for the first time, have been known to refuse, spit out, or even blow it in the feeder's face. Moving up to a more advanced food can cause colic or other stomach discomfort; many a babe who has just been introduced to new foods has cried through the night, at such times many a parent has sleepily walked the floor with the sufferer. 'More solid' spiritual food may also be the cause of unhappiness and discomfort. But wise spiritual guides realize that it is an unpleasant stage which both the developing Christian and her or his teachers must endure.

What are spiritual 'milk' and 'solid food'? The New Testament gives only vague clues. In 1 Corinthians, Paul fed 'milk' by condemning divisiveness and personality cults, denouncing improper sexual conduct, litigation against other Christians, improper attitudes toward and treatment of Christian leaders, unacceptable conduct at worship, overemphasis on certain spiritual gifts, and lack of proper theological knowledge and understanding. Children need correction!

'Milk' also involves positive instructions. Paul, therefore, focused attention on Jesus Christ and reminded the Corinthians that it was in his person and work that they believed (1 Cor 1:21–2:2). He reviews the essential elements of the 'gospel' for the Corinthians (1 Cor 15:1ff.) He reminds them of the radical difference between spiritual and earthly standards, wisdom, and thinking. In dealing with 'immature behavior and thought' Paul gave specific directives and instructions.

The Book of Hebrews summarizes 'the elementary doctrine of Christ' by listing a number of points where the line between Judaism and Christianity could be blurred. 'Laying again a foundation of repentance from dead works and of faith toward

God' involved the critical point – 'dead works.' The old way of life must be replaced by 'faith in God'. For Christians, growth requires that the revelation through Christ must be added to 'the elementary doctrines' available in the Old Testament. It is essential that the uniqueness of Christianity, the significance of Jesus, be repeated over and again as the basics of the answer to the 'What must I do to be saved?' question; evangelistic activity is essential and believers need to be told time and again 'the old, old story of Jesus and his love'. Yet, there is more to the Christian life and the believer needs to be building upon, rather than constantly examining and admiring the 'foundation'.

Next, the writer of the Epistle to the Hebrews lists 'instruction about ablutions' as a part of spiritual 'milk'. The Greek word translated 'ablutions' (*baptismos*) is from the same root as 'baptism'. Here, the reference is probably to teachings and disputes about a wide range of primarily Jewish cleansing rites, but may also include excessive concerns about Christian baptism and traditions which quickly sprouted in the early church but were not necessarily inherent in the scriptural teachings about it.

'The laying on of hands,' the next 'elementary doctrine', was, in the early church, sometimes associated with the coming of the Holy Spirit (Acts 6:17-19; 19:6), healing of the sick (Acts 9:12; 28:8; cf. Jas 5:14-15), or the recognition and installation of a person for leadership in the Christian community.[4] All are important parts of Christian teaching and experience, but the growing believer does not dwell upon them too long.

Finally, 'the resurrection of the dead, and eternal judgment' are associated with the end of the world and the consummation in the broader fields of teaching in both Judaism and Christianity. The epistle's writer seems to understand that preoccupation with such can hinder growth by diverting attention from other matters that are also essential.

---

[4]Acts 6:6; 13:3; 1 Timothy 4:14; 5:22; 2 Timothy 1:6. Acts 9:17, 'Ananias ... laying his hands on him he said, 'Brother Saul, the Lord Jesus who appeared to you on the road by which you came, has sent me that you may regain your sight and be filled with the Holy Spirit,' may refer to both healing and setting aside for Christian ministry.

These indications of spiritual 'milk' must be recognized as examples, not the whole of it. All basic teachings which clarify the uniqueness of the New Testament faith from both Judaism and pagan religions, are a part of the 'ABCs' of Christianity. As parents teach by censuring improper attitudes, words, and activities, so too did the apostles as they dealt with 'baby' Christians. As parents seek to replace unacceptable behavior with good, so Christian 'milk' included positive instructions for meeting the situations which had evoked improper responses. The epistles are full of both prohibitions and positive directions; apostolic writers give both reproof and correction and teaching and training in righteousness (cf. 2 Tim 3:16).

Descriptions of 'solid food' are even more difficult to find. Hebrews presents the fact and implications of Jesus as 'a high priest for ever after the order of Melchizedek' (Heb 5:6, 10; 7:11, 17) as one example of such. Perhaps the word 'implications' should receive special emphasis. The implications of the fact of Jesus' unique priesthood are far-reaching and profound; it is here that much of the 'solid food' is to be found. These teachings involved not a few simple statements, but a deeper understanding of the whole of Salvation History, the proper place of Old Testament offices and institutions, the implications of Jesus within that framework, and what all this has to say about the Christian's present and future.

Perhaps here is a hint of the type of thing for which we are to look in seeking 'solid food' – the place and implications of Jesus in the total scheme of 'the whole counsel of God'. A couple of examples might help. Ephesians 1:3-23 tells of blessing, choice, grace, redemption through his blood, mystery, and revelation accomplished and made available by Christ; but all these were planned and purposed according to the counsel of the will of God 'before the foundation of the world'. Colossians 1:13-23 again speaks of the victory over evil and the Christian's transferral 'to the kingdom of his beloved Son'. Christ, the image of the invisible God and the first-born, was active at creation. Now he is the one in whom 'all things hold together', the head of the church, the risen and pre-eminent one, in whom 'all the fullness of God was pleased to dwell'. It is through him that all things have been reconciled; in his incarnation Jesus was 'making peace by the blood of his cross'.

In each of these presentations of 'solid food' Jesus Christ is central and pre-eminent. Each adds to our knowledge and understanding of him and his work. Each goes on to develop implications for daily thought and conduct from these truths. We would, however, be amiss if we failed to note that each assumes that Jesus both reveals and does the work of God. The 'meat' of the maturing Christian is the means of getting to know God better. To know him better should lead to loving him more and serving him more completely. Maturity involves knowledge, response, and actions resulting from an ever deepening relationship with the Creator of the Universe, the King in the Kingdom of God, the Christian's Father who is in heaven.

Resources for Growth

The purpose of God's work of salvation is to re-establish a positive, prior relationship with those whom he created to share his fellowship but who rebelled. The one Triune God – Father, Son, and Holy Spirit – willed, planned, and carried out the plan for human salvation. Reconciliation turns enemies into friends. We must stress that the believer grows within the friendship and the friendship grows through association. Growth in the image and likeness of God is pre-eminently stimulated by spending time with him, thinking about him, seeking to know him better, and by conforming thoughts, ambitions, and activities to those which please him. Spending time with one another is essential if any relationship is to grow. Hence, our major resource for living and developing in the Christian life is regular association with *God himself.*

The Bible is a major resource for getting to know God better and thereby developing as Christians. It is the book which God authored, working through chosen, Spirit-filled people. It is the account of his words, deeds, activities among people, and reactions to them. In short, it presents God as he wants to be known; it shows him in the way we are accustomed to getting to know persons – by being with them and seeing them in action.

The Bible is the Word of God. However, it is not a magical book. The inspired Paul said to Timothy: 'Make zealous effort to show yourself proven to God, a workman with no reason to be ashamed, one who is guiding the word of truth straight to its goal' (2 Tim 2:15). The Bible must be used properly or Christian growth may be stifled or abnormal. The Bible reveals God and his will by showing him at work, responding to various situations, as well as by making direct statements and giving specific instructions. It also shows people reacting to God in various ways and his responses to them.

It is important to seek the reasons behind the way that God is shown doing or saying this or that. What is it in God's nature that prompted this statement, action, or response? What are the basic moral and spiritual principles and procedures that determine and control what is being done? How can those same moral and spiritual principles be applied to situations and issues in the modern world? Just as there are appropriate ways for reading, understanding, and applying human books, so too there are for handling God's book. Growing Christians need to be aware of proper principles for Biblical interpretation.

Biblical literacy should be the goal for all Christians. Regular, systematic reading and study make important contributions to Christian growth. Reading, studying, and meditation upon favorite or significant books and passages certainly have an important place in the discipline of Christians. However, it is essential to grasp an adequate overview of Biblical content in order to see how the parts relate to the whole and to each other. There is no substitute for the kind of saturation with Biblical content which comes from reading and rereading it, and from reading large sections of the Bible at a time; it builds strength and resources for both daily life and emergencies.

Perhaps a word about my own experience may help others. I had learned Bible stories in my boyhood home, had Bible courses for two years in a Christian high school, majored in Bible in college, and spent three years obtaining a degree from a theological seminary. During my first year as a pastor I realized that I still did not know my Bible; that is, I did not have a view of the whole. I set out on a campaign which resulted in reading through the Bible seven times in two years. Also, I began seeking to understand the outline of the major periods of Biblical history in both the Old and New Testaments and how the parts fit together. I sought to grasp the essential teachings of each Biblical book. The result was a foundational knowledge of the whole of Scripture that is invaluable. Although I do not always continue reading the volume I did during those two years, I continue to find reading large chunks at one time an important part of my devotional life. Numerous friends and students have testified to the benefits they have gained from similar programs.

Prayer is essential for Christian growth. The Christian life is, as we have said, life in relationship with God. Relationships are built and grow through association; conversation is an important part of associations. There are several types of, parts to, and reasons for prayer. A common list of the elements of prayer includes: (1) *adoration* (praising God for who he is), (2) *thanksgiving* (praising God for what he has done), (3) *confession* (acknowledging sin, repenting from it, and asking for forgiveness), (4) *petition* (asking on behalf of ourselves), (5) *intercession* (asking on behalf of others), and (6) *consecration* (yielding to God's will and dedicating ourselves to him). Adoration and thanksgiving combined are often thought of as worship; this we shall consider shortly. Prayer is also sharing, discussing, asking, listening. What are the types of things children talk about or ask for from their parents? Those are also the types of things Christians can bring to God.

Children are to 'honor' their parents; this includes speaking and asking with proper respect. We, even more so, are to have the proper honor, respect, and reverence when we address God. In prayer we are speaking to another person, but we are not equals; God is supreme and sovereign. We are told as we ask to 'have no anxiety about anything, but in everything by prayer and supplication with thanksgiving let your requests be made known to God' (Phil 4:6). But asking, requesting, must not be demanding. God often answers in ways we do not expect. Like human parents, he reserves the right to say, 'No.'

One of the more important illustrations of prayer in the Bible is the case of King Hezekiah. His enemy, the Assyrian king, had written Hezekiah a letter which said in essence, 'I'm going to beat up and defeat both you and your people and there's nothing you can do about it.' In 2 Kings 19:14-19[5] Hezekiah took the letter 'to the house of God, and spread it before the LORD, and Hezekiah prayed.' Hezekiah knew that God was aware of the contents of the letter, but Hezekiah needed to share it with God. Hezekiah also expressed his own feelings to God and asked for help. He did more than ask, he talked over the issue with God. That is an important part of prayer, to talk through issues with him, to express our feelings and frustrations, to ask for help.

Also, prayer is, reverently speaking, the 'love talk' between humans and the One who 'so loved'. It is the expression of our emotional response and gratitude to him.

But prayer is also constant communion, always being in touch. This certainly does not mean going through the day with eyes closed and hands folded. It is living in conversational reach of God. An old gentleman I know, who has lived long in the presence of his Lord, as he faces decisions, difficulties, or even the minor issues of life can frequently be heard to mutter, 'Stay with me, Jesus!' He has learned the meaning of Paul's directive, 'Pray constantly' (1 Thess 5:17).

Worship is a resource for growth. Worship is simply ascribing worth to God; it is recognizing and expressing who God is, what he does, and one's own submission to and love for him. The great hymn, 'Holy, Holy, Holy, Lord God Almighty,' based on glimpses of worship in heaven given in Revelation 4:8, is a marvelous expression of worship. But so too is the simple recognition that, 'The LORD is my shepherd, I shall not want' (Ps 23:1). Worship need not be limited to Biblical words, it is expression of the realization of who God is, of aspects of his nature, what he does, and what he means to us.

God desires our worship. But, worship is also good and necessary for us. It directs our attention to God himself. Worship is an important resource for spiritual maturity because it reorders priorities away from our interests, wants, needs, and activities to the person and work of him in whom we 'live, and move, and have our being' (Acts 17:28).

---

[5]The account is repeated in Isaiah 37:14-20.

We will look specifically at the body of believers, the church, in chapter 8. Here, we must note that just as the human person develops in relation to other people so also Christian maturity is aided by *fellowship with other Christians*. Hebrews 10:23-25 points to one aspect of this.

> Let us hold fast the confession of our hope without wavering, for he who promised is faithful; and let us consider how to stir up one another to love and good works, not neglecting to meet together, as is the habit of some, but encouraging one another, and all the more as you see the Day drawing near.

Association with other Christians is of help in remaining steadfast in the faith, for mutual encouragement in doing what is right, and for encouragement during the present phase of Salvation History.

In addition, aid, correction, support, counsel and advice, sympathy, and companionship are but some of the other benefits of regular fellowship with other Christians. Other believers have different personalities and perspectives, have been thrust into situations dissimilar from ours, have different experiences, and possess gifts and abilities unlike ours. Their perspectives can enrich, broaden, and provide controls for ours.

Older Christians can contribute wisdom and caution which comes from broad perspectives and much experience. The younger bring a freshness of excitement, enthusiasm, innovation, and strength. Within the body there is corporate wisdom and the checks and balances against wrong headedness, foolish mistakes, excess, and imbalance. The process of Christian maturation moves forward better, and usually more quickly, as the individual lives in concert with others of like faith. A wise person of a previous age said that one can neither be married nor a Christian in isolation.

The fellowship of other Christians is not limited to those now living. Great benefit can be derived from *the history of God's people*. The New Testament writers make frequent reference to the experience of ancient Israel, God's people of the past. That same resource is available to modern Christians. In addition we also have at our disposal the history of the church. We are part of a continuum;

we can, must, learn from the victories and defeats, the mistakes and accomplishments of those who have gone before. It is not without reason that more than one revival movement or period of rapid advance and noteworthy accomplishment in the past has featured a renewed interest in the study of church history.

Many Christians complain of lack of time for the kinds of activities which promote Christian growth. God has established the principle of one day in seven as a day for change of pace, change of focus, rest, and the opportunity for worship and using other means for Christian growth. Some past and present uses of the *Lord's Day* are often characterized by excessive legalism on the one side and either relativism or complete disregard of it on the other. Legitimate demands of modern life prohibit insistence that all observe the same day or do so in the same way. I, for one, am hesitant to prescribe do*s* and don't*s* for others. This is one of the issues of which Paul says, 'Let every one be fully convinced in his own mind' (Rom 14:5). Yet, the principle of observing one day a week in a different way remains as one of God's directives for our own good. More careful use of it could provide a resource for Christian growth in itself and more time for distinctly Christian service.

Additional chance for special opportunity for growth may be found by taking *times of withdrawal for meditation, contemplation, and rest.* Many moderns, caught up as we are in the fast pace of life and the pressures of the assumed necessity and urgency of our tasks and callings, cannot contemplate the need for such. Some may wonder if they could tolerate even brief sustained reduced activity or withdrawal from contact with many numerous other people. Yet, in the middle of his busy schedule and mission Jesus said to his disciples, 'Come away by yourselves to a lonely place, and rest a while' (Mark 6:31). He gave the example of one who found such withdrawal necessary. It may take reordering of priorities, resources, and personal preferences, but yielding to Christ's admonition is worth the effort and cost to promote fellowship with God, personal self-examination, and spiritual growth.

Fasting was a well established part of the piety of Judaism of Jesus' day. His criticism of it was not because of the act itself, but of the motives he saw behind the fasting of many of his contemporaries. They disfigured their faces 'that their fasting may be seen by men' (Matt 6:16). He also says his disciples did not fast because he was with them (Matt 9:15; Mark 2:19; Luke 5:34). In the verses immediately following, he says that after 'the bridegroom' is taken from his disciples, 'then they will fast.' In Matthew (6:17-18) he gives instructions for procedures for fasting that win God's approval. The New Testament records that both Jesus and Paul went without food for periods of time. Elsewhere fasting is mentioned only in Acts. In 13:2 it is associated with worship and in 13:3 and 14:23 with prayer.

Throughout the history of the Church fasting has been a part of the spiritual discipline of some believers. It has been more prevalent in some times and places than others. It has been subjected to abuses. Its continuing voluntary practice has Biblical precedent. Many continue to find it a helpful aid in spiritual growth, primarily when carried out privately and always with spiritual wisdom and moderation.

The words of Jesus, 'Give to him who begs from you, and do not refuse him who would borrow from you' (Matt 5:42; cf. Luke 6:30) and 'It is more blessed to give than to receive' (Acts 20:35), point to another stimulus for Christian growth, *Christian giving*. However, not all giving by Christians is necessarily Christian giving. Christian giving is giving that is not for personal acclaim but for the glory of God. Jesus instructed his disciples,

> When you give alms, sound no trumpet before you, as the hypocrites do in the synagogues and in the streets, that they may be praised by men. Truly, I say to you, they have received their reward. But when you give alms, do not let your left hand know what your right hand is doing (Matt 6:2-3).

Giving obviously helps others, both individuals and the greater body of Christ. Here we call attention to the benefits for the giver. It turns one's attention away from self toward God, and to others. Giving can remind the giver of God's provision for him or herself and the needs of someone else. Sacrificial giving by the Christian is a 'gracious work', a following of the example of Christ (2 Cor 8:7-9). Philippians 4:15-17 implies that the giver shares in the Christian work to which she or he gives and accrues 'fruit'.

Witness, service, and day-to-day Christian living provide challenges and experiences which are important in Christian growth. Involvement in telling others about new life through God's grace in Jesus, working as members of and for the furthering of the Kingdom of God, often force growth. The need to better understand and explain are occasions for learning more and thinking through more completely that which we believe. Facing the issues of life brings not only threats to our faith, but also the opportunity and responsibility to live it out in our daily relationships, work situations, and in making choices in the world. Life in the world brings about that kind of growth which cannot come in isolation. Hebrews 5:14 describes the mature as 'those who have their faculties trained by practice to distinguish good from evil'." The words 'by practice' reminds us that 'real life' situations provide opportunity for a quality of growth that cannot be obtained in any other way. Christians learn and develop on the battlefield! Difficulties, challenges, and threats must be recognized as opportunities for growth. We learn by doing, by practice and experience.

Expectation and *hope* provide both stimulation and direction for growth. It always helps to know where one is going or what the anticipated end product of a project is. Our expectation and hope of full maturity and eventually of being 'made perfect' before God's presence contributes to spiritual development. It is for this reason that early in this chapter we sought to give some indication of what the Bible portrays as the final outcome of Christian growth and development.

We have already noted that Christian growth involves God's work. This is the special domain of the Holy Spirit. In the next chapter we will look at the role and work of the Holy Spirit in the Christian life. We mention it here as a reminder that *the Holy Spirit* is an important, our most important, resource.

Perils of the Christian Life

Nowhere does the New Testament promise Christians an easy, prosperous, comfortable life in this world. Instead, it warns of the dangers of living in *a hostile environment*. We have already made a number of observations about the Christian's present position. Believers live 'between the times', between the arrival of the Final Age and the completion of God's work; we live as aliens and pilgrims, as Jesus said, 'in the world but not of it' (John 15:18-25; 17:14-16). Paul, recognizing that his readers were on a spiritual battlefield, called upon them to 'be strong' and 'put on the whole armor of God ... and having done all, to stand' (Eph 6:10-17); in likening the Christian to the 'soldier in service,... an athlete,... the hard-working farmer' (2 Tim 2:5-6) he implies that the believers are in a dangerous, demanding position which requires a twenty-four hour a day, seven days a week commitment.

In speaking of his readers' former companions in pagan pursuits and immoral living, Peter says, 'They are surprised that you do not now join them in the same wild profligacy, and they abuse you' (1 Peter 4:4). The apostle refers to Christians as 'aliens and exiles' (2:11) and warns, 'Be sober, be watchful. Your adversary the devil prowls around like a roaring lion, seeking some one to devour' (5:8). James, aware that the hostile environment in which we must live is a very real detriment to Christian living, writes, 'Do you not know that friendship with the world is enmity with God? Therefore whoever wishes to be a friend of the world makes himself an enemy of God' (4:4).

Yet, because we are human, most of us want to be accepted by our fellow humans; we recoil from the idea of being 'different'. We may well fear the consequences of living as growing Christians in the midst of the world. We are not immune from the allure of evil, fleshly pleasures and material rewards. The persecutions and other sufferings of many in the past and present testify to the reality of the price that frequently must be paid by those standing 'in Christ'.

A factor related to our environment, is the constant presence of *temptation*. The Synoptic Gospels depict Jesus' face-to-face confrontation with the devil in his temptation. Christians too may sometimes have such momentous struggles in which the presence and power of Satan is obvious. However, most temptation is more subtle, inherent in our environment, and even within our own desires. This James points out,

> Let no one say when he is tempted, 'I am tempted by God'; for God cannot be tempted with evil and he himself tempts no one; but each person is tempted when he is lured and enticed by his own desire. Then desire when it has conceived gives birth to sin; and sin when it is full-grown brings forth death (1:13-15).

In the imaginary correspondence between 'Uncle Screwtape,' an official in his Satanic majesty's 'lowerarchy,' and 'Wormwood,' a junior tempter working with a 'patient' on earth, C. S. Lewis depicts constant efforts by the forces of Satan to render the Christian ineffective.[6] Lewis is insightful in stressing the subversive powers of even 'nice' sins – spiritual pride, jealously, and the rest – in addition to moral felonies which would be denounced in any respectable society.

Failure to take advantage of what is provided for growth leads to stagnation in Christian development – and, not only to stagnation, to retrogression as well – limbs, muscles, abilities, and skills weaken and atrophy when not used. The New Testament writers' constant urging to grow is not only so that their readers may enjoy all that God has for them, it is also a safeguard against slipping back into their former manner of life. The weary mother who frequently had to put her young son back into bed several times each night after he had fallen out finally asked, 'Johnny, why do you fall out of bed so often?' With trembling lips, he replied, 'I don't know, Mommy. Probably because I stay so close to where I got in.' Growing beyond the point at which we were born into the Christian life does not eliminate all problems, but it certainly lessens the danger of staying too close to the point of entering the Christian life and the temptation for 'doing what the Gentiles (heathen) like to do' (1 Pet 4:3).

---

[6]C. S. Lewis (1942), *The Screwtape Letters* (London: Geoffrey Bles).

Perhaps, we may expand this peril by recognizing *immaturity* itself, especially self-centeredness, the quest for success in human terms, preoccupation with earthly pleasures and possessions, as a hindrance to Christian living. Jesus spoke of 'the cares of the world, and the delight in riches, and the desire for other things, [which] enter in and choke the word, and it proves unfruitful' (Mark 4:19).

Specific sins, particularly those recognized as sin but persisted in by the individual, are major perils of the Christian life. Were we to start listing such sins, we would certainly omit more than we could include and, perhaps, give comfort to a reader living in 'known sin'. The subjects addressed in the ten commandments (Ex 20:3-17), those things listed as the 'works of the flesh' (Gal 5:17), and the like, would certainly be among the specific sins from which all Christians should recoil and repent. Paul insists that the Corinthian Church deal firmly with such sins (note 1 Cor 5). But there are sins of omission; 'Whoever knows what is right to do and fails to do it, for him it is sin' (Jas 4:17).

Again, we cannot seek to be either all inclusive nor deal at length with some of the common problem areas which may be perils in the Christian life. *Guilt* is one such area. All are guilty before God, but in his eyes, the death and resurrection of Jesus has removed the guilt of believers. Guilt is a problem when we refuse to believe that God has really forgiven or when we are unable to forgive ourselves. The cure is not to dwell upon our past sins and guilt, but upon God's grace and the love he has made known in Christ. The degree with which 'God so loved the world', on the basis of which 'he gave his only Son', is more than adequate to remove all of the sin and guilt of 'whoever believes in him' (John 3:16).

Ignorance has always been a problem for Christians. The New Testament speaks of ignorance of 'the righteousness which comes from God' (Rom 10:3; cf. 2 Pet 2:12) as characteristic of the non-Christian. It is also a characteristic of immature Christians (Heb 5:2; 2 Pet 3:16). We are to be aware, not ignorant, of the designs of Satan (2 Cor 2:11). Paul had to deal with ignorance of certain basic Christian teachings (1 Cor 15; 1 Thess 4:13).

All Christians are called to be 'disciples'. A disciple is a learner, a student. Learning is, first of all, learning of Jesus who said, 'Come to me ... learn from me' (Matt 11:28-30). He is both the teacher and the curriculum for the believer; there is an interpersonal aspect of overcoming ignorance. There is also the need to learn facts, 'the whole counsel of God,' to learn from others, and from our own experience of living the Christian life. Failure to overcome ignorance is a peril we must work to avoid.

Earlier we spoke of *imbalance* as a mark of an immature Christian. It is one of the most common perils into which Christians fall. It can be an insidious and debilitating evil producing warped, deformed, abnormal Christians.

Intolerance is a problem area not completely separate from imbalance. Non-believers often view the Christian conviction that theirs is the only way to God as intolerance. But we are speaking here of intolerance of a Christian for a fellow believer. Specifically, we refer to that intolerance which all too often demands conformity beyond the bounds of limitation placed by Scripture. Such thinking tends to indicate belief that all Christians must have the same experiences, must always see, do, and think alike. An imbalanced person frequently demands that all share his or her unbalanced view and actions. It is a peril which has frequently brought blotches upon the name of the church, pain within it, and has hindered well-rounded Christian living.

There is yet another common problem area that must be mentioned – that of overly *dominating persons and the presence of personality cults* within the church. Some individuals either seek leadership positions in the church, or once they have it, use it wrongly and harmfully. They seek to be personally recognized and honored, to gratify their own desire for power, or to dominate others – all for their personal aggrandizement. (Leaders' greed for money, sex, and power are not limited to the secular realm![7]) Jesus condemned such traits in the religious leaders of his day (Mark 12:28-38; Matt 23:2-7;

---

[7]Cf. Richard J. Foster, *Money, Sex and Power: The Challenge of the Disciplined Life* (San Francisco: Harper and Rowe, 1985); Philip Turner, *Sex, Money, and Power: An Essay in Christian Social Ethics* (Cambridge, MA: Cowel Publications, 1985).

Luke 20:46-47). Paul seems to have such persons in view when, in writing to the Corinthians, he speaks of one who 'makes slaves of you, or preys upon you, or takes advantage of you, or puts on airs, or strikes you in the face' (2 Cor 11:20). He alludes to those who preach Christ to spite him while he is in prison (Phil 1:15-18). In 3 John 9-10, the beloved apostle refers to a classic example,

> Diotrephes, who likes to put himself first, does not acknowledge my authority ... prating against me with evil words. And ... he refuses himself to welcome the brethren, and also stops those who want to welcome them and puts them out of the church.

In 1 Corinthians 1:10-17 Paul faced the issue of personality cults. It is likely that these groups centered themselves not only around noted leaders, but also upon certain doctrines, procedures, or activities. It is significant that Paul does not try to say who is right or wrong, rather, in essence he says, 'Cut it out!' He then proceeds to direct their attention where it rightfully belongs, upon the person and work of Jesus Christ (1 Cor 1:18–2:2).

The weak, imbalanced, ignorant, the immature are especially susceptible to domination by the Diotropheses present in every age. They may be easily sucked into a group centered upon a human leader or a particular doctrinal emphasis or practice. It is a peril of major proportions; the safeguards are watchfulness, personal growth, having one's 'faculties trained by practice to discern good from evil' (Heb 5:14).

The New Testament has a *holistic* view of human persons. Jesus developed in all areas (cf. Luke 2:52). Paul desires that God will sanctify his readers 'wholly,' that their 'spirit and soul and body be kept sound and blameless' (1 Thess 5:23). I recount the following incident to illustrate that *physical health and emotional conditions* can affect our Christian lives, or at least our perception of them.

A student came to tell me of his (use of this pronoun does not necessarily reflect the person's gender) decision to drop out of college. The reason given was the assumption that he was not passing his work and particularly that he had no chance of passing a course

I was teaching. My evaluation of his work was a bit different – a solid 'A' rather than 'F.' He went on to tell of doubts about many spiritual issues, including his own salvation. In the following conversation I discovered he was getting much too little sleep. I persuaded him to remain in college for the rest of the semester (since money already paid for food, lodging, and tuition was not refundable), to make getting eight hours of sleep every night the first priority, and doing the best possible in academic work in the time left (since he was already convinced failure was inevitable, there was nothing to lose). Weeks later both academic and spiritual problems were all but forgotten.

In dark nights of either soul or body the Christian is especially vulnerable to the fiery darts of Satan. Such times are not occasions for making avoidable major decisions. Such times are occasions for trust. A young man lay in a hospital bed, in pain, discouraged, and a bit bitter at God. An old friend and teacher visited him, cut short his complaints with the words, 'Hush, God is still on the throne.' In the confidence of the sovereignty of a loving God the young man, although not pain-free, has for nearly forty years been able to live an active life, including writing this book. Afflictions of body and mind can be turned to times of finding, with Paul, that when one trusts God's grace to be sufficient, then 'when I am weak, then I am strong' (2 Cor 12:9-10).

Chapter 7

How Should Believer Live?
Sanctification and the Christian Life

Sanctification has long been assumed to be synonymous with growth and development in the Christian life. Differences of opinion about the nature of sanctification, the possibility of attaining full maturity or perfection, and how it is achieved are major issues dividing denominations and other Christian groups.[1] Lutheran and Reformed (including Presbyterian, some Baptist, and other) groups hold that sanctification is a continuing process within which both God and the individual are active but which is completed only in heaven, never in this life.

Other views believe that in one way or another sanctification (either as a process or as an instantaneous act) is a realizable goal before death. Some insist that God works in such a way as to make this possible and a reality, or that the believer is able to attain holiness (complete sanctification) through exercising the means of grace and growth.

John Wesley taught that on the road from sin to salvation the Christian seeks to attain perfect love, the Christian's love for both God and for other people. Nevertheless, that road is characterized by willful rebellion against both human and divine law. Yet, he insisted, one must attempt to take seriously the command to holiness. His followers often speak of two crises; the first brings the conversion experience and justification in which one is freed from past sins he or she has committed. The second experience, or the second work of grace, brings 'full salvation' in which the believer is liberated from

---

[1] See Donald A. Alexander, ed., *Christian Spirituality: Five Views of Sanctification* (Downers Grove, IL: InterVarsity, 1988). Lawrence Richards, *A Practical Theology of Spirituality* (Grand Rapids, MI: Zondervan, 1988), 35-48, offers a simple summary of the Reformed, Wesleyan, and Dispensational views with his own suggestions.

flaws in moral nature which cause sin. For Wesley, the emphasis was on the expectation of perfect love for God. In his thought 'sinless perfection never means a claim to flawlessness . . . [but rather] the sanctifying and purgative action of the Holy Spirit' enabling the believer to be relieved and cleansed of the disordered contents of the subconscious mind.[2]

Pentecostal views usually have much in common with that of Wesley. They tend to place even more emphasis upon 'experience'. The higher levels of sanctification are usually associated with a separate experience, the 'baptism' or 'filling' with the Holy Spirit.

The church has frequently faced views which affirm the possibility of sinlessness on the basis that sin is only law breaking. There is now no law for the Christian, therefore nothing a Christian can do is sin. Antinomianism (no law), as this teaching is called, usually has a broad view of Christian liberty and a narrow view of sin;[3] sin, it argues, consists only of overt acts by sinful people. Antinomians frequently lean heavily upon selected verses in 1 John which in some translations seem to say that Christians do not sin (e.g., 3:4-6, 9; 5:18). A careful study of the Greek verb tenses relating to sin in this epistle shows that the author is not saying that a Christian never sins, but that a continuing lifestyle of sin is foreign to the mature Christian's experience. Rather, to claim we are sinless is self-deception (1:8) and treats God as if he is a liar (1:10). The goal is sinlessness, but forgiveness is available when it is not achieved; 'My little children,' says John, 'I am writing this to you so that you may not sin; but if any one does sin, we have an advocate with the Father, Jesus Christ the righteous; he is the propitiation for our sins, and not for ours only but also for the sins of the whole world' (1 John 2:1-2).

In the previous chapter we noted briefly that sanctification (*hagios, hagiasmos*) carries the basic meaning *to set apart for and dedicate to God, to make holy, consecrated, be hallowed;* it may denote either a ceremonial state or moral fitness. It comes

---

[2]Alexander, *Spirituality: Five Views*, 98 – quoting from Wesley, *Clinical Theology* (1966 edition), p. xxv.

[3]The latter phrase adapted from the title of a song by Robert H. Scott, 'A Broad View of Freedom and a Narrow View of Sin,' (unpublished, 1994).

from the same root word as the noun *saint*. As such it seems to focus more upon the result and goal of salvation rather than the fact of Christian growth and the means of achieving it. As George E. Ladd puts it, 'Sanctification is not a term designating the totality of the good life as such, but one that denotes the dedication of Christians to God in contrast to the prevailing evils of their society.'[4]

Again, a study of Greek verb tenses in relevant passages is instructive. Some verses refer to sanctification as having taken place in past time so that it is *now completed (*1 Cor 1:2; 6:11; Heb 10:10, 14). Furthermore, many of the epistles address their readers as 'saints' – assuming that they have already been sanctified – but then go on to deal with the 'unsaintly' life the writers assumed many of these 'saints' to be living. Thus, the past tense appears to be used to refer to the believer's position in Christ in which every provision has already been made for a holy life. However, for the New Testament writers there may still remain a difference between provision and possession.

Other passages depict sanctification as a *present* process, one that is *still continuing.*[5] To my knowledge the word *sanctify* (and its various forms) is not found in future tense in the New Testament.[6] Nevertheless, the concept of a perfection *complete only in the glorified state* is found in such passages as 1 John 3:2 ('Beloved, now are we the sons of God, but it does not yet appear what we shall be; but we know that when he shall appear, we shall be like him') and Jude 24 ('... to present you without blemish before the presence of his glory).[7]

Hence, it appears that from God's point of view sanctification

---

[4]George E. Ladd, *A Theology of the New Testament*, rev. ed., 565.

[5]1 Thessalonians 5:23; Hebrews 2:11; 10:14; note also the expectations and admonitions for continuing growth in 1 Corinthians 3:18; 1 Thessalonians 3:12; and 2 Peter 3:18.

[6]However, note 1 Thessalonians 5:23: 'May the God of peace sanctify you wholly; and may your spirit and soul and body be kept sound and blameless at the coming of our Lord Jesus Christ.' The two verbs, *sanctify (hagiasai)* and *keep (tērētheiē),* are in the optative mood and certainly look forward to a future fulfillment and that for which Paul prays.

[7]See also Ephesians 5:27.

has been completed, it is an accomplished fact. From the human point of view it is still in process of full realization. The final stage of sanctification will be realized only in the resurrected body which will then be completely holy in the presence of God.

In 2 Thessalonians 2:13 Paul makes a particularly interesting, and a bit puzzling, statement: 'God chose you from the beginning to be saved, through sanctification by the Spirit and belief in the truth.' Here salvation and sanctification are closely linked, although not equated. The agents of sanctification are the Spirit and faith in the truth. Sanctification is a part of God's election, it is realized through the activity of the Spirit, and involves the intellectual-volitional commitment of faith or trust in the truth. Such an understanding of sanctification does nothing to settle the debate about whether the fullest level of maturity and holiness are 'realizable' in this life, or if the believer is glorified only in the presence of God in heaven. It does not solve the question of whether maturity comes through God's work alone or as a result of human effort, or whether it is a combination of human and divine effort and work. It does place proper emphasis upon the fact that the Christian is set apart by and for God and that holiness in being and in conduct is an important feature of the Christian life.

From earlier discussions in this book, the reader will detect that the writer believes that both Biblical data and experience depict Christian growth as a continuing process in which both human and divine energies must be active. Furthermore, it appears that the process will be complete only in the consummation, as a part of the conclusion of God's work in Salvation History. However, there are two points closely associated with this view which should be stressed.

First, although the new birth and the Christian life must be distinguished, they cannot be separated. Birth is birth; it is the point at which life begins; the one being born is passive; it is God's saving work. The Christian life can only begin after birth has been accomplished. Numerous preachers properly insist, 'Don't try to live a Christian life unless you have a Christian life to live.' Once life has come, growth must follow. Human growth demands a cooperative effort between the newborn and those caring for him or her. Spiritual life is also a cooperative effort, the believer must be actively involved in furthering growth in it. God, through his Spirit, is at work, but also the commands to grow and develop must be taken seriously.

This leads to the second point, progress in the Christian life requires conscious human effort. It requires discipline, courage to stand against the tides, submission to the sovereignty of God, and the work of the Holy Spirit within. The Christian is to use the means of growth, to do good, and 'declare the wonderful deeds of him who called you out of darkness into his wonderful light' (1 Pet 2:9). That 'declaration' is for all Christians, not just the wives to whom Peter specifically refers; it involves living so that 'they [who] do not obey the word, may be won without a word by the behavior of ...' believers with whom they come in contact. (cf. 1 Pet 3:1). Even so, the most experienced Christian should humbly say to others, and to him or herself, 'Please be patient, God is not yet finished with me.'

But, how does one live in that way? What are the directives for Christian living?

Standards for Life and Conduct

Paul, in Colossians 1:10, establishes the criteria for Christian behavior when he says, 'We have not ceased to pray for you, asking that you may be filled with the knowledge of his will in all spiritual wisdom and understanding, to lead a life worthy of the Lord, fully pleasing to him, bearing fruit in every good work and increasing in the knowledge of God.'

The criteria that conduct must be 'worthy' (*axios*) of the Christian's relationship with God is a recurring one. Paul says, 'Let your manner of life be worthy of the gospel of Christ' (Phil 1:27); 'lead a life worthy of the calling to which you have been called' (Eph 4:1); 'lead a life worthy of God, who calls you into his own kingdom and glory' (1 Thess 2:12). He commends the Thessalonians' 'steadfastness and faith in all your persecutions and afflictions which you are enduring. This is evidence of the righteous judgment of God, that you may be made worthy of the kingdom of God, for which you are suffering' (2 Thess 1:4-5).

He directs that Phoebe, a Christian sister, be received 'as is worthy of the saints' (Rom 16:2). Likewise, 3 John 6 says of visiting Christian teachers, 'You will do well to send them on their journey as befits (or 'is worthy of') God's servants.'[8]

It is evident from such statements that the Christian's conduct is to be determined in relation to God. It is God's name and nature that must determine what one does or refrains from doing. Are there more specific guidelines or expansions on this principle in the rest of Scripture?

The Teachings of Jesus: General

In the Synoptic gospels discipleship is commitment to Jesus. He says, 'Come to me' (Matt 11:28; 19:21), 'Follow me,'[9] 'Learn from/of me' (Matt 11:29). It is a radical commitment; the disciple is to leave all to follow Jesus (Matt 10:37-39; Luke 14:26-27), to take up the cross, deny self, and give up life itself (Mark 8:34-38; Matt 16:24-26; Luke 9:23-26). Jesus, as recorded in John's Gospel, makes it very explicit that his disciples are to obey his commands: 'If you love me, you will keep my commandments' (14:15); 'If a man loves me, he will keep my word' (14:23); 'If you keep my commandments, you will abide in my love, just as I have kept my Father's commandments and abide in his love' (15:10).

Of special importance in understanding Jesus' standard for conduct is his answer to the scribe's query, 'Which commandment is first [or, most important] of all?'[10] His answer insists that 'The first [commandment] is ... "love the Lord your God".... The second is this, "You shall love your neighbor as yourself"' (Mark 12:28-33; Matthew 22:36-40; Luke 10:25-27). Matthew 22:40 records that

---

[8]In the period immediately following the New Testament, the 'Apostolic Fathers' express similar sentiments: 1 Clement 21:1, 'be citizens worthy of him'; in Polycarp's letter to the Philippians, he says, 'we ought to walk worthy of his commandments and His glory' (5:1); 'if we conduct ourselves worthily of Him we shall also reign with him' (5:2); the Epistle to Diognetus 11:1 speaks of the 'teacher of gentiles, ministering worthily to them.'

[9]Mark 1:17 = Matthew 4:19; Mark 2:14 = Matthew 9:9 and Luke 5:27

[10]Some Jewish scholars of the day sought the 'first commandment', meaning the one which if kept would assure the observance of all the rest.

he also said, 'On these two commandments depend all the law and the prophets.' Within the context of the question, Jesus rejects a legalistic standard for twofold relational guidelines. But, not just any relationships. First, conduct is determined on the basis of love for God – the perfect, holy One for whom right and wrong make a difference. Good is that which is in harmony with God's nature and which pleases him; wrong is that which is out of harmony with his nature and displeases God. The second relationship is love for other people. The parable of 'The Good Samaritan' (Luke 10:29-37) defines 'neighbor' as anyone whom we might meet who is in need. In John, Jesus' statement is even broader, 'Love one another.'[11]

In the earlier phases of Salvation History God expressed his will with do*s* and don't*s*. In Christ, God's revelation was completed. God now directs his children by asking that their love for him affect all areas of life. He says, 'Know me, love me, honor me in your actions, and don't do anything that would disgrace me, whose name you bear.' To live by such an ethic one must strive to know more and more about God, to constantly increase one's awareness of his person, his likes and dislikes, in short to seek to know God better. One must also be sensitive to those about him or her. Hence, the 'love ethic' for the Christian life is neither legalistic nor relativistic. It is personal, based on the Christian's relation with God; it has specific content, God's nature and will.

One further fact about Jesus and the law is that he subjected both the law itself and the traditions and customs about it to his own person and authority. Matthew 12:1-5 (cf. Luke 6:1-5) records that in response to criticism of his disciples picking and eating grain on the Sabbath Jesus cited two examples of legitimate exceptions being taken to the law – David's eating the bread of the Presence and priests performing their duties on the day. He continues, 'I tell you, something greater than the temple is here. And if you had known what this means, "I desire mercy, and not sacrifice," you would not have condemned the guiltless. For the Son of man is lord of the sabbath' (Matt 12:6-8).

---

[11]John 13:34; 15:12,17; cf. 1 John 3:11, 23; 4:7, 11; 2 John 5.

He also exercised the right to heal on the Sabbath;[12] in John 7:23 he cites the practice of circumcising on the Sabbath as another recognized justification for his 'working' on the seventh day. Likewise, he claimed the authority to challenge accepted practices about laws dealing with things clean and unclean and even annulled the Old Testament basis of them; Mark says, 'he declared all foods clean' (7:19). Jesus' actions displayed a concern for the intent rather than the letter of the law and the traditions that had grown up around it. The needs of people, he insisted, take precedence over a strict interpretation of the law. Jesus is Lord, even of the law; the king in the Kingdom has the right to interpret and apply his law as he sees fit.

The Teachings of Jesus: The Sermon on the Mount[13]

It is generally agreed that Jesus' Sermon on the Mount is a part of his teachings regarding life and conduct. The exact nature and purpose of the Sermon is much debated. Some see it as a statement of what Jesus requires; a collection of simple commands intended to be obeyed explicitly; thus, the Sermon is the law or a new legalism through which one is to earn God's favor (salvation). Others argue that it portrays an impossible ideal, a sample of God's requirements in their fullest sense which shows how stringent God's law really is and how impossible it is to keep. Thus, the Sermon on the Mount forces people to seek salvation through some other means, i.e. by grace through faith. Some insist that in the Sermon on the Mount Jesus gave teachings for a specific, limited period of time. Perhaps it is a temporary law to hold jurisdiction only between the time of Jesus' coming and the end of the world. Or, maybe it is the law for the coming millennium to govern the world during some future period in which Jesus will establish his reign on earth prior to the final overthrow of evil forces and the beginning of the eternal state. Another view suggests that the Sermon on the Mount is law for

---

[12]Mark 3:1-5 = Matthew 12:9-14 and Luke 6:6-11; Luke 13:16; 14:1-5; John 5:2-18; 9:1-30.

[13]Matthew 5:1–7:29; cf. Sermon on the Plain, Luke 6:16-49.

Jewish Christians; Gentile believers are governed by another standard.

A careful study suggests that the Sermon on the Mount[14] is a selected sampling of Jesus' teachings which demonstrate in general and by example the type of life and attitudes expected of those who are citizens of the Kingdom of God. It provides illustrations of what it means to love God supremely and one's neighbor as oneself. It describes his disciples, the Blessed ones, as those who are poor in spirit, who mourn, are meek, who hunger and thirst for righteousness, are merciful, pure in heart, peacemakers, and are persecuted for righteousness (5:3-17). Nevertheless, it is just such unlikely persons (by the world's standards) who are the salt of the earth, the light of the world, the city which cannot be hidden (5:13-16).

Jesus' own attitude toward the Law is recorded in Matthew 5:17-20. His affirmation of the permanence of the Law, 'Think not that I have come to abolish the law and the prophets; I have come not to abolish them' (vs. 17), is limited by his coming 'to fulfill them' and the phrase, 'until all is accomplished' (vs. 18). Understanding what Jesus meant requires the clarification of several points, the first of which is the meaning of *Law*.

The word *Law* (*nomos*) is used by the various New Testament writers in a number of different ways. Paul seems to have the most variety in the ways he employs the term, but Jesus also appears to stress first one and then another possible aspect of it. The major alternatives which emerge from study of the relevant texts suggest *law* may refer to:

1. The expression of the revelation and the nature and will of God;
2. The Old Testament, Mosaic legislation;
   a. The Ten Commandments;
   b. The Pentateuch;
3. The whole of the Hebrew (Old Testament) Scriptures;

---

[14]Joachim Jeremias, *The Sermon on the Mount,* Norman Perrin, trans. (Philadelphia: Fortress Press, 1963).

4. The orderly, governing principles of nature and/or society;

5. The Pharisaic interpretations (additions) to the Old Testament Law, the Oral Law;

6. Human constructed regulations as means for obtaining a favorable relationship with God;

7. The law of sin and death;

8. The law of the Spirit and of Christ; and

9. It is possible that in some contexts 'law' may refer to:

    a.   that which controls or has dominance in life (see Romans 7:1; 8:2); or

    b.   basic guidelines for life.

Jesus' meaning in the Sermon on the Mount is probably in keeping with the common usage of the day which did not clearly discriminate between such options. Rather, he affirmed the legitimacy of the principle of divine law but insisted that numerous current attitudes, some additions, and many contemporary practices failed to realize God's intent.

This raises the issue of the meaning of *to fulfill* (*plērosai*). In Jesus' statement *fulfill* is the opposite of *to destroy* (*katalusai*) in verse 17. When put in the context of what follows in the Sermon and the rest of his ministry, *fulfill* indicates that in his life and words Jesus rejected all deviation from the divine intent, whether it be by excessively legalizing or disregarding it. He assumes the religious leaders of the day were guilty of both. In Matthew 5:19 Jesus warns against relaxing 'one of the least of these commandments' and teaching others to do so. Instead, he says, 'Unless your righteousness exceeds that of the scribes and Pharisees you cannot enter the kingdom of heaven' (5:20). In the 'antitheses' (5:21-48), which appear to be directed against the religious lawyers of the day (the Jewish religious professionals, the 'theologians'), he emphasizes and places the inner attitude on the same level with the deed. Thus, anger is as bad as murder, lust as adultery, and he equates divorce with adultery. He says faithfulness and dependability must make oath-taking unnecessary. The Old Testament principle of an eye-for-eye[15] – a restraint upon excessive violence – should be replaced with the principles and attitudes of non-resistance and giving; rather than hating one's enemy and loving the neighbor, love must be for all. The divine intent in Old Testament regulations and a guide for Christian conduct is further stated in the so-called 'Golden Rule'. 'Whatever you wish that men would do to you, do so to them; for this is the law and the prophets' (Matt 7:12; also Luke 6:31).

In summary, Jesus says, 'Be ye perfect even as your Father in heaven is perfect' (5:48, RSV). The word translated here as *perfect* (*teleios*) is the same used elsewhere to mean *complete, mature, full grown, grown up.* In the parallel passage, Luke 6:36, the injunction is, 'Be merciful, even as your Father is merciful.' Elsewhere, the same idea, that attitudes and conduct should reflect God's nature, is expressed in similar grammatical structures; those who have entered the Kingdom of God through Jesus must be forgiving because God forgives (Matt 6:14), and be loving because God is love (1 John 4:7).

In Leviticus 11:44-45 (cf. 19:2; 20:7, 26) Israel is to 'consecrate yourselves therefore, and be holy, for I am holy. You shall not defile yourselves with any swarming thing that crawls upon the earth. For I am the LORD who brought you up out of the land of Egypt, to be your God; you shall therefore be holy, for I am holy.'

This injunction has to do with Israel's separate, distinct status because of her special relation with God (Lev 20:24-25), which was to be reflected in her ceremonial observances. In fact, justification for demanding Israel's obedience of God's commands, both in general (Lev 18:1-5) and specific injunctions (throughout the book of Leviticus), is that Israel is in covenant relationship with God – 'I am the LORD,' 'I am the LORD your God,' or some similar statement occurs time and again. The totality of Israel's life was to be governed by the implications of the nature of God with whom she had a special relation.

Earlier we saw that, as Jesus summarized the Law, he expressed the expectation that his disciples would be governed by their relationship with God, 'Love the Lord your God ...'; love to God

---

[15]Exodus 21:24; Leviticus 24:20; Deuteronomy 19:21. This is often called the *lex talionis,* the law of restrained retaliation.

and neighbor is the fulfilling of the Law. It is unlikely that 'perfect,' in the traditional translations of Matthew 5:48, means that Jesus is calling for the impossible, the absolute moral perfection and holiness which exists only in God. Rather, like Israel of old, Christian conduct is based on a special relationship with God, it is human response to God's love and a demonstration of the Christian's love for him. From the larger context of the verse, it seems reasonable to assume that in Matthew 5:48, Jesus is saying that his followers are to have the same type of 'mature' understanding of the nature and intent of the Law with which God views it; this includes both attitudes and actions, the spirit must not be separated from the letter.

Jesus builds on the same principle; that the invisible, the spiritual, is at least as significant as the external and visible when he addresses some of the major practices of the pious Jewish lay people – almsgiving (6:1-4), prayer (6:5-15), and fasting (6:16-18). Likewise, in instructing his own disciples, Jesus replaced the outward, material manifestations of true religion with God's perspectives which includes spiritual concerns. At the same time Jesus does not reject the necessity of their outward manifestation and practice (6:19-7:12). This, he recognizes, is not the popular, the broad, but the narrow way (7:13-14). As the minority, Jesus' disciples must be especially vigilant and discerning because of the presence of false prophets and false disciples (7:15-23). They are to build upon rock, the lasting foundation (7:24-27).

Law Versus Grace Controversy, Continued (Implications for Ethics and Life)

In a previous chapter we looked at the Jerusalem Council of Acts 15 as it dealt with the primary issue of the Law versus Grace Controversy, 'What must I do to be saved?' and its answer, 'By grace through faith.' There was also a *secondary issue*, involving the practical implications of this decision for grace. If salvation is apart from law, what about moral and ethical conduct and the living of life from day to day? Are there ethical and moral standards for the Christian; if so, where and how are they to be identified? Perhaps, the Jewish laws and ceremonies have no part in salvation but are required for Christian living. If not, is there some other form of legalism which prescribes all obligations and questions of conduct by clearly stated laws and rules? On the other hand, maybe there are no regulations of any kind for Christians; they have complete freedom to follow the dictates of their redeemed wills.

The Jerusalem Council seems to have accepted none of these extremes. To understand what it did we must note both its pronouncements and the implications of those actions for its culture and time.

What did the Jerusalem Council do? It listed four classes of activities, Christians are to 'abstain from': 'the pollution of idols,... unchastity (fornication), from what is strangled, and from blood' (Acts 15:20, 29; cf. 21:25). These are sometimes called the Council's 'Decrees.' There is disagreement as to whether abstaining from 'blood' means murder or ingesting blood, that is, eating improperly drained meats.

What is involved in these decrees? The answer has long been a point of debate and disagreement among scholars. In seeking an understanding, two points need be remembered. First, the issues arose in the racially mixed early Christian church. Although Jewish Christians were still in the majority, the number of Gentile believers was rising rapidly. Christians coming from Jewish environments shared certain basic religious commitments and behavioral norms – belief in monotheism, agreement that certain basic moral principles are reflected in the Old Testament law, and an acceptance of some fundamental elements of a Jewish 'lifestyle'. On the other hand, Gentiles accepted the existence of many gods and believed that one could worship and serve more gods than one. Their moral and ethical codes could be quite different from the Jewish ones; the relationship between religion and behavior was not well established. Finally, some Gentiles tended to both look down upon Jewish customs and often tried to trick Jews into compromising them.

Second, in ancient thought, a part often stood for a whole. So, for an example, the directive to abstain from 'the pollution of idols' could mean 'idolatry and everything associated with it.' The prohibitions against unchastity and blood (if it refers to murder) speak to the whole of Gentile ethical systems which were contrary to God's law; these items were points of obvious and significant difference. 'Things strangled' and 'blood' (if it refers to eating meat not properly drained) would thus imply reference to the whole system of Jewish ceremonies, of which the concept of 'clean and unclean' foods, was an important part. Thus, the decrees may address the religious problem by protecting against any form of Gentile syncretism which might permit holding Christianity and some form of paganism at the same time. The ethical instructions insist both that there is a relation between the Christian's faith and behavior and, in fact, there are moral absolutes. The ceremonial prohibition recognize problems faced by Jewish believers at that time and insist that Gentile Christians be sensitive toward them.

To put the matter in a way more evidently related to the question, 'How should believers live?' we suggest the Jerusalem Council applied to its situation some basic principles which are eternally valid although they may have different applications in other times and places.

First, the Old Testament insistence that God is a 'jealous God'[16] remains eternally constant. There is but one God and he will not share his place with any pretenders or figments of human imagination; Christianity, like Judaism, is committed to an exclusivistic concept of God. The prohibition against 'the pollution of idols' spoke directly to this religious-theological truth which was not clear to some new Gentile converts. It is also relevant in the face of the less evident but real forms of modern 'idolatry' (giving anything in life and thought a higher place than that ascribed to God – including personal fulfillment and satisfaction, material possessions, economic success, personal prestige, pleasure, and the like).

In the ethical and moral realm there are basic principles which are rooted in the nature of God. The Christian, the individual in personal relation with God, must determine to conform life and actions to these principles. In so doing she or he seeks to avoid doing anything offensive to God. Sexual matters, murder, and others

---

[16]Exodus 20:4; 34:14; Deuteronomy 4:24; 5:9; 6:15; Nahum 1:2.

covered in the Ten Commandments are among those which come in this category. The apostles, elders, along with the whole church address these issues in the 'decrees' as they call for abstinence from 'fornication' and possibly from 'blood'.

There is still another type of attitude and conduct which the Council addressed. The prohibition against 'things strangled' and 'blood' (if it is a dietary restriction) speaks to a matter rooted in local and cultural practices and attitudes which, although important in some groups and communities, were not eternally relevant, absolute spiritual or moral and ethical principles. Here, and elsewhere in the New Testament, these matters appear to be addressed within the context of Christian *freedom*, but limited by *love* and *responsibility*.[17] Although in local customs and cultural preferences not involving basic, absolute principles, the Christian person is free, she or he must be aware of the effects upon others of exercising this freedom. How will the consequences of actions reflect upon the God whom she or he serves? How will such deeds affect the non-Christian's opinion of God or the church? Freedom is also limited by concern for one's fellow Christian. The Christian is to act lovingly and with sensitivity toward these who might have special concerns for the matters in question.

Standards for Conduct in the New Testament Epistles

Standards for life and conduct in the epistles are extensions of the teachings of Jesus and that which is implied in the decrees of the Jerusalem Council. Jesus' summary of the law calls for complete love and devotion to God and, second, love for neighbor as one's self. The first part of this general guideline is the same as Paul's admonition to 'walk worthy' of God and to 'please God' (1 Thess 2:4; 4:1). Paul explicitly says:

> Owe no one anything, except to love one another; for he who loves his neighbor has fulfilled the law. The commandments, 'You

---

[17]Note F. F. Bruce (*Commentary on Romans*) speaks of Paul expounding the principles of liberty in Romans 14:1-12 and charity in Romans 14:13–15:6.

shall not commit adultery, You shall not kill, You shall not steal, You shall not covet,' and any other commandment, are summed up in this sentence, 'You shall love your neighbor as yourself.' Love does no wrong to a neighbor; therefore love is the fulfilling of the law (Rom 13:8-10).

Elsewhere he affirms, 'The whole law is fulfilled in one word, "You shall love your neighbor as yourself"' (Gal 5:14).

On this point Paul and James are in virtual word-for-word agreement. James also summarizes the law with reference to Jesus' Love Command, 'If you really fulfill the royal law, according to the Scripture, 'You shall love your neighbor as yourself,' you do well' (2:8).

For Paul, as for the Jerusalem Council, the principle that when basic moral and spiritual principles are not involved, conduct should be determined on the basis of freedom limited by love and responsibility. This is what Paul has in mind when, speaking of food offered in sacrifice to idols, which he believes to be of no consequence to the mature Christian,[18] but says, 'Take care lest this liberty of yours somehow become a stumbling block to the weak' (1 Cor 8:9).

The Christian may need to alter conduct out of deference to those who are fellow members of the household of God or in view of how actions might be perceived by outsiders. This is quite clear, not only in 1 Corinthians 8 but also in the way Paul deals with a variety of matters in Romans 13–15 and 1 Corinthians 10:23–11:1. In this latter passage, Paul faces the inevitable question, 'Why should my liberty be determined by another man's scruples?' (vs. 29). Paul gives no direct answer but simply says,

> Give no offense to Jews or to Greeks or to the church of God, just as I try to please all men in everything I do, not seeking my own advantage, but that of many, that they may be saved. Be imitators of me, as I am of Christ (1 Cor 10:32–11:1).

Of course, somebody, somewhere, will probably always be offended by anything we might do. The use of common sense along with

---

[18]Note the whole context of 1 Corinthians 8 and Romans 14:14.

responsibility and love is appropriate. Probably, the stronger, more mature Christian, should usually yield to the younger and weaker, at least in public. There may also be occasions when it would be helpful to assist the objector in seeing the issue more clearly. A friend of mine, when confronted by another Christian who claimed to be offended by some action or attitude of my friend, replied, 'Oh! are you my weaker brother?' Such a blunt response can hardly be considered the loving one by those who see confrontation and love as incompatible. Nevertheless recounting this incident helps keep the matter in proper perspective.

Determining God's Will in Day-to-Day Situations

Thus far our focus has been upon the theory for determining the standards for life and conduct. Now we ask, 'How is the Christian to make day-to-day decisions?' Like any kind of life commitment there must be an initial period of training, learning the basic data and concepts, skills, and applications. There needs also to be continuous conditioning, keeping up and fresh in the field of one's life and work. So too in the Christian life. The resources for growth are also those for maintaining competence in it.

Of course first, and foremost, the relationship between the Christian and God must be intact and fresh. Since God and his nature are our guide, we need to keep in contact with him. This provides resources for both the daily grind and the emergency situations. The story is told of a little boy walking with his grandfather. They came to a rain–swollen stream that threatened to wash away the bridge they had to cross. As they started over the boy cried, 'Grandaddy, don't you think we should pray?' The reply came, 'I try to stay prayed-up for such times as this.' To this we would add the need to stay 'read up' in the Bible so that we have immediate access to both the power of prayer and the input from Scripture as we face the flood-endangered bridges of life.

Still, we must face many situations for which there is no direct divine guidance in Scripture and God seldom speaks audibly. What then? Earlier we said that there are basic moral and spiritual principles, rooted in the nature of God, to which those in a right relationship with him must conform their thoughts, words, and deeds. We mentioned the Ten Commandments in the Old Testament and the Love Command in the New Testament as conveyors of such principles. In addition to these the Bible gives other, often less concrete, prescriptions and guidelines. A commitment to these must be a part of the Christian's decision-making equipment. In countering the legalistic interpretations and demands of the day, Jesus twice refers to the Old Testament teaching in which God says, 'I desire mercy, and not sacrifice' (Matt 9:13; 12:6-8). Later, in the same spirit he said, 'Woe to you, scribes and Pharisees, hypocrites! for you tithe mint and dill and cummin, and have neglected the weightier matters of the law, justice and mercy and faith; these you ought to have done, without neglecting the others' (Matt 23:23). In so doing he makes reference to a number of Old Testament passages which 1) condemn the outward practice of religion, including sacrificing and other ceremonial acts, which have no effect on daily life[19] and 2) make specific statements about 'what God requires.' At least some of these latter statements should be included here:

> Fear the LORD your God,... walk in all his ways,... love him, serve the LORD your God with all your heart and with all your soul (Deut 10:12) ... glory in this,... understand and know me, that I am the LORD who practices steadfast love, justice, and righteousness in the earth... (Jer 9:24) ... I desire steadfast love ... the knowledge of God (Hosea 6:6) ... let justice roll down like waters, and righteousness like an ever-flowing stream (Amos 5:24) ... do justice,... love kindness,... walk humbly with your God (Micah 6:8).

To these statements we must add the LORD's condemnation of Israel in Isaiah 59:4-19 because she had rejected peace, justice, righteousness, and truth. Certainly, along with the features of the Christian's mind-set in Philippians 4:8, listed above, here we have an excellent foundational list of those qualities that should guide the Christian's daily walk.

---

[19] 1 Samuel 15:22-23; Psalms 40:6; 51:17-19; Proverbs 21:3; Isaiah 1:11-15; 43:22-24; Jeremiah 7:21-22; Hosea 6:6; Amos 5:21-27; Micah 6:6-8.

Although doing so might be misunderstood as implying that other qualities are less significant, we must comment specifically on two qualities. The Hebrew behind the phrase rendered 'steadfast love' (*chesed*) in Hosea 6:6, is notoriously difficult to translate; *mercy* and *loving kindness* are other popular renderings of it. When used of God it speaks of his love and tenderness extended through and because of his covenant. When used of human beings it assumes that appropriate behavior is expected as a response to the covenant-love God has extended to us. The concepts of *righteousness* and *justice* are closely related. Throughout the Old Testament the call for justice by God's people occurs over and over again. Both the Old Testament and the New Testament frequently state that 'God is not a respecter of persons,'[20] that he is not partial, that he does not discriminate against anyone. Justice is the demand for the same policy and conduct by his people. Leviticus 19:15 (also in Exodus 23:3, 6) exemplifies what it means, 'You shall do no injustice in judgment; you shall not be partial to the poor or defer to the great, but in righteousness shall you judge your neighbor.' In a mature Christian life concerns for justice and mercy are not electives!

Furthermore, in seeking God's guidance, Paul's experience in Acts 16:6-10 is instructive. He had finished his immediate task of delivering the decrees of the Jerusalem Council in Syria, Cilicia, Derbe, and Lystra (15:41–16:4). He then had no clear instructions for further activity. He sought to go into the Roman province of Asia (in modern Turkey) but 'was forbidden by the Holy Spirit' (16:6).

---

[20]E.g., Deuteronomy 10:17; 1 Samuel 16:7; 2 Chronicles 19:7; Acts 10:34; Romans 2:11; Galatians 2:6; Ephesians 6:9; Colossians 3:25; 1 Peter 1:17; James 2:1.The Greek word *prosōpolēmptēs* is used only here in the New Testament. Literally it means *a receptor of the face or person*. It is part of a larger group of similar words which combine to form an idiom which refers to the principle of non-discrimination, one being not a respecter of persons, and the like. Other words or phrases expressing the concept of impartiality in the Greek New Testament are *ou lambaneis prosōpon* (*not receive the face*, as in the Greek translation of the Old Testament, Luke 20:21); *prosōpolēmpsia* (show partiality, Rom 2:11; Eph 6:9; Col 3:25; Jas 2:1); *diastrolē* (distinction or difference, Rom 11:12); and *prosklisis* (inclination [with *kata* = in the spirit of partiality], 1 Tim 5:21).

He then looked toward Bithynia, but again his way was blocked
(vs. 7). He kept going until he reached Troas (vs. 8). There he stopped
because further progress in the same direction would have carried
him into the Aegean Sea. At Troas he came to understand that God
wanted him to go to Macedonia. He then realized he had been going
in the right direction all along. God guided Paul by closing doors.
This was possible because Paul was trying to go somewhere but
was willing to have his mind and direction changed. There come
times when, using our best God-given common sense and our best
analysis of the situation, we must make a move, try to go somewhere,
to do something, but be open to redirection. Movement, however,
is important – it's difficult to steer a parked car!

There are less dramatic, less monumental decisions that confront
us daily. Are there direct Biblical guidelines for these? In many cases,
no. Yet, we make some observations for those committed to Christ
and to live for his glory.[21] It is important to remind ourselves of the
characteristics of the Christian life discussed above; for Christian
living choices and decision made in that life should be consistent and
in harmony with these qualities and traits. Ephesians 4:2-3 will serve
as a quick summary and reminder, for in his life Christ showed that
these are qualities of the life of one who is 'of God.' Here Paul says
that leading a 'life worthy of the calling' of God involves living 'with
all lowliness and meekness, with patience, forbearing one another in
love, eager to maintain the unity of the Spirit in the bond of peace.'
These are not normal characteristics for those seeking success,
power, and notoriety by worldly standards. They are, however, the
framework within which the Christian is to operate.

With commitment to please God and walk worthy of him, the
determination of many decisions and actions should be made on the
basis of simplicity and confidentiality. After all, most of our decisions
and actions never need be exposed to public scrutiny. However, in
making decisions, especially when the matter at hand is close to the
line between right and wrong, we suggest the Christian might ask

---

[21]I gratefully acknowledge the help of my brother, David W. Scott, a
Christian businessman, in stating these suggestions for making decisions
when there seems to be no direct guidance from Scripture.

her/himself some questions. If actions based on this decision were publicly exposed, what would be my reactions? Would I be embarrassed? If so, then this is most likely the wrong decision. If my actions were made public would I be prepared to defend them, even if they were unpopular? If so, then it is a course of action I probably could take. Most of all, how would public awareness of my action reflect upon the God I claim to worship, honor, and serve, and upon his people, the church, of which I am a part? Any decision which would defame the name of God or cast the church into a negative light is wrong. As Paul says,

> Try to learn what is pleasing to the Lord. Take no part in the unfruitful works of darkness, but instead expose them. For it is a shame even to speak of the things that they do in secret; but when anything is exposed by the light it becomes visible, for anything that becomes visible is light. Therefore it is said, 'Awake, O sleeper, and arise from the dead, and Christ shall give you light' (Eph 5:10-14).

A couple of Old Testament passages provide a helpful framework for life and work. Proverbs 1:7 says, 'The fear of the LORD is the beginning of knowledge.' *Fear*, in this context means something like, *reverence, awe, a healthy respect for,* or *in right relation to.* It is within that relationship and attitude we are to live and make decisions. Proverbs also provides our other guideline.

> Trust in the LORD with all your heart, and do not rely on your own insight. In all your ways acknowledge him, and he will make straight your paths. Be not wise in your own eyes; fear the LORD, and turn away from evil. It will be healing to your flesh and refreshment to your bones (Prov 3:5-8).

It is the first part of this passage that is usually remembered in seeking guidance. Certainly, complete trust in the LORD is essential; it is he who rules and over-rules to accomplish his will in the life of his own people. The latter two verses are also important; they emphasize the folly of our own wisdom, the following of which is, in fact, a failure to trust God.

Permit another personal experience as an example. As a teenager I endured a list of where not to go and what not to do each time I was permitted to take the car out by myself. Then came the day when my mother, as she handed me the keys, said, 'Remember what family you're from and don't do anything that would disgrace us.' That was a much harder 'command' to obey than like former ones – my conduct was to be based on the implications of the name and standards of my family relationship!

What have we said? We have repeated points made earlier, that the guidelines for Christian action is the nature of God himself. The Christian life is 'walking worthy' of him and what he has done for us. Our conduct must be based upon full awareness that we are God's children and we must remember what family we're in and do nothing to disgrace the head of that family or the family as a whole.[22] Paul admonishes the Corinthians that in their lifestyle they should 'give no offense to Jews or to Greeks or to the church of God' (1 Cor 10:32).

As a last point, in living the Christian life we are not alone. Relationship with God means having an ear tuned to 'the voice of the Good Shepherd'; Jesus said, 'My sheep hear my voice' (John 10:27). Jesus promised the Holy Spirit, who bears witness to him, will guide his own into 'all truth'. That promise was kept, beginning with Pentecost. The Holy Spirit is a person who is really present in the life of the Christian. Second, the Christian is part of a family, the corporate body of all others who belong to Christ, the church. In living the Christian life, including decision making, believers are not 'Lone Rangers'; they have the privilege and the safety-factor of consulting with others of like faith.

Power (Enablement) and Guidance: The Role and Work of the Holy Spirit in the Christian Life

What may be said about the role and work of the Holy Spirit in the life of the Christian? Toward the end of the previous chapter we

---

[22]Compare Psalm 69:6, 'Let not those who hope in thee be put to shame through me, O Lord GOD of hosts; let not those who seek thee be brought to dishonor through me, O God of Israel.'

summarized the work of the Holy Spirit in the application of salvation. At the outset of this chapter we saw that a characteristic of the Christian life is that it is dominated by the Spirit of God. His presence and activity saturates the entirety of the Christian's experience, both individually and within the church, even before the new birth and until the completion of God's work.

We come now to try to pull together some of the basic New Testament teachings about the work of the Holy Spirit, the unseen, but real person, presence, power, and activity of God – as we described him earlier – in the life of the Christian. The New Testament teaches that it is impossible to be a Christian without the presence and work of the Holy Spirit: 'Any one who does not have the Spirit of Christ does not belong to him' (Rom 8:9). In Galatians 5:25, Paul associates both spiritual birth and life with the work of the Holy Spirit, 'If we live by the Spirit, let us also walk by the Spirit' – since the Holy Spirit has brought us into new life in Christ, that life must also be lived in association with and under the control of that same Spirit.

Two general points should be made at the outset. Peter cites the presence of the Holy Spirit in a unique way as proof that the Final Age is present and is an active force in the world (Acts 2:16-21). Furthermore, he affirms that the Holy Spirit in the believer is the seal and guarantee (down payment) of our future inheritance promised by God (Eph 1:13-14; 2 Cor 1:22; 5:5). The presence of the Holy Spirit identifies the present phase of Salvation History and assures believers of their reward at its consummation.

In the Synoptic gospels Jesus assured his followers of the future presence of the Spirit, 'If you then, who are evil, know how to give good gifts to your children, how much more will the heavenly Father give the Holy Spirit to those who ask him!' (Luke 11:13). More specifically he promised the presence of his Spirit in times of crises brought on by their witness for him, 'When they bring you to trial and deliver you up, do not be anxious beforehand what you are to say; but say whatever is given you in that hour, for it is not you who speak, but the Holy Spirit' (Mark 13:11; Matt 10:19-20). The Holy Spirit is part of the name (note the singular) of the Triune God in which his disciples are to baptize (Matt 28:19).

In the Fourth Gospel, John records that Jesus said believers would be given the Spirit, although 'as yet the Spirit had not been given, because Jesus was not yet glorified' (7:39). He assured them that God does not give the Spirit quantitatively, 'by measure' (3:34) – one either has or does not have the Holy Spirit!

As the earthly ministry of Jesus drew to a close, during his last meal with his disciples he again promised that the Holy Spirit would be sent to them and described something of his function. At times he referred to the Spirit as the 'Paraclete' (*paraklētos* = advocate/ instructor or comforter/helper); that he equated the two, Spirit and Paraclete, is clear in John 14:16-17, 'The Paraclete [RSV has 'Comforter'] . . . even the Spirit of truth' and 14:26, 'the Paraclete (Comforter), the Holy Spirit, whom the Father will send in my name.' He was to be sent by both Jesus and the Father (14:26; 15:26). He will 'teach you all things, and bring to remembrance all that I have said to you' (14:25). The work of the Spirit is to 'guide you into all the truth' but does 'not speak on his own authority, but whatever he hears he will speak, and he will declare to you the things that are to come' (John 16:13). Specifically, the Spirit 'shall bear witness to Jesus' (15:26). The presence of the Spirit will be to the Christian's 'advantage . . . [and he shall] convince the world of sin, righteousness, and judgment' (16:7). Jesus further says that the Holy Spirit is both present in and recognized by only Christians (John 14:17).

The Holy Spirit is mentioned over fifty times throughout Acts. In 1:8, Jesus promised his apostles that the Holy Spirit would give them 'power' (*dunamis*) for witness. The rest of the book is virtually a commentary on Jesus' promise as it shows the Holy Spirit at work through his representatives.

Comment was made above on 2 Thessalonians 2:13, where Paul refers to the Holy Spirit as the agent of sanctification. We may assume that it is through the Spirit that God works in believers 'both to will and to work for his good pleasure' (Phil 2:13). The Spirit gives power and strength for Christian growth and development. It is significant that the dominant features of the Christian character and life are called 'the fruit of the Spirit' (Gal 5:22-24) and are immediately followed by the admonition, 'Let us ... walk (conduct our lives) by the Spirit' (vs. 25). In considering the work of the Spirit in salvation we noted that he makes Christians; here we affirm that he grows Christians.

Jesus taught that blaspheming the Holy Spirit, including failing to acknowledge his presence and to submit to his work, is the sin which 'never has forgiveness, but is ... an eternal sin.'[23] Stephen accused the Jews of resisting the Holy Spirit (Acts 7:51). Christians are warned against *grieving* (Eph 4:30), *quenching* (1 Thess 5:19), and *outraging* (Heb 10:29) him.

A consideration of the Holy Spirit in the work in the church is reserved for the following chapter. This includes comments on the 'baptism of the Spirit' and/or 'being filled with the Spirit,' for it seems likely that those are more often to be understood as promises and experiences of the whole body than of the lone individual. It seems best to discuss the 'spiritual gifts' in that context as well.

Conclusion: Life in a Distinctively Christian 'Lifestyle'

Much more could (and probably should) be said about how Christians should live. Here we must try to pull together certain Biblical teachings. Hopefully, this will stimulate further thought and study. There are at least five basic principles which must influence the way one approaches this new life in Christ.

First, Christianity is essentially a relationship between God and the sinner who has been saved by grace. The fact and implications of that relationship dominate and control the whole of the Christian's being and life.

Second, Christians are 'new persons (creations)' in Christ, old things are (or should have/should be in the process of) passed away (or be passing away). A mature (or maturing) Christian life will result in a real, discernable difference in lifestyle from that of non-Christians. This is not something the Christian should force, it is something that will inevitably occur as the fruit of the Spirit and other Christian

---

[23]Mark 3:29; Matthew 12:31-32; Luke 12:10; cf. 1 John 5:16.

character traits, attitudes, and activities become evident.

Third, the Christian lives in a hostile environment. There will be temptations and pressures to which one will yield, seek compromise, or resist and reject. Misunderstanding and opposition are bound to occur. Persecution is an ever-present possibility. Opposition and persecution may be subtle, showing themselves in social, economic, intellectual, or other forms; they may also be open, blatant, and even include imprisonment, physical suffering, and death. In prayer, Jesus said to his Father, 'I have given them your word; and the world has hated them because they are not of the world, even as I am not of the world' (John 17:14). To his disciples he said, 'If the world hates you, know that it has hated me before it hated you' (John 5:18); 'you will be hated by all for my name's sake';[24] 'they will deliver you up to tribulation, and put you to death; and you will be hated by all nations for my name's sake' (Matt 24:9). Consequently Jesus warned potential disciples to 'count the cost' before making a commitment (Luke 14:25-33).

Fourth, conduct must be determined on the basis of the character of the God with whom the Christian is now in relation. Decisions and actions must be made and taken within the framework of this relationship. What is appropriate for a Christian, a person who bears the name of Christ? The ultimate standard is 'what pleases God!'

Finally, 'Faith without works is dead' (Jas 2:26). Christians are not saved **by** works, but they are saved **for** works. Works, the outward evidence of the Christian life, is the normal, natural, expected result of a living, vital faith. (Note that James' example of 'works' are 'things needed by the body,' food and clothing, 2:16. This is a parallel to the spirit of Jesus of that given or withheld from 'one of the least of these' in the judgement scene in Matt 25:31-46.) There is no difference between James and Paul at this point. The latter expressed it differently, 'Work out your own salvation with fear and trembling; for God is at work in you, both to will and to work for his good pleasure' (Phil 2:12-13) and 'We are created in Christ Jesus for good works, which God prepared beforehand that we should

---

[24]Mark 13:13; Matthew 10:22; 24:9; Luke 21:17.

walk in them' (Eph 2:10). An individual in whom the marks of the Christian life are absent is either not a Christian, a very immature Christian, or an abnormal and deformed one.

The New Testament implies that the Christian life is marked by growth in Christ and freedom in Christ. The former comes as a result of the presence of the new life and the efforts of both the Spirit of God and the spiritually newborn him or herself. Freedom in the Christian life is tempered and controlled by love and responsibility.

Christian conduct is based on relationship, not a rigid legalism. Its freedom does not lead to a 'do as I please' antinomianism or relativism. It is based on what pleases God. Hence, Christian ethics require an ever-growing knowledge of God, of him personally, of his nature and character, and, on the basis of this, of his likes and dislikes. The Christian ethic is determined by what constitutes 'walking worthy' of God.

From knowing God comes the recognition that there are basic *moral and spiritual principles* which must apply in all situations; hence, there are absolutes, but not in the sense of Platonic ideals, rationally defined universals, or the like. They are personal absolutes because they are founded in the nature of the personal God.

Christian ethics further take into account that there are also *cultural and personal matters of preference or tradition*. When these do not involve basic moral and spiritual principles the Christian's freedom must lovingly and responsibly take into account the possible effect of his or her actions on others.

The Christian life is not lived in isolation. It is lived 'in Christ', and with the presence, control, power, and direction of the Holy Spirit. The Christian life is also life 'in community,' in fellowship with other believers; it is life in the church. What is the church? It is to this question that we now turn.

Chapter 8

What is the Church?
The Corporate Life of the Believer

The church is the community into which the believer is 'born', grows, and lives. A person is never an isolated entity apart from his or her family. We cannot understand the Christian, his or her growth, life, service, worship, or any other part of the believer's existence apart from the church. It is within the church that we are united with Christ, the Head of the church, and here the Holy Spirit is active in very special ways. Yet, the word 'church' is beset with so many ideas that it is not only difficult to get a clear understanding of its nature but also to try to look objectively at the New Testament data. At the same time it has a definite emotional content for some, it should for all. For the Christian it is 'home'![1]

If we can learn anything about the church from the New Testament, it is clear that we must begin our study by trying to eliminate any notions of the church as a building,[2] a denomination,

---

[1] 'There is a word that, when a Catholic hears it, kindles all his feelings of love and bliss, that stirs all the depths of his religious sensibility, from dread and awe of the Last Judgment to the sweetness of God's presence; and that certainly awakens in him the feeling of home; the feeling that only a child has in relation to its mother, made up of gratitude, reverence, and devoted love, the feeling that overcomes one when, after a long absence, one returns to one's home, the home of one's childhood.

'And there is a word that to Protestants has the sound of something infinitely commonplace, more or less indifferent and superfluous, that does not make their heartbeat faster, something with which a sense of boredom is so often associated, or which at any rate does not lend wings to our religious feelings — and yet our fate is sealed, if we are unable again to attach a new, or perhaps a very old, meaning to it. Woe to us if that word does not become important to us again, does not become important to our lives.

'Yes, the word to which I am referring is "Church"' (Eberhard Bethge, *Dietrich Bonhoffer* [New York: Harper and Row, 1970], 42).

[2] Excessive concentration upon the Church building in the West is

or some broad or particular organization as we now know them. The church is more than its officers whether they be a group, one or more pastors, bishops, a pope, or patriarchs. The church transcends the limits of a single cultural, ethnic, or nationalistic group or those of one group, congregation, or selective groups of congregations. It is more than a doctrinal statement, a particular plan or program, or set of specified religious experiences. Other debates throughout church history have centered around such issues as the claim of a particular normative organizational structure, the nature, types, and authority of church leaders, forms of worship, its relation to secular society and government, and other matters too numerous to mention. The church may have or contain one or more of these but none of them are of its essence.

The Church is a single body, united in Christ, its head. It is the Christian community which exists at all times and in all places. The Church includes all whom God has accepted because of their relation to him through Jesus Christ. This is possible because God has made salvation available through Jesus to those who accept Christ as their God, Savior, and Lord according to the Scriptures. For Protestants the Scriptures are the authoritative witness of God's revelation of himself in the universe, history, and supremely in Christ. In these writings the church finds the inspired proclamation of the prophets, apostles, and Jesus himself afresh in each successive generation. The church is made up of people, people who bear the marks, scars, and defects of their first parent, Adam. Within it also reside Jesus Christ, our second Adam, and the Holy Spirit; therefore the church is also perfect, righteous, and holy.

Much of what has already been said about the growth, development, and life of the Christian as an individual must also be said about the church. But, there are distinctive aspects as well. We will seek to survey the information about the church in the New Testament, most of which is found in Acts and the Epistles. Our

---

frequently a detriment to understanding the true nature of the Church. Often, in areas in which the Church is restricted by governmental, religious, or other powers, Christians are not permitted to gather outside of an approved building. This casts the function of the building in a different light.

objective is to form from the Scriptures a general idea, an impression, about the church before attempting to seek a more precise understanding.

Data and Disagreements

In the Revised Standard Version of the Bible, the words 'church' or 'churches' occur 86 times in Acts and the New Testament epistles (the Greek word appears even more). The majority of these are general references to 'the church,' a designation for the collective body of Christians. It is sometimes called 'the church of God and/or of Christ'.[3] Christ has a special relation to the church; he is its head and it is his body (Eph 5:23; Col 1:18, 24), he loves it (Eph 5:25, 29); he is 'made head over all things for the church' (Eph 1:22). The work of Christ was carried out 'that he might present the church to himself in splendor, without spot or wrinkle or any such thing, that she might be holy and without blemish' (Eph 5:27). Yet, although the church is inseparably bound to Christ, she is not Christ and cannot demand the same authority or allegiance as he. The relation between Christ and the church remains something of a 'mystery' (Eph 5:32).

There are numerous references to the church or churches in a particular city or region. Romans 16:4 speaks of 'the churches of the Gentiles.' There are four specific references to churches in homes or houses;[4] 1 Corinthians 14:33 mentions 'all the churches of the saints.' Either directly or by allusion New Testament writers refer to the organization and human leaders in the church and are concerned for order in life, thought, and worship. Some specific issues they mention include judging wayward persons, collecting and using money, healing, speaking in tongues, the activity and role of women in some congregations, and accuracy in understanding and applying the teaching of the faith.

Only Matthew, among the Gospel writers, refers to the church. Following his acknowledgment of Jesus as the Messiah, Jesus says to Peter, 'On this rock I will build my church' (Matt 16:18). In

---

[3] Acts 20:28; Romans 16:16; 1 Corinthians 11:16, 22; 15:9; 2 Corinthians 1:1; Galatians 1:3; 1 Thessalonians 2:14; 2 Thessalonians 1:4; 1 Timothy 3:15.

[4] Romans 16:5; 1 Corinthians 16:19; Colossians 4:15; Philemon 2.

18:17 he directs that disagreements between believers are to be referred to the church.

The word *church* is used in Revelation only in chapters 2 and 3, in the letters to each of the churches in seven cities of Asia Minor to whom Christ wrote. However, there are other images in the book which are assumed to refer to the church. Most noteworthy is that of 'the bride of the Lamb' (19:7; 21:9; 22:17), although 'the new Jerusalem' is also designated as the 'bride' (21:2).

We also learn of the church as we see it in action. From this we may discern reflections of its nature and internal affairs.

Information about the details of the life and structure of church in the New Testament is scanty, general, and not always clear. In Acts, for an example, we learn generalities. The Twelve Apostles held important places in it, but most of them vanish from the narrative of the book fairly early. The Church was composed of individual members in various locations who formed groups or congregations. There were a number of different types of leaders, some related to only a single locale, others engaged in travels in which they both evangelized and gave direction to scattered Christian communities. Luke indicates that the church experienced both rapid growth and persecution. Its activities included teaching and learning, worship, preaching, and fellowship.[5]

The difficulty of answering the question 'What is the Church?' is further complicated by a long history of conflict and controversy about virtually everything associated with her. Hence, many of us come to the question with deep-seated preconceived ideas which color our considerations of the evidence.

We will not be able to ignore the debates and opinions of the past and present. We certainly will not be able to solve all problems nor settle all disputes. Conscientious, honest Christians come from different cultures and societies, and have had diverse experiences with the church. They see different meanings in the texts, place

---

[5]Note Carey C. Newman, 'Images of the Church in Acts,' *The People of God* (Nashville: Broadman, 1991), 133-147, who insists the early Church in Acts was more of an 'apocalyptic community' than a clearly recognizable, structured organization.

different weights on traditions and church pronouncements. The church is composed of people, imperfect people, unique people with their own personalities, outlooks, and experiences. Its members are pilgrims whose journey has not yet reached its end; diversity therefore, is probably inevitable.[6] It should not be surprising that this diversity includes their understandings about the nature and mission of the church or that these matters may evoke deep emotional responses.

We will attempt to focus attention upon what can be learned from the Biblical data. This means that we will try to limit matters of historical theology and philosophical and/or systematic theology to a secondary role.

It should be noted that unfortunately the English language has no way to distinguish between the singular and plural second personal pronoun, 'you' (except in the version spoken in the southern part of the United States, where 'y'all' indicates precisely that the speaker intends the plural). English readers are frequently tempted to assume the singular in many references which, being in the plural in the Greek, were intended for the whole group, the church. Thus, some of the

---

[6]A French writer of the nineteenth century, J. H. Merle D'Aubinge, *(History of the Reformation of the Sixteenth Century.* H. White, trans. [New York: American Tract Society, 1847], 220-223), observing the diversity spun off by the Reformation of the sixteenth century observed,

'Unity in diversity and diversity in unity is a law of nature as well as of the Church.

Truth is like the light of the sun: it descends from heaven one and ever the same; and yet it assumes different colors upon the earth, according to the objects on which it falls. In like manner, formularies [statements of Christian truth] somewhat different may sometimes express the same Christian idea considered under different aspects...

Divine unity has its rights, so also has human diversity....

The Reformation, by restoring liberty to the Church, was destined also to restore its original diversity, and to people it with families united by the great features of resemblance they derive from their common parent; but different in their secondary features, and reminding us of the varieties inherent in human nature. Perhaps it would have been desirable for this diversity to exist in the Universal Church without leading to sectarian [denominational] divisions. Nevertheless, we must not forget that these sects are but the expression of this diversity.'

New Testament data which could help in understanding the nature
and mission of the church is obscured.

A second observation is necessary as we will frequently make
reference to the early, New Testament church in this chapter. It is
the Biblical principles which guided the forms and activities of the
early church that are normative, not those forms and activities
themselves. Modern Christians sometimes believe it necessary to
duplicate as nearly as possible the exact practices and activities of
the first church. This is impossible; ours is another day, another
culture. The New Testament indicates that even in the first century
forms and activities probably differed from place to place. In any
case, it is impossible to duplicate the experiences of the early church.
To do so we would have to do away with church buildings,
automobiles, and other parts of modern culture and civilization. Some
of the external features of the primitive church were responses to
persecution by Jewish authorities and the Roman empire. Our world
is very different from theirs; our responses, if appropriate in our
world, may be quite different from those who are our forerunners in
the faith. It is the message, the presence of the Holy Spirit, and the
commitment to Christ that establishes our continuity with the past.

Biblical Vocabulary and Images of the Church

One traditional, and often helpful, way of approaching our question
about the nature of the church is to look at the vocabulary and images
used of it in the Bible.[7]

Vocabulary

The English word *church* is the usual translation of the Greek
ekklēsia which itself is the combination *klētos, (called, chosen,
select, elect)* and the preposition *ek (out of, from)*. **Ekklēsia** has

---

[7]There are many good books and articles which deal with these subjects.
I have found two particularly helpful: Lothar Coenen, 'Church, Synagogue,'
The New International Dictionary of New Testament Theology, English
trans., Colin Brown, ed., (Grand Rapids, MI: Zondervan, 1975) Vol. I, 291-307
and Paul S. Minear, *Images of the Church in the New Testament* (Philadelphia:
Westminster, 1960).

a history of specialized use in classical Greek where it designates some kind of an assembly, be it military or judicial, the citizens of a city, or some other special group. In the Septuagint, the pre-Christian translation of the Old Testament into Greek, it is the translation for the Hebrew word *qāhāl* (but not the only translation for it). By contrast, another Hebrew word (*'ēdâh*) is usually translated by the Greek *sunagōgē (synagogue)*. The distinction between the two Hebrew words helps in understanding what the New Testament writers have in mind when they use the word *ekklēsia* (church). *Synagogue* (*'ēdâh*), the broader of the two terms, refers to a congregation in general, to Israel as a nation wherever she may be; a permanent community into which one was born. *Church* (*qāhāl*) is more specific and refers to an assembly of those who, bound to the LORD by his covenant and law, have heard and obeyed the call. The assembly may come together for any one of several reasons, including political, judicial, learning, or for worship.

Synagogue is used in the New Testament to refer to a Jewish community, congregation, or building.[8] The New Testament writers build upon traditional meanings of *ekklēsia*, but by modifying them they make it a distinctively Christian term as well. Those who have heard the proclamation of salvation in Christ and have responded by faith are *The Chosen Ones* (*klētoi*), that is, the Christian group or community. The distinguishing feature of this group is the call by which God separated them by his own actions and for his own glory. Theirs is a special relationship with God, that results in their incorporation in the group, community, institution of *The Chosen Ones* (*eklētoi*). Those in this group or community have a relationship with each other, as well as their corporate and individual relationship with God; hence Paul says, 'We, though many, are one body in Christ, and individually members of one another' (Rom 12:5). The word *ekklēsia* thus refers to both the event and the resulting institution.

Although Jesus seems to have introduced the concept of the church (and the term *ekklēsia*), it does not appear to have been used to describe his followers until after his crucifixion and resurrection

---

[8]Only in James 2:2 is it used of a Christian gathering.

(earlier they were called 'disciples'). The early Christians understood they had been called to accept Jesus, [the] crucified, 'as Lord and Savior' (cf. Acts 2:36); their commission was to proclaim him as such to others. The church of God is also the church of Christ, more specifically, 'the church of God in Christ Jesus' (1 Thess 2:14).

The church, then, finds salvation in Christ, lives in union with him, serves under his lordship, bears the stigma of his crucifixion, proclaims his person, his past, present, and future work, and awaits his return. As the church yields to Christ's reign, his sphere of influence and power, it belongs to the Kingdom of God, but it is not that Kingdom. The Kingdom is greater than the church; the church announces the presence of the Kingdom and its future consummation.

The church has specific location and limits; it is on earth. The full church can be present in a plurality of places at the same time; hence Paul can speak of *the* church in various cities. Even a small group in a single home is called *church*. Yet the church is one, it is *the church*. The unity of the church lies in Jesus Christ. There may be local differences, including variations in patterns of church life and expression, but, as Paul says, Christians must

> with all lowliness and meekness, with patience, forbearing one another in love, [be] eager to maintain the unity of the Spirit in the bond of peace. There is one body and one Spirit, just as you were called to the one hope that belongs to your call, one Lord, one faith, one baptism, one God and Father of us all, who is above all and through all and in all (Eph. 4:3-6).

In 1 Corinthians, a letter written to a church plagued with divisiveness, Paul says, 'By one Spirit we were all baptized into one body – Jews or Greeks, slaves or free' (1 Cor. 12:13). There is only one Christ, one faith, and a common body of general instructions and directives made known by the apostles (1 Cor. 1:17; 11:16; 16:1). 'What counts is the presence of Christ ... (cf. Gal 3:1) and faith nourished by him.'[9]

---

[9]Coenen, 'Church, Synagogue' *Dictionary of New Testament Theology*, (Grand Rapids, MI: Zondervan, 1975) Vol. I, 301.

This unity must be recognized and, in some way, expressed. In the New Testament the successes, growth, victories, needs, suffering, order, and doctrine of the church in one location was the concern of the whole body of Christ. The apostles exercised a unique mission and authority for all; yet, the churches in specific places also recognized a responsibility to those elsewhere, exemplified by famine relief aid and other gifts sent by Gentile churches to Jerusalem.[10]

The church is the spiritual people of the Final Age. They have a new citizenship in heaven and look for a future inheritance. Yet those in the church remain in the present world and social order. Here, although all people are biologically equal through the creative work of God, differences between groups remain. Such categories as Jew or Greek, freeman or slave, male or female, citizen or foreigner are socio-economic or biological realities. However, in Christ a new set of relationships is set up alongside the earthly structure. This new order obliterated the kinds of distinctive aspects which establish class and power levels or promote distinctions of personal worth and, thereby, are barriers to unity, harmony, and fellowship (Gal 3:28; Col 3:11).

At the same time there were distinctions between leaders and people. The epistles make frequent reference to various groups of officials. Hebrews 13:17 says

> Obey your leaders and submit to them; for they are keeping watch over your souls, as men who will have to give account. Let them do this joyfully, and not sadly, for that would be of no advantage to you.

Peter admonishes leaders to 'tend the flock of God ... being examples' (1 Pet 5:2-3) and charges others to 'be subject to the elders' (5:5). Paul's final words to the Ephesian elders he met at Miletus were in the same vein (Acts 20:28-31). But leaders were appointed to serve (Mark 10:43-44), they are warned against lording it over others (Mark 10:43-44) or being domineering

---

[10]Acts 11:27-30, cf. Galatians 2:10; Romans 15:25; 1 Corinthians 16:1ff.; 2 Corinthians 8:1ff.; 9:1ff.

(1 Pet 5:3) in their actions. The church is an egalitarian assembly; all in the church are 'brethren' (the NRSV catches the true intention by translating the word 'brothers and sisters') – although this spiritual equality should not disrupt such relationships as that between husbands and wives (Eph 5:22-33), parents and children (Eph 6:1-4), and master and slave (Eph 6:5-9; 1 Tim 6:1-2). Yet, there is no place for a church office to become a platform for power, personal prestige or aggrandizement, or financial gain (1 Tim 3:6; Titus 1:11). Leaders, after all, are called, as was their Lord, not for greatness, but to serve (Mark 10:43-45). The model is Jesus, who humbled himself (Phil 2:8) and, after washing his disciples feet, said, 'You also ought to wash one another's feet. For I have given you an example, that you also should do as I have done to you ... a servant is not greater than his master' (John 13:14-16). Leaders and the rest are equal before God; subordination of function is only to maintain good order. Within the church, Paul says 'you are all one' (Gal 3:28); Hebrews 2:11 insists 'those who are sanctified have all one origin' (better, 'are all out of one').

In summary, the New Testament depicts the church as a unique group of persons who have been 'mustered' by God's call to have a special relationship with him in Christ and to fulfill the purpose of his will. Those in the church are 'in God the Father and the Lord Jesus Christ' (1 Thess 1:1; 2 Thess 1:1). They have been set apart, are 'saints together with all those who in every place call on the name of our Lord Jesus Christ, both their Lord and ours' (1 Cor 1:2). Jesus is 'the head of the church, his body, and is himself its Savior' (Eph 5:23). God's ultimate purpose is 'that he might present the church to himself in splendor, without spot or wrinkle or any such thing, that she might be holy and without blemish' (Eph 5:27).

Images of the Church

Paul Minear, in his book *Images of the Church*, discusses ninety-six images of the church in the New Testament. Although all make important statements about the church, it is questionable that all which he lists are images in the strictest sense of the term. We will not mention even most of those which are unquestionably images.

Nevertheless, it will be helpful to note a selection of them.

Minear classifies the images under five headings. He discusses thirty two *minor images*, including 'The Salt of the Earth,' 'A Letter from Christ,' 'The Boat,' 'The Ark,' 'One Loaf,' 'The Branches of the Vine,' 'The Fig Tree,' 'The Building on the Rock,' 'The Elect Lady,' 'The Bride of Christ,' 'Citizens,' 'Exiles,' 'Ambassadors,' and 'The Poor.'

Next he notes images built around the church as *the people of God*, such as 'Israel,' 'A Chosen Race,' 'A Holy Nation,' 'Abraham's Sons,' 'The Remnant,' 'The Elect,' 'Little Flock,' 'The Holy City,' 'The Holy Temple,' and ten more.

Among the sixteen classified under the general heading *the new creation* are 'New Creation,' 'The [corporate] Son of Man,' 'Fighters Against Satan,' 'Light,' 'The Tree,' and 'The Communion in the Holy.'

Among those images classified as *the fellowship in faith*, Minear includes 'The Common Life of the Sanctified,' 'The Faithful,' 'The Justified,' 'Disciples,' 'The Road (Way),' 'Slaves,' 'Friends,' 'Servants,' 'The Household of God,' and 'Sons of God.'

Finally, Minear's category *the body of Christ* encompasses 'The Body of Life,' 'Spiritual Body,' 'Head of the Elemental Cosmic Spirits,' 'The Body of this Head,' and 'The Fullness of God.'

Any consideration of Biblical verbal images must proceed with the understanding that they are useful only in that they point toward a basic, general feature. Misunderstandings and even harm can result from trying to make the images say too much; that is, to push details to conclusions never intended.

Probably the best known images are those which affirm that the church is the body of which Christ is the head (Col 1:18), the branches of which he is the vine (John 15:5), God's building (1 Cor 3:9; 2 Cor 5:1), the flock of which Christ is the Shepherd (John 10:11), the bride for whom he is the Bridegroom (Eph 5:23-32; Rev 19:7; 21:9; 22:17), citizens (Eph 2:19), slaves, servants, and friends. 'Body and branches' imply an organic union which, if severed, results in death. 'Building' speaks not only of God, who constructs the structure, but also the one who keeps it in repair. 'Shepherd and bridegroom' refer to relationships which are impossible without both parties. 'Citizens' reminds the reader of both the part the church has in the Kingdom of God and the Christian's membership in that city of which Hebrews speaks, 'which has foundations, whose builder and maker is God' (Heb 11:10). 'Slaves' and 'servants' depict the church's relation to its superior and the nature of its role. 'Friends,' in Jesus' words to his disciples, describes a very special relationship,

> Greater love has no man than this, that a man lay down his life for his friends. You are my friends if you do what I command you. No longer do I call you servants, for the servant does not know what his master is doing; but I have called you friends, for all that I have heard from my Father I have made known to you (John 15:13-15).

In 1 Peter 2:9-10, potent images are used which liken the position of the church to that of the nation Israel.

> But you are a chosen race, a royal priesthood, a holy nation, God's own people, that you may declare the wonderful deeds of him who called you out of darkness into his marvelous light. Once you were no people but now you are God's people; once you had not received mercy but now you have received mercy.

These words could raise the debate about the relation between Israel and the church; are they separate entities, did the church replace Israel, or, in some way, are the two parts of the same body? Whatever case, it is clear that the church is 'the People of God' and has the same priestly responsibility as Israel (cf. Ex 19:6). Paul draws the relationship even closer when he insists,

> The Scripture, foreseeing that God would justify the Gentiles by faith, preached the gospel beforehand to Abraham, saying, 'In you shall all the nations be blessed.' So then, those who are men of faith are blessed with Abraham who had faith.... If you are Christ's, then you are Abraham's offspring, heirs according to promise (Gal 3:8-9, 29).

The images of the church show it has the same, if not a closer, relationship to God as that enjoyed by Old Testament Israel. It is dependent upon God and upon ongoing contact with him for both its life and continuance. Its function involves close communion, service, and worship.

Our look at the words and phrases used of the church have pointed us in a direction, but have hardly provided a clear, crisp definition. This is probably a helpful realization. The church is a corporate body, made up of individual believers in Christ, who have a relationship with God in Christ. In addition to this individual relationship they also have one with Christ as a part of the corporate group, and relationships with other Christians both through Christ and as a part of the church structure. We may describe, but hardly define, such human institutions as family, nation, race, or the relationship within a business corporation. So too we cannot precisely define the church. The best we can say is that it is a collective entity that is completely dependent upon Christ for its existence and as its absolute authority. The church and its members need also the ministry of individuals both to each other and to the whole. Within this entity there is a network of complex relationships, privileges, responsibilities, and activities which could never be reduced to an organizational chart nor adequately described in a corporate manual.

Perhaps a good question might be, 'Why is the word *ekklēsia* appropriate to designate this particular group or body?' It names a particular group of people, Christians, who are distinct from but have continuity with the Old Testament society; hence, they are 'The People of God.' The word conveys an element of novelty: it is free from limitations that would restrict it to a single racial or nationalistic group. It is adaptable for a group with a messianic consciousness; it is able to express the deepest religious concepts of a relationship between God and his people. *Ekklēsia* carries a community concept but is also open to the needed individualistic aspect which maintains and shows personal responsibility. It also carries the concept of wholeness necessary to demonstrate the unity of God's people.

Distinctive Aspects of the Church

The Church's Relation to God and to Jesus Christ
It would be superfluous to repeat what is said above concerning the
relationship between the church and God. However, even a casual
reading of Acts indicates that the unique feature of early Christianity
is what it believed about Jesus of Nazareth. There are two interesting
features about this belief. First, there was virtually unanimous
agreement that Jesus Christ is the central focus of the faith and life of
the church. Second, there was progressive clarification and
expression of precisely what the church believed about him and the
implications of that faith.

There is no need to repeat the outline of the apostolic evangelistic
preaching, the *kērugma*, given in chapter 5. It is enough to remind
ourselves that it centers upon the person and work of Jesus. Again, we
have summarized the early church's view of Jesus in answering our first
question, 'Who is Jesus?' It is sufficient here to note the elements of
things said about Jesus in some of the sermons recorded in Acts. He is
1) a 'man/human being' (Acts 2:22), 2) attested by God (2:22), who is
3) the Lord, 4) the Christ (= Messiah, 2:36; 9:22), 5) the savior (5:31),
6) Jesus is God's Son (9:20; 13:33; 20:28), 7) who was crucified (2:23,
36; 4:10; 5:30), 8) raised from the dead (2:24, 31; 4:2, 10, 33; 5:30),
9) and the ascended one (2:33).

Jesus is the church's risen, ascended Lord, the subject of her
proclamation. She understood that in order to realize her own calling
and function she had not only to be aware of, but also to grasp the
significance, the interpretation, and implications of these facts. This
included seeing both Jesus and the church itself within the totality of
God's work (especially Old Testament). The church had to make
adjustment for the absence of the physical Jesus. How were his
past functions as teacher and leader to be fulfilled when he was no
longer visible among them? What was the place of memory and
tradition? They provided continuity with Jesus, but what was their
place? The church was acutely aware of the present activity of the
Holy Spirit in its life. A part of the answer to the question, 'What is
the church?' was the early church's answer to the question, 'Who is
Jesus?' – the church's Savior and Lord.

Role of the Holy Spirit in the Church[11]

The Holy Spirit and the Church in the Final Age
Whatever the answer to the perennial question, 'When did the church begin?' the events of Pentecost, as recorded in Acts 2, played a pivotal role in the early Christians' belief and actions in regard to the church. Previously the Holy Spirit came only upon prophets, judges, and kings. Now he had come upon the whole congregation. Visible and audible signs accompanied and authenticated his presence.

Peter's explanation of the events and unusual phenomena are clear. The coming of the Holy Spirit in the way he did proved that the Final Age was already a present reality. To catch the flavor of his opening statement, a translation must emphasize the demonstrative pronoun, 'This is what has been spoken through the prophet Joel' (2:16). And, Joel had predicted the coming of another phase in God's Salvation History, the Final Age. The undeniable presence of the Holy Spirit in their midst gave (and still should give) the church the conviction that she was/is 'The People of God of the Final Age,' 'God's Eschatological Community.'

The Continuation of the Ministry of Jesus
In John 14:12 Jesus spoke of the 'greater works' his followers would do after he was no longer with them. As we have seen, he promised that he and the Father would send the Holy Spirit. Through the Spirit they would carry on his ministry. The Spirit would perform something of the same function Jesus had during his earthly ministry; he would remind and guide, speak and declare, and glorify Jesus (John 14:26; 16:13-15). Through the Spirit they would do the 'greater works;' indeed, Jesus said, 'It is to your advantage that I go away, for if I do not go away, the Paraklete (*paraklete*) will not come to you' (John 16:7).

His function in the life and experience of the church, as noted in the previous chapter, includes applying the benefits of the work of

---

[11]This is the third topic under which we have considered the work of the Holy spirit. To summarize, the Holy Spirit is active in 1) the application of salvation, 2) the Christian life, and 3) the Church.

Christ to the believer, his presence is the guarantee ('down-payment') of the church's inheritance until it acquires possession of it at the consummation (Eph 1:14; cf. 2 Cor 1:22; 5:5). Throughout the New Testament we see the Holy Spirit working, sometimes overtly, more often behind the scenes (for his task is not primarily to call attention to himself), to fulfill the promise of Jesus and to work through his followers.

The Holy Spirit and the Church
After his resurrection Jesus specifically stated that the Holy Spirit would empower his followers, the church (Acts 1:8). This is another of the places where the second person plural of the pronoun is important. The promise of 'power' in this verse is to the church as a body. This is true also of most, if not all, of the promises and references to the coming, being 'baptized with' or 'filled' with the Holy Spirit.[12] The Spirit does come upon individuals, but his primary vehicle for action is the body of Christ, the church.

In addition to reminding, guiding, speaking, declaring, and glorifying Jesus, in the Book of Acts we see the Spirit confirming God's guidance and indicating approval of action taken, especially as the Gospel spread to new groups and locations. This played an important role in the experience of the church as she sought to clarify her nature, role, mission, and responsibilities.

The 'Gifts' of the Holy Spirit

The 'Gifts' in General. The empowerment of the Holy Spirit includes his provision of the so-called 'Spiritual Gifts.' The word 'gift' (*dōrea*) when used in the same context with the Holy Spirit refers to the Holy Spirit himself as the gift (Acts 2:38; 10:45), not to something he gives. The special abilities he makes available are designated as 'spiritual things' (*pneumatika*) or 'a grace thing or endowments' (*charisma*).[13] Paul made it clear that they are not

---

[12]See the appendix at the end of this chapter for notes on 'the filling' and 'baptism' of the Holy Spirit.

[13]In Ephesians 4:11, RSV, apostles, prophets, evangelists, pastors, and teachers are listed as 'his gifts.' They probably should be understood 'Christ's

primarily to enhance the spirituality or reputation of the individual[14] but for the benefit of the church;[15] these abilities are 'for building up the body of Christ' (Eph 4:12).

There are a number of lists of these 'spiritual things' in the New Testament. The lists are never the same and only a few abilities are mentioned more than once. This is evident in the following summary.

LIST OF SPIRITUAL [GIFTS] THINGS

Rom 12:6-8	1 Cor 12-14	1 Pet 4:10-11	Eph 4:11ff.
	1. Wisdom (12:8)		
	2. Knowledge (12:8)		
	3. Faith (12:9)		
	4. Healing (12:9, 28, 30)		
	5. Miracles (12: 10, 28, 29)		
1. Prophecy	6. Prophecy (12: 10, 28, 29;	2. Prophets	1. Speaks oracles of God
	7. Discerning spirits (12:10)		
	8. Tongues (12: 10,28, 30; 14:2ff.)		
	9. Interpretation of tongues (12:10, 30; 14:27ff.)		
	10. Apostles (12:28,29)	1. Apostles	
2. Teaching	11. Teachers (12:28)	5. Teachers	
	12. Helps (helpful deeds, 12:28)		
	13. Governments (administrators, 12:28)		
	14. Love (chap. 13)		
3. Service			2. Service
4. Exhortation			
5. Contributing			
6. Acts of Mercy			
		3. Evangelists	
		4. Pastors	

gifts' (cf. vs. 7, 8); in vs. 11 *gifts* in Greek is not a noun but a verb and should be translated, 'And he himself gave ...'

[14]Although he is well aware that they may come upon a single person in private (1 Cor 14:18).

[15]'For the common good' (1 Cor 12:7); 'strive to excel in building up the church' (14:12).

It is probably questionable that these twenty-one abilities constitute a complete list. In the Old Testament the Spirit came upon individuals to enable them to lead, to make war, to give wisdom, and the like. The point seems to be that the Holy Spirit makes available to the People of God those abilities needed at a particular time and place to accomplish the task God wants done then and there.

Paul discusses the spiritual things in 1 Corinthians 12–14 because there was misunderstanding and, he believed, misuse of them in that church. The issues seem to have included what someone under the control of the Holy Spirit might be expected to say. There also seem to have been questions about which are the more important 'grace things': Should all be able to speak in tongues? In what structure or order should the 'grace things,' particularly speaking in tongues, be utilized?

Paul's answer assumes that God does give such abilities to various individuals, but he also seems to be aware of counterfeits or look-alike abilities that are not from God. John's statement, 'Do not believe every spirit, but test the spirits to see whether they are of God; for many false prophets have gone out into the world' (1 John 4:1), seems to be what Paul has in mind in 1 Corinthians 12:3, 'no one speaking by the Spirit of God ever says, "Jesus be cursed!"'[16] and in 14:32, 'the spirits of the prophets are subject to the prophets.' Paul does appear to give some kind of rank order of abilities and offices: apostles, prophets, teachers, workers of miracles, then healers, helpers, administrators, and tongues speakers; but he also insists that the greatest ability or quality is love. He admonishes, 'Earnestly desire the higher gifts' (12:31).

Speaking in Tongues

Evidently the ability to speak in tongues was highly prized in the Corinthian church. Paul says, 'I want you all to speak in tongues' (14:5), but assumes that they do not – the Greek construction of the

---

[16]Evidently, the situation of 1 Cor 12:3 is that some Corinthians, when threatened with persecution, exclaimed 'Jesus is cursed.' They later claimed when they did so they were speaking in the Spirit. Paul responded,

questions in 12:29-30 assumes a negative answer, hence, 'All are not apostles, are they? All are not prophets, are they? All are not teachers, are they? All do not work miracles, do they? All do not possess the grace-ability of healing, do they? All do not speak in tongues, do they?'

Such abilities are not given for the benefit and prestige of the individual. They are made available at the behest of the Giver, to whom, when, and for the purpose God desires. 'The same Spirit ... apportions to each one individually as he wills' (12:11). The abilities are 'church gifts;' individuals are 'given the manifestation of the Spirit for the common good' (12:7). Paul says he would like all to be able to speak in tongues. However he says he wishes even more that all could prophesy, for this he believes to be a higher gift since through prophecy the church is edified (14:5). In 14:26-40 Paul insists that in public meetings all spiritual abilities should be employed in an orderly fashion; thus he assumes that a person with one or more spiritual endowments has some control over their use.

Prophecy in the New Testament

A word, then, need be said about prophecy in the New Testament. The Old Testament prophets were 'spokespersons for God'. On occasions the prophets did speak to particular individuals and offered guidance for personal problems. Their main task was to the nation as a whole, (1) to remind Israel of God's past revelation (especially in the Covenant, Law, and events of the Exodus); (2) to call attention to and condemn sins in the lives of persons and communities of their contemporaries – these sins demonstrated that there was something wrong with the people's relation with God; (3) to warn of punishment and promise blessing, depending upon how Israel responded to their message; and (4) to promise restoration after times of punishments. Their predictions of the future and giving of new information about God, his will, and acts (revelation) usually came only in connection with this final aspect of their work.

In the New Testament, apostles were the primary authorized spokespersons for God. Theirs was the responsibility to give revelation, new information from God, as they reported the facts of the life and ministry of Jesus and told the significance (interpretation) of those facts. The epistles also show the apostles applying the teachings of both Old Testament and New Testament revelation to the situations and lives of those to whom they wrote.

The New Testament mentions Christian prophets. Jesus occasionally implied he was a prophet and he was frequently recognized as such. Christian prophets and prophetesses are mentioned, but with only a single exception, without any description of their activities or message.[17] The prophet Agabus warned Paul against going to Jerusalem and predicted his arrest if he did so (Acts 21:10-11). After Paul had instructed certain individuals at Ephesus and laid hands on them, 'the Holy Spirit came upon them; they spoke with tongues and prophesied' (Acts 19:6). This association of prophecy as one of the endowments of the Holy Spirit is noted in two of the lists given above.[18]

We have then the following facts. The primary (but not exclusive) function of Old Testament prophets was to interpret and apply previously given revelation to God's people. We have no evidence of any New Testament prophet (other than the Apostolic writers) giving any revelation save the words of Agabus to Paul, which Paul, a spirit-filled person, felt free to disregard. The New Testament is clear that God's revelation reached its completion in Jesus Christ. It would seem, then, that Christian prophets are essentially interpreters and appliers of revelation already given in the life and ministry of Jesus and in the written Scriptures. Their messages may well be from God, but recipients are to test them against previously given revelation. God's revealing and saving work is complete. Since God does not change, valid contemporary interpretations and applications cannot contradict what God has already revealed of himself and his will. The message of contemporary prophets must be tested on the basis of previously given revelation available in Scripture and especially in the person, teachings, and work of Jesus Christ.

---

[17] Acts 13:1; 15:32; 21:9; cf. Revelation 22:6.
[18] 1 Corinthians 12:28-29; 14:29, 32, 37; Ephesians 4:11.

The Function and Continuance of Spiritual 'Gifts'

In discussing spiritual endowments Paul uses the illustration of the body in which the many members are all necessary to make up the whole and work together to complement each other. Likewise, he says, the various spiritual grace-given endowments must function together for the benefit of the whole (1 Cor 12:12-27). Paul hints that a failure to grasp these facts about the spiritual abilities, to recognize their legitimate existence and the way they are to be employed, as well as the necessity for order are all evidence of immature thinking (14:20).

Although Paul had no question of the validity of the spiritual qualities, the point is debated in the modern church. The major line of reasoning for those who question their validity in our day is that these abilities were given to confirm the authority of the apostles and their message; they validated the new, authoritative revelation (both facts and interpretations) that God was giving during that time period. Now, God's revelation is complete, the church has the New Testament; as the writer of Hebrews says again and again, in Christ God has worked 'once and for all'.[19] There is, therefore, no new revelation to validate. Furthermore, 1 Corinthians 13:8, 'as for prophecies, they will pass away; as for tongues, they will cease,' is often cited as proof that Paul anticipates the soon cessation of these abilities.

However, the same verse says the same thing about knowledge as it does about tongues; to assume it has now passed away, leaves both individual believers and the church in dire straits. Rather, the total passage seems to be referring to the consummation, when we 'shall understand fully' (13:12).

The concern to maintain and protect the completeness of God's revelation in Christ is a legitimate one. The problem often comes by failing to understand the difference between 'revelation,' 'illumination,' and 'application.' Revelation speaks of new information and its interpretation given by God to the church. What more could God do to make himself known than become flesh, take the form of

---

[19]Cf. Hebrews 7:27; 9:12, 26-28; 10:10.

humanity, to live and move among us that humans might behold his glory (John 1:14, 18; Phil 2:7-8)?

In Jesus Christ God has spoken and acted once and for all. However, God still speaks through the Holy Spirit. His task is now that of illumination and application. The former involves better understanding the revelation already given; hence Jesus promised the disciples that the Spirit would guide them into 'all the truth' (John 16:13-14). Application is the ability to see the meanings and implications of God's revelation and to use them in the situations we face in the modern world. This too is a part of the work of the Spirit as he gives wisdom and guidance. Revelation is complete, illumination and application continue – thank God!

The Holy Spirit in the Modern Church

Whatever one believes about the continuance of certain of the special manifestations of the Spirit, the continuing presence and activity of the Holy Spirit in both individual believers and the Christian community, the church, cannot be doubted by any Bible-believing Christian. Earlier we pointed out that one cannot be a Christian without the person and work of the Holy Spirit. So too we must stress that without the Spirit no group can be a true church. The presence and work of the Holy Spirit is the most important 'mark' or evidence of the church. The church is the place where God is at work; God works through the Spirit. Without the Spirit a so-called church is merely a group of human beings.

Throughout Scripture the word and the Spirit are portrayed as working together. In Acts, as the church prayed, 'they were all filled with the Holy Spirit and spoke the word of God with boldness' (4:31) and in the house of Cornelius 'the Holy Spirit fell on all who heard the word' (10:44). In Ephesians Paul reminds his readers that they 'heard the word of truth, the gospel of your salvation, and have believed in him, were sealed with the promised Holy Spirit' (1:13) and that they should take 'the sword of the Spirit, which is the word of God' (6:17). He tells the Thessalonians 'our gospel came to you not only in word, but also in power and in the Holy Spirit and with full conviction ... and you became imitators of us and of the Lord, for you received the word in much affliction, with joy inspired by the Holy Spirit' (1 Thess 1:5-6; cf. 1 Pet 1:12). The word provides an objective standard against which the presence and work of the Spirit can be validated; the Spirit empowers the written word (the law, the Scriptures) which would otherwise be a 'dead letter' (cf. Rom 7:6; 2 Cor 3:6).

The work of the Spirit in the church is often invisible; he works as he chooses. The metaphor with which Jesus likens the Spirit to wind which 'blows where it chooses, and you hear the sound of it, but you do not know where it comes from or where it goes' (John 3:8) is appropriate here. The words 'where it chooses' are particularly important; the presence and work of the Holy Spirit are beyond human control and often may go undetected. The presence and fruit of the Spirit include emotional responses such as 'love, joy, and peace' (Gal 5:22). But he cannot be manipulated by human actions or through set procedures which 'assure' his coming or endowments. Emotional states and feelings may (or may not) be legitimate evidence of the Spirit at a particular time or place. All evidence of the Spirit is divine and comes at God's initiative and discretion. Those which are self- or group-induced do not necessarily bring nor guarantee his presence. This is no insignificant matter.

Perhaps an additional word is appropriate here. Human persons have intellectual, volitional (the element of will), and emotional facilities. Some persons emphasize one or two of these more than the others. When, as often happens in the modern church, persons of similar inclinations band together those parts of the Body of Christ which emphasize the intellect or the will are deprived of the contribution of those for whom experience, emotion, and feeling are important. And these miss the contribution of the others. In discussing the Christian life we have already noted that fellowship with other Christians helps maintain a balance in the church and in the lives of individual believers.

Jesus taught that blaspheming the Holy Spirit, including failure to acknowledge his presence and work and refusing to submit to him,

---

[20]Mark 3:29; Matt 12:31-32; Luke 12:10; cf. 1 John 5:16.

is the sin which 'never has forgiveness, but is ... an eternal sin'.[20] The context for such statements indicate that this 'unforgivable sin' is the ultimate resistance and rejection of the Holy Spirit by those outside the circle of believers. It seems that there comes a point at which God's Spirit ceases to call, woo, and convict the one who continually hardens the heart against him. It is comforting to know that it is the very persons who are fearful that they may be beyond forgiveness who are most certainly those who have not committed the unforgivable sin. The danger is that those who no longer are concerned about the things of God may (but not necessarily) be among those with whom he has ceased to convict and call. Nevertheless, throughout her history the church has struggled to find proper ways to 'test the spirits' (cf. 1 John 4:1) and to discern the true Holy Spirit from counterfeits and false spirits without resisting or quenching him.

Not infrequently one is asked, 'Why do we not hear more about the Holy Spirit? Why do we not see and experience more of his presence in the world today?' That some Christian groups need to pay more attention to the New Testament's teaching about the Holy Spirit is beyond doubt. Yet, there are answers to these questions which need be remembered.

First, we have just noted that the Spirit's work is often invisible. It is not the kind of phenomena which can be tested and proven by reason or the methods of science. It is spiritually discerned (cf. 1 Cor 2:14).

Closely related to this is the fact that lack of awareness of the Holy Spirit may be understood from the words of Isaiah and then of Jesus as they speak of those who have ears but do not hear and eyes but do not see (cf. Isa 6:9-10; Matt 13:13). Paul says that 'the god of this world has blinded the minds of unbelievers, to keep them from seeing' (2 Cor 4:4). In this modern secular, mechanical world unbelievers, and at times even Christians, fail to see God at work through the Holy Spirit. The temptation is always present to seek naturalistic explanations for what may well be the work of the Holy Spirit.

Third, the Holy Spirit is the one member of the Godhead who's job is not to call attention to himself. In John 16:13 Jesus, the greatest authority on the work of the Holy Spirit, said, 'He will not speak on his own ... He will glorify me.' The Spirit does not call attention to himself; He calls attention to and glorifies Jesus. Where Jesus is proclaimed, where work is being carried on in his name, where Jesus is glorified, there is the Spirit.

Finally, it is important to come before God both individually and corporately with both awareness of the Spirit and the expectancy of activity among us. Christ promised the presence of the Spirit for the benefit of his people and church. His promise is enough for us to expect that the Spirit is and will be with us always. God's people should come together expecting the Spirit to move among us in ways which he chooses.

External Features

Although the church is a spiritual body in which the Holy Spirit dwells, it is also visible. What are the characteristics of this visible aspect of the church?

The church consists of sinners who have been saved by faith in Jesus Christ, who are growing in grace, and who are being sanctified through the work of the Holy Spirit. They are a part of the people of God, members of God's kingdom and family, the body of Christ. They outwardly confess Christ as Savior and Lord. Members of the church are recognized because they 'love one another' (John 13:34-35). Their life and community, as they grow in grace, become progressively more distinct from those of unbelievers.

Such relationships and qualities are only partly visible and the New Testament writers are well aware that not all who claim to be a part of the church are truly members of it. The New Testament writers are assured that believers 'by God's power are guarded through faith for a salvation ready to be revealed in the last time' (1 Pet 1:5). Paul says, 'I am sure that he who began a good work in you will bring it to completion at the day of Jesus Christ' (Phil 1:6) and 'I have believed, and I am sure that he is able to guard until that Day what has been entrusted to me' (2 Tim 1:12). Yet they are aware that even as the betrayer of their Lord was one of the Twelve, external appearances may be deceiving, 'that it is not the children of the flesh who are the children of God, but the children of the promise' (Rom 9:8). John, speaking of some who had deserted the faith says, 'They went out from us, but they were not of us; for if they had been of us, they would have continued with us' (1 John 2:19). Even Paul saw the need to discipline himself lest he should become a castaway (1 Cor 9:27; cf. Phil 2:12, 16); Hebrews constantly calls its readers to 'pay the closer attention ... lest we drift away (2:1), to 'hold fast our confession' (3:6; 4:14), and patiently endure (10:36, 38; 12:1). Indeed, the consistent affirmation of the Scriptures is that persistence and continuance in the faith is the final proof of true faith.

Such realities caused later Christian writers (e.g., Augustine, Wycliffe, Luther, and Calvin) to make a distinction between the 'visible' and the 'invisible' church. Although they stressed the importance of church membership, they were all too aware of weeds among the wheat (Matt 13:24-43), goats among the sheep (Matt 25:31-46), and deceit and hypocrisy among those who outwardly claimed to be a part of the church. They argued that God knows who are his; this, the *real* church, is invisible to human eyes. Some want to include in the 'invisible church' those who were in Christ but are now dead; the Book of Revelation seems to give some support to this claim.

Worship and Organization as Visible Features of the Church
The most obvious external features of the church are its worship and organization. Wars have been fought between proponents of different views on these matters; they remain among the more powerful reasons for divisions among Christians. It is likely that within the current ecclesiastical and scholarly climates solutions to these controversies are impossible. Even dispassionate, impartial discussions are difficult. We come to such conversations from our own experiences of church and worship, we have different personalities which incline toward one type of organization or form of worship, and we live in cultures which predispose to one type in exclusion of others. These investigations frequently move quickly from the New Testament to information in Christian sources outside

it. Here the situation appears to have been both fluid, highly polemical, and moving toward the essentially hierarchal and more liturgical models which eventually gained majority acceptance. In addition to noting these outcomes, it is also important to contemplate the possible influence of the specialized environment and conditions in which the early Christians lived – including its move from a predominantly Jewish/Semitic culture to the Greco-Roman societies of the Gentile world, the fact of persecution by the empire, the widely scattered locations in which Christians lived, the presence of only a few recognized leaders, and the lower socio-economic level and limited literacy of the majority of the early believers.

Issues regarding worship and organization are not easily solved by limiting the study to the pages of the New Testament. The fact that all groups can find some (they feel conclusive) support for their views of the proper form of worship or church government in Scripture, should at least raise the possibility that the views of the ancient writers were not as unvarying as some modern interpreters claim.

Worship

The models for worship from the ancient world included formality and ceremony in both Jewish and traditional pagan religions. Judaism, as well as some mystery and other oriental religions, had place for both spontaneity and freedom of expression in worship. Such diversity has influenced developments within the Christian church so that Greek and Roman Catholics and Anglicans focus upon liturgical and sacramental elements in worship. Traditional Protestants have stressed the centrality of the Word of God in worship; hence, the reading, preaching, and study of it maintains an important place. They have also emphasized the importance of the participation of all believers, but not without human leadership. They have also observed rituals, ceremonies, or have followed some customary patterns or forms. The worship of other groups is largely informal and spontaneous with a minimum of directives or leaders.

The examples of worship found in the New Testament are contained largely in the prayers recorded there. We know very little about the mechanics of worship of the earliest church. Even Jewish Christians would have had a variety of different traditions in their backgrounds emanating from the temple and synagogues. The fact that worship usually took place in small houses or in the outdoors must have affected what could be and was done.

The Old Testament conveys the fact that not all worship is acceptable. The prophets condemn idolatry in two forms: (1) worshiping a wrong (false) god and (2) worshiping the right God in the wrong way. Use of idols or images, occult pagan ceremonies involving sex, and excess emphasis upon the material side of worship, especially when not accompanied with a godly life, are among improper ways of worshiping the Jewish and Christian God.

Tradition, culture, that to which one is accustomed, or that which appeals to a particular person or group usually plays a significant part in determining the content and form of worship in the modern world. Such influences are unavoidable. Yet, ultimately worship must be based upon an understanding of God, it must be founded upon an understanding which comes as close as possible to who and what he really is. In the final analysis, for Christians as well as Jews, it is not what appeals to the worshiper but what pleases God that counts.[21] Extra-biblical features, especially those springing from cultural or social ones, should not be so discriminatory as to drive away or make unnecessarily uncomfortable any member of the family of God. The admonitions in James 2:2-6 clearly condemn socio-economic discrimination within the church. The withdrawal from table-fellowship (possibly including participating in the Lord's Supper) with Gentile Christians by Jewish believers in Antioch was on the basis of what they believed to be religious principle. Yet, Paul denounced the action as cultural with negative implications (Gal 2).

---

[21]Note, 'The Lord said: Because these people draw near with their mouths and honor me with their lips, while their hearts are far from me, and their worship of me is a human commandment learned by rote: so I will again do amazing things with this people, shocking and amazing' (Isa 29:13-14, NRSV). The NIV also uses the word 'worship', the RSV has 'fear' and the NASB 'reverence'. In each case the meaning is the same; God is to be approached on his own terms.

If our understanding of the request to abstain from 'things strangled' in the settlement of the law versus grace controversy in Acts 15 is correct, Gentile Christians were asked to be sensitive to Jewish ethnic and cultural sensitivities. Hence the leaders of the Reformation of the sixteenth century agreed and insisted that worship activities must be directed by Scripture. Unfortunately, they, no less than moderns, could not always agree just what those Scriptural directives might be.

Organization

The theoretical or theological concept of church organization or government affirms that Christ, as Lord and Head, governs and works in and through the church, through the Holy Spirit whom he, with the Father, has sent. Human leaders are individuals who have been called and enabled by God[22] and recognized by the church. Church leadership is not for one who happens to want it, it must not be decided on the basis of having representation from certain groups within the church. The only criteria is evidence of the call and enablement of God.

The church is a society in which all persons are equal before God and in which there is to be no discrimination on external grounds.[23] Yet, there are leadlers in the church who, although they are equals with other Christians, because of their function in the Body of Christ, are to receive respect (1 Tim 5:17; Heb 13:7),

---

[22]Old Testament leaders were called by God either by birth or as he designated them for specific tasks. Of some individuals their appointment and provision for office is described with the phrase 'the Spirit of God came upon him;' some prophets seem to have experienced a special 'call vision' through which they were inducted into office (1 Kngs 22:19; Isa 6:1; Jer 1:4ff.; 23:16ff.; Amos 3:7). In the New Testament Paul refers to his 'call to be an apostle' (Rom 1:1). In 1 Peter 5:2 elders are 'charged' with tending 'the flock of God.' Leadership offices and endowments are among the spiritual endowments listed above. It is said of Timothy that he received 'the gift of God ... through the laying on of hands,' a statement which seems to imply the recognition of spiritual leadership abilities by the church as a whole.

[23]Galatians 3:28; Colossians 3:11; cf. Acts 10:34; 1 Timothy 5:21; James 2:1-7.

honor, and obedience as they discharge the duties given them by
God and confirmed by the church. But, just as the spiritual
endowments or gifts are for the good and growth of the church, so
too are the positions of leadership. Paul says, God's gifts of church
officers is

> to equip the saints for the work of ministry, for building up the body
> of Christ, until we all attain to the unity of the faith and of the
> knowledge of the Son of God, to mature manhood, to the measure
> of the stature of the fullness of Christ; so that we may no longer
> be children, tossed to and fro and carried about with every wind of
> doctrine, by the cunning of men, by their craftiness in deceitful
> wiles. Rather, speaking the truth in love, we are to grow up in
> every way into him who is the head, into Christ, from whom the
> whole body, joined and knit together by every joint with which it is
> supplied, when each part is working properly, makes bodily growth
> and upbuilds itself in love (Eph 4:12-16).

The New Testament solves this apparent paradox of leaders with
some sort of authority in an egalitarian group by insisting that leaders
are servants. Their objective is to work 'not for shameful gain'
(1 Pet 5:2) nor be 'domineering ... but ... [be] examples' (1 Pet
5:3).[24] Jesus said to his disciples, 'Whoever would be great among
you must be your servant, and whoever would be first among you
must be slave of all' (Mark 10:43-44).

The titles and responsibilities of the church officers of the various
modern church groups and denominations have been set almost as
much by tradition and custom as by Scripture. If we initially restrict
ourselves to the New Testament we find leaders called by different
names; it is not always clear whether some functions listed, such as
healers and miracle-workers, are regular church officers or abilities
given by the Spirit. If we initially look at Acts we find that apostles

---

[24]Paul warns those in danger of being made subservient to other humans,
'You were bought with a price; do not become slaves of men' (1 Cor 7:23).
Although earlier (vss 20-22) he is speaking of social-economic slavery,
perhaps his words could be extended to those Christian leaders who would
force their own authority on others.

are the first to be mentioned. Then, chapter 6 recounts the election of the Seven who are usually assumed to be deacons. The office of elder was present in the Jerusalem Church.[25] Paul and Barnabas appointed elders during their first missionary journey (14:23). In chapter 20 Paul addresses the elders of the Church of Ephesus (vs. 17). Philip appears to function as an evangelist in Acts 8 and is called by that title in 21:8. Agabus is called a 'prophet' (21:10). Ephesians 4:11 says that God's 'gifts were that some should be apostles, some prophets, some evangelists, some pastors and teachers.' We have already seen that some of these positions are also listed among the spiritual endowments made available by the Holy Spirit. The other possible major leadership position mentioned in the New Testament is that of 'stewards' (*oikonomoi*), agents or employees who act in this capacity. They are mentioned in 1 Corinthians 4:1-2; the word also occurs in 1 Peter 4:10, but it is not clear in the latter case whether it refers to an office or a function.

The term 'apostle' (*apostolos*) most often refers to 'The Twelve'. The word designates one sent out as an official representative, one who has the authority to speak for another. The names of the initial twelve are given in the New Testament in four different places.[26] These names and the order of them vary slightly from list to list. We know no more than the name of most of them; all save Peter and John fade from the events of the New Testament fairly early in the church's history. It seems that it is the number, twelve, that is most significant. In calling this group, just as 'Old Israel' had been founded upon twelve tribes, so Jesus founded the 'New Israel' upon these twelve apostles.

Nevertheless, the office of the apostle was highly significant. They were witness to the life, ministry, death, resurrection, and ascension of Jesus (Acts 1:21-22); Paul asserts his apostleship was based on his special call (Gal 1:15-16), the fact that he had seen the risen Lord (1 Cor 9:1), and his performance of the 'signs of an apostle' (2 Cor 12:12). After the death of Judas Iscariot the number of the

---

[25] Acts 11:30; 15:2, 4, 6, 22-23; 16:4; 21:18.
[26] Matthew 10:2-4; Mark 3:16-19; Luke 6:13-16, and Acts 1:13.

apostles was brought back to twelve by the election of Matthias (Acts 1:23-26). As far as we know, no later efforts were made to maintain that number. In addition to the twelve, Matthias, and Paul, the title is also ascribed to James, the relative of Jesus (Gal 1:19), Barnabas (Acts 14:4; 1 Cor 9:6, implied), Epaphroditus (Phil 2:25), Andronicus (Rom 16:7),[27] Junias (masculine) or Junia (feminine) (Rom 16:7), 'our brethren' (or messengers (*apostoloi*), an undefined group in 2 Cor 8:23), and Jesus himself (Heb 3:1). The apostles, as the official spokesmen for God, the successors of the Old Testament prophets (hence, the references to 'prophets and apostles'), declare the revelation of God – as we have said, both the facts and the official interpretation of it. They too had the responsibility for spreading the good news and, as Paul says, 'the daily pressure ... of ... anxiety for all the churches' (2 Cor 11:28).

The Seven of Acts 6 who were selected to serve are usually assumed to have been 'deacons,' but the noun is not used of them. Qualifications for deacons are given in 1 Timothy 3:8-13; the masculine noun, which could be translated either 'deacon,' 'minister,' or 'servant,' is applied to Phoebe (a woman) in Romans 16:1. The church of Philippi had deacons as well as bishops (Phil 1:1). Elsewhere in the epistles the word *diakonoi* (deacons/ministers) occurs, although it is debatable whether some of these refer to an office, function, or characteristic.[28] On the basis of Acts 6 it is usually assumed that deacons are responsible for the

---

[27]For a discussion of the textual, grammatical, history of interpretation, cultural background, and an attempt to bring all this together in a suggested statement of what Epp thinks the passage is saying, see Eldon Jay Epp, *Junia. The First Woman Apostle.* (Minneapolis: Fortress, 2005).

[28]Apollos and Paul 'are through whom people believed' (1 Cor 3:5). In 2 Corinthians Paul says, 'God has equipped us to be *diakonoi* of a new covenant' (3:6) and 'we commend ourselves as *diakonoi* of God' (6:4), that 'Satan's *diakonoi* are transformed into *diakonoi* of righteousness' (11:15), and that if his (Paul's) opponents are *diakonoi* of Christ, so is he! Paul claims to be 'a *diakonos* of Christ' (Eph 3:7), 'a *diakonos* of the gospel' and 'of the church' (Col 1:23, 25). Paul says 'Epaphras is a *diakonos* of Christ' on behalf of the Colossians (1:7) and calls Tychicus a 'faithful *diakonos*' (Eph 6:21; Col 4:7). Timothy will be 'a good *diakonos* of Christ Jesus' if he 'puts these instructions before the brethren' (1 Tim 4:6).

material concerns of the church, but this is nowhere stated explicitly in the New Testament.

'Elders' (*presbuteroi*)[29] occupied an established office in Judaism of both the Old Testament and Intertestamental periods; the office was prominent in the leadership of the church. We have just noted references to elders in Acts; they are especially prominent at Jerusalem during the Council of Acts 15, where they were active in clarifying doctrine and policy. They appear again during Paul's final visit to that city in chapter 21:18-25, when they exercised some sort of administrative oversight. The writer of 2 and 3 John identified himself as 'the elder', the church of Ephesus had elders (Acts 20:17), and elders 'laid hands on' Timothy to appoint him to his work (1 Tim 4:14). James 5:14 directs sick persons 'to call for the elders of the church'. There are general references to 'the elders' in a number of passages.[30] In Revelation elders in heaven are mentioned at least a dozen times.

1 Timothy 5:17-20, while not detailing the responsibility of elders, provides insights into the status and nature of the office. Paul says,

> Let the elders who rule well be considered worthy of double honor, especially those who labor in preaching and teaching; for the Scripture says, 'You shall not muzzle an ox when it is treading out the grain,' and, 'The laborer deserves his wages.' Never admit any charge against an elder except on the evidence of two or three witnesses. As for those who persist in sin, rebuke them in the presence of all, so that the rest may stand in fear.

Hence, elders 'rule,' have administrative responsibilities, 'preach and teach,' can expect some sort of compensation,[31] and are not to

---

[29]From whence comes the word 'presbyterian'.

[30]1 Timothy 5:17, 19; Titus 1:5; and 1 Peter 5:1, 5 – note that Peter identifies himself as an elder.

[31]The precise type of compensation intended is not clear. The reference to 'double honor' might/ imply respect and status. The not necessarily complimentary comparison implied in Paul's use of the quotation from Deuteronomy 25:4, likening the rights of the elder to that of an ox threshing grain, could suggest some form of material 'honor.' The latter is more likely since in 1 Corinthians 9:4-14 Paul also quotes the same passage from Deuteronomy as part of his argument that 'those who proclaim the gospel

be lightly accused of misdeeds.[32] Paul instructs the Ephesian elders
to care for (or provide for) the 'flock' and 'shepherd the church of
God' (Acts 20:28); Peter also exhorts elders to 'tend the flock of
God that is in your charge' (1 Pet 5:2). We will comment on the
church leader as shepherd below.

Mention of the office designated by the Greek word *episkopos*[33]
occurs only in Acts, Philippians, 1 Timothy, and Titus. The term can
be translated as 'bishop' or 'overseer.'[34] Philippians 1:1 notes that
there were bishops in the church of Philippi. The office is called a
'noble task' (1 Tim 3:1), and qualifications for the office are given in
1 Timothy 3:1-7.

The same group of leaders of the church at Ephesus is called
elders in Acts 20:17 and bishops or overseers in verse 28.[35] Titus
1:5-9 presents data that is sometimes perplexing. It is helpful to
quote the entire passage:

---

should get their living by the gospel' (9:14), a right of which Paul himself did
not make use.

[32] 1 Timothy 5:1 may reflect the same idea, 'Do not rebuke an older man
but exhort him as you would a father.' The phrase 'older man' is the same
word translated elsewhere as 'elder.'

[33] The word from which comes 'episcopal'.

[34] Sometimes neither translating philosophy, theological perspective, nor
disagreements regarding the original texts account for differences in
translations. Rather traditional, sectarian (denominational) matters, and
custom may be involved. The following 8 words used in 17 translations of
episkopos in 1 Timothy 3:1 provide an example.

> bishop, KJV (1611), American Standard Version (1901), The Douay-Rheims
> (a Roman Catholic translation, 1941), RSV (1971), New KJV (1982) adds in a
> footnote Literally *overseer*, 1999), God's Word (1995);
>
> Bishop (note capitalization), English Revised Version (1881);
>
> overseer, Berkeley (NT 1945, OT 1959), New Americam Standard Bible (1960;
> Updated edition [1997]), NIV (1973), NIV (inclusive language, 1995), ESV
> (2001);
>
> leadership, New English Bible (1961/76);
>
> church leader, Good News Bible/Today's English Version (1966);
>
> a presiding elder, Jerusalem Bible (1966), New Jerusalem Bible (1985-90);
>
> pastor, Living Bible (1971);
>
> elder [Gr, 'overseer'], New Living Translation (1996).

[35] The same phenomenon of leaders being called both *presbuteroi* (elders)
and *episkopoi* (bishops or overseers) occurs in the First Epistle of Clement
44 (ca. AD 95), one of the documents called 'the Apostolic Fathers'.

This is why I left you in Crete, that you might amend what was defective, and appoint elders (*presbuterous*) in every town as I directed you, if any man is blameless, the husband of one wife, and his children are believers and not open to the charge of being profligate or insubordinate. For a bishop (*episkopon*), as God's steward (*oikonomon*), must be blameless; he must not be arrogant or quick-tempered or a drunkard or violent or greedy for gain, but hospitable, a lover of goodness, master of himself, upright, holy, and self-controlled; he must hold firm to the sure word as taught, so that he may be able to give instruction in sound doctrine and also to confute those who contradict it.

The passage begins with reference to Paul's instructions to Titus to appoint elders and gives some basic moral qualifications for candidates of that office. In verse 7 he speaks of 'a bishop, as God's steward' and adds additional lifestyle and doctrinal requirements. Do these passages in Acts and Titus mean that the titles elders, *episkopoi* (bishops/overseers), and stewards are synonyms for the same office? Do they refer to two or three separate offices? Is it significant that the qualifications in Titus are much more specific than those for an elder in 1 Timothy 5? These questions are among the imponderables in discussions of church leadership.

In the same category is the issue of rank order between the various leaders mentioned in the New Testament. Elders or bishops, elder-bishops, seem to have positions with more authority than others. This seems to include the ability to teach others,[36] but Stephen and Philip, among the Seven of Acts 6 (deacons?), engaged in similar activities.

The term *pastors* requires some comment. The noun form appears in the RSV only in Ephesians 4:11, a translation for the Greek word *poimēn*, *shepherd* or *sheep-herder;* this is the same word frequently used of Jesus in his role of Shepherd. In its natural sense it carries such ideas as one who tends, leads, guides, protects, cares for, and nurtures sheep. We have already noted the use of

---

[36] 1 Timothy 5:17; cf. 2 Timothy 2:2.

shepherd language ('care for the flock ... shepherd the church') in the description of the duties of the elder-bishops of Ephesus (Acts 20:28) and by Peter (1 Pet 5:2). There is no doubt that all Christians have the opportunity and duty to minister to, to shepherd, fellow-members of Christ's flock. Yet it is apparent that this function is a special responsibility of church officers. Is *pastor-shepherd* another term for *elder-bishop/overseer-steward*? It is noteworthy that neither elder, bishop, or steward appears in the list with pastor-shepherd in Ephesians 4:11. Still, it may be a separate office, primarily concerned with shepherd-like responsibilities for the church as a whole and/or for individual believers. Then again, as seems implied in Acts 20, 'shepherding' may be a further clarification of the duties of the elder-bishop-steward office. In any case, just as a shepherd lived with his flock, so too the elder-bishop/overseer-steward seems to be a local officer, one who lives with and among the flock as it faces the joys and sorrows of life.

The Pastoral Epistles contain lists of qualities of both life and spirit which should be present in a Christian leader.[37] All point toward qualities of godliness and holiness that are evident in the external life of the person. Even so, not all godly and holy people are necessarily called to leadership; administration is but one of the special spiritual-grace endowments given as God wills (cf. 1 Cor 12:28). As already noted, it is those whom God has designated and equipped and who have been so recognized by the church that are proper candidates for church office. In all cases spiritual maturity is essential; hence, Paul, speaking of installing individuals in church offices, says, 'Do not be hasty in laying on of hands' (1 Tim 5:22).

It is worth noting that with the possible exception of the apostles, in the New Testament church, officers exercise leadership authority as a group, not as an individual. Strong argument for the authority of a single leader does not seem to be present in Christian literature until the writings of Ignatius (martyred about AD 117). The insistence with which he argues for the authority of a single bishop-overseer in each area may betray the fact that there were those who disagreed with him.

---

[37] 1 Timothy 3:1-13; cf. 5:17-21 and Titus 1:5-11.

The issue of gender requirements and limitations for leadership in the church is often the subject of controversy. The New Testament knows of both men and women rendering effective service in the early church. We do not always know in precisely what capacity each served. Throughout the history of the church some groups have and do accept members of both genders into some or all levels of their official leadership, others restricted it solely to men. The commitment to submit to Biblical teaching is not the only issue. The role of women in the church is not the only point of disagreement among Christians on matters of faith and practice. The human limitations of interpreters with different backgrounds, presuppositions, and hermeneutical methods[38] often engender lack of agreement on what the Biblical writers intended on this as well as other matters. Both church history and the tenor of recent debates do not offer much hope for the soon emergence of a widely accepted agreement on the numerous issues involved in question of feminine leadership in the church.

This writer wishes that the following elements could be permitted to guide the continuing discussion of the place of women in the body of Christ.

First, it is on the basis of Biblical exegesis, not tradition nor contemporary political, social, or cultural pressures, that the issue must be studied. As this is done, as is true for all textual studies, sound interpretative procedures require that the entirety of the Biblical data be examined. This means that the evidence which seems to include women in leadership positions as well as that which seems to restrict it[39] must be investigated. Both clear statements and examples which imply one or other assumption or practice must be included in studies of this topic. The honest interpreter does not come to the text with his or her mind already made up.

---

[38]The British scholar, R. T. France, *Women in the Church's Ministry. A Test Case for Biblical Interpretation* (Grand Rapids, MI: Eerdmans, 1995), shows how differences of opinion on this issue, even among those who hold the same evangelical-conservative view of Scripture, can rest in different methods of interpreting the Bible.

[39]Especially 1 Corinthians 11:3-16; 14:33-36; and 1 Timothy 2:11-15.

Second, whatever the conclusion, there must be a clear understanding that leaders have a role (function) that in no way implies they are of superior 'stuff' (in their being) to others. We are all one in Christ (Gal 3:28; cf., Rom 12:5) and are to 'be subject to one another out of reverence for Christ' (Eph 5:21).[40]

Third, the order and effectiveness of the church must have priority over the rights of any individual or group. Paul was concerned for the welfare and reputation of the church as well as for the individual. He could even advocate the voluntary abdication of a Christian person's rights or the pursuit of justice, if need be, to maintain peace and order in the fellowship or to protect it from offence.[41] In short, love for the church, including those within it with whom one disagrees, is a dominant feature of the life of believers and should be evident in this debate as well as in all other aspects of the life of the community.[42]

---

[40]This statement is subject to several possible meanings; most English translations further confuse the point. The first word, 'subject or submit' *(hypotassomenoi)* is a present, middle or passive, participle and it is not repeated in verse 22. Hence, the meaning is something like, 'As you are being submissive to one another out of reverence for Christ, wives to their own husbands as to the Lord.' This construction could mean (1) the three groups which follow this statement (wives, children, and slaves) are to be submissive; (2) submission is a characteristic of the Christian life in general, but there is a special submission required of wives, children, and slaves; or (3) since there are no superiors or inferiors in the church all believers are to be submissive to each other. This includes even the closest relationships although there is a 'rank order' which must be allowed to function, but in a way different from that of the world – husbands are to love and give themselves up for their wives, parents are not to provoke their children but to bring them up in Christ, slave-owners are not to threaten because in Christ 'there is no partiality' (Eph 6:9).

[41]1 Corinthians 6:6-7; 10:32; 11:22; 14:12; 14:40.

[42]Note the appeal of F. F. Bruce. He argued that all persons upon whom the Holy Spirit bestows gifts for the benefit of the church should be permitted to exercise them. This led him to views of the place of women in the church that were different from the majority of those with whom he regularly worshipped and had fellowship. He said, 'Nothing should be done to endanger the unity of the local church. Let those who understand the Scriptures along the lines indicated in this paper have liberty to expound them thus, but let them not force the pace or try to impose their understanding of the Scriptures until that understanding finds general acceptance with the

Fourth, no matter what the titles or formal structure may be, the different perspectives from which men and women can contribute and balance each other is as essential within the church even as in marriage where 'the two shall become one.'[43] Some means should be found for that contribution to be made.

Finally, as we noted above about church leadership in general, here too we must remember that a church office is a position in which one serves; it must not be a platform from which one can assume superiority, power, control over another or satisfy personal ambitions.

The issue of organizational structures or governmental forms found in the New Testament is still hotly debated. Three broad models have developed throughout church history. The *Episcopal or Monarchial* form has centralized control in the hands of one or more persons, usually called 'bishops'. The Greek and Roman Catholics and Anglican communions have some type of this hierarchical oversight and stress that both authority and unity are in some way related to the organizational structure. In the *Presbyterial* form leadership stems from New Testament references to 'elders' who, it is assumed, lead through a representative administrative structure. *Congregational church government* is a democratic form. In it each member of the congregation has an equal vote in all matters.

As previously stated, each group argues for its church government from the New Testament, often claiming it to be the only structure found there. We suggest that there may not have been a single form of church government in the New Testament era. Rather what we may have is leadership in the hands of persons whom God called and gifted, and who were so recognized by the church. Second, the organization of leaders and the relation between churches in an area may have developed on the basis of the leadership available and possibly patterned after the particular form of secular government

---

church – and when it does, there will be no need to impose it' ('Women in the Church: A Biblical Survey,' *A Mind for What Matters* [Grand Rapids, MI: Eerdmans, 1990], 264).

[43]Matthew 19:5; Mark 10:8; Ephesians 5:31.

functioning in that locale. Hence, in Asia minor and Rome the church gravitated toward a more centralized, hierarchal, monarchial, episcopal form of administrative structure. In Jewish areas the representative model, that of government by elders as found in synagogues, seems to have emerged. In Greek areas, such as Corinth, the tradition of the Greek city-states, in which all citizens participated in government, may have led to some form of congregational form of church government.

It appears to me that the essentials of church government include recognizing

(1) Christ as the sole, authoritative head of the church, the presence and activity of the Holy Spirit in carrying out the plan and purpose of God, and the authority of the Scriptures.

(2) God calls and equips individuals for special leadership roles and responsibilities. These the church should search out and permit them to carry out their call. Their authority must always be circumscribed by that of Christ, the head of the church. Although they are to be respected, they must be held accountable to the dictates of the revelation of God and his will in Scripture.

(3) Although the whole church is present wherever Christ is present with two or more of his own (Matt 18:20), the church is unlimited by the boundaries of a single congregation, geographical location, race, nation, culture, social grouping or the like. It is one body. Some means should be found to recognize and exercise this unity, a unity which lies first and foremost in Christ rather than in outward forms. The accountability of both individual leaders and ecclesiastical units to the Head should be safeguarded by accountability to other church units, yet solely on the basis of conformity to Scripture.

The New Testament depicts the church gathering wherever it could. Homes, schools, possibly synagogues and public buildings, and the open air were all utilized. There is some evidence of existing structures being adapted for church use fairly early in the church's history. The construction of buildings exclusively for church use probably did not begin until the third century; erecting elaborate buildings was not possible until the Emperor Constantine legitimized Christianity in AD 313.

Added Note: The 'Filling' and 'Baptism' of/by/with the Holy Spirit

The purpose of this note is to look at the data relating to the baptism and/or filling with the Holy Spirit through the eyes of Biblical theology. Hopefully, this study will clarify some of the issues often raised in discussions of these terms. We will focus upon the occurrences of the relevant terms and related data in the New Testament and seek conclusions that may be drawn from them.

The occurrences of the actual vocabulary involving baptism or filling with the Holy Spirit are limited. If we exclude those references which apply to the circumstances of the births of John the Baptist and Jesus and look only at those places where baptism or filling with the Spirit involves a specific group, individual Christians, or the church as a whole, the evidence is even less.

Each of the Synoptic Gospels relates John the Baptist's announcement that the One to come after him would baptize with the Holy Spirit and with fire (Matt 3:11; Mark 1:8; Luke 3:16). All also record that the Holy Spirit came upon Jesus when he was baptized by John (Matt 3:16-17; Mark 1:10-11; Luke 3:21-22). After testifying that he saw the Holy Spirit come upon Jesus at his baptism, John the Baptist said explicitly, 'I myself did not know him; but he who sent me to baptize with water said to me, 'He on whom you see the Spirit descend and remain, this is he who baptizes with the Holy Spirit'' (John 1:33).

In Acts 1:5 Jesus tells his disciples, 'John baptized with water, but before many days you shall be baptized with the Holy Spirit.' The actual phrase 'baptized with the Holy Spirit' does not occur in the following chapter, in the description of the disciples' experience at Pentecost. Apparently we are to understand that the promise was fulfilled when 'they were all filled with the Holy Spirit' (Acts 2:4). This 'filling' was accompanied by both unusual visible and audible phenomena. The coming of the Holy Spirit is described as 'the gift' (*dōrea*). At the conclusion of his sermon at Pentecost Peter urges his hearers, 'Repent, and be baptized every one of you in the name of Jesus Christ for the forgiveness of your sins; and you shall receive the gift of the Holy Spirit' (Acts 2:38). Here receiving the Holy Spirit is assumed to be a part of the hearer's conversion to Christianity.

After Peter and John had been released from imprisonment and interrogation by the Jewish council they, and 'their friends' prayed, praised God, and asked for boldness while God stretched out his hand to heal and perform signs and wonders 'through the name of thy holy servant Jesus' (Acts 4:23-30). In response, 'The place in which they were gathered together was shaken and they were all filled with the Holy Spirit and spoke the word of God with boldness' (vs. 31). At least some of those who had been previously filled with the Holy Spirit (at Pentecost) were again so filled.

In Samaria new converts believed and were baptized; Philip's preaching was accompanied by the casting out of demons and the healing of paralyzed or lame persons (8:7) and by 'signs and great miracles;' no other specific evidence is mentioned (8:12-13). However, the Holy Spirit came upon the Samaritan believers later, only after Peter and John had come from Jerusalem, prayed that the new converts would receive the Spirit, and laid hands on them (8:14-17). There is no further indication of signs or miracles.

Three days after Saul-Paul's confrontation with Jesus on the Damascus road Ananias laid hands on him that he might regain his sight and 'be filled with the Holy Spirit.' His sight was restored, presumably, although the text does not explicitly say so, he was filled by the Spirit, and was baptized (Acts 9:17-18).

Peter's preaching of Jesus in the house of Cornelius was interrupted when 'the Holy Spirit fell on all who heard his word.' They then spoke in tongues and extolled God (Acts 10:46). They were then baptized in the name of Jesus Christ because, as Peter said, they had 'received the Holy Spirit just as we have' (Acts 10:47-48). Again the Holy Spirit is called 'the gift' (*dōrea*). Later, in Jerusalem, Peter defended his association with uncircumcised Gentiles on the grounds of both the Spirit's directing him to do so and that 'the Holy Spirit fell on them just as on us at the beginning' (11:4-12;[44] see also 15:7-9). Peter associated the coming

---

[44]Undoubtedly he was referring to the experience of the Jerusalem Christians at Pentecost (Acts 2).

of the Holy Spirit upon these Gentiles with Jesus' promise of the baptism with the Holy Spirit and as evidence of God's approval of this new racial-cultural group now being included among the number of the believers. Again, the coming of the Spirit is described as 'the gift' (11:16-17).

The two incidents in Acts 18:24–19:7 are both interesting and somewhat puzzling. Apollos, although 'he had been instructed in the way of the Lord ... and taught accurately the things concerning Jesus' (18:25), knew only 'the baptism of John'. The remedy was additional instruction by Priscilla and Aquila. There is no mention of baptism or of any special indication of the presence of the Holy Spirit. However, in Ephesus Paul found some disciples whom, for some reason, he asked 'Did you receive the Holy Spirit when you believed?' (19:2). Their negative answer was followed by profession of ignorance about the Holy Spirit and that they had received only John's baptism of repentance (19:4). Paul, as had Priscilla and Aquila in dealing with Apollos, gave additional instruction. When he laid hands on them 'the Holy Spirit came on them; and they spoke with tongues and prophesied' (19:6).

Strictly speaking the New Testament never describes an event in which a person or group was 'baptized with the Holy Spirit'. This phrase always refers to either a future or a past event or experience. The words used to describe the coming of the Spirit are that he 'fell upon' or 'came upon' them or that the individual or community were 'filled' or 'full of' the Holy Spirit. This raises the question of whether baptism and filling of the Holy Spirit refer to the same or different events.

Predictions of a future baptism with the Spirit were made by John the Baptist and later by Jesus just before his ascension. With the exception of Pentecost, the 'coming,' 'filling,' or 'receiving' the Spirit occurred with persons as they initially came to faith in Jesus or upon those who were already believers.

In the epistles Paul speaks of believers being baptized into Christ and his death as a symbol or synonym for identification with Christ.[45] There is no direct reference to the Holy Spirit in these contexts and Paul may have water baptism in mind.

---

[45]Romans 6:3; Galatians 3:27; Colossians 2:12.

In 1 Corinthians 12:13, Paul, speaking of the common heritage and unity of the church, says: 'For by one Spirit we were all baptized into one body – Jews or Greeks, slaves or free – and all were made to drink of one Spirit'; and in Ephesians 4:4-6, he writes: 'There is one body and one Spirit, just as you were called to the one hope that belongs to your call, one Lord, one faith, one baptism, one God and Father of us all, who is above all and through all and in all.' The reference to baptism in the Corinthian passage is probably to that of the Holy Spirit; the 'one baptism' in Ephesians may refer to baptism by water, with the Spirit, or both. In any case, Paul stresses the unity of the church which comes and is expressed through baptism, of either kind. Acts also probably would have the reader understand that as diverse groups of believers participate in the same Spirit they are a part of the one church.

Paul suggests the fullness of the Holy Spirit as a corrective for improper behavior when he says, 'Do not get drunk with wine, for that is debauchery; but be filled with the Spirit' (Eph 5:18). He further admonishes, 'Do not grieve the Holy Spirit, in whom you were sealed for the day of redemption' (Eph 4:30) and, 'Do not quench the Spirit' (1 Thess 5:19).

Although I realize it will not be granted by all, it seems apparent that, as noted in our earlier discussion, in some sense the Holy Spirit is present in the life of all Christians. Paul says, 'Any one who does not have the Spirit of Christ does not belong to him' (Rom 8:9). This statement seems to indicate that it is impossible to be a Christian without the person and work of the Holy Spirit in the individual. As we have seen, the New Testament teaches that it is the Holy Spirit who applies the work of Christ to the believer.

A further point must be made. John 3:34 states, 'He whom God has sent utters the words of God, for it is not by measure that he gives the Spirit.' Evidently God does not give the Holy Spirit quantitatively; hence, the terms 'baptism' and 'filling' cannot refer to the amount of the Spirit one receives. On the other hand individuals who are 'filled with the Spirit' may have different capacities; both a pint and a gallon container may be 'full' but contain different amounts.

The term *baptism with the Holy Spirit* seems to indicate the identification of the individual or group with God through Christ. It probably refers to the work of the Spirit in the new birth, the presence of the work of the Spirit as he brings and applies salvation. At times outward evidence of the baptism with the Holy Spirit occurs after the conversion experience. Visible and/or audible evidence do not always occur; in fact some evidence may indicate that these manifestations are associated only with new or special events in the experience of the Christian community.

The cases of Jesus and of the 120 disciples at Pentecost may indicate that the baptism and filling of the Holy Spirit are synonymous; these could also be interpreted as special cases in unusual circumstances. It is noteworthy that, except in the case of Jesus, the baptism of the Holy Spirit was always the experience of a group. Furthermore, the New Testament never speaks of the same group being baptized with the Holy Spirit more than once. It does report a repeated filling of the Holy Spirit upon some persons who had previously experienced it.

Hence, as stated above, the evidence seems to point toward the conclusion that usually baptism and filling of the Holy spirit refer to different phenomena. There are, however, additional questions. Should, must, this be a common, normative experience of all believers? Or, is this, in some way, an experience of only some individuals who have a special awareness of the presence of the Spirit in their lives? Is/are this/these experience(s) for the individual or only for the group? Are we speaking of acts and experiences limited to the Apostolic Age or should they be expected as an ongoing part of the life of the church?

The interpretation of the evidence of the Book of Acts is crucial. Four distinct comings of the Holy Spirit are recounted: (a) upon the Jewish believers in Jerusalem (2:4), (b) Samaritans (8:17), (c) Gentiles in the house of Cornelius (10:44), and (d) the disciples of John the Baptist (19:2-7). The laying on of hands is mentioned in connection with the second and fourth. Speaking in tongues is present in the first, third, and fourth. The coming of the Spirit was unexpected at Pentecost and in the house of Cornelius and so there was no laying on of hands; however, when it was expected the Christian leaders did lay hands on those who were to receive the Spirit. Does the silence about speaking in tongues in Samaria mean that sign does not necessarily accompany every incident of the coming of the Spirit or, since tongues were present at the other three, is the reader to assume it was present in Samaria as well? A further question is whether the experiences and phenomena of these occasions provide a pattern for what each or all Christians should expect or whether their occurrence had some other significance.

Some contend that all believers should/must have this experience with visible and/or audible confirming signs. They believe that people become consciously aware of the presence of the Holy Spirit either as the result of a crisis experience or as the conclusion of struggle and progress within the Christian life. Some Christians, especially those in Pentecostal and/or Holiness traditions insist that the baptism/ filling (frequently assumed to be synonyms) with the Holy Spirit comes in a special, distinct action of the church and/or of God; they often refer to this as 'the second work of grace' or 'the second blessing'. Formula-sequences, such as, (1) believe, (2) undergo water baptism, (3) pray, asking for the Spirit, (4) laying on of hands by a spirit-filled person or persons, and then, (5) the coming of the Holy Spirit (often accompanied by one or more 'gifts of the Spirit'), are sometimes put forth as the process through which a person is filled with and indwelt by the Spirit.

Other Christians argue that incidents such as those recorded in the Book of Acts were limited to special situations. Some (especially among those holding to the Reformed tradition) argue that 'signs and wonders' were given to validate new revelation from God. Now that the New Testament era has come to a close and in Christ God has given his final self-revelation, these external confirming events are no longer needed and do not occur. Others note that each of the four comings of the Holy Spirit in Acts accompanied a new phase of the geographical and/or racial expansion of the church. These comings of the Spirit, with various external signs, indicated God's approval of each new step. Consequently the experience may or may not be subsequently duplicated.

In other words, we face the question, are the experiences described in the New Testament, primarily in Acts, normative for the whole church and for all Christians in all times and places, or were or are they special divine acts given to provide confirmation at important junctures of the church's experience (past, present, or future), and/or in response to some specific needs?

My present opinion is that, in general, the New Testament evidence implies that the baptism with the Holy Spirit and the filling with the Holy Spirit refer to different occurrences. The baptism of the Spirit is his coming and/or presence which is the activity of God in his work of regenerating a person. The baptism of the Spirit is the activity of the Spirit in the new birth and in identifying the individual with the community of the People of God. As George E. Ladd says, 'The baptism with the Spirit is the act of the Holy Spirit joining together into a spiritual unity people of diverse racial extractions and diverse backgrounds so that they form the body of Christ – the *ekklēsia*.'[46]

The filling of the Holy Spirit may come at the time of conversion or on later occasions. Its purpose is to meet some special need or to provide some special ability for the benefit of the Christian community. It may be repeated when God considers it advantageous. Outward signs or abilities too may or may not accompany the filling of the Spirit depending on what is necessary 'for the common good' (1 Cor 12:7) of the church.

However, I refuse to judge the validity of another's claim of an experience of the Holy Spirit – 1 Corinthians 14:32-33 calls for the evaluation of what seems to be Spirit-given activities and abilities, but only by the church. I am among neither those who restrict the special activities and fillings with the Spirit to only one period of church history nor those who believe it to be prescriptive and normative for all. It is God who determines when, to whom, and for what purpose he makes these things available, 'The things of the Holy Spirit are distributed according to his own will' (Heb 2:4).

I cannot accept the implication that the Biblical data in referring to the filling of the Spirit is speaking of an initial coming of the Holy

---

[46]George E. Ladd, *A Theology of the New Testament*, 384.

Spirit upon those who are already Christians but are without the Spirit. (A Spiritless Christian, one not born of the Spirit, is a contradiction in terms.) Nor does it seem that the phrase 'filled with the Spirit' refers to a quantitative presence of the Holy Spirit.

I place considerable weight on the words 'yield,' 'do not resist' nor 'quench' the Spirit. Perhaps, the Biblical data may refer to two things. First, it may refer to receiving the Spirit in the sense of becoming consciously aware of his presence and activity. We may know of the presence of a guest in our home, but not until we walk into the same room with him or her and 'receive' our guest do we begin to reap the full benefit of his or her presence. So too awareness of the presence of the Spirit is necessary for him to have full control. Second, a container may be 'full' but still not hold as much as another, larger one. As the Christian grows, the capacity for awareness of and the work of the Holy Spirit within grows as well.

Receiving the Spirit, becoming consciously aware of his presence, involves both knowledge (as was necessary in Acts 19:2-7) and experience. The concept of more of the Spirit, which may be implied in the forms of the word 'fill,' may refer to growth, enlarged capacity.

The significance of the construction of the verb in the statement given above from Ephesians 5:18, translated, 'Be filled (*plērousthe*) with the Spirit,' is too often overlooked. It is in the imperative mood, thereby expressing a command or strong admonition. The passive voice denotes something that is done to rather than by the subject and the present tense denotes a continuing action. It is directed to the church, for it is second person plural. The call is for a constant, continuing yielding, letting God, through his Spirit, be sovereign in the life of the community, 'You (plural) be continually filled with the Spirit.'

Finally, whatever the details, the church needs to become more aware of and yield to the person and work of the Holy Spirit. The power of the church is not her organization, the brilliance of her leaders, the effectiveness of her methods and techniques, the efficiency of her advertising, or the oratorical skill of her preachers. Let it be clear that the power of the church is the presence and activity of the Holy Spirit working within her, both as individuals and as the body.

Chapter 9

What is the Church?
The Mission, Task, and Activities of the Church

Mission, Task, and Activities in General

The mission and task of the church are to worship, honor, and serve God as she makes known God's person, will, and work through Jesus Christ. It is significant that Acts (1:3) records that one of the main activities of Jesus during the forty days between his resurrection and ascension was 'speaking of the kingdom of God.' The kingdom was a primary focus of the teachings and activities of Jesus. The question of the disciples about 'restoring the kingdom to Israel' (1:6) indicated they still didn't get it – they continued to think of the kingdom in earthly, political, nationalistic terms. The ascension and coming of the Holy Spirit at Pentecost brought that idea to an end. The controversy associated with the conversion of the Gentiles clarified that the Jesus-Son of Man, now at the right hand of the Father, exercises 'dominion and glory and kingdom, that all peoples, nations, and languages should serve him; his dominion is an everlasting dominion, which shall not pass away' (Dan 7:14).

The church's mission, task, and activities were similar to those of Jesus, to live under the sovereignty of God and to announce, explain, and call people into the kingdom. This, of course, was possible only because God had extended his love and grace in Jesus, through whom forgiveness of sins and reconciliation are possible.

Acts 2–6 gives a summary and introduction to the life and activities of the earliest Christian community. It engaged in (1) preaching, (2) baptizing, (3) teaching, (4) fellowship, (5) breaking bread, (6) 'the prayers,'[1] and (7) praising God. Their life and attitude was

---

[1] Possibly meaning continuing use of the times for and wording of prayers in Judaism as well as distinctive, spontaneous Christian prayers such as those recorded in these chapters.

characterized by (8) fear, that is, a reverential awe, a healthy respect for God and his work among them, and (9) joy. They (10) gathered both in the temple and at home. As the need arose they (11) shared their goods with other believers. These activities of the church were carried on by both individuals and the group as a whole as they were keenly aware of the presence of the Holy Spirit within them. He was a part of all they did; when he was not so acknowledged, the church got into trouble.

More detailed information about the activities of the church is scattered throughout the New Testament. We learn of these more often in descriptions of her endeavors, as we see the church in action, than in statements of principles or abstract discussions. It is helpful to summarize briefly the work of the church under the headings of those to whom its activities were directed – God, believers, the church itself, and the world at large.

The Church's Obligation to God

The first obligation of the church is to God. Paul includes reference to the amazing scope of the responsibility of the church as he speaks of his own duty 'to preach to the Gentiles the unsearchable riches of Christ, and to make all men see what is the plan of the mystery hidden for ages in God who created all things' (Eph 3:8-9). However, his work is a part of the broader mission of the church, carried out

> that through the church the manifold [many sided] wisdom of God might be made known to the principalities and powers in heavenly places. This was according to the eternal purpose which he has realized in Christ Jesus our Lord, in whom we have boldness and confidence of access through our faith in him (Eph 3:10-12).

The church's obligation to God includes its responsibility to be the means of communicating to all, including evil 'principalities and powers' what God has been doing since eternity past and which has now reached its crisis point in Christ. The church is God's 'new thing' which participates in his age-old plan and purpose that affects all nations, all the world, and beyond! This it does as it carries out a number of more specific functions and duties.

The church owes to God its worship, adoration, thanksgiving, and complete obedience. To do so she must, as we have often said, be continually getting to know him and his will better. To accomplish this the first church pored over what we now call the Old Testament and reflected upon the words and work of Jesus Christ. Contemporary Christians still have the Old Testament and also the New Testament; the tragedy is that these Scriptures are used more often to meet our immediate needs and to find help for present situations than to become better acquainted with God. The second duty of the church to God is to participate in his work. The church has distinct responsibilities as the people of God in the Final Age, the latter part of Salvation History. It is within the church that God continues to work; to her, as his 'special possession', he has given directives for proclamation, instruction, activities, and life.

The church has the obligation to make God known and to carry out his work. As just noted Paul explains his own mission as the proclamation of 'the unsearchable riches of Christ ... to make all men see what is the plan of the mystery hidden for ages in God who created all things' (Eph 3:8-9). This is surely the church's responsibility as well. But there is more. Paul speaks of God's design, 'that through the church the manifold wisdom of God might now be made known to the principalities and powers in the heavenly places. This was according to the eternal purpose that he has realized in Christ Jesus our Lord' (Eph 3:10-11). From the beginning God intended that the church make known God's person, wisdom, and power to spiritual powers, including evil ones, as well as to people.

The Church's Obligation to Individual Christians

Teaching
The church has obligations to believers, that is, to individual Christians. Significantly, the first activity of those converted at Pentecost, following their receiving the word and baptism, is that 'they devoted themselves to the apostles' teaching' (Acts 2:42). The church is a teaching-learning society. After its duties to God, the first obligation of the church is to its own, and instruction must have high priority.

Learning is hard and laborious work (Eccles 12:12). Modern Christians often prefer to have their 'felt needs' addressed first – improving self-image, fellowship, support, help with specific problems – but the 'real needs,' which must be met include instruction, 'teaching,... reproof,... correction, and ... training in righteousness' (2 Tim 3:16). (If priority were given to 'felt needs' in rearing children many would seldom eat vegetables, go to school, practice elementary hygiene.)

What should the church teach? Scholars have been more successful in outlining the basic content of the church's preaching for conversion (its evangelistic preaching), the *kērugma*, than identifying the content of its teaching (*didachē*). Nevertheless, it is possible to get some idea of the curriculum, the content of educational work in the New Testament church. Certainly, it sought to teach the broader implications of the basic message, the *kērugma*. This seems evident from the fact that potential Jewish converts at Beroea examined 'the Scriptures daily to see if these things were so' (Acts 17:11). 'The Scriptures' mentioned here were the Old Testament; Jewish converts would come to the faith with a basic knowledge of it. This was not the case with Gentile believers. Yet, the New Testament epistles, including those written to predominately Gentile churches or individuals, assume the readers are familiar with the contents of the Hebrew Scriptures – its history, people, and basic teachings. Furthermore, the writers of the Epistles proceed with the assumption that their readers have a basic understanding of how the Old Testament should be interpreted. They could not have done so had they not been sure that in some way Gentile converts had been instructed in these matters. Early Christian education, it seems, included solid 'courses' in Old Testament survey and principles and methods for interpretation (hermeneutics).

Basic Christian teachings or doctrines also appear to have been a part of the church's teaching ministry. Exposition of the essential message, the *kērugma*, would have provided the first level of this. The language of 1 Corinthians 15:1 suggests that in preaching the gospel Paul was aware of passing on established tradition, the essential teachings of Christianity. This also seems to be assumed elsewhere in the New Testament. The first eleven chapters of Paul's own letter to the Romans presents something of a sketch of Christian doctrines; perhaps here we may get some idea of another part of the content of 'the apostles' teaching'.

In our previous chapter on 'How Should Believers Live?' we had much to say about ethics, directives and guidelines for conduct. We noted two important points: first, the Christian conviction that there are moral, ethical, behavioral implications for the lives of believers. There is a connection between faith and life. Although Jewish converts would have assumed as much, the notion of the necessary connection between religion and behavior was initially foreign to many Gentile believers. Second, under the guidance of the Holy Spirit, the early Christians recognized specific 'dos and don'ts' and guidelines for areas in which Christian freedom is to be exercised with responsibility. Again, the certainty that these things were well known to the readers of the epistles leads us to conclude that the teaching of the early church included ethical instruction to new converts.

Matthew 28:18-20, the 'Great Commission,' spells out the church's responsibility for evangelizing, proclaiming the gospel, to 'all nations ... to the close of the age,' that is, during the whole of the Final Age. This commission may outline areas of Christian teaching as well. The command is to 'make disciples', that is 'to make learners or students.' Then follow elements of disciple–making, baptizing (presumably including an explanation of what the act means) and teaching observance of the commandments of Jesus. Winning converts and instructing them in the faith may be distinguished (the one from the other), but never separated!

Fellowship

Another part of the ministry of the church to its own is to provide an atmosphere for fellowship, that is the mutual up-building, help, and the support that comes from other believers who 'love one another.' Psalm 68:6 says, 'God gives the desolate a home to dwell in' ('God sets the lonely in families,' in the NIV). At the dawn of human existence God recognized, 'It is not good that the man should be alone,' and so woman was created and marriage instituted (Gen 2:18, 21-24). Humans also need broader associations, with groups and communities. When God began his special work in Salvation History he selected a man and his family, Abraham, through whom he would provide the blessing of salvation. The nation Israel became the community of the People of God. So too the church. In its internal relations, described in Acts 2–6, 'fellowship' is one of the initial features of its life.

Fellowship (*koinōnia*) means more than simply getting together or associating. The root of the Greek word carries both the ideas of *common* and *sharing*. Hence, the idea behind it is sharing that which is held in common; in the case of the first Christians it was faith in Jesus Christ which they held in common. In Acts 2:42, where the word is first used of the church, 'fellowship,' was based on the apostles' teaching, included 'the breaking of bread' (probably, 'having meals together'), prayer, and holding goods in common (2:44). Although included in fellowship, this sharing does not refer exclusively to material goods. Paul does use the word at least partly in that sense in Philippians 4:15 – there he insists that because the Philippians shared their material goods with him, they also participated (shared together) in his ministry. Perhaps the word *commonality,* including sharing all of life in the bonds which held them together in Christ, catches the idea of what 'fellowship' meant in the early church.

Meeting Material Needs
The statement in Acts 2:44-45, 'All who believed . . . had all things in common; and they sold their possessions and goods and distributed them to all, as any had need,' requires some comment. Is the church essentially a communal society in the sense that all material possessions of its members should be merged into a central treasury? This has certainly been one of the models that some Christians have followed throughout history. Nevertheless, several observations should be made to keep in perspective the experience and practice of the Jerusalem Church described in the early chapters of Acts.

This sharing of goods was an expression of (1) enthusiasm and love in the fresh flush of the excitement at the beginnings of Christians' fellowship together.

(2) There is some indication that it may have been practiced in view of the expectation of the soon return of Christ, under which circumstances, long range planning for material needs would have been considered unnecessary.

More important, these acts of generosity were probably (3) responses to an emergency situation; many of the new converts were not residents of Jerusalem but had come to celebrate the Passover festival. Their stay was prolonged, possibly so they might become better informed of 'the apostles' teaching' and to enjoy fellowship with other believers. In any case, these new believers from afar had only limited resources available to them. At least some Jerusalem Christians generously shared with them.

It is essential to remember that, unlike many communal experiments and twentieth century Communism, contributions were (4) voluntary. Ananias and Sapphira were punished, not for holding back part of their funds, but for deception, for seeking credit for a higher level of generosity than they actually offered. Regarding their property, Peter clearly states, 'While it remained unsold, did it not remain your own? And after it was sold, was it not at your disposal?... You have not lied to men but to God ... you have agreed together to tempt the Spirit of the Lord' (Acts 5:4, 9).

(5) The long-term result of these actions was the impoverishment of the Jerusalem Church. Although there may be much more involved in the gifts of Gentile churches to Jerusalem,[2] such assistance was needed and the 'Pillars' of that church, through Paul and Barnabas, requested the Church of Antioch, 'Keep on remembering the poor' (Gal 2:10).

Finally, (6) this form of communal living did not become the norm or only model for Christians, either in the New Testament era or afterwards.

Nevertheless, the New Testament writers are clear that those in the family of God are to respond to the needs of those about them.

---

[2]Acts 11:27-30; 1 Corinthians 16:1-4; 2 Corinthians 8:1–9:15; Romans 15:15, 25-27.

Concern for justice, ministry to the needs of the hungry and thirsty, strangers, the naked, sick, and imprisoned (cf. Matt 25:34-45), the orphans and widows is at the heart of attitudes and concerns stemming from the new nature in Christ.

The Church's Obligation to Herself

The activities of the church toward herself, as a body, include seeking to maintain her peace, order, purity, and focus.

Maintain Peace

New Testament expressions of the desire and necessity of peace in the church are far too numerous to even begin to record. They are contained in the opening of virtually every epistle and many of their closing sections. 'Peace,' a characteristic of the fruit of the Spirit, is expected in the corporate as well as the individual expressions of Christianity (Gal 5:22). Peace in the church is a reflection of the nature of her God; in appealing for peace Paul reminds the Corinthians, 'God is not a God of confusion but of peace' (1 Cor 14:33); the Ephesians, he says, should be 'eager to maintain the unity of the Spirit in the bond of peace' (Eph 4:3). He charges the Thessalonians, 'Be at peace among yourselves' (1 Thess 5:13) and 'may the Lord of peace himself give you peace at all times in all ways' (2 Thess 3:16). The Epistles to the Hebrews charges, 'Strive for peace with all men, and for the holiness without which no one will see the Lord' (12:14), and James says, 'The harvest of righteousness is sown in peace by those who make peace' (Jas 3:18). Peter admonishes the churches to whom he writes, 'Seek peace and pursue it' (1 Pet 3:11). The goal of the church is that finally it might 'be found by him without spot or blemish, and at peace' (2 Pet 3:14). The contentiousness so often found within the church is a denial of her oneness and unity and a detriment to fulfilling her mission and task.

Maintain Order

Paul's well-known admonition, 'All things should be done decently and in order' (1 Cor 14:40), speaks clearly of the church's responsibility to maintain order. Elsewhere in the epistles, time and again, the writers seek to establish or maintain order in those churches to whom they write. Order also includes proper relationships within Christian households. The epistles give instruction to maintain order among husbands, wives, children, masters, servants, and slaves.[3]

Maintain Purity and Discipline

The concern for the purity of the church is reflected in 2 Peter 3:14, quoted just above. The apostle desires that the church be 'without spot or blemish.' By the 'purity of the church' we have in mind the moral uprightness of her members, but much more as well. The church must be concerned for her own purity of worship, of doctrine, and of her relation to the world.

The church best maintains her peace, order, and purity by maintaining Jesus Christ as the center of her focus. Paul reveals his personal focus to the Philippians,

> Not that I have already obtained this or am already perfect; but I press on to make it my own, because Christ Jesus has made me his own . . . forgetting what lies behind and straining forward to what lies ahead, I press on toward the goal for the prize of the upward call of God in Christ Jesus (Phil 3:12-14).

To the Colossians he says,

> If then you have been raised with Christ, seek the things that are above, where Christ is, seated at the right hand of God. Set your minds on things that are above, not on things that are on earth. For you have died, and your life is hid with Christ in God. When Christ who is our life appears, then you also will appear with him in glory (Col 3:1-4).

The verbs in this and the following passage are plural; they refer to the church as a whole. The writer to the Hebrews admonishes,

---

[3]Ephesians 5:21–6:9; Colossians 3:18–4:6; 1 Peter 2:18–3:12.

Let us run with perseverance the race that is set before us, looking
to Jesus the pioneer and perfecter of our faith, who for [instead
of] the joy that was set before him endured the cross, despising
the shame, and is seated at the right hand of the throne of God.
Consider him who endured from sinners such hostility against
himself, so that you may not grow weary or fainthearted (Heb
12:1-3).

The more the church turns away from focusing upon the person,
work, and commission of Jesus Christ, the more she turns aside
from her mission and task.

The word *discipline* has a number of meanings. It may refer to
teaching or instruction in general, to a particular branch or field of
study, or training which corrects, molds, and strengthens. Discipline
may refer to the control and enforcement of order and conduct or
to the punishment which follows breaking rules or disrupting order.
The church is to discipline herself and her members in each of these
senses of the word. Here we will mention two specifically.

The church must discipline by correcting wrong thoughts or
doctrines. Paul told the Ephesian elders that even from among
themselves would come persons who would speak 'perverse things,
to draw away the disciples after them. Therefore be alert' (Acts
20:30-31). He informed Titus that church officers (and in this context
he mentions elders, 1:5, and a bishop as a steward, 1:7) must 'be
able to give instruction in sound doctrine and also to confute those
who contradict it' (1:9).

Right doctrine is not determined by majority vote, by compromise
as a result of discussion, by reason, or by political manipulations. It
is to be evaluated on the basis of its conformity to the word of God.
Right doctrine, sound words, are those which are in agreement with
Jesus Christ.

If any one ... does not agree with the sound words of our Lord
Jesus Christ and the teaching which accords with godliness, he is
puffed up with conceit, he knows nothing; he has a morbid craving
for controversy and for disputes about words, which produce envy,
dissension, slander, base suspicions, and wrangling among men

who are depraved in mind and bereft of the truth, imagining that godliness is a means of gain (1 Tim 6:3-5).

The church has sometimes suffered from overly zealous 'heresy hunters' who want to quibble about minutia. Nevertheless, to the church as a whole Jude appeals, 'Contend for the faith which was once for all delivered to the saints' (vs. 3). Discipline, in the sense of instructing in the truth and guarding against error, is a part of the mission, task, and assigned activities of the church.

While the purity of the church includes *orthodoxy*, right doctrine or belief, it also requires *orthopraxy*, right conduct and actions. The church must 'discipline,' guide, and direct its members so that their lives are in harmony with their belief, the teachings of the church; that their lives are worthy of Jesus Christ. Jesus himself sketched out procedures for dealing with a sinning fellow Christian in Matthew 18:15-20. Paul too gives some guidelines in 1 Corinthians 6:1-11 and insists that one who persists in open sin is to be 'removed from among you' (excommunicated! 1 Cor 5:1-13). He also speaks of the 'other side' of discipline when he calls for forgiveness and the restoration of a repentant offender (2 Cor 2:5-11). It requires a delicate balance. For, furthering the peace and unity of the church cannot be done at the expense of its purity. Hers cannot be an 'anything goes' unity; it must be a unity based on Jesus Christ and the Scriptural teachings about him and his will.

The Church's Obligation to the World

The mission, task, and activities of the church contain also a responsibility to the world at large. Most obvious is the privilege and task of evangelization, of announcing the 'good news' of salvation in Christ, of proclaiming the *kērugma*. We have commented on the fact of this responsibility as we considered the 'Great Commission' (Matt 28:18-20) and outlined the content of evangelistic preaching. We must mention two other parts of the church's mission to the world that are corollaries to proclamation.

First is Godly living. As 1 Peter 4:15 says, 'Let none of you suffer as a murderer, or a thief, or a wrongdoer, or a mischief-maker.' This, to say the least, is a rather negative way to present the Christian life. However, earlier, the same apostle admonished women married to unbelievers to live so that their mates 'may be won without a word by the behavior of their wives' (1 Pet 3:1-2). The same principle holds true for other Christians. A consistent Christian life, exhibited before the world, can be a powerful tool for attracting non-Christians to Christ.

The defense and explanation of the gospel is a part of the church's obligation to the world. This duty is often called the *apology* or *apologetic*.[4] This does not mean to make an excuse for Christianity. Rather it refers to giving a careful explanation or making a clear defense for it. This is what is envisioned in 1 Peter 3:15, 'Always be prepared to make a defense (*apologian*) to anyone who calls you to account for the hope that is in you, yet do it with gentleness and reverence.' The church owes the world a clear explanation of what it is and what it is doing.

In the parable of the 'Good Samaritan' (Luke 10:25-37) Jesus makes it clear that the 'neighbor' is any person in need whom the believer may encounter. The victim to whom the Samaritan ministered was a member of another ethnic group and religion. To say to the destitute, 'Go in peace, be warmed and filled' is not enough, such springs from that faith which by itself is dead (Jas 2:16-17). The summary of the Christian ethic which includes, 'love ... your neighbor as yourself' includes the church's ministry to the suffering in the world at large.

The mission, task, and activities of the church are summed up in being faithful to her Lord and Head. The church must recognize herself as his servant, to do his bidding. This includes responsibilities to Jesus Christ, to herself, to the believers who are in her, and to those without, be they friend or foe.

---

[4]From the Greek *apologia*.

A Healing Community[5]

Jesus assumed that his followers are in the world but not of it (John, chapters 14–17). He predicted they would be misunderstood, hated, despised, isolated, tortured, and killed; even as was he mistreated, maligned, rejected, and executed (Matt 10:25; John 15:18). Being treated unjustly, wounded, feeling helpless, alone, and abused by society is an experience not restricted to Christians. Many non-believers as well as believers are inwardly, if not also outwardly, lonely, abused, afraid, angry, and traumatized in general. Hence, in summary, the church has the obligation and the privilege of addressing this situation and need.

Jesus called, 'Come to me, all who labor and are heavy laden,... learn from me.... I am gentle and lowly in heart, and you will find rest for your souls' (Matt 11:28-29). Healing was an important part in his ministry and that of the early church. Jesus said he was sent to the sick and to call 'not the righteous but the unrighteous' (Matt 9:12; Mark 2:17; Luke 5:31-32). As the Great Shepherd he ministered to the lost, the confused, the hurt, and the dying. The word for 'pastor' and that for 'shepherd' are the same (*poimēn*); the pastor not only does the work of the shepherding but works in a community that carries on the same function. It is not without significance that the grace/spiritual things, the so-called gifts of the Spirit, which are intended to assist the church carry on her work, include helps, ministering, healing, and the like.

One of the ways to summarize the mission, task, and activities of the church is to do so under the metaphor of 'healing community.' This has implications for the individual within the group as well as the community itself. In her work of evangelism, to the unrighteous the church issues the invitation to receive righteousness through Christ. The new Christian finds this community to be composed of those like themselves, who have been brought in by the grace of God in Jesus Christ.

These new believers, upon entering the church, bring their old wounds with them. Here they also find sufferings for a different set

---

[5]See also *A Generation Alone*, 71-114.

of reasons. Christians suffer because although not of it they are still in the world – abused, rejected, mistreated, traumatized in many ways simply because they belong to Christ. A dominant feature of Christians is that they 'love one another'[6] no matter how humble, objectionable, or revolting 'the other' may be. All within the church-community should find acceptance by the body, personal value because they have been bought with a price (1 Cor 6:20) ... ransomed ... with the precious blood of Christ (1 Pet 1:18-19).

Both the body and each person within it has the responsibility for the healing and nurture of these babes in Christ and for support for all within the church. The community with the great shepherd/ physician as its head is a shelter in the midst of hostile forces to provide safety, rest, comfort, acceptance, assistance, learning, fellowship (*koinōnia*) in its fullest form, in short, for healing.

Ordinances/Sacraments of the Church

There are certain rites or ceremonies, instituted by Christ, which are to be observed and practiced by the church. Their use should bring Christians closer to their Lord and to each other. In fact they have often been the cause of deep and bitter divisions within the church. The first area of disagreement involves the name given these rites or ceremonies, ordinances or sacraments. An *ordinance* is simply that which has been commanded. The observers believe themselves to be obeying the command of Christ. There is nothing more involved than remembering and obeying. Those who employ the term *sacrament* see an element of spiritual mystery involved in participating in the ceremony. Not only are they remembering and obeying Christ, but something inexplicable is taking place; a sacrament makes something happen.

Another area of controversy involves the number of such special rites or ceremonies. Both the Roman Catholic and the Eastern Orthodox churches recognize seven: baptism, confirmation, the Eucharist (Mass), penance, extreme unction (last rites for the dying), ordination to holy orders, and marriage. Others insist that only two

---

[6] 1 John 3:11, 14, 24; 4:11, 12.

of these, baptism and the Lord's Supper (or any of its many other designations) alone are clearly designated as an ordinance or sacrament in the New Testament. It is with these we will deal.

There are also a number of controversies about both baptism and the Lord's Supper that set some Christians apart from the other. Although not strictly a part of Biblical theology, we will try to summarize briefly the major elements of those disagreements. But first we will briefly look at the Biblical evidence pertaining to baptism and the Lord's Supper.

Baptism

What has the Biblical student to say about baptism? She or he is likely to argue that the Biblical data is insufficient for giving a final, dogmatic answer to any of the debated questions. However, such a person might want to focus study upon the Bible in its linguistic and historical setting, minimizing the issues and opinions that have been associated with discussions of baptism in post-Biblical Christian history.

If a person with no previous contact with Christianity began reading the Bible through consecutively, he or she would meet the word *baptism,* or some form of it, first in Matthew 3:1, 'In those days came John the Baptist' and 3:5, which states that those who came to him 'were baptized by him in the river Jordan, confessing their sins.' Later, our new Bible reader would learn that John said, 'I baptize you with water for repentance, but he who is coming after me is mightier than I ... he will baptize you with the Holy Spirit and with fire' (Matt 3:11). Continued reading would indicate that in addition to baptism 'with fire,' noted here, that baptism by the Holy Spirit, mentioned in John's preaching, is also found in Acts 1:5 and 11:16 (quoting John the Baptist). In addition, baptism may be a symbol for martyrdom (Mark 10:38-39; Matt 20:22-23) and the Israelites were said to have been 'baptized unto Moses in the cloud' (1 Cor 10:2). Jesus made a cryptic statement, 'I have a baptism with which to be baptized; and how I am constrained until it is accomplished' (Luke 12:50). There are in Acts and the epistles accounts of believers being baptized, but only twice, Acts 8:36-38 and 10:47, is water specifically mentioned as a part of the ceremony. Hence, if the claim is accepted that the Greek word *baptizō* always refers to 'immerse,' 'dip,' 'cover with,' or 'submerged in,' then some, if not all, of these non-water references must be taken figuratively.

Romans 6:1-11 is another significant passage often cited in the discussion of baptism. Paul says the Christian has 'been baptized into Christ Jesus ... baptized into his death' (vs. 3). The following verse speaks of dying, being buried, and rising with Christ. Paul's central focus is that Christians who in union with Christ have 'died to sin' must not 'still live in it ... [but] walk in newness of life' (vss. 2, 4). He sees baptism as significant in union with Christ. But, does he anywhere assume that it is baptism which effects that union, testifies to it, or makes a general reference to it? Some interpreters argue that Romans 6 indicates Paul believed that baptism actually initiates the individual into the death, burial, and resurrection of Jesus. Others believe that it refers more generally to one's acceptance and commitment to Christ as savior and Lord. In any case, baptism is seen here as an indication of a special point which should signal a radical change of lifestyle.

A new Bible reader might thus conclude that baptism is a religious act which may, but not necessarily, involve the application of water. It seems to be an act which is associated with the forgiveness of sins[7] and the identification of the baptized with the triune God (Matt 28:19) and/or with Christ (Acts 2:38; 8:12; 10:48; Rom 6:3; Gal 3:27).

Our novice Bible reader might remember that in the Old Testament, water was frequently applied in the various cleansing rituals in which a Hebrew who, having become unclean, was made clean and once again able to associate with other Hebrews. If this were an enquiring person she or he might also be aware that application of water was a part of the life of some Jewish groups or parties, such as the writers of the Dead Sea Scrolls, who used it both as a part of their ritual for initiating new members into the group and as a regular part of their religious observances. The problem lies that in both the Old

---

[7]Acts 2:38; cf. Mark 1:4; Luke 3:3.

Testament and Intertestamental Judaism the application of water was frequently repeated, except in initiation ceremonies. There is no New Testament evidence of Christian baptism ever being repeated.

Further, an observant reader might note that there was a difference between the baptism of John the Baptist and Christian baptism. The former was in preparation for someone who was coming, the Messiah; the latter because he had already come.

On such minimal evidence, a person first meeting Christianity, might conclude that Christian baptism (1) is a religious ceremony, (2) it relates both to identification of the person with Christ and to the forgiveness of sins, (3) it usually involves the application of water, and (4) through baptism the one who is an 'outsider' (either unclean or a non-member) is brought into and recognized as a part of the community. Its emphasis is upon identification with Christ and with his people.

Regarding infant baptism, many of those who baptize infants argue that just as (they believe) the Lord's Supper succeeds the Jewish Passover, so baptism replaces Old Testament circumcision. Circumcision was administered to male babies of the covenant community (females were represented in the male head of their families). Without instruction to the contrary Jewish Christians would have assumed their children were included in the new covenant community and, therefore, baptism was available to children of Christian parents. Romans 4:11, so they argue, indicates that circumcision was not just a nationalistic sign, but also religious, Abraham 'received circumcision as a sign or seal of the righteousness which he had by faith.' Colossians 2:9-15 may associate circumcision and baptism. All persons whose baptism is related in the New Testament were first generation Christians; we have no information concerning whether or not the children of Christian parents were baptized.

Contemporary controversy about the meaning of this New Testament data centers around four major questions. The first is 'What does baptism mean or do?' Does it make something happen? And if so, what? Of those who argue that baptism really does something, one opinion holds that it actually washes sins away, that the act of baptism saves the person.[8] Others insist that baptism identifies the individual with the death and resurrection of Christ, and it is Christ, in his death and resurrection, who washes sins away. A second group insist that baptism itself does nothing other than to testify that something has already or is in the process of taking place. Again, we face a difference of opinion: to what does it testify? Some argue that it signifies the coming of the Holy Spirit or his presence in the individual; others argue that the individual has previously established a relationship with God.

The second major question is, 'Is baptism necessary?' The majority would answer, 'Yes,' but there the agreement ends. Some Christian groups insist that it is a required condition for salvation, others that it is necessary as a testimony that one has come into a relationship with God. A third group believe baptism is mandatory in order to obey Christ who commanded it. Some argue that baptism is not necessary because (1) it is optional, (2) it is now obsolete, or (3) it is for another period of time within God's work on Earth to provide salvation.

The third question is, 'How should the water be applied?' Roman Catholics, Lutherans, Anglican-Episcopalians, Reformed Protestant Christians, and Methodists baptize by sprinkling or pouring water on the head of the individual – as was frequently done in Old Testament washing ceremonies.[9] A second opinion, held by Baptist and Anabaptist communions, Pentecostals, and many independent congregations is that proper baptism involves totally submerging the individual in water – as was done in some Jewish cleansing rites and in the ceremonies of some first century Jewish groups. Others, believing the mode of baptism to be optional, will accept either of these two.[10]

---

[8] As is implied in the word 'christen', which means 'to make Christian'.

[9] Note that Old Testament cleansing rituals, as described in Exodus, Leviticus, and Numbers, often involved sprinkling blood, oil, or water. Ezekiel 36:25 makes direct reference to this mode of applying water.

[10] As is the position in the *Didache*, an early church manual dating about AD 100.

Our final controversial area involves the question, 'Who should be baptized?' One group asserts that proper subjects for baptism must be old enough to understand what is happening and to believe in Jesus. Other Christians insist that both believers and their families, including children, are to be baptized.

The purpose of infant baptism, however, is defined in different ways, even among those who practice it. Some baptize the very young believing that by it the child is saved. Others believe that as baptism is performed the Christian community recognizes that this child has been born into the family of faith and claims for it the faith of the parents. Yet a third group holds that in presenting their child for baptism, parents are recognizing the need of the child for salvation, claiming God's promises on her or his behalf, requesting the work of the Holy Spirit in the life of the child, and acknowledging and calling on the Christian community to have a part in bringing this person to the point of personal faith and commitment.

A few, believing baptism saves the individual, argue that everyone should be baptized, whether they are aware of it or not. This idea and practice were common in the Middle Ages, but are not now prevalent.

The Lord's Supper

In the night in which he was betrayed,[11] Jesus took bread, broke it, gave it to his disciples saying, 'Do this in remembrance of me.' He also took the cup, gave it to them saying, 'Drink, all of you, of it.' His other words on that occasion speak of his desire to eat with them, include that the broken bread was 'my body broken for you,' the cup was 'the blood of the new covenant shed for you, for the forgiveness of sins,' the command to do this 'in remembrance of me', 'as often as you eat this bread and drink the cup, you proclaim the Lord's death until he comes,' and 'from now on I shall not drink of the fruit of the vine until the kingdom of God comes.' These actions and words of Jesus are the basis for an important observance by contemporary Christians that is called by a number of different names:

---

[11]A summary of the record in Mark 14:27-25; Matthew 26:26-29; Luke 22:14-22; and 1 Corinthians 11:23-26.

Eucharist, Communion, the Holy Communion, Mass, Lord's Supper, The Last Supper, The Love Feast, and others.

In our chapter on salvation we noted the three tenses of the verb in New Testament passages relating to the Lord's Supper. It is a memorial of the life and ministry, and death and resurrection of Jesus in the *past*, a communion and fellowship with him who is with us both here on earth and also at the right hand of the Father in the *present*, and an anticipation of his *future* return when he will eat and drink with his own in the Kingdom of God.

The meaning of Jesus' statement that his body was 'broken for you' is seldom discussed. Most probably assume it is a synonym for his death. The treatment Jesus received between his arrest and crucifixion was brutal torture his body bore. Crucifixion was the most painful and degrading death to which a person could be subjected. As the shedding of his blood speaks of Jesus' death (nb., Lev 17:11, "...the life of the flesh is in the blood ... for it is the blood that makes atonement by the life"), so may the breaking of his body refer to the awful suffering his body bore.

As was true of baptism, there is considerable diversity of opinion regarding a number of features of this observance. The most significant disagreement centers around the meaning of Jesus' words, 'This is my body, this is my blood' in referring to the bread and the wine. The major opinions hold some form of one of the following interpretations. In the ceremony, the body of Christ is, in some sense, actually present; but, in what sense? The four major views hold that:

(1) the bread and wine are miraculously transformed into the actual, physical body and blood of Jesus;

(2) the actual physical body of Christ is present along with the bread and wine (the partaker receives both the physical elements of bread and wine and the real body and blood of Christ);

(3) as believers partake of the bread and wine the spiritual presence of Christ is with his followers in a unique way; or, finally that

(4) in the communion the presence of Jesus is limited to the minds and memory of his followers; some insist this is simply a memorial service of the life and death of Jesus.

These disputes must not be allowed to blind us to the fact that in this ceremony the church gathers with its Head, the bride dines with her Husband, and the Lord with his friends and disciples. It is the Lord's table. Its place in the life of the church reminds again that for all its limitations, foibles, fallibility, faults, and failures it has a matchless Head. It is he whose broken body and shed blood bought her forgiveness; it is he who gives the church her life and meaning, and it is through the Spirit whom he has sent that she has power. 'The church's one foundation is Jesus Christ her Lord!'

Liabilities (Dangers for) the Church

The glory of the church is her Lord; its true treasure, the gospel, the good news, that all who repent are already forgiven.[12] Unlike all other earthly organizations, the church is a spiritual community. But she is indeed earthly and so has liabilities and faces dangers.

All hindrances to individual Christian growth, some of which are noted in a preceding chapter, are also liabilities for the church. She must live and work in a hostile environment. Her enemy is defeated but not yet eliminated. Yet her biggest problem is that she is comprised of people, sinful human beings, saved, forgiven human beings, yes, but still human. Her members are pilgrims still in progress. Their final sanctification, perfection, lies yet in the future. And these humans are, oh, so human! And humans are capable of unbelievable atrocities, including the barbarism of the Crusades in the Middle Ages and anti-Semitism which continues to our own day. The church has too often failed to stand for righteousness, justice, truth, mercy, and peace which are the bedrock of the society of the people of God in both testaments. A seminary professor of mine once told our class, 'You will never be in a perfect church, because you will be in it.' And through the ages the church has endured, suffered through, the growing pains of God's children.

The next chapter is devoted to the relation between the church and society and culture. Here we make comments about a few perennial problems. Earlier we noted the case of 'Diotrephes, who likes to put himself first' (3 John 9) and the 'personality cults' in

---

[12]This last phrase is a summary of Martin Luther's 'Ninety Five Theses.'

Corinth. The church is not the only organization humans have sought
to use for their own self-ends – to enhance their own prestige, power,
wealth, or personal pleasure and gratification. Some of these may
be genuine Christians, others counterfeit believers; we often have
no way of knowing which – only God can judge hearts.

Nevertheless, Paul is sure that at least some falsely name the
name of Christ. He speaks specifically of some who hold 'the form
of religion' but deny its power and 'make their way into households
and capture weak women, burdened with sins and swayed by various
impulses' (2 Tim 3:5-6). History provides ample proof that it is not
just 'weak women' who are subject to the deceptions of these. Far
too many Christian leaders, appearing to be respectable, make prey
of all types of saints. Paul diagnosed such as

> false apostles, deceitful workmen, disguising themselves as apostles
> of Christ. And no wonder, for even Satan disguises himself as an
> angel of light. So it is not strange if his servants also disguise
> themselves as servants of righteousness (2 Cor 11:13-15).

Equally dangerous is imbalance in either doctrine or actions. History
indicates that 'heresy' is seldom that which is completely incorrect
or wrong. Rather, it is usually truth taken to an unwarranted extreme.
The protection against such is the type of discerning maturity of
those 'who have their faculties trained by practice to distinguish good
from evil' (Heb 5:14). Also, when decisions are made within the
context of the believing community, the group, should provide checks
and balances. The church, the body as a whole, must seek answers
by listening for the leading of the Holy Spirit; it must evaluate
suggestions and options, as those who rightly handle 'the word of
truth' (cf. 2 Tim 2:15).

And, Biblical illiteracy and its corollary, doctrinal ignorance, is an
ever present liability to the church. When its members do not know the
Scriptures and their teachings, they are vulnerable to being led away by
any smooth tongue or attractive personality that might come along. It
was for their protection as well as for edification that Paul was careful to
declare 'the whole counsel of God' to the Ephesians (Acts 20:26-31).

We might also speak of lack of self-discipline, procrastination, and laziness in using the means for spiritual growth and development, both by some individuals and the corporate body itself. But, perhaps the most common liability of the church is the combination of distraction by concerns of the affairs of life and of our environment and weariness in doing well. It is not without reason that Galatians 6:9 (cf. 2 Thess 3:13) encourages believers not to 'grow weary in well-doing, for in due season we shall reap, if we do not lose heart.' The Christian church, as well as the Christian life, requires persistence and demands conscious effort to perform its mission and task – this is a major part of the message of Hebrews, as it is addressed to a church under stress in the first century.

Summary: What is the Church?

What is the church? In this chapter and the previous chapter, we have looked at a number of her features and offered partial definitions along the way. But, defining the church is like trying to define marriage or family. The externals are easy to enumerate and relationships readily defined. But still there is more – the inner core which can be approached only through symbol or poetry. As a result an attempt to paint a picture of the nature and mission of the church must first cleanse the canvas by clarifying what the church is not. We attempted this at the beginning of the previous chapter in the partial list of features we gave which the church may possess, or may be secondary features but are not of her inner being.

Noting the major vocabulary related to the church, *called out, assembly, fellowship,* is helpful but does not completely answer our question. Perhaps reminding ourselves of certain facts will begin to get at the issues with which the New Testament writers seem to be most concerned: the church

(1) involves the relation between Christ, the Savior, Lord, and Head and people who by faith have committed themselves to him;

(2) involves the relation between the people who have made such a commitment and that physical, social, cultural, national, and other external features make no difference;

(3) involves local, individual groups or congregations, but it is also a universal body in which all believers are united;

(4) has leaders who are servants;

(5) is in the world and subject to the features which make up its many societies and cultures, but it is distinct from the world and subject to its hostility;

6) has an agenda which is set, not by people, but by Christ, its Lord.

The church is first and foremost centered in Jesus Christ. And so the New Testament writers refer to it as she who is loved, who has been 'ransomed with ... the precious blood of Christ' (1 Pet 1:18-19), the family of God, the body of Christ, the innumerable host, the bride adorned for her husband. Beyond such figures are spiritual realities so allusive that human efforts to oversimplify, externalize, organize, or redefine have not only been inadequate but often wrong.

Christ is Lord. He is to be acknowledged as such, and the chief function of the church is to worship. The authority in the church is his. The church's lifestyle, mission, methods, and activities must be those he has set.

The church is the people of Jesus Christ now living in the Final, the Eschatological, Age. Hence, she is the people living 'between the times', between the first and second comings of Christ, the period between his victory in the decisive battle between God and Satan and the day of final victory. But, now the church lives on the battlefield, and battlefields are always dangerous; those on them must be alert and careful. The church must never forget that because she is his body, she is on the winning side!!!

The church is the people of Jesus Christ living in the light and expectation of the consummation. The church prays that the Lord will make her to increase and abound in love ... that the Lord will establish the hearts of her members blameless in holiness before himself, at the coming of the Lord Jesus with all his saints (1 Thess 3:12-13). As members of the church we look for that time when 'we shall be like him, for we shall see him as he is' (1 John 3:2).

Because the church is also made up of person-to-person and human group-to-human group relations it has responsibilities to acknowledge as brothers and sisters those believers who may be different in external features. She is to minister in concrete ways to fellow believers in peril, need, or danger.

At the beginning of this study of 'What is the Church?' we spoke of the church as a single body existing in many times and places. We noted that it is associated with the past through the testimony of the apostles in the Scriptures. Finally, although made up of imperfect beings it is also perfect and holy because of its association with Christ, its head, and the Holy Spirit who indwells it. We were there influenced by the language of early Christian thinkers who, after the New Testament period, spoke of 'the one, holy, catholic, and apostolic church.' Such language is not found in the New Testament itself, but, as we have tried to show in our study of the New Testament data, it reflects what that document presupposes.

The church, as she lives in the world, is to take her place in it, bear witness to Christ by both word and example and minister to needs as he did during his incarnation. This issue, the relation and responsibility of the church in the world is important and difficult. It must be the New Testament theme we consider next.

Chapter 10

What is the Church's Relation to Society?

Introduction: Some Alternative Models

Once again the need for clarification requires that we introduce an issue with reference to development of views in the past. Various positions relating to the answer to the question, 'What is the Church's Relation to Society' have been outlined by H. Richard Niebuhr in a little book that has become something of a modern classic, *Christ and Culture*.[1] He sets forth five positions which have been prominent at one time or another in history. But, he warns, it is not uncommon to find two or all of these positions existing at the same time and in the same geographical areas.

The 'Christ Against Culture' model assumes a two-way opposition between Christ and the customs of human societies. This attitude presents Christians with an either-or model, either embrace the current society and its culture or oppose and, if necessary, withdraw from it. This is frequently a response to society's opposition toward Christianity. Hence, in the early centuries of the Church's existence many Christians placed themselves in opposition to the cultures of both Judaism and the Roman world. Later groups, during medieval times, abandoned the 'world' and founded their own societies. Even in the twentieth century many Christians oppose the structures and customs of societies to the extent that they either withdraw mentally and emotionally or even physically as they form their own little communities with their own cultures. The assumption is that worldly society and all that pertains to it is thoroughly corrupt and must be rejected and opposed by Christians.

The 'Christ of Culture' response stresses agreement. Jesus, it is argued, was a part of society and its culture; his life and teachings

---

[1] H. Richard Niebuhr (1951), *Christ and Culture,* New York: Harper and Row.

are the pinnacle of human achievement. He is the statement of the
values toward which all should strive. Thus, Jesus is himself a part
of the great social heritage of the world that must be preserved and
passed on from generation to generation. Often holders of this view
assume that Jesus represents their own political, social, economic,
or intellectual views. He is thus made the champion of Western
civilization, democracy, capitalism, socialism, the spirit of Marxism,
or others.

The remaining three models all seek to hold both the difference
between Christ and culture while at the same time maintaining some
sort of contact or even unity between them. The first of these, Niebuhr's
third answer to the question of the relation between Christ and society,
stresses that although Christ enters into human life and society, he
transcends it, enters it from above. Hence such advocates of 'Christ
Above Culture' such as Thomas Aquinas and his followers, insist the
church lives in tension, tension between the above and the below. Christ
is indeed the great model for society and came to restore it to the divine
intention. Yet, he is distinct from it. Society and its culture may lead
persons toward Christ, but they must reach beyond culture and all
societal institutions to reach him. Indeed, the intended design and full
potential of society lies beyond even the best human achievement, values,
and institutions. Christ must enter into human life from without and bring
a supernatural society and values which could not even be imagined by
humans, much less achieved by their efforts. For Aquinas since grace
completes nature, medieval Western Christianity is perhaps the ultimate
paradigm for this model.

Martin Luther is an example of those who see 'Christ and Culture
in Paradox.' Both the authority of Christ and that of society, especially
the state, are legitimate. Nevertheless there is frequently, usually,
conflict between them, and both the individual Christian and the
church are caught in that struggle. Those who hold this view refuse
to compromise or accommodate the claims of Christ to secular
society, yet they understand that God requires obedience to the
institutions of society, especially to human government. The Christian
is like a person with dual citizenship when both countries of which
he or she is a citizen are at war with each other. Those who hold this

position maintain that ultimate authority and supremacy belong to Christ who will be the final judge of society. But now, the Christian lives in tension, lives precariously, looking for final justification and vindication beyond history.

The 'Christ, the Transformer of Culture' approach fully recognizes the reality and seriousness of sin. It is cognizant of its all-pervasive effects on the individual and society. Its advocates recognize that these effects upon society are transmitted as culture passes from one group to another. Yet, they remain in and active in society, its institutions and cultures, seeking the radical transformation, the salvation of culture. Those with this view affirm that Christ, the Savior of believers, is also the redeemer of society. This, they believe, need not await the consummation; it is possible in the present, in this world order. They are committed to work for that end. Augustine seems to have outlined this approach; John Calvin and those who followed him developed and continue to advocate it.

Niebuhr's categories do not cover all possibilities. My Wheaton College colleague, Dennis Okholm, has made an important addition, 'Culture Against Christ.'[2] He noted that this is probably actually the position Niebuhr would have ascribed to the Anabaptist, although modern members of that group have pointed out that their forefathers founded independent societies, not by choice but because they were forced to do so. Okholm went on to suggest this is actually the situation in which Christianity, especially its Evangelical wing, found itself as the twentieth century wound to its close and the twenty-first dawned. Previously there was something of consensus, even among non-Christians, which accepted the basic elements and language of the Judeo-Christian values and ethics. This has now broken down because of a shift in society which has produced two important results. First, the concept of objective, absolute truth is no more assumed. The majority in contemporary society believe in

---

[2]Paper read at the National Meeting of the Evangelical Theological Society, 1992. Now published as *Recommendations for the Family*, the final chapter of Timothy Philips and Dennis Okholm, *Family of Faith* (2d ed; Grands Rapids Baker, 2001), 262-272.

relativism and/or normative pluralism which insists that persons may define truth as they see fit. Even if an individual's definition conflicts with another's idea of truth, it is still truth for that person. Okholm continued:

> This becomes significant when one realizes that what underlies much of the debate over abortion, homosexuality, and active euthanasia is the failure to arrive at a common definition of what it means to be human and what the purpose of human existence is. Dealing with these issues in a moralistic manner or attempting to pass statewide legislation prohibiting such behaviors may have worked thirty or forty years ago. It will not work today. The dominant culture, characterized by relativism, is at odds with the church on a more fundamental level than ... [leaders of such attempts] seem to realize.

Second, Okholm noted that 'the prevailing culture is characterized by a "post-Enlightenment" public atheism'. Christians hold beliefs and moral values which are based on assumptions not shared by contemporary society. This places society in a position diametrically opposed to the Christian and church. He argues that the church should see to it that God-given cultural institutions and gifts (such as the family and the arts and sciences) are made 'Christian', that is transformed, but to expect the transformation of the 'prevailing culture' is another matter. We cannot hope to transform the 'prevailing culture' or ethos, but Christians and the church as a whole can still live out an alternative culture (call it counter-culture, but that term might not capture the point as well as 'alternative culture').

Biblical Evidence Related to the Position of the Church in the World

The Biblical data on the church's relation to society is scattered; no single writer or literary group comes even close in presenting a complete view. We can at best note what is available in various parts of the New Testament and seek the principles behind them. Furthermore, it is difficult to summarize the relevant data without prejudicing the case in favor of one or the other above alternatives. Closely connected are the relations between the church and society and the church's relation to a specific element of society, the state. We will look at this latter issue at the end of this chapter.

As we approach the Biblical evidence relating to church and society there are two points to remember. First, there is a difference between the position of Old Testament Israel and the church. Israel was a conscious theocracy, a nation and society founded and governed directly by God. Theoretically there was no difference between the expressed will of God and that of the religious-political body. Of course, there were many times when the relation between society and God was disharmonious, but for the Old Testament writers these were aberrations. In the New Testament the church is never viewed as synonymous with society, dominating it, nor really having much, if any, direct influence upon society. Political and social realities made anything else impossible. Use of the example of Old Testament Israel as a model for the church's relation to society is not always appropriate.

Second, the real issue is not what the early church did, but what does the New Testament present as the way Christians and the church should relate to society? Of course, the New Testament writers expect the final resolution of the matter at the consummation when the Kingdom of God will have absolute and uncontested control, when rebellious elements will have been banished. But what about the here and now?

First and foremost, the New Testament assumes that Christians, and the church as a corporate entity, are a part of and citizens of the Kingdom of God. Their prior allegiance must always be to God. When confronted with the issue of their relation to the Jewish state, even with its special claim for divine sanction, Peter and John applied the principle that must govern all relations between church and society, namely, that when conflict arises involving loyalty or obedience to either God or the state, it is God, rather than any human institutions, who must be obeyed (cf. Acts 4:19).

Jesus

As we have already noted, Jesus clearly teaches that his disciples are '... in the world ... but not of the world ... therefore the world hates...' (John 15:18-19; 17:14-16). In other words, although Jesus saw an obvious distinction and even a separation here between the church and society, that hardly means Jesus advocated complete withdrawal. He lived in society, taught persons who were a part of it, and sent his representatives into the societies of his day and following years, even 'to the end of the age.'

Jesus taught that rulers, both political and religious, have their rights and dues. Matthew 23, although it contains scathing denunciation of scribal and Pharisaic practices, says that Jesus insisted 'The scribes and the Pharisees sit on Moses' seat; so practice and observe whatever they tell you' (vss. 2-3). On the rights of civil government, even a foreign, pagan one, he said, 'Render therefore to Caesar the things that are Caesar's, and to God the things that are God's' (Matt 22:21).

On the same principle he denounced any person or group that sought to usurp the place and prerogatives of God. For an example, the Jewish leaders recognized themselves as the unjust tenants in the parable of the vineyard in Mark 12:1-12.

The Epistles

Paul makes a number of important contributions to our search for an answer to the relation between the church and society. In Romans 1 he states that the present condition of both non-Christian persons and their societies is a result of 1) failing to acknowledge evidence about God, available to all in nature (vss. 19-20), by honoring and giving thanks to him (vs. 21) – this includes God's 'eternal power and deity' (vs. 20); 2) 'they became futile in their thinking and their senseless minds were darkened' (vs. 21) and 'God gave them up' (vs. 24); 3) the result is, religiously, that 'they exchanged the truth about God for a lie and worshiped and served the creature rather than the creator' (vs. 25) and, morally, that society is given over to 'dishonorable passions' and all kinds of wickedness (vss. 26-32); and 4) they stand under the wrath and judgment of God, partly revealed now, but to be fully visited upon them at the consummation. Hence, human society as now known has rejected God and is living out that rejection. At this point, in answering the question, 'What is the relation between the church and society?' Paul assumes that they are very different because of the contrasting ways they have responded to God's self-revelation.

Next, in 2 Thessalonians 1, Paul states that human society is in opposition to the church and persecutes Christians because people of the world 'do not know God;' they want to live without God. This is a normal, expected relation; society is fundamentally against the church. He goes on to say the world wants to live apart from God and eventually it will get what it wants, *exclusion* from God.

> They shall suffer the punishment of eternal destruction and exclusion from the presence of the Lord and from the glory of his might, when he comes on that day to be glorified in his saints, and to be marveled at in all who have believed, because our testimony to you was believed (2 Thess 1:9-10).

A passage to which we have referred in a number of contexts, 1 Peter 4:3-5, states that pagan society abuses Christians because they are different. Although before converting to Christianity Peter's addressees shared the lifestyle of pagan society, they do not now do so and this evokes persecution. However, a persecuting society itself will face judgment.

Society cannot tolerate non-conformity to itself, at least when refusal to conform is open and evident. The passages at which we have looked show this and remind Christians that the hostile, negative reaction they experience from society is to be expected.

Summary

The whole orientation of the New Testament writers assumes that the present condition of society is abnormal. The Biblical doctrine that God's creation was originally 'good' establishes that. But the effects of sin are not limited to nature and the individual. Society too is not now as it was meant to be. Along with the natural order, the structures within which humans live and relate to each other do not recognize, honor, and serve God and do not submit to his rule and will. Furthermore, the Biblical writers teach that this abnormal condition of society will not continue. The New Testament is alive with the reality that Christ's atonement was directed to all that was affected by sin, 'God so loved the *world*' (John 3:16). The sovereignty of God and the in-breaking of his rule subjects society to his redeeming influence. To say the least, Christ does transform culture, although not necessarily directly in this phase of Salvation History. He transforms people in culture and they, in turn, spread the claim and implications of his rule over society. But, 'as it is, we do not yet see everything in subjection to him' (Heb 2:8). The tension between 'Christ and Culture in Paradox' and 'Christ the Transformer of Culture' will reach resolution at the consummation. The time will come when God will 'subject all things to himself' (Phil 3:21), when 'at the name of Jesus every knee [shall] bow, in heaven and on earth and under the earth, and every tongue [shall] confess that Jesus Christ is Lord, to the glory of God the Father' (Phil 2:10-11).

The redemption and reconciliation purchased by Christ includes all of creation, 'God so loved the world' – in all its parts: natural, societal, and human persons. Thus, the fact and scope of salvation prohibit Christians from being unconcerned about all that is about him or her. We have learned something of the nature of the present context and relationship between church and society, but we have not answered the question of this chapter.

Witness of the Church to the Saving Work and Lordship of Christ
Both in 'The Great Commission' of Matthew 28:18-20 and in his parting words, recorded in Acts 1:8, Jesus made clear that the church is to bear witness to society of the nature of the spiritual situation, including its rebellion against God and the fact of his saving work and Lordship. We noted this command when summarizing the mission and task of the church. A part of the church's relation with society is its prophetic role; a role which will often result in resentment and hostility by society. Nevertheless, the church has the responsibility to relate to society in this way.

In describing the root cause of the difference between the false and the true prophet, Jeremiah records God's stating that the true prophet has 'stood in the council of the Lord' (23:18). That is, the true prophet has been made aware of the very person and character of God. The prophet's word must be based on the awareness of God's nature. Then, God continues, speaking of the false prophets, 'If they had stood in my council, then they would have proclaimed my words to my people, and they would have turned them from their evil way, and from the evil of their doings' (23:22). The true prophet speaks against sin in order to turn hearers away from it. So too the true church calls attention to societal (as well as individual) sins, denounces them, and calls for repentance. This is precisely what Paul did before Felix, the representative of Roman society and government, as 'he argued about justice and self-control and future judgment' (Acts 24:25).

Church history is replete with accounts of those who have taken this responsibility seriously, and delighted in doing so. But denunciation of sin and warning of judgment must come from those who have learned that the greatest of the spiritual endowments is love (cf. 1 Cor 13:13). Tears, not glee, befit the preacher of impending doom who would follow him who wept over Jerusalem. Another side of the relation between the church and society must be her compassion for those blinded and bound by the evil one, even though the object of that compassion is her persecutor.

The church bears witness, not only to society's sin and eventual judgment, but also to the fact of the presence of the Kingdom of God. It joyfully affirms that light has shined in the face of Jesus Christ who has brought forgiveness and freedom from enslaving evil. It also proclaims the victory won by the death and resurrection of Christ and the fact of the coming consummation.

The church is responsible to bear witness, to announce the good news to society. Hers is not the responsibility for the response. Little matter if, after being faithful in discharging her duty, the church suffers a like fate from those who killed the prophets, or receive a response similar to that of Felix to Paul's witness, 'Go away for the present; when I have an opportunity I will summon you' (Acts 24:25).

The church is to relate to society as witness with all the available methods appropriate to the message she gives. These include words, the preachment, but also behavior. Included too are deeds which show to the world Christian concern, love, justice, and mercy even in the face of the exact opposite from society. There is also the witness through lifestyle, of which we have spoken. Yes, it may evoke hostility and abuse; it may also bring admiration, conviction, and conversion.

The Early Church and Cultural Diversity

Introduction

The fact of the tension between the church and her earthly environment always presents challenge. There will always be those with differing opinions of how to respond and hence, alternative answers to the question posed in this chapter.

At the risk of restating and oversimplifying Niebuhr's alternatives, we suggest that in general the early church chose one or another of three general alternatives as it faced secular culture. The first involved as completely as possible the physical or emotional rejection of the world, its society and culture, and the establishment of its own segregated ones. The monastic movement is an example of just such a response. A second option is adaptation to the culture without compromising those distinctive elements Christians hold because they emanate from her allegiance to her Lord and Head. This usually involves seeking 'Christian' outlooks, attitudes, actions, and answers in the circumstances within which they lived. The New Testament church in the Roman empire seems to have followed this alternative. The third attempt, of which English Puritanism provides an example, seeks to change culture until it complied with the church's norms and values.

Change, of course – change of society and culture – is the desired goal of the church's prayers and witness. However, her effects usually come slowly at best. Cases of immediate society-wide changes following proclamation are rare; Jonah's case was an exception. The example-lifestyle type of witness provides light, salt, and leaven for society. The imperceptible rising of dough by the action of the leaven (Matt 13:33; Luke 13:21) is a more common model than switching on an electric light.

Hence, when in position to do so, the church, or some parts of it, have not infrequently employed confrontation and militancy to achieve her ends. Most extreme are the 'conversions' brought about at the point of sword or gun or with the torturer's rack or scourge. Such are most inappropriate for representatives of him who meekly accepted rejection and even personal suffering, awaiting vindication from his heavenly Father. More aptly, in the past Christians have confronted society by becoming involved in social activism and in the political process, they have contributed to prison reforms, regulation of child labor, abolition of slavery, the elevation of the status of women, correctives in judicial systems, and more. In recent decades demonstrations and civil disobedience have become tools for attempting social change.

Of course, society itself largely controls the forms of relationships the church may have to it. Society may hinder, make difficult and dangerous, and thus restrict witness, but it cannot eliminate it entirely. Or in more subtle ways it can resist militancy by the church or close the socio-political processes to Christians and otherwise limit efforts for change. It is not difficult to guess how the Roman empire might have dealt with a Christian demonstration for religious rights, one advocating the elimination of explicit sexual material in theaters, or the abolition of blood games in coliseums.

The New Testament Church and Cultural Change

We must repeat what was said in the previous chapter about the proper and inappropriate ways the New Testament church be employed as a model for the modern one. We learn from the theological principles (which are often only implied) which the New Testament church applied to the situations it faced. We cannot expect to duplicate its responses, because our cultures and societies are different from theirs.

The New Testament shows the church responding to two distinct major cultural forms. These were the many sided cultures of the

Jewish and then the Greco-Roman worlds. Both, in the long run, were hostile to the church and her message.

During the Apostolic Age, Christianity's entry into the Greco-Roman world precipitated an internal identity crisis, involving particularly her relation to the Jewish society and religion. The law versus grace controversy was a major response to it.

The Jewish background and environment from which the first Christians came gave expression to the conviction that the old Jewish order had been given by divine revelation and operated under divine sanction. There was a definite need to clarify the Christian position in relation to the distinctive elements of the church and their relation to what had gone before. Galatians and Hebrews, as well as Acts 15, show the early Christians responding to this challenge. The implication of these passages is that while the society, institutions, and customs of the past had indeed, at least partly, come at divine directive, the arrival of Jesus introduced a new situation – Christians lived in a new period of Salvation History! Hebrews, for an example, makes explicit that Judaism and Christianity are not equally valid alternatives. Because 'Christ has offered for all time a single sacrifice for sin (10:12) ... there is no longer any offering for sin' (10:18). Consequently, if a Jewish Christian, or anyone with knowledge of the truth about Christ and the Final Age, sins by turning away from trusting Christ and the adequacy of his atonement, there no longer remains an Old Testament-Levitical sin offering, only the prospect of judgment.[3]

On the other hand, observance of traditional customs which were rooted in culture appears to have been permitted only if they did not conflict with the will and revelation of God in the Final Age. Specifically, those customs or practices observed not in a vain attempt to obtain salvation, but only as personal preference, seem to have been regarded as matters of the individual's conscience.[4]

In the greater Greco-Roman world the church faced a challenge quite different from that posed by Judaism. First, there was an intellectual-doctrinal threat – not only blatant paganism, but also

---

[3]My paraphrase of Hebrews 11:26-27.
[4]Note Romans 13:11–15:13.

that of syncretism, the cojoining of Christianity with various forms from pagan systems. Colossians, 1 and 2 Peter, and 1 John all seem to combat some form of pagan thought, probably a proto-Gnosticism, which challenged such truths as creation of the material world by a good deity and the material reality of the physical body of Christ during his incarnation. They claimed that salvation comes by knowledge rather than by grace through faith. The entirety of the pagan thought-world was essentially at enmity with the assumptions and values of Christianity. This pagan approach and mind-set were the foundation of first century Gentile society.

The issue of morals and ethical standards raised the question, 'Is there a distinctive Christian "lifestyle"?' Although there was some difference between the moral-ethical codes of Jewish society and Christianity, these differences were minuscule compared with those the church faced in Gentile societies. Here, as previously noted, there were not only dissimilar codes, but also lack of agreement about any necessary relationship between religion and conduct.

Even in the face of persecution and death, none stood more firm than Paul for basic moral and spiritual principles as they affect the essentials of Christian thought and life. Yet, he displayed a remarkable adaptability in matters of societal customs. His classic statement is 1 Corinthians 9:19-23:

> Though I am free from all men, I have made myself a slave to all, that I might win the more. To the Jews I became as a Jew, in order to win Jews; to those under the law I became as one under the law – though not being myself under the law – that I might win those under the law. To those outside the law I became as one outside the law – not being without law toward God but under the law of Christ – that I might win those outside the law. To the weak I became weak, that I might win the weak. I have become all things to all men, that I might by all means save some. I do it all for the sake of the gospel, that I may share in its blessings.

So, what did the church do, what was its basic method of facing cultural challenge? It stressed its distinctive aspects as summarized in the Christ-centered *kērugma* and clarified its belief in salvation by grace through faith. In a legalistic environment it proclaimed the priority of relationships arising from God's grace – relationships, first with God, then with others. It boldly proclaimed faith in Jesus as the only true religion in societies committed to pluralism and syncretism; 'There is salvation in no one else, for there is no other name under heaven given among men by which we must be saved' (Acts 4:12). It also insisted on absolutes in a relativistic environment.

In Jewish societies, it could build on past revelations and commitments. In Gentile areas it had to first construct a foundation through its own teachings.

In summary, we may say that as the first Christians faced the societal and cultural forms of its day, they displayed willingness to adapt in *form* and *emphasis* but were uncompromising in the *content* of its faith and life. An illustration will both support this statement and demonstrate how the church went about relating to society in this way.

The implications of Paul's dealing with Onesimus and Philemon provide some insight in how he dealt with a specific social ill, that of slavery. The issue was not only a social matter, but also an ethical one. Onesimus, the runaway slave, seems to have stolen some of his master's property. In a strictly Hebrew society, the runaway slave was not to be returned to his master (Deut 23:15). For some reason, possibly because Onesimus lived in a Gentile culture, Paul and/or Onesimus believed it to be essential for this runaway to return to Philemon.

In the normal course of things in the Roman world, a returned slave could expect a severe beating at best; a slow death by torture was also a possibility. Paul sought to change the slave's situation with his Christian master by personal intervention and involvement on behalf of Onesimus. His letter to Philemon itself is such. In it Paul identifies himself with the slave saying, 'I am sending him back to you, sending my very heart' (vs. 12) and requesting a favorable reception for Onesimus as a personal favor – 'receive him as you would receive me' (vs. 17). Paul stands ready to compensate for Philemon's loss, 'If he has wronged you at all, or owes you anything, charge that to my account ... I will repay it' (vss. 18-19), but feels Philemon should forgive the obligation because of his benefit from Paul's ministry (vss. 19-20).

Paul further appeals to Philemon for love's sake (vs. 9), on the ground that Onesimus was now a Christian (vs. 10). As a Christian, although still a slave, Onesimus is now 'more than a slave,... a beloved brother ... both in the flesh and in the Lord' (vs. 16).

The implications of these last statements are far reaching. They involve nothing less than the basis for a new structure of relationships among Christians, relationships based on equality among believers. The ancient structure was hierarchical. At the top were nobles, the wealthy, and citizens. At the bottom were foreigners, the poor, women, children, and slaves. The latter groups were usually regarded as inferior 'things' (Aristotle referred to the slave as a 'human tool'), to be used for the benefit and pleasure of those at the top of the structure. Paul designated Onesimus, the slave now become a Christian, as a 'brother,'. Thus, Paul immediately elevates him to the status of a *person* who is *equal*. Should such a notion prevail, the whole structure of Roman society would be reordered.[5]

Paul did not order the dissolution of the institution of slavery in the Roman world as a whole. He had no authority, power, nor the influence to do so. He did not even demand that Christians immediately free their slaves. Rather, in the church he insisted upon the recognition of a new society in Christ. Slaves are brothers! Elsewhere Paul insisted that social, economic, political, racial, and cultural distinctions no longer count; in Christ even gender differences have no spiritual significance. All Christians are one and equal before God (Gal 3:28; Eph 2:11-21; Col 3:11).

At the same time, Paul and Peter insisted that earthly, socio-economic relationships were not to be instantaneously overthrown.

---

[5]What happened to Onesimus? We do not know for sure. At least two early Christian writers, Ignatius and Eusebius, refer to an early second century bishop of Ephesus with that name. Onesimus was a common slave name, we cannot be sure the bishop was once Philemon's bondsman. He would have had to be a young boy when converted and at least in his seventies when Ignatius refers to him. This is a good possibility; the likelihood that the two are the same is strong. The name 'Onesiphorus' (2 Tim 1:16-18) is related to 'Onesimus' etymologically; it could conceivably designate Paul's convert.

In our study of the church we noted that the epistle writers counsel maintaining the proper, respectful relationship between the various elements of society.[6] In 1 Timothy 6:1-2, Paul also speaks specifically to Christian slaves, urging that they honor their masters 'so that the name of God and the teaching may not be defamed' and the fact that Christian masters and slaves 'are brethren' should not be grounds for disrespect by Christian slaves, but for more zealous service.

Regarding social situations Paul says, 'Let every one lead the life which the Lord has assigned to him, and in which God has called him' (1 Cor 7:17). This certainly is a general statement advocating contentment, not an absolute rule – one called to Christ while a child could not remain in that state. Furthermore, Paul allows for improvement of one's lot as he continues, 'Were you a slave when called? Never mind. But if you can gain your freedom, avail yourself of the opportunity' (1 Cor 7:21).

The attitude of the New Testament writers seems to be that society at large must not be allowed to hinder consistent Christian living. Even though secular structure may be unjust by Christian standards, Christians, so much as it depends upon them, should find a way to live contentedly and peacefully within it (Rom 12:14, 18). If Christians can improve their lot in society, then they should do so, but that should not become such a prevailing preoccupation that it hinders the living of daily life for the glory of Christ. Christian society within the church is another matter. Christians are equals and share the designation of 'children of God'.[7] Here believers are 'subject to one another out of reverence for Christ' (Eph 5:21). Larger society cannot prevent the Christian community from living as equals, subject to one another in Christ.

For those early Christians outside the boundaries of the Land of Israel, living as they did as a minority in a secular, pagan society and culture, there was no possibility for the church to effect a fast, radical transformation of culture. Consequently, these early Christians sought

---

[6]Ephesians 5:21–6:9; Colossians 3:18–4:6; 1 Peter 2:18–3:12.

[7]Although some of these 'equals' have positions of leadership in the church.

to find a Christian answer to the situation, which included undesirable social and cultural situations, in which they found themselves. (The New Testament gives no real information regarding the attitudes and actions of the church when the situation is different from that found in the first century.)

In the long run, in areas where the Christian ideal has been influential, social structures have been slowly changed and are being altered. As salt and leaven have done their work, the implications of the light of the gospel has shined; even those in darkness have at times seen the rightness of the way Christians live in relation to each other. In short, the church's relation to society must at least involve living before the world as Christians both in society at large and in the church.

Some Elements of God's Ideal for Society

In considering the Christian life we looked at some Old Testament statements about 'what God requires' – love, steadfast love, justice, righteousness, kindness, peace, truth, and walking humbly with God. The prophets insisted on these as marks of society as well as (really more than) an individual in covenant relation with the LORD. These should certainly be hallmarks of the Christian society, the church. They are also that which any Christian who has the opportunity must seek to implement in society as a whole. This may not be as easy as might appear; it might involve loving enemies, turning the other cheek or suffering personal loss in order to maintain peace. It might also involve supporting the elimination of unjust structures which have protected one's privileged status, or involving oneself in the needs of the needy, and more.

Such qualities are at the heart of the New Testament social model. Jesus rebuked the political-religious establishment for developing and furthering a religious-social order which served its own benefit at the expense of the people. Jesus placed the authority of his own person over that of the leaders. He turned the tables by identifying himself with the poor, lowly, despised, the oppressed, and enslaved.

As noted in chapter 4, the principle of non-discrimination – 'God is not a respecter of persons ... [Christians are] ... not respecters of persons,' – must be the norm for Christian behavior. It is the stated basis for

determining proper candidates for inclusion in the church.[8] The principle
is also cited in the New Testament in (a) determining the nature of
relationships between Christian masters and slaves (Eph 6:9), (b) the
basis for church administration (1 Tim 5:21), (c) the administration of
divine punishment in judgment (Col 3:25), and (d) the esteem and
treatment to be given the poor in the Christian community (Jas 2:1-9).
The model society maintains equality and justice.[9]

The religious ethic of both Old Testament and New Testament is
to love God supremely.[10] In the New Testament the individual and
corporate social ethic also calls for love for other humans. Time and
again, the words *love one another*[11] and *love your neighbor as
yourself* echo from various sections of the New Testament.[12] The
disciples are admonished to love even their enemies.[13] Following
the teachings of Jesus,[14] both Paul and James declare that love is
the fulfillment of the law.[15] Such are the underpinnings of that society
for which Christians yearn and pray.

If the divine ideal for society is not now present, what then is the
Christian's responsibility to further it? What is the Christian's social
responsibility? To what extent, if any, is the Christian to work for the
implementation and realization of the divine ideals in this world?

The fact of the Lordship of Christ over the universe is a truth the
church cannot escape. Its goal is for the recognition and

---

[8]Becoming Christians, as it is in Acts 10:34; 15:19.

[9]The Biblical view of equality and justice does not necessarily comport
with those of the 'politically correct' mentality. Leviticus 19:15 summarizes
the expectation of complete non-partiality, 'You shall do no injustice in
judgment; you shall not be partial to the poor or defer to the great, but in
righteousness shall you judge your neighbor.' The secular culture of late
twentieth century North America seems to ask for favoritism and the need
for the empowerment of minorities and disadvantaged.

[10]Deuteronomy 6:4-5; Mark 12:28-30 = Matthew 22:35-38; Luke 10:27.

[11]John 13:34; 15:12, 17; Romans 12:10; 13:8; 1 Thessalonians 4:9; 1 Peter
1:22; 1 John 3:11, 23; 4:7, 11-12; 2 John 5.

[12]Matthew 19:19; Mark 12:31 = Matthew 22:39; Luke 10:28; Romans 13:9;
Galatians 5:14; James 2:8.

[13]Matthew 5:44; Luke 6:27, 35.

[14]Mark 12:28-31 = Matthew 22:34-40; Luke 10:25-28.

[15]Romans 13:8, 10; Galatians 5:14; James 2:8.

implementation of this all-encompassing Lordship, to seek to establish Christ as the 'Transformer of Culture.' The church has the responsibility of continuing proclamation of the reality of Christ's Lordship. It must pray for its realization. What more must it do?

The question of the social responsibility of the church[16] must center around the examination of three points: (1) the specific goals or objectives to be sought, (2) the bases and motives upon which these goals are identified, and (3) the means to be employed in achieving them. Although there may be agreement that a certain objective or ideal is good, just, and even necessary, there may still remain wide disagreement on why it is so considered and how it is to be achieved. Practically speaking, for the church, questions of motives and means are of equal importance with objectives. Objectives involve external programs; motives and means relate to the theory and theology on which the programs are designed.

Here again we reach a point on which there is widespread disagreement. The disagreement is at least partly based upon theological matters such as the nature of human persons, of sin, salvation, the church, and the final chapter of universal history. Carl F. H. Henry has summarized four strategies for social change which have been employed at one time or another throughout church history: (1) Revolution: 'the radical change of social patterns through violence and compulsion,' (2) Reformation: 'a gradual but pervasive ethical amendment of prevailing social character and forms,' (3) Reevaluation: 'a fresh intellectual comprehension and direction, whereby social life and structures are critically reassessed in the light of transcendent moral norms,' and (4) Regeneration: 'the transformation by a supernatural impulse in individual lives whereby the social scene is renewed through spiritual motivations.'[17]

---

[16]Cf. J. Julius Scott, Jr., 'Race Relations, Social Change, and the Church,' *Presbuteron* 3 (Spring, 1977), 20-29; 'Acts 10:34, A Text for Racial and Cultural Reconciliation Among Christians,' *The Gospel in Black and White. Theological Resources for Racial Reconciliation*, Dennis L. Okholm, ed. (Downers Grove, IL: InterVarsity Press, 1997), 131-39.

[17]Carl F. H. Henry, *Aspects of Christian Social Ethics* (Grand Rapids, MI: Eerdmans, 1964), pp. 16ff.

Perhaps we should not think of one strategy to the exclusion of the other. Witness and prayer must be neither dismissed as 'insignificant cop-outs' nor as an excuse for doing nothing more when more is possible. Both the 'Good Samaritan' and Paul became personally involved in cases of need. Where free voting on issues which impact society is permitted, Christians must be sure that such Biblical social principles as those outlined above inform their choices and vote, even above personal self-interest. The impact of even the lone Christian voice through the halls of government is not insignificant. The modern world needs both the contribution and example of public officials who resist the temptation to use power for personal gain, who stand for right regardless of political or personal consequences, who seek to determine the common good on the basis of Scriptural principles and through prayer, who, as Christ, seek to serve rather than be served.

Christians in government? Christians in government! The question raises one of the most important and most difficult of all questions with reference to the relation of the church to society. It is that of the relation of church and state. Few recognize that New Testament writers address the matter with an implied question, one associated with ultimate authority.

Church and State: Who is Lord?[18]

The Biblical evidence for discussing the relation between church and state is scattered and varied. As we have already recognized,

---

[18]Summary of views of the relationship between Church and State:

1. Until Constantine, state was the enemy of the church.

2. Constantine, as emperor, was head of the pagan Roman religion. After he began favoring Christianity he continued as religious leader of the realm; only now it was Christianity that he led.

3. With the movement of the Capital from Rome to Constantinople (330) there developed different concepts of Church-State relations.

a. In the East: Caesaropapism – the Ruler is the supreme authority, even in doctrinal matters.

b. In the West: the Church had more freedom, but the state was weak [n.b. Bishop Gelarius I (429) – doctrine of the two swords].

4. Reformation

a. Luther – distinguished the temporal and spiritual powers but not the administrative, etc., which is essential.

b. Erastian system – the prince supervises the Church.

Old Testament Israel was an unusual case. She was, in a unique way, 'the People of God,' limited to a particular race, nation, and society. As such her government was that of a theocracy, a governmental form which, from the Christian point of view, is not and cannot be duplicated in the contemporary world. Also in the Old Testament world the non-Hebraic (Gentile) nations were essentially hostile to God's people. The Old Testament writers often portray them as the tools, if not the embodiment, of evil.

The Teachings of Jesus

Jesus recognized the authority of Jewish leaders and authorities as legitimate. He faulted them for refusing to recognize him as God's Messiah and so standing in opposition to God's presence and work. As noted above, the leaders recognized that Jesus depicted them as the 'bad guys' in his parable of the vineyard and the unworthy tenants (Mark 12:1-12). He condemned their abuses of power, their neglect of the law, and their circumvention of the letter and intent of God's law. He challenged the interpretation, use of, and additions to Old Testament law by Jewish officials (Mark 7:1-23), but he acknowledged the authority of the positions they held. On one occasion he said, 'The scribes and the Pharisees sit on Moses' seat; so practice and observe whatever they tell you, but not what they do; for they preach, but do not practice' (Matt 23:2-3). Furthermore, Jesus paid his temple tax, so as 'not to give offense' (Matt 17:24-27). Later Jesus submitted to arrest and trial by Jewish officials.

Surprisingly, Jesus was apparently less critical of Roman government and officials. He treated a centurion with respect and healed his servant.[19] When an attempt was made to put Jesus in a position of supporting either governing God's people by the Jews or by the Romans, he replied, 'Render to Caesar the things that are Caesar's and to God the things that are God's' (Mark 12:13-17 =

---

c. Calvin – distinguished between temporal and the spiritual; the state maintains peace, protects, but follows Biblical principles in civil affairs.

d. Anabaptist – complete separation of Church and State.

[19]Matthew 8:1-13; Luke 7:1-10; John 4:43-54.

Matt 22:15-22; Luke 20:20-26). On trial before the Roman governor Pilate, Jesus stated, 'He who delivered me to you has the greater sin' (John 19:11).

The Book of Acts

The best known statement about church-state relations is in Acts 4:19, 'Peter and John answered them [the Jewish Council], "Whether it is right in the sight of God to listen to you rather than to God, you must judge."' Actually, the relation between church and state in Acts is quite complex. There is always respect for the state. Jewish officials are portrayed in a less favorable light than those of Rome. Official Judaism is always hostile to the church, although some individuals, such as Gamaliel (5:34), were more reasonable. Acts shows that Christians, when accused by their enemies before Roman officials, usually received a favorable, or at least not a negative decision; when the facts were clear, Romans permitted the continued preaching of the Christian message. The execution of James, the brother of John, by King Herod Agrippa I (12:1-23) may be an exception, although Agrippa was regarded as Jewish by the Romans.

The Epistles

Key church-state passages in the epistles are well known. The two most clearly dedicated to the subject are in the writings of Paul and Peter. In Romans Paul says,

> Let every person be subject to the governing authorities. For there is no authority except from God, and those that exist have been instituted by God. Therefore he who resists the authorities resists what God has appointed, and those who resist will incur judgment. For rulers are not a terror to good conduct, but to bad. Would you have no fear of him who is in authority? Then do what is good, and you will receive his approval, for he is God's servant for your good. But if you do wrong, be afraid, for he does not bear the sword in vain; he is the servant of God to execute his wrath on the wrongdoer. Therefore one must be subject, not only to avoid God's wrath but also for the sake of conscience. For the same reason you also pay taxes, for the authorities are ministers of God, attending

to this very thing. Pay all of them their dues, taxes to whom taxes are due, revenue to whom revenue is due, respect to whom respect is due, honor to whom honor is due (13:1-7).

This passage is set in the context of a number of important exhortations. 'Bless those who persecute you (12:14) . . . Live in harmony with one another . . . If possible, so far as it depends upon you, live peaceably with all (12:18) . . . never avenge yourselves, but leave it to God (12:19) . . . Do not be overcome by evil, but overcome evil with good' (12:21). In Romans 13:5 Paul explains, 'One must be subject, not only to avoid God's wrath but also for the sake of conscience.' In submission to government, even a less than perfect one, is part of a broader concept of goodness and goodwill which must, to the extent possible, be a characteristic of the Christian community, even in an alien environment.

Peter's admonition is similar:

Be subject for the Lord's sake to every human institution, whether it be to the emperor as supreme, or to governors as sent by him to punish those who do wrong and to praise those who do right. For it is God's will that by doing right you should put to silence the ignorance of foolish men. Live as free men, yet without using your freedom as a pretext for evil; but live as servants of God. Honor all men. Love the brotherhood. Fear God. Honor the emperor (1 Pet 2:13-17).

The following verses in 1 Peter admonish servants (domestic servants[20]) to be submissive and respectful to their masters, even if they suffer wrongfully. Peter may see the two directives, one regarding submission to higher governmental authorities and the other calling for the same attitude by servants toward masters, as applications of the same principle. The instructions to servants to endure undeserved punishment being 'mindful of God' (2:19), assuring them 'you have God's approval' (2:20), and reminding them that 'Christ also suffered for you, leaving you an example' (2:21) are equally applicable to the church. *God's servants*, the church, will at times undergo persecution by the government, their earthly master.

---

[20]*oiketai,* not necessarily slaves.

Both Romans and 1 Peter call for submission to and respect for human government. Paul goes a step further by insisting that human government has God's authorization; obedience to the authorities is a Christian duty. However, both statements appear to reflect a situation when the state was not engaged in official, systematic persecution of the church (1 Peter moves from discussing persecution as a theoretical future possibility to a present fact at 4:12).

One additional reference in the Biblical epistles deserves comment: 2 Thessalonians 2:6 mentions 'he who restrains' or (as the RSV says) 'what is restraining him' ('the man of lawlessness,' vs. 3). The grammatical construction leaves uncertain whether Paul is referring to a person or an impersonal institution or force. The major possibilities are that Paul is confident that, in contrast to modern readers, the Thessalonians will understand whether he refers to (1) a supernatural power, (2) Satan himself, or (3) the Roman empire and emperor. An alternative form of the third option suggests that it is the rule of law in general which restrains. If Paul is referring to either the Roman empire or the political structure in general, as seems likely, then we have here another piece of Biblical evidence relating to the Christian view of the state.

Two points are important in considering this information from the epistles. First, they were not written about an ideal political situation; the Roman Empire was hardly a Christian, or even an 'enlightened,' state. The Thessalonian letters were written ca. AD 50, during the reign of the emperor Claudius (AD 41-54). Claudius was a rather benign ruler as far as the church was concerned. However the whole fabric of society was pagan. As Roman historians tell us, Claudius expelled Jews from Rome (Acts 18:3) because they were constantly rioting under the leadership of 'Chrestus,' almost certainly a misunderstanding of the name 'Christus' or 'Christ.'[21] During Claudius' reign incidents of persecution of Christians flared up from time to time.[22] Romans and 1 Peter were written while Nero ruled,

---

[21]What probably occurred were disruptions in the Jewish communities of Rome over 'Christ.'

[22]See F. F. Bruce, 'Christianity Under Claudius,' *Bulletin of the John Rylands Library*, 44/2 (March 1962), 309-26.

a cruel egomaniac, who in AD 66 unleashed the first great empire-wide, official persecution of Christianity.

Second, none of these Biblical statements come from times of official persecution by the Roman state. As Acts in particular shows, Christianity was at least tolerated, and sometime protected by Roman officials. Such conditions could explain the 2 Thessalonians reference to the restraining influence, if it is indeed pointing to the political structure. The question thus arises, what would the New Testament writers say about the state if they wrote during those times when the government was engaged in an official campaign to eliminate the church? The 'mixed' attitude toward Jewish officials in the New Testament is no realistic clue; the Jewish nation, although it misused its authority, did, after all, have divine legitimacy behind it.

Revelation

The sole possibility for examining what might be the Biblical view toward an openly anti-Christian state lies in the Book of Revelation. Here, any conclusions will be problematic. The book is written in a literary form, the apocalyptic, which by design is figurative, allusive, and imprecise. Furthermore, throughout Christian history, interpreters have viewed the book through different eyes – is it (1) an idealized, figurative depiction of the struggle between good and evil in general? (2) a veiled portrayal of the church's experience of persecution by Rome in the first century? (3) a symbolic presentation of the experience of the church from Apostolic times until the second coming of Christ? or as (4) a description of times and conditions immediately prior to, including, and immediately following the second coming of Christ as well as at the end of the world?

An Expository Model by Oscar Cullmann

If the Book of Revelation does refer to events both contemporary and future to its writer, then the imagery of Revelation provides insights into the Christian view of the state when it is a persecutor. Of the many who have sought to work out the details of this option, the most helpful to me is the Swiss New Testament exegete and theologian, Oscar Cullmann.[23] A summary of his work is relevant here.

Biblical Salvation History includes and gives meaning to all periods of the time, but the New Testament is primarily interested in the *present* period. This was so because of the function of Christ as Lord in it. Underlying the writings of the New Testament is the conviction that all history must be understood from the perspective that they and their readers are living in the future age although the end has not yet come.

The presence of the Holy Spirit is the sign of the presence of the final age but also of the tension characteristic of it. In the death and resurrection of Christ the Kingdom of God has been provisionally realized, but it can only be believed in, not seen. The new life of the Kingdom of God, which *will come* finally at the end of the world, *is already* realized in its members.

The church is made up of individuals who are still sinners. It has the responsibility to call all people to accept the good news that the decisive battle was won on Good Friday and Easter and that Christ already rules effectively over sin and death. It gives both the promise and warning of Christ's coming final victory and judgment.

By its proclamation the church actually participates in and carries forward the divine redemptive activity in history; it is also the earthly center of Christ's Lordship. The church then is the clue to what is going on in the world and what God is doing in church history; it is also the clue for understanding secular history.

The problem of the relationship between church and state actually reflects the issue of the relation of Salvation History and world history. Like the church, the political state exists 'between the times.' Christ's

---

[23]'The Kingship of Christ and the Church in the New Testament,' *The Early Church: Studies in Early Christian History and Theology* (A collection of essays). Edited by A. J. B. Higgins (Philadelphia: Westminster, 1956); *Jesus and the Revolutionaries* (New York: Harper, 1970); *The State in the New Testament* (London: SCM, 1956). See also his *Christ and Time: The Primitive Conception of Time and History,* rev. ed. (Philadelphia: Westminster, 1964) and 'The Relevance of Redemptive History,' Soli Deo Gloria: *New Testament Studies in Honor of William Childs Robinson* (Grand Rapids: Eerdmans, 1968), 9-22.

lordship includes his rule over the world of political powers as well as the church. However, behind the state also stand demonic powers[24] which are the enemies of Christ. Christ won the victory over the 'princes of the world' who were ultimately responsible for his death.

Cullmann insists that the difference between church and state is simply that the former knows of the lordship of Christ and willingly serves Him. The state, on the other hand, does not know of the lordship of Christ but still serves Him unconsciously and against its will. The state exists to maintain peace and order so that prior to *The End* the church can carry on its preaching. Therefore, Christians must have respect and concern for the state.

The demonic 'powers' are now only 'subjected' to God, they have not yet been destroyed; they can still do damage to the church, the representative of the Kingdom of God on earth. They constantly threaten to free themselves from the authority of Christ and sometimes appear to do so. Then, instead of creating peace and order, the state may be used by 'the powers' and become totalitarian, become the persecuting beast (cf. Rev 13). At that point the church must refuse to give *absolute* obedience to the state. Absolute obedience belongs to Christ alone.

The Christian's responsibility is to respect and obey the state as the instrument of God. It must also be watchful for signs of self-deification in the state because the Christian knows that there are always demonic forces threatening to break loose. When this happens, the church is obligated to disobey the state, for in such circumstances obeying the state would be rebellion against the lordship of Christ.

Eventually the demonic powers will be eliminated. Then all will be truly subject to God.

Then comes the end when he [Christ] delivers the kingdom to God the Father after destroying every authority and power. For he must reign until he has put all his enemies under his feet. The last enemy to be destroyed is death. 'For God has

---

[24]Note Ephesians 6:12; 1 Peter 5:8-9; James 4:7.

put all things in subjection under his feet.' But when it says, 'All things are put in subjection under him,' it is plain that he is excepted who put all things under him. When all things are subjected to him, then the Son himself will also be subjected to him who put all things under him, that God may be everything to every one (1 Cor 15:24-28).

Cullmann's approach has much to commend it. He, rightly I think, adopts the point of view that the Book of Revelation both anticipates the consummation, the return of Christ, while it also, at least partly, portrays the experience of Christians during Roman persecution in the first century. Yet his overall analysis assumes the Lutheran position on the issue of the relation between Christianity and culture and which Niebuhr labels 'Christ and Culture in Paradox.' Cullmann's understanding of Revelation could have opened the door for him to show directly how a change in the relationship between Christ and culture, such as culture against Christ, might alter the Christian's attitude and response. He implies an answer, but does not address the issue directly.

To me, the major weakness of Cullmann's analysis of the relation between church and state is that it provides only limited guidance for determining precisely when the Christian community is to refuse to obey the state. He speaks of the point at which the state becomes the persecuting beast and when it deifies itself, demanding the worship due only to God. These, he believes, accompany the failure of the state to provide a peaceful and orderly society in which the church can preach the gospel. When the state demands its head be worshiped, as did Rome in the first century and Japan in the twentieth, it has obviously deified itself and must be disobeyed. Hitler's attempt to dominate the church would certainly call for Christian resistance. Totalitarian states that prohibit the open and free proclamation of the gospel have, according to Cullmann's analysis, become the tools of the demonic powers. At what point, short of such open signs of self-deification by the state, is the church to withdraw its support? Doubtlessly, Cullmann would answer that the Christian community must determine that for itself in every age.

An important implication of Cullmann's view of the relationship between church and state could easily be overlooked. Both entities operate under the authority of God and both have their God-given spheres of activities. The state is not responsible to preach the gospel; that is the responsibility of the church. It only provides a setting in which that can take place. Furthermore, the church, as a corporate body, is not to control the state. While its members may participate in human government, the church is to perform its own task in its own sphere. The church is loyal to and supports the state as it operates in its sphere. At the same time the church must be ever being watchful for signs that the demonic powers may be breaking out in the state.

Christians in 'Neutral' or Nominally Christian States

The Biblical 'Worldview' affirms the presence of the sovereignty of God, the reality and presence of the Kingdom of God, and also the reality and threat of demonic powers who have been defeated but not yet eliminated. There is an unquestionable divine sanction for the state. Yet, even though the nation Israel was chosen and favored by God, she rejected the Messiah and persecuted the church. Her case reminds us that even the best of states can turn against God's sovereignty and the lordship of Christ. The state, any state, is (often unconsciously) subject to being used by evil powers. It is important to note that in Acts 4:25-26 the early church, quoting Psalm 2:1, applies to Israel a statement first made of the Gentiles, the heathen who 'gathered together against the Lord and against his Anointed.' Nevertheless, God remains sovereign; he can and does work through the state. The gist of Cullmann's discussion provides helpful guidelines for formulating the Christian attitude toward a particular state and government . One must indeed ask whether the state permits the church to acknowledge and live under its prior loyalty to the lordship of Christ and, secondly, whether the state permits free proclamation of the gospel. Yet, as implied above, he provides little guidance in determining when the lines have been crossed. In addition, more needs be said to benefit Christians in situations less extreme than those with which he deals.

Most modern western governments are not obviously the persecuting 'beast' or committed to Christian principles. Okholm's analysis, described at the beginning of this chapter, which suggests that although Christians may not be able to overthrow or change the 'prevailing culture', is probably close to the situation in which most readers of these words live. His call for the church to live out an alternate culture is close to Jesus' instructions to pray for enemies, persecutors, and for those in authority, to love enemies, feed the hungry, clothe the naked, visit the sick, orphans,, widows, and imprisoned. Nevertheless, I find Okholm's view a bit too pessimistic.

Above, in summarizing Henry's four strategies for social change we noted one is 'Regeneration: the transformation by a supernatural impulse in individual lives whereby the social scene is renewed through spiritual motivations.' Rather than seeking to organize political parties, action groups, resistance movements, or the like, this strategy looks for transformation from the inside. It avoids the danger of Christianity becoming contaminated by associating too closely with any type of political position.

What was said above about elements of God's ideal society should be the 'platform' for Christian desires for his or her political as well as social situation. Somehow, usually by example but sometimes by participation in government Christians have a unique responsibility. They, as a part of the Church, are the agents under God's guidance to be a voice for order and morality. Christians can provide examples of concern and active care for the poor, sick, disabled, and other disadvantaged in the name of Christ. God's people are to call for justice because he is the God of justice. It is not coincidental that such Christian spokespersons as Paul appealed to the state for justice (Acts 25:1-12). And, then, there is love. The Christian message calls for love because God first loved us. Christians are to love one another, but also those different from themselves, and even their enemies and persecutors.

The unique job of the Church within any state is to lift high the cross of Christ, to call for repentance and moral renewal. This is not accomplished through legislation, manipulation, force, or other human political schemes but by prayer, love, Christian living, and the spread of the Gospel. The humanistic, materialistic, secular, and even a hostile state is to be confronted, 'Not by might, nor by power, but by my Spirit, says the Lord of hosts' (Zech 4:6).

Conclusion

The question contained in the title of this section of our exploration of 'What is the Church's Relation to Society?' is 'Who is Lord?' It is always the question for every situation the church faces, especially that of her relationship to the state. The church must always affirm her prior loyalty to God and that she 'cannot but speak of what . . . [she has] . . . seen and heard' (Acts 4:19-20). When confronted with attempts to enforce national, religious-cultural traditions which violated the intention of God, Jesus said, 'The Son of man is Lord of the Sabbath' (Mark 2:28); he could have added, 'and of everything else.' The Christian sees Christ, not only as the 'Transformer of Culture,' but also as the one who triumphs over it.

Chapter 11

How Shall It End?

Definition and Scope of Eschatology

The word *eschatology* comes from the Greek adjective *eschatos* which means *last* or *end.* Traditionally, discussions of eschatology, *The End,* deal with such topics as the end of all things and the fate of individuals. Hence, Christian eschatology includes discussions of physical death, the events preceding the second coming of Christ, including the last struggle(s) with evil forces, and the second coming of Christ itself. It may consider the millennial issue, intermediate state and immortality, resurrection(s), and judgment(s). The end of nature (the cosmic order) and of humanity, rewards and punishments (heaven and hell), the new heaven and earth, and the final state of the universe may also be among topics included under the category *eschatology.*[1]

---

[1]*Eschatology* is currently used in other ways. It is frequently used to refer to anything which has to do with the Final Age, from the beginning of Jesus' ministry onward.

Much contemporary non-evangelical theology proceeds on assumptions which de-emphasize or deny the intervention of supernatural forces into the natural order and claims of the end of the material world. It tends to focus attention upon other issues under the heading *eschatology.* These, for an example, may include discussions of assumptions about the final stage of moral, social, intellectual, physical, and spiritual development. The result, it assumes, is utopia on earth, brought about largely by naturalistic processes.

Even more likely, since *end* may refer to *goal* or *purpose,* some contemporary theologians view the subject matter of eschatology as the attainment of meaning, purpose, self-awareness and the authenticity of the individual. Note the way Rudolf Bultmann uses the term in his existential interpretation of the New Testament in 'The New Testament and Mythology,' *Rudolf Bultmann: The New Testament and Mythology and Other Basic Writings.* Trans. by Schubert M. Ogden (Philadelphia: Fortress, 1984), 1-43.

Before beginning a general summary of the New Testament's teaching about *The End*, there are three issues of which we must be aware. They have contributed to the mass of confusion which, at least from the time of the Montanists in the second century to the present, has often arisen about *The End*.

Most of the New Testament statements about *The End* utilize some of the ideas and language of Intertestamental Jewish thought and writings. There are, however, differences. First, only some strains of contemporary Jewish eschatology are found in Christian teaching. Even more important, the Christian writers consider *The End* from a distinctly different point of view; for them the Final Age is already in effect. Oscar Cullmann in commenting about the Book of Revelation, puts it succinctly,

> Unlike Jewish apocalypses oriented towards the future only, John's revelation is characterized by the Christian notion of time according to which the center of divine history is by anticipation already reached in Jesus Christ. Thus the present time is already the time of the end, although the end itself must still be achieved. The author shows the celestial aspect of present events, just as he describes the celestial aspect of future events. This is the key for understanding the whole book.[2]

Christian writers also employ a literary form that is frequently found in Intertestamental Jewish writings.

The *Apocalyptic literary form* occurs in the Old Testament and Intertestamental Jewish writings as well as in parts of the New Testament. As mentioned in our statements about the Book of Revelation in the previous chapter, this is a distinct literary genre which utilizes much symbolism and visions. The Biblical student must become familiar with the apocalyptic as a whole in order to deal adequately with this material; it must be interpreted with methods which are appropriate for this distinct and unique form of writing.

Christians have and often do assume that the apocalyptic form is always to be taken as an indication that the writer is referring to the

---

[2]*The New Testament: An Introduction for the General Reader*. Trans. by Dennis Pardee (Philadelphia: Westminster, 1968), 120-21.

end time, in the restricted sense of the phrase, that which has to do with the very end of human history, the second coming of Christ. This can be a misleading assumption. The apocalyptic writers often have in view their own day, the immediate future, as well as the more distant future. At times their primary concern is with doctrines other than eschatology (such as theodicy, the problem of why/how a just, loving, and all-powerful God permits evil to exist).

In considering the question 'How shall it end?' Christians have often been preoccupied with questions and issues with which the New Testament text shows little concern – chronological schemes, identification of people, events, and institutions, and the exact time of Christ's return.[3] The New Testament is much more concerned to make general affirmations than to provide a 'map' of the sequence of the final pages of human history and to identify precisely the time of the second coming of Christ and the consummation of Salvation History.

Jesus criticizes his contemporaries for not being able to interpret 'signs of the times' (Matt 16:3). But, in Mark 13:31-33, he also said,

> Heaven and earth will pass away, but my words will not pass away. But of that day or that hour no one knows, not even the angels in heaven, nor the Son, but only the Father. Take heed, watch; for you do not know when the time will come.

This statement makes as clear as possible that human responsibility relating to *The End* is to 'watch,' to be ready, not to seek to set dates. To claim knowledge which God has reserved for himself is one of the attitudes or actions which the Biblical writers assume constitute blasphemy. In this context Oscar Cullmann says,

---

[3]'Some much canvassed questions, such as the chronological relation of the parousia to the great distress of Mark 13:19, to the manifestation of the man of lawlessness of II Thess 2:3-8, or to the millennial reign of Rev 20, are marginal to the main course of NT eschatological teaching, belonging rather to the detailed exegesis of the passages concerned'(F. F. Bruce, 'Eschatology,' *Evangelical Dictionary of Theology*, 365, Walter A. Elwell, ed., 2d ed; Grand Rapids Baker, 2001).

The limitation of the knowledge of the Son is asserted only with reference to the question of chronology. The reckoning of hours and days is regarded as a completely blasphemous undertaking, which even the possession of the Spirit cannot justify.[4]

New Testament Eschatology: the Presence of the Future in Jesus Christ

Paul summarizes the essence of the New Testament's teaching about *The End*, with the words, 'Christ Jesus our hope' (1 Tim 1:1) and 'Our Savior Christ Jesus,... abolished death and brought life and immortality to light through the Gospel' (2 Tim 1:10). As we have frequently mentioned, the Biblical view of time and of the nature of the Kingdom of God forces a broader view of eschatology than usual theological approaches. It assumes that the eschatological period is *already present* but also looks for *future aspects*.

New Testament eschatology cannot be separated from our view of God, his revelation, and theology in general; especially from the perspective framework of Salvation History. A Christian philosophy of history must include the assumptions that (1) the sovereign God, who is both creator and redeemer, remains active in the affairs of his created and redeemed order; (2) history is not an endless, meaningless cycle, but is moving toward a predetermined end; (3) the chief purpose of humanity is to be realized and fulfilled in what lies ahead, both for the individual and all creation.

In the New Testament view in which both time and the Kingdom of God lie within Salvation History, Jesus Christ is

---

[4]*Christ and Time*, 77. 'The anti-Christian feature in the apocalyptic evaluation of events in time, as we find this evaluation in the later apocalyptic sects down to the present day, is not the fact that such events are in some way interpreted as 'preliminary signs,' but that from them the time of the end is reckoned. Such a reckoning stands in contrast to the Primitive Christian belief that the fixing of the *kairoi* [= 'times'] belongs solely to the sovereign power of God, and that men, even by their knowledge, have no control over it. Viewed from this standpoint, it is not a falling away from the Primitive Christian attitude when ever and again, in the course of the centuries, this or that phenomenon is judged to be a manifestation of the Antichrist; but it is such a falling away when such a phenomenon is regarded as his *final* manifestation and so is used to reckon the date of the end' (*Ibid.,* 156-57).

central. This included its special view of *The End;* that since the life and ministry of Jesus the present situation is different from that existing before his earthly ministry – the Final Age, including the kingdom of God and the Messiah, is a present reality. Hence, the Christian worldview, distinct from that of unbelievers, is both eschatologically charged and changed. We may speak of 'realized eschatology' or 'eschatology being realized', but also we assume that 'the end is not yet'; there is more to be accomplished in God's work. The consummation is still future; God's great 'Victory Day' lies ahead! As we have previously noted, the coming of the Holy Spirit at Pentecost was proof that the Final Age is already here (Acts 2:16-17); his continuing presence in the church is 'the guarantee (or down payment) of our inheritance until we acquire possession of it' (Eph 1:14; cf. 2 Cor 1:22; 5:5). We live within the Final Age, aware of the reality of the invisible, realizing that the future is now.

A Summary of Biblical Data: Major New Testament Words and Other Sources of Information about Still Future Aspects of the Final Age

Vocabulary

There are at least seven words or phrases used of Christ's second coming in the New Testament. It is important to note them because each throws into the spotlight a different aspect of the event.

(1) *Revelation, reveal, disclose (apokalupsis)* speak of 'unveiling of that which is already present although unseen,' 'a removal of that which now obstructs.'[5]

(2) *Appearing, appearance (epiphaneia),* from which comes the word *epiphany* (often used of the Christmas season), means 'appearance,' 'manifestation of that which is already present although unseen,' or 'coming out from a hidden background.'[6]

(3) *Presence (parousia)* speaks of a 'closeness,' 'nearness,' or 'proximity,' 'the appearance of that which is new,' or 'that (usually

---

[5] 1 Corinthians 1:7; 2 Thessalonians 1:7; 1 Peter 1:7, 13; 4:13.
[6] 2 Thessalonians 2:8; 1 Timothy 6:14; 2 Timothy 1:10; 4:1, 8; Titus 2:13.

something new) which proceeds or results from something which is present.'[7]

(4) *The end* or *conclusion* (*to telos*) is occasionally used to refer to the culmination or to God's work of salvation as renewal (Matt 24:6).

(5) *The Day of the Lord* (*hē hēmera tou kuriou*) designates a point in time at which God acts in a decisive way, usually in judgment.

(6) *Our gathering together* or *our meeting* (*hēmōn episunagōgē*) is a term for the final collecting of God's people (2 Thess 2:1).[8]

(7) and, finally, *the blessed hope* (*tēn makarian elpida*) is a metaphor for the believer's future (Titus 2:13).

A couple of observations are in order about three of these words.[9] The New Testament writers believed Christ, although invisible, is spiritually present with the church from the ascension onward. Therefore the early Christians viewed the second coming as the revealing, the becoming visible of him who is, in fact, already present. The words *revelation* (*apokalupsis*) and *appearance* (*epiphaneia*), when used of this event, convey this idea. But the kind of visibility implied by these words need not be that of a physical body; it could be in a spiritual body which only appeared to be physical. However, the early Christians expected Christ to return in the resurrected-physical body, 'in the same way' (*houtōs*, Acts 1:11), in which he had ascended. This physical, visible return is the 'new element' involved in the second coming. It is conveyed by the word *presence* or *parousia*. The so-called 'delay of the *parousia*' (delay of the second coming[10]) was not an unexpected delay of the return of

---

[7]Matthew 24:3, 27, 37; 1 Corinthians 15:23; 1 Thessalonians 2:19; 3:13; 4:15; 5:23; 2 Thessalonians 2:1-9; James 5:1, 8; 2 Peter 1:16; 3:4, 12; 1 John 2:28.

[8]The verb is used in Matthew 24:31.

[9]I am indebted to my long-time colleague and friend, Dr. Walter A. Elwell, for help with the following suggestions.

[10]Some scholars argue that the early Christian expected the return of Christ in a very short period of time. When this did not occur, the scholars hold, the early Christians either gave up the expectation of a second coming or had to revise their theology to 'fit' the situation as they now perceived it to be.

Christ; the early Christians believed him to be already present, spiritually but invisibly. Rather, if there was indeed a 'delay' in the minds of some early Christians, it merely required an adjustment for living longer than expected with 'only' the spiritual presence of their Lord while they awaited the physical, visible manifestation.

Other New Testament words describe another aspect of *The End,* the eternal state itself. (1) *Age (aiōn)* means a distinct major period of time, and is used about 122 times in the New Testament. It may either stand alone or, in combination with other words, refer to a number of different periods of time. These include

(a) the present world or period of time, often meaning the present evil age (e.g., Gal 1:4). Other references may have more positive or neutral implications, as in Matthew 12:32, 'And whoever says a word against the Son of man will be forgiven; but whoever speaks against the Holy Spirit will not be forgiven, either in this *age* or in the *age* to come;'[11]

(b) sometimes *age (aiōn)* may refer to 'the end (completion, close) of the age;' note, Matthew 13:39, 'the enemy who sowed them [weeds in a field] is the devil; the harvest is the close of the *age*, and the reapers are angels.'[12]

In other New Testament passages *age* may refer to (c) *the coming age;*[13] (d) *the age to come;*[14] or (e) *eternal life* or, literally, *life of (or into) the ages (eis ton aiōna)* – this phrase looks forward into eternity;[15] the opposite, *from the age (ek tou aiōnos),* looks backwards from eternity (John 9:32).

Other major words referring to the eternal state include (2) *rebirth, restoration,* or *regeneration;*[16] (3) the *resurrection*

---

[11]See also Luke 20:34; 1 Corinthians 1:20; 2:8; 3:18; Galatians 1:4; Ephesians 1:21.

[12]See also Matthew 13:40, 47; 24:3; 28:20; Hebrews 9:26.

[13]Matthew 12:32; Ephesians 1:21; Hebrews 6:29.

[14]Luke 18:30, no one who has left all for Christ 'will not receive manifold more in this time, and in the *age* to come eternal life.'

[15]Mark 10:30; Luke 18:30.

[16]*Palingenesia,* as in Matthew 19:28 (RSV = 'new world;' NIV = 'restoration' – the same word is used in Titus 3:5 for 'born again.'

(*anastasis*, Matt 22:30); and (4) Acts 3:19-21 contains a phrase which refers to the end time that is a difficult passage to translate.[17] The RSV renders it,

> Repent therefore, and turn again, that your sins may be blotted out, that times of refreshing may come from the presence of the Lord, and that he may send the Christ appointed for you, Jesus, whom heaven must receive until the time for establishing all that God spoke by the mouth of his holy prophets from of old.[18]

Finally, Revelation 21:1 speaks of *The End* as (5) 'A New Heaven and a New Earth.'

The Teachings of Jesus

A large part of Jesus' teaching about *The End* is contained in what he says about the future aspects of the kingdom of God in the Synoptics, and about eternal life in John. His teaching concerning what happens after death is found mainly in the implications of the parable of 'The Rich Man and Lazarus' (Luke 16:19-31). He affirms that after death both the good and the evil have a conscious existence. The former enjoy peace, security, and happiness in 'Abraham's bosom' while the evil, in 'hades,' are, in the words of the rich man, 'in anguish in this flame.' The parable seems to indicate that those in one place are aware of those in the other and also of at least something of what is taking place on earth. There is no access from 'Abraham's bosom' to 'hades' or vice versa.

Matthew 19:23-29 tells of Jesus' statement, 'It will be hard for a rich man to enter the kingdom of heaven . . . it is easier for a camel

---

[17]*Kairoi anapsuxeōs apo prosōpou tou teeou ... cheonōn apokatastaseōs. Anapsusis* carries such ideas as 'to cool,' 'refreshing,' 'breathing space,' and 'relaxation' and *apokatastasis,* 'restoration.'

[18]Note that other English translations have different verse divisions and translations; KJV = 'times of refreshing ... the times of restoration of all things;' NIV = 'times of refreshing may come from the Lord ... until the time comes from God to restore everything;' NASB = 'times of restoration of all things ... the period of restoration of all things;' and the NRSV = times of refreshing ... the time of universal restoration.'

to go through the eye of a needle than for a rich man to enter the kingdom of God.' The disciples then ask, 'Who then can be saved?' and mention their leaving everything and following Jesus. Jesus replies,

> Truly, I say to you, in the new world, when the Son of man shall sit on his glorious throne, you who have followed me will also sit on twelve thrones, judging the twelve tribes of Israel. And every one who has left houses or brothers or sisters or father or mother or children or lands, for my name's sake, will receive a hundredfold, and inherit eternal life. But many that are first will be last, and the last first. (vss. 28-30)

The word here translated *new world* (*palingenesia*) means either *restoration* or *rebirth*. Hence, in addition to affirming the coming in glory of the Son of man, the reward of those who have made a total commitment to him, and the complete reversal of human values, Jesus makes an important statement about the future. It is the time of the ultimate return of all things to the conditions and situations God intended at creation.

John, too, records Jesus speaking of the future and of his assuring his followers of their eventually being with him. 'If I go and prepare a place for you, I will come again and will take you to myself, that where I am you may be also' (14:3), is probably his best known statement. Other than affirming that in his 'Father's house are many rooms' (14:2) and that he will return for his own, he makes a tantalizing statement. He insists that his going away, his ascension, the coming of the Holy Spirit, and the time preceding his return, are important parts of the whole drama of redemption (John 16:7). The church's present existence is no accident nor mistake; it plays its role in that which culminates at *The End*. Exactly what that role might be is left for us to surmise from the rest of Jesus' words and the activities and writings of the apostles.

Jesus' Olivet Discourse regarding *The End*[19] is the most often discussed part of his eschatological teachings. Its context is

---

[19]Mark 13; Matthew 24; cf. 25:31-46; Luke 21:5-38; cf. 19:41-44.

important. Jesus had just predicted the destruction of the Jerusalem temple, saying, 'Do you see these great buildings? There will not be left here one stone upon another, that will not be thrown down' (Mark 13:2). Some of his disciples ask 'When will this be, and what will be the signs when these things are all to be accomplished?' (Mark 13:4). Plainly, their questions enquired about events we now know were fulfilled when the Romans destroyed Jerusalem in AD 70.

Equally plain is the fact that the disciples assumed the destruction of the temple and the consummation of Salvation History would occur simultaneously. Matthew's account makes this clear, 'The disciples came to him privately, saying, "Tell us, (1) when will this be, and (2) what will be the sign of (a) your coming and (b) of the close of the age?"' (24:3). Furthermore, Jesus' answer was not limited to the historical destruction of Jerusalem. He seems to combine into a single unit the various times of physical and spiritual disruptions culminating with 'the Son of man coming in clouds with great power and glory ... [when] ... he will send out the angels, and gather his elect' (Mark 13:26-27). He referred to the early stages of the blooming cycle of a fig tree to admonish his hearers to be aware of future signs of the nearness of events (Mark 13:28-30) but warns against attempting to use the 'signs' to establish the exact time of his coming (Mark 13:32). The disciples are to 'take heed, watch' (vs. 33) and to be ready because, even for those who look for him, the coming of the Son of man will be 'sudden' (vs. 36). Matthew adds, 'You do not know on what day your Lord is coming .... The Son of man is coming at an hour you do not expect' (24:42, 44).

In referring to 'wars and rumors of wars' and other political, social, and natural disturbances (Matt 24:6-8) Jesus may have in mind events near to his own time, to the destruction of Jerusalem, as well as to the distant future. 'The desolating sacrilege' and flight from Jerusalem may well refer to the fall of Jerusalem in the first century AD (Mark 13:14). Luke's version of the discourse includes reference to 'Jerusalem surrounded by armies' (21:20); the same gospel records Jesus' earlier statement of coming doom upon Jerusalem in which, he said, 'The days shall come upon you, when your enemies will cast a bank about you and surround you, and hem you in on every side, and dash you to the ground' (19:43-44); events which parallel the description of the destruction of Jerusalem by the Romans related by the Jewish historian Josephus.

At the same time, the Olivet Discourse contains references to events which evidently have not yet occurred. The universal proclamation of the gospel (Mark 12:10) may be one of these; the return of the Son of man is certainly another case in point.

It appears that Jesus is making predictions about both the near and the distant future without indicating the time-gap between them.[20] It is also likely that Jesus' words imply a 'Salvation History pattern' in which God's dealing with people at one time and place is reflective of the way he deals with others in later times (some of Matthew's Old Testament quotations also seem to be examples of this).

Within the history of the church, the Olivet Discourse has been interpreted in many ways. Without going into details, we will miss the essential truths of this part of Scripture if we fail to recognize some important elements of Jesus' teaching. He insists that God will judge, even his own people, and human symbols of religious devotion, such as the Jerusalem temple, will not be exempt from that judgment. Furthermore, even times of trouble and the apparent triumph of evil are not beyond God's knowledge and control. His plan will be carried out, and the return of Jesus, the Son of man, is an essential part of its conclusions. The church is to 'watch' and 'be ready' for her Lord's return.

The Writings of Paul

1 Thessalonians 4:13–5:11 and 2 Thessalonians 2:1-12 contain direct references to *The End* and are probably Paul's earliest comments on the subject. The former comes in answer to questions asked about the role and fate of Christians who had already died in the return of Christ and subsequent glory. Paul affirms that

(1) Christ will indeed return, accompanied with 'a cry of command ... the archangel's call, and with the sound of the trumpet of God' (1 Thess 4:16).

---

[20]Apparently in the synagogue at Nazareth (Luke 4:16-21), he interpreted Isaiah 61:1-4 in this way.

(2) Dead believers will arise and actually precede those still living into heaven (1 Thess 4:14-15, 17).

(3) 'The day of the Lord' will come suddenly and unexpectedly (1 Thess 5:2-7).

(4) Believers are, therefore, to be watchful and ready (1 Thess 5:4-8).

(5) The fact of Christ's return is to be a source of comfort and encouragement (1 Thess 4:18; 5:11).

The 2 Thessalonians 2 passage is evidently an attempt to correct misconceptions, especially the report that 'the day of the Lord' had already come (vs. 2). Paul, referring to teaching previously given his readers, reminds them of some 'signs' which must precede that event, the coming of 'the rebellion' and 'the man of lawlessness ... the son of perdition' (vs. 3).[21] Since these had not occurred, the Thessalonians could be assured that the Lord's return was still in the future. He warns that 'the lawless one by the activity of Satan' will work 'with all power and with pretended signs and wonders, and with all wicked deception' and will lead the wicked astray (vss. 2:9-12). By implication, he warns believers not to be deceived by 'pretended signs and wonders'.

We will consider the major thrust of 1 Corinthians 15 in connection with Paul's view of immortality and resurrection. There are also

---

[21]Although the original readers of the epistle doubtlessly knew full well to what Paul referred in mentioning 'the rebellion' and 'the man of lawlessness... the son of perdition,' we do not. F. F. Bruce (*Word Biblical Commentary: 1 and 2 Thessalonians* [Waco, TX: Word Books 1982]), notes that the word translated 'rebellion' denotes either a political or a religious defection. He observes, 'Since the reference here is to a world-wide rebellion against divine authority at the end of the age, the ideas of political revolt and religious apostasy are combined' (p. 166). He assumes that 'the man of lawlessness' and 'the son of perdition' are the same individual. The language the writer uses here 'suggests that he is in some sense a rival Messiah, the *antichristos* of 1 John 2:18 ('you have heard that AntiChrist is coming')' (p. 167). See also J. Julius Scott, Jr., 'Paul and Late-Jewish Eschatology – A Case Study, I Thess 4:13-18 and II Thess 2:1-12,' *Journal of the Evangelical Theological Society* Vol XV, Part 3 (Summer 1972), pp. 133-43.

comments in this chapter germane to our more general survey. After speaking of the resurrection of Christ, the first fruits, then concerning believers, Paul goes on to say that the rule of Christ will result in the complete subjugation of all things to himself. He will destroy all enemies; the last enemy to be eliminated is death. Christ will then deliver the kingdom to God the Father, 'that God may be everything to every one' (vss. 24-28).

At the end of 1 Corinthians 15 Paul speaks of a 'mystery' (vs. 51), an instantaneous resurrection and change from the mortal to the immortal. As in 2 Thessalonians, he refers to the sound of the trumpet (vs. 52). The result will be the final 'victory through our Lord Jesus Christ' (vs. 56). Again, he insists that knowledge of all this calls the believer to steadfastness and awareness that 'in the Lord your labor is not in vain' (vs. 58).

Paul also speaks of immortality and the resurrection in 2 Corinthians 5:1-10, but without the apocalyptic imagery of 1 Corinthians 15. There Paul refers directly to coming judgment and uses it for motivational purposes, 'We make it our aim to please him. For we must all appear before the judgment seat of Christ, so that each one may receive good or evil, according to what he has done in the body' (vss. 9-10).

The last Pauline passage at which we will look is Romans 8:18-30 in which references to *The End* are woven into a discussion of the broader fabric of the final aspects of the work of Christ in salvation. He speaks of future glory (vs. 18) and of the liberation of all creation (vss. 19-22). The Apostle specifically mentions the final redemption and adoption of believers (vss. 23-25). He gives assurance that God's ultimate purposes will prevail and 'that in everything God works for good with those who love him and are called according to his purpose' (vs. 28). The passage ends with Paul's assurance of the believer's position, that nothing 'will be able to separate us from the love of God in Christ Jesus our Lord' (vss. 31-38).

2 Peter and Jude

The problem with which Peter deals in his second epistle is clearly the fact that the second coming had not occurred as soon as some had expected. He refers to 'scoffers ... saying, "Where is the promise of his coming?... all things have continued as they were from the beginning of creation"' (3:3-4). Peter's reply involves the difference we noted above between the words *revealing* (*apokalupsis*) (1 Pet 1:7) and *presence* (*parousia*) (2 Pet 3:4). The former speaks of the making visible that which is already present although invisible, the latter, while not denying the reality of a spiritual presence, carries the idea of *newness*, a distinct appearing which is yet to come. Peter asserts that the Christ who is now spiritually present will return visibly, and that will be a definite, discernable event.

The delay of God's judgment is no argument at all. He delayed judgment but eventually unleashed it in the time of Noah (2 Pet 3:5-6). The same principle explains the present situation; divine delay is a gracious act to give time for repentance (3:9, 14). Quoting Psalm 90:4, Peter demonstrates that the Lord's time is different from that of humans; 'one day is as a thousand years, and a thousand years as one day' (3:8).

With Jesus and Paul, Peter affirms that 'the day of the Lord will come' and that it will be unexpected, 'like a thief' (2 Pet 3:10). He says the material world as now known will be destroyed and replaced with 'new heavens and a new earth in which righteousness dwells' (vss. 10-13). Peter also gives practical admonitions, calling for 'lives of holiness and godliness' (3:11), for awaiting 'and hastening (or 'earnestly desiring') the coming of the day of God' (3:13), and for zeal 'to be found in him without spot or blemish, and at peace' (3:14).

Jude adds little information about New Testament teachings concerning 'The End'. He quotes the intertestamental Jewish book, 1 Enoch 1:9, to support his contention that the Lord is coming for judgment (Jude 14-15). With 2 Peter he uses the word 'scoffers' to describe false teachers who will come 'in the last time' (vs. 18). He is sure that God is 'able to keep you from falling and to present you without blemish before the presence of his glory' (vs. 24).

The Book of Revelation

No attempt to answer the New Testament question, 'How shall it end?' can be complete without attention to the Book of Revelation. In mentioning its possible relevance for the issue of church versus state we commented on some of the special problems associated with Revelation – the obscurity of its literary form, philosophical orientation, and precisely with which historical situation it interacts or intends to present. We noted too the interpretative question which asks whether it refers to *The End* or to some other period or concept. The history of interpretation of Revelation provides adequate proof that different opinions on these matters will result in a plethora of conclusions about the nature and details of its relevance to the issue at hand.

This is not the place for a detailed examination of the book nor a defense of a particular interpretative stance. I tend to see Revelation as an example of the type of prophetic writing which addresses and alludes to events of the author's own time and *also* to the future. It does so as it sees in the writer's situation patterns and shadows of that which is yet to come. The book, I believe, refers to, draws imagery from, and addresses directly the experiences of Christians living at the end of the first century, during the time of persecution by the Emperor Domitian (*ca.* AD 90-96). At the same time, the inspired writer alludes to the types of experiences and events that will occur when the restraint mentioned in 2 Thessalonians 2 is removed. Then God will gather together the various strands of his work in Salvation History and bring it to its end in the consummation.

We are not able to identify nor understand all the imagery and allusions in the book; yet, its overall message is crystal clear. Revelation attests that God's people are living 'between the times', after the decisive victory won by Jesus in his death, resurrection, and ascension, but before the final victory which will be his at his coming. The earthly, although affected, is not the only, nor even the most important scene of events in the ongoing conflict between God and Satan. During this 'between-the-times' period, God's people are subject to the wrath of the defeated, but not yet subdued enemy who still ranges afar, seeking whom of God's own he may destroy.

God is not unmindful of the plight of his own. Yet, for reasons not fully revealed, he chooses to let the beasts, harlots, Babylons, and others through whom Satan carries on his hopeless struggle, play out the tragedy of rebellion until its bitter end.

And the end is sure to come. The writer can already see the divine judgments borne with broken seals (Rev 5–6) and trumpet blasts (Rev 7–11). Plagues and wars may come, beasts arise, martyred souls cry from beneath the throne, the pregnant woman must flee, witnesses are killed, and the saints are called to 'endurance and faith' (13:10). The angel bearing 'an eternal gospel' already flies through the heavens and calls 'to every nation, and tribe and tongue and people' to 'Fear God and give him glory, for the hour of his judgment has come' (14:6-7). The coming of 'the great day of God the Almighty' is already decreed, and it will come 'like a thief!' (16:15). The field and outcome of the final battle is even now determined; at Armageddon (16:16) 'the Lamb will conquer ..., for he is the Lord of lords and King of kings' (17:14). As Babylon falls the kings of the earth cry, 'Alas, alas!' (18:10). But 'the voice of a great multitude in heaven, cries,

> Hallelujah! Salvation and glory
> and power belong to our God...
> He has avenged ... the blood
> of his servants ...
> Praise our God, all you his servants,...
> Hallelujah! For the Lord our God
> the Almighty reigns' (19:1-6).

The victory is won. At the judgment from 'a great white throne' books are opened. The enemies of God and the Lamb are cast into 'the lake of fire,' the second death. Those who dwell in 'a new heaven and a new earth ... [in] ... the holy city, new Jerusalem' are called, with language reflective of the covenant made with Abraham, 'his [God's] people.' From the throne, with even more direct covenantal language, the voice declares, 'I will be his God and he shall be my son' (21:3, 7). God's cosmic work of salvation will be complete, for there the leaves of the tree of life are 'for the healing of the nations' (22:2). The restoration of the church and individual believers will reach its climax when God's

> servants shall worship him; they shall see his face, and his name shall be on their foreheads. And night shall be no more; they need no light or lamp or sun, for the Lord God will be their light, and they shall reign for ever and ever. (Rev 22:3-5)

In spite of its literary and historical obscurities, the Book of Revelation speaks clearly of God, of his salvation, of his relation to his church (even during times of suffering), of God's final victory, and of his judgment of the wicked. It regards as future, yet certain, the culmination and restoration, the final realization of God's original intents for creation, in the new heaven and new earth. Then will be redemption in its fullest sense. Then will be the complete realization of the promises contained in the covenant and the proclamation of the kingdom.

The primary purpose and message of Revelation is to speak about both the present and 'The End.' It affirms that God is present and active in the history of the world and that in the end he will be victorious and conform the universe to His purpose, under His control. This is how it shall end!

Summary: The Church's Responsibility

Already we have observed that most of the eschatological passages throughout the New Testament contain both admonitions and statements of responsibilities for those who await the consummation. Discussions about *The End* in the New Testament are not idle speculations. They are eminently practical – to encourage the readers to be faithful and zealously to live the lives given by God in their new birth in Christ.

Time and again we have encountered the command to 'watch,' to be prepared. Although the Lord's coming is sure, its time is unknown and will not be known by mortals. In Mark 13:34 Jesus alludes to his coming like that of a householder who returns unexpectedly from a journey and as a thief (Matt 24:43). Paul (1 Thess 5:2, 4), Peter (2 Pet 3:10), and Revelation (3:3; 16:15) also liken Christ's return to that of the coming of 'a thief.' Deceivers and deception will be a constant threat, even signs, wonders, and what appears to be prophecy will not be trustworthy indicators of the Lord's work (Matt 24:11; Luke 21:8; 2 Thess 2:9). Consequently, believers are to be ready, to watch, to be prepared. Of what do watchfulness and preparation consist? Matthew 24:46 (cf. Luke 12:43) makes clear that the blessed servant is the one who will be found doing his or her assigned tasks when the Lord comes.[22] In view of the dangers and sufferings ahead for God's people, to Jesus' admonition to watch, he adds, 'Praying that you may have strength to escape all these things that will take place, and to stand before the Son of man' (Luke 21:36).

Godliness, holiness, righteous living are also preparations for the Lord's coming. In fact, the New Testament writers assume that awareness and conviction of the Lord's return will radically affect both one's worldview and daily life. They proclaim it, not only as an important element of Christian knowledge, but also as a motivation for proper behavior. The uncertainty of the time of its occurrence is all the more reason for constant, consistent Christian living.

Some Eschatological Themes and Issues

We have already said enough to answer the question, 'How shall it end?' There are, however, a number of themes and issues which are significantly important to address, even at the risk of redundancy.

The Return of Christ

All sections of the New Testament leave no doubt that 'the blessed hope' is that Jesus will return to earth and bring God's work of salvation and restoration to its consummation. As the apostles stood

---

[22]A student once came to my office to tell me of an itinerant Bible teacher who was speaking at a nearby church. He responded to my obvious lack of enthusiasm by informing me that the teacher said positively that the Lord would return in 1975. I replied that I was not surprised because as a junior high school student I had heard the same person affirm that the second coming would occur in 1956. With disgust the student asked what I would do if I knew for certain the Lord would come at 1:30 that day. I replied, 'Teach my 1:00 class.'

gazing at the cloud which had received their ascending Lord, angels assured them that he would return 'in the same way as you saw him go into heaven' (Acts 1:11). What does this mean? As his disciples had little warning of his ascension, so his return will be sudden and unexpected. He was taken up in his resurrected physical body; certainly his return will be physical. Also, his return will be visible, for Revelation 1:7 says 'every eye shall see him.' Perhaps there are other parallels; clouds may accompany his return; Zechariah 4:4, when compared with Acts 1:12, suggests that it may occur at the same location.

The expectation of the return of Christ is a future fact with present significance. It is significant for both Salvation History and universal history. Much contemporary despair and meaninglessness is related to the suspicion that human kind is locked in an endless, irrational, purposeless cycle. For the Christian, belief about *The End*, based upon Scripture, gives hope and comfort. It also provides an ethical mandate and motivation. There is a living, loving God at work in history; good and evil make a difference to him; there is a heaven to gain and hell to shun.

Life and Death

Both *life* and *death* are used by New Testament writers with a variety of meanings. There are three Greek words which are usually translated *life*. Life[23] can refer to present, earthly existence. *Zōē* can also mean something more, a unique quality of life which comes in union with Christ through faith. In combination with *ages* (*aiōn*), *zōē* means everlasting life, a synonym for the immortal state. The word often translated *soul* (*psuchē*) has a variety of meanings which are often impossible to distinguish. They include *physical existence*, or something like *very being*; it is often thought to refer to the psychological and/or emotional aspects of humans. The Greek word for *spirit* (*pneuma*) can also mean breath, or wind. Occasionally it refers to physical life (as it clearly does in Revelation 11:11; 13:15). More often it is used of the new spiritual life, life by and in the Spirit of God.

---

[23]*Zōē* and occasionally *bios*.

The term *life*, then, may refer to that which animates the human body or that which distinguishes a human being from an inanimate object. It also speaks of that new quality of existence which comes in union with God through Christ.

The opposite of life is *death*. Of course it may designate the end of human life, physical death. It is also used of spiritual conditions such as separation from God, the source of all life. Death is the principle which dominates all persons separated from God and is the state of human spiritual helplessness (Eph 2:1; Col 2:13). Revelation 20:14; 21:8 define eternal punishment, meaning permanent separation from God, as *the second death*.

These terms indicate important aspects of New Testament eschatology. They inform us that in *The End* lies the culmination of life and death. True, never-ending life is evident only after the consummation. The full implications and meaning of death are also revealed at the conclusion of universal and Salvation History.

Resurrection and Immortality

'Resurrection' refers to the return to life of a physical body, 'immortality' to life after death, a never-ending, incorruptible existence. The Biblical writers assert that only God has immortality, a never-ending, incorruptible existence. They also teach that in Jesus Christ Christians receive immortality and survive and function after death. However, they provide but little detail about the nature of this state of existence beyond physical death.

The concept of immortality is present in the Old Testament, but there is no Hebrew word for it. In Proverbs 12:28 (NASB), 'In the way of righteousness is life, and in its pathway there is no death.' *Immortality* (as the last word is translated in the NIV) is, literally, the phrase *no-death*.[24] *Sheol*, which occurs many times throughout the Old Testament, denotes an obscure, shadowy, gloomy place of existence, but also one of forgetfulness, after death. The Old Testament Hebrew hoped for deliverance from sheol (Pss 26:10; 49:15; 86:13). Job 10:20-22 anticipates only a sheol-like state after death but in 19:25-26 he seems to

---

[24]Hebrew, *'al-māwet*.

look for something more. Isaiah's prophecy may end with a vague expectation of continued existence for good and evil (Isa 66:22-24; cf. Isa 26:16; Ps 23:6); such is made clear in Daniel 12:2. During the intertestamental period there arose a variety of views of immortality and resurrection.

Discussions of immortality are closely associated with those dealing with the nature of human persons. There are traditionally at least three major alternatives. Each of these is related to different views about the effects of death and the nature of the beyond. The traditional view within Christianity, acknowledging either a dualist or tripartite view of persons (that people are composed of either body and soul-spirit or body, soul, and spirit), holds that between death and the resurrection there is some sort of an intermediate state in which the immaterial part of the individual continues a conscious existence apart from the physical. Others emphasize that persons are a composite whole and assume that at death there is an immediate resurrection of a new spiritual body and union with God. Others with a similar holistic understanding of human persons propound a form of re-creationism, a temporary extinction at death which ends at the resurrection in a new creation. An associate issue, *soul sleep* (*psychopannychy* – an unconscious existence), could be a corollary to either the traditional view or that of re-creation. The New Testament writers present the idea of immortality with (1) nouns translated with such phrases as not-perishable, incorruptibility, or immortality;[25] and no-death, deathlessness, or immortality;[26] (2) with adjectives imperishable, incorruptible, immortal;[27] and (3) the phrase *eternal life* (literally, *life of the ages, zōē aiōnios]*.

Eternal life occurs only occasionally in the Synoptics,[28] but is a favorite expression of John.[29] It is never used in Revelation, but is

---

[25]*Aphtharsia,* as in Romans 2:7; 1 Corinthians 42, 50, 53-54; Ephesians 6:24; 2 Timothy 1:10.

[26]*Athanasia,* as in 1 Corinthians 15:53-54; 1 Timothy 6:1.

[27]*Aphthartos* in Romans 1:23; 1 Corinthians 9:25; 15:52; 1 Timothy 1:17; 1 Peter 1:4, 23; 3:4.

[28]Matthew 19:16, 20; Mark 10:17, 30; Luke 10:25; 18:18, 30.

[29]John 3:15, 16, 36; 10:38; 17:2-3; 1 John 1:2; 2:25; 5:11, 13, 20; etc.

frequently employed by Paul.[30] Passages, such as 2 Corinthians
5:1-10, refer or allude to the concept with metaphors. Immortality
is a corollary to belief in existence after death,[31] or resurrection in
general.

Throughout his teachings, Jesus assumes a continuing existence
after death. Certainly the future aspects of the Kingdom of God
imply as much. He speaks of it directly in the parable of 'The Rich
Man and Lazarus' (Luke 16:19-31) and in the judgment scene of
Matt 25:31-46. To make 'everlasting life' available is at the heart of
his mission in John, 'I came that they may [have life], and have it
abundantly' (10:10; cf. 5:40; 20:31). In John 14:1-3 Jesus assumes
not only a continuing existence, but also that for believers it will be
with him.

Peter says that Christians 'have been born anew to a living hope
through the resurrection of Jesus Christ from the dead, and to an
inheritance which is imperishable, undefiled, and unfading' (1 Pet
1:3-4). Later he states that this new birth is 'not of perishable seed
but of imperishable' (vs. 23). The judgment scenes of Revelation
20–22 predict an eternal life of bliss for believers and punishment
for those who refuse to believe.

It is Paul who gives the clearest explanation of immortality. In
Romans 2:7, he says God will give eternal life (*zōē aiōnios*) to
those who seek glory and honor and immortality (*aphtharsia*).
Paul, in Ephesians 6:24, blesses with grace those loving Christ in
immortality (*en aphtharsia*) – a phrase which could refer to an
immortal, incorruptible or undying love, to a state of immortality, or
simply *forever*. In 2 Timothy 1:10, the writer affirms that our Savior
Christ Jesus abolished death and brought life and immortality
(*aphtharsia*). The adjectival form of the word (*aphthartos*),
that can be translated imperishable, incorruptible, immortal refers to
God (Rom 1:23; 1 Tim 1:17) and to the lasting reward of the believer
in contrast to the perishable wreath won by the athlete (1 Cor 9:25);

---

[30]E.g., Romans 2:7; 5:21; 6:22-23; Galatians 6:8; 1 Timothy 1:16; 6:1; 2
Timothy 2:10; Titus 1:2; 3:7.

[31]E.g., Philippians 1:20-24; 3:10-21.

elsewhere it appears only in 1 Peter 1:4, 23; 3:4. *Eternal life* (literally, *life of the ages, zōē aiōios*) occurs frequently in John and the Johannine epistles (but never in Revelation), nine times in Paul's letters (the references are given above), and in Acts only in 13:26, 48, a context in which Paul is prominent. The New Testament writers clearly teach that there is an existence beyond the one people now have and that it will never end.

In 1 Corinthians 15 Paul's focus is upon the resurrection of Christ in particular and that of humans in general. He deals with immortality by both word (vvs. 42, 50, 52-54) and inference. Immortality is the opposite of perishable or mortal (*phthartos*); it is also a description of the nature of resurrected bodies. He argues that as there are different types of earthly, physical, perishable bodies (fish, fowls, animals, human), so there is a difference between earthly bodies and heavenly, spiritual bodies. The perishable is equated with dishonor and weakness, and is physical; the immortal is equated with glory and power, and is spiritual (vss. 42-44). Since the physical, earthly, 'cannot inherit the Kingdom of God,' nor does the perishable inherit the immortal, a change is necessary. This Paul describes as 'not being asleep,' (vs. 51), 'being raised' (from the dead) and 'putting on' the imperishable (vs. 52). The result is God's final victory over death (vss. 54-57). Thus, on the subject of immortality, Paul, in 1 Corinthians 15, asserts the fact of an incorruptible, permanent existence in contrast to our present condition, that it will involve different *bodies* (but in continuity with present ones), and that immortality will be the believer's full and final possession at the final resurrection.

The passage in 2 Corinthians 5:1-10 also adds light to the teaching on immortality. The future, eternal, heavenly 'house' is the present possession of believers.[32] In spite of the present undesirable state, a mortal one in which 'we groan' (vss. 2-4), the Spirit is 'the guarantee' (*arrabōn*) of the better state which awaits the believer (vs. 5). Furthermore, Paul asserts that to be 'away from the body' is to be 'at home with the Lord' (vs. 8). Thus, again Paul is confident

---

[32] 'We have' (vs. 1).

of a conscious immortal existence in a changed or different body. His belief regarding what lies between death and the 'putting on' of the heavenly house is the subject of a variety of interpretations.

Philippians 1:20-21 strengthens the conviction of 2 Corinthians 5 that in the believer's union with Christ, the future (immortal) life is a present possession. Galatians 3:27, using the same metaphor of 'putting on clothes' as 2 Corinthians 5, suggests that the 'baptized' are already 'clothed ... with Christ'. The expectation of enjoying the presence of Christ after death is also stated in Philippians 1:20-24. Philippians 2:10-21 concludes with the same expectation as that of the Corinthian correspondence – of a changed or transformed body, which is by implication immortal.

Many contemporary investigations stress that immortality, as well as other features of Paul's eschatology, must be viewed within the context of his total thought. Ladd says, 'The believer lives the life of the new age.... To be 'in Christ' means to be in the new age and to experience its life and powers.'[33] Indeed, Paul assumes immortality is a permanent, incorruptible, never-ending state and life. Not only awaiting the Christian after death but is already the present possession of the believer. Changes will occur after death which will make immortality evident, in appropriately different bodies, because it is now obscured in corruptible ones.

Thus far our discussion has been rather technical. In the face of the death of our loved ones or in contemplating our own fate, we want to know what lies beyond the grave. The Bible clearly teaches a continuing existence after death for all. For believers this will be eternal and imperishable, marked by that glory and honor which comes from union with Christ. Because immortality is now obscured in corruptible bodies, changes will occur. Believers will have different bodies, appropriate for their immortal state. Paul indicates that these 'bodies,' although different from those we now possess, will have some continuity with them.[34] What is assured is that our personality,

---

[33]George E. Ladd, *A Theology of the NT,* (1993), 596.

[34]The nature of the resurrected body is unclear. The disciples usually recognized the resurrected Jesus only as a result of their relation with him in which they talked with him and saw his actions. Through this his personal

personhood, or whatever it is that makes us unique and recognizable by others will be a part of our perfect, glorified state. All this Paul sees as certain because of the Spirit's guarantee, the defeat of death, and the ultimate victory of God through Jesus Christ (1 Cor 15:54-57).

Judgment(s)

'It is appointed for men to die once, and after that comes judgment' (Heb 9:27); 'We must all appear before the judgment seat of Christ, so that each one may receive good or evil, according to what he has done in the body' (2 Cor 5:10). These verses explicitly state the New Testament proclamation regarding the certainty of divine judgment upon all. There are over fifty-five direct references to divine judgment in the New Testament. If places where God or Christ are referred to as 'judge' and other indirect references were included, the count would be much higher.

In a survey of this sort, it is not possible to go into a detailed discussion of even the major passages related to judgment. Certainly we cannot consider the details of the countless controversies relating to who is to judge and be judged, the time of judgment, the basis for judgment, the nature of pronouncements (rewards and punishments), or even the number of judgments.

Some general statements must be made at the outset of our consideration of this topic. In the Old Testament judgment is spoken of in general terms, affecting both Israel and the Gentile nations, but it shows little concern for judgment after death. In the New Testament judgment after death and the role of the Messiah in judgment are, if not new concepts, then certainly especially emphasized features. Every part of the New Testament, gospels, Acts, the epistles, and Revelation, both assume and, to some degree, discuss judgment. There are references to judgment in the past (e.g., Rom 5:16), in the present (e.g., John 8:15; 9:39; 12:31), as well as a future act. Nevertheless, while there does seem to be an ongoing divine judgment

---

being shone through. At the same time, the rich man recognized Lazarus from afar.

of all people, the New Testament clearly ties the Great Judgment to the second coming of Christ.

Essentially judgment is on the basis of relationship with God through Christ. A proper understanding of judgment must recognize that condemnation is not some future, arbitrary act. The nature of creation, in which God's moral nature is reflected in the very fabric of the universe as he intended it to be, and the necessity of his continuing sovereign rule over it, make judgment essential. To reject God's rule, to refuse to abide by the morality which was originally inherent within his creation, mean that offending groups and persons are 'condemned already . . . he who does not obey the Son shall not see life, but the wrath of God rests upon him' (John 3:18, 36). Future judgment will only confirm an existing legal state. Release from condemnation requires acceptance of the Judge's means of acquittal, a restoration of the intended relationship between God and his creatures, for 'He who believes in him [Jesus Christ] is not condemned . . . He who believes in the Son has eternal life' (John 3:18, 36). Note that believing in Jesus Christ is synonymous with obeying the Son; belief is active faith which obeys.

Matthew has more to say about judgment than the other Synoptic Gospels. His portrayal of it crescendos in 25:31-46, the great judgment of all the nations by the Son of man upon his glorious throne. Note that judgment, in the sense of determining guilt or righteousness, appears to have already been made; those gathered around the throne have already been placed in their proper group. There the 'sheep,' the acquitted to whom eternal life is granted, have already been separated from the 'goats,' who are condemned and sent away into eternal punishment. Here we have more of a scene of sentencing than determination of guilt. This is in harmony with what we have just noted about those who have rejected God and his Christ being 'condemned already.'

Judgment is on the basis of how one has related to the Judge's 'brethren.' Hence, the question of who are 'the brethren?' Opinions vary. Are they a collective group or individuals? Are they the Judge's own people, the Jews, or Christians? Or are they a 'remnant' of one or another of these groups? It is nations who are gathered

(25:32), but judgment is on the basis of individual response to the need of 'one of the least of these my brethren' (25:40, 45). Whatever the answer, the essential element is not general social concern, but relation to Christ exhibited through social concern for his own in their times of need.

The question of the basis for segregating the 'sheep' from the 'goats' remains. The two passages already mentioned in John 3 assert that such distinction is on the basis of believing 'in the name of the only Son of God.' Elsewhere, in the same gospel 3:16 says, 'whoever believes in him should not perish but have eternal life' and 12:48 records Jesus' statement, 'He who rejects me and does not receive my sayings has a judge; the word that I have spoken will be his judge on the last day'. The whole of our consideration of the question, 'What must I do to be saved?' is relevant here. Forgiveness, justification, reconciliation to God, through faith in the person, words, and atoning work of Jesus Christ, places one among the 'sheep.' But the language of Matthew 25 and other judgment passages strongly emphasize that faith in Christ is no mere intellectual or emotional response. It is an active response, a total life-changing commitment, which affects every aspect of our relation to God, of our daily life, and our relationship with his people (both his and the Christian's 'brothers and sisters').

Still, those passages which we quoted at the beginning of this section, and many more, especially in Revelation, heighten the expectation of a great, final judgment. The words of 20:11-13 speak for themselves,

> Then I saw a great white throne and him who sat upon it; from his presence earth and sky fled away, and no place was found for them. And I saw the dead, great and small, standing before the throne, and books were opened. Also another book was opened, which is the book of life. And the dead were judged by what was written in the books, by what they had done. And the sea gave up the dead in it, Death and Hades gave up the dead in them, and all were judged by what they had done.

The word 'judgment' does not occur in 1 Corinthians 3:10-15 but the implication of it is evident. Paul says he has 'laid a foundation . . . which is Jesus Christ' (vss. 10-11). He continues,

> Now if any one builds on the foundation with gold, silver, precious stones, wood, hay, straw – each man's work will become manifest; for the Day will disclose it, because it will be revealed with fire, and the fire will test what sort of work each one has done. If the work which any man has built on the foundation survives, he will receive a reward. If any man's work is burned up, he will suffer loss, though he himself will be saved, but only as through fire (vss. 12-15).

Although it is not quite certain what he means by the various kinds of 'building materials,' the affirmation that even those whose works will be destroyed will be saved suggests some sort of evaluation of Christians, not for salvation but for reward.

Jesus' parable of the servants whose master would return unexpectedly and his comments which follow it (Luke 12:47-48), when considered along with the 1 Corinthians 3 passage, raise the possibility of degrees of both rewards and punishments.

> That servant who knew his master's will, but did not make ready or act according to his will, shall receive a severe beating. But he who did not know, and did what deserved a beating, shall receive a light beating. Every one to whom much is given, of him will much be required; and of him to whom men commit much they will demand the more.

Such could apply to the judgment both of Christians and unbelievers. Although Romans 2:2-16 asserts that those who have never heard the good news of salvation through Christ will not be exempt from punishment, Jesus' words in Luke may imply that the punishment of such persons will be less severe.

Although the Biblical data never deviates from the fact of judgment, it contains a variety of both description and details about it. It is, therefore, not surprising that some Bible students have suggested there will be several judgments – sometimes as many as four, the judgment of 1) believers, 2) Israel, 3) of the Gentile nations, 4) and the Great White Throne. The Biblical data is certainly open to such interpretations. It is also possible, I think probable, that the evidence could fit a single final judgment. This would confirm the judgment already in effect of those who have rejected or submitted to the rule of God and his saving work through Christ. It would then dispatch all human kind to their final place and also be the occasion for the reward of believers.

The Eternal State

Three major elements are involved in considering the eternal state which will follow the return and final victory of Christ. These include the Kingdom of God, the change and renewal of the created order, and the assignment of human persons and spiritual beings to different places on the basis of their obedience to God.

The return of Christ will bring in the Kingdom of God in its fullest sense. At his last supper with his disciples, Christ spoke of the passover being 'fulfilled in the kingdom of God' and his not drinking 'of the fruit of the vine until the kingdom of God comes' (Luke 22:16, 18). In discussing the relation between church and state we were reminded of God's eventual victory over all powers, including the demonic. Then, all things are put into subjection to God, 'that God may be everything to every one' (1 Cor 15:28). The consummation will witness the completion of the work of Christ to establish God's kingdom. Then will come the final victory and visible manifestation of the kingdom, the eternal, uncontested reign of God.

As we have previously noted, the created order will experience its full redemption in the eternal state. Isaiah's imagery of the taming of nature, when 'they shall not hurt or destroy in all my holy mountain; for the earth shall be full of the knowledge of the Lord as the waters cover the sea' (11:6-9), may be reflected in Romans 8. Here Paul says 'the creation itself will be set free from its bondage to decay and obtain the glorious liberty of the children of God' (8:21). Peter predicts the destruction of the earth and its works to be replaced by 'new heavens and a new earth in which righteousness dwells' (2 Pet 3:10, 13). The same sort of renewal is found in Revelation 21.

Details are few and images are general and perhaps vague at times. The fact seems clear. The Creator is redeeming his creation, all of it! The natural order which was affected and cursed at the first sin in Eden (cf. Gen 3:17-21) will share in God's final victory over sin. Its eternal state is described with the word 'new.'

Where will you spend eternity? The question assumes the answer is either heaven or hell. The Biblical writers would agree, but their language is not quite so simple. It is also involved with the questions of what happens immediately after death and of an 'intermediate state.'

Some Biblical words for the place of exclusion and punishment include (1) *gehenna*, (2) *hadēs*, (3) *tartarus*,[35] (4) outer darkness,[36] and (5) 'the lake that burns with fire and sulfur (brimstone), which is the second death.'[37] Both *gehenna* and *hadēs* are usually translated as *hell* in English Bibles. The place of blessedness is called (1) *heaven* or *the heavens*, (2) *paradise*,[38] and (3) 'Abraham's bosom' (Luke 16:22).

These are 'picture words'; our concern is to what they refer. A survey of all Biblical evidence confirms two general alternatives. *Heaven* refers to the presence of God with the blessedness and joy of his servants as they remain in that presence, characterized as righteousness, holiness, and purity.

The other alternative is complete exclusion from God's presence; it involves condemnation, *death*, and punishment. Some question whether or not God really does condemn, whether references to condemnation are to be taken literally or figuratively, and whether divine punishment is eternal or temporary. The Biblical data does not seem to leave room for the doubts implied in such questions.

The word *gehenna* arises from a location in Jerusalem, the Hinnom Valley, or Valley of the Sons of Hinnom. It is a ravine just beyond the western limit of the old city. As a place for executions,

---

[35]Which occurs only in 2 Peter 2:4, here only in the verb form, and refers to fallen angels awaiting punishment.

[36]Matthew 8:12; 22:13; 25:30.

[37]Revelation 21:8; cf. 19:20; 20:10, 14-15.

[38]Luke 23:24; 2 Corinthians 12:3.

pagan worship, garbage, unburied bodies, and unclean persons it came to symbolize disgrace, that which is repulsive, and separation. Jewish popular belief associated it with the place of the last judgment, punishment, and a place of continual burning. It seemed an apt picture for what we call *hell*, the place of condemnation, separation, and unimaginable eternal punishment; note 2 Thessalonians 1:8-10, describing God's 'vengeance upon those who do not know God and upon those who do not obey the gospel of our Lord Jesus. They shall suffer the punishment of eternal destruction and exclusion from the presence of the Lord and from the glory of his might, when he comes on that day to be glorified in his saints, and to be marveled at in all who have believed, because our testimony to you was believed.'

In the Greek world *hadēs* designated the underworld, the place of the dead, much like *she'ol* in Hebrew. It was also linked with death, as in Revelation 6:8; 20:13-14. The New Testament seems to use *gehenna* and *hadēs* as synonyms for the counterpart for heaven.

All parts of the New Testament assume the condemnation of the wicked; in referring to it most writers use either *gehenna* or *hadēs* as their place of punishment. It is especially strong in the teaching of Jesus in the Synoptic Gospels and in Revelation. Paul, in Philippians 3:19, says the enemies of the cross will suffer 'destruction.' His uses of 'anathema' (1 Cor 16:22; Gal 1:9) implies a strong curse, rejection, and probably assignment to 'hell'.

Paul also speaks of 'the wrath of God',[39] the response of an absolutely pure and just being to anything short of his perfection and glory. The phrase assumes eventual condemnation and punishment. In Revelation the wicked are confronted with the wrath of the Lamb (6:16), the day of wrath (6:17), and the wrath of God.[40] Earlier John the Baptist had called for his hearers to 'flee from the wrath to come' (Matt 3:7; Luke 3:7).

---

[39] Ten times in Romans, but also in Ephesians 5:6; Colossians 3:6, and 1 Thessalonians 1:10, 26.

[40] Revelation 11:18; 14:10, 19; 15:1, 7; 16:1, 19; 19:15.11.

Fire is often associated with the fate and punishment of the wicked. It is frequently a general symbol for judgment.[41] Matthew twice refers to the 'hell of fire' (5:22; 18:9). The wicked will suffer in 'eternal fire' (18:18; 25:41; Jude 7) and 'unquenchable fire' (Mark 9:43, 48). The ultimate punishment in Revelation is the 'lake of fire'. Hence, the question arises if 'hell' contains literal fire. Of course we do not know for sure, but we must remember that burning is the most painful torture the ancients could imagine. They had no language to describe anything worse than eternal, unquenchable burning. Perhaps, with their symbolic language, they intend us to understand that eternal separation from God is far worse than the worst human mind can comprehend.

It is much more pleasant to think about heaven. *Abraham's bosom* and *paradise* are either synonyms for heaven or refer to some temporary intermediate state of joy and blessedness, such as that which existed prior to the resurrection of Jesus. In the Gospels Jesus constantly affirms that heaven is where God is. In his teaching the emphasis is more upon heaven as God's presence than upon it as a place. He describes God as 'Father in heaven', 'heavenly Father,' 'my Father in heaven,' and, speaking to his disciples, 'your Father in heaven.' Heaven is not necessarily up or down, rather it is transcendent, that is, both different and separate from the material world. This difference is emphasized by Jesus when he says to the Sadducees that those who have risen from the dead 'neither marry nor are given in marriage, but are like angels in heaven' (Mark 12:25).

Paul also stresses that heaven is the presence of God. He once speaks of being caught up into 'the third heaven' where he received revelations from God (2 Cor 12:1-4). There is no way to determine whether he was speaking literally, figuratively, or employing common language of the day; certainly he was referring to 'where God is'.

Hebrews speaks of heaven more as a place. In this epistle the New Testament writer locates God's throne, the symbol of his presence, majesty and rule as being in heaven. His symbolism also

---

[41]E.g., Matthew 3:10, 12 = Luke 3:9; 13:42, 50; Mark 9:49; Hebrews 10:27; Revelation 8:7; 14:10.

includes references to the tabernacle as the heavenly worship center (8:2; 9:11-12), the heavenly country and Jerusalem (11:10, 16; 12:22). His use of imagery should caution against assuming that his references to heaven as a place are radically different from other New Testament writers.

Revelation makes reference to heaven more than any other New Testament book. It is the place of God's presence, the place he is worshiped, where his servants, both angels and saints, await his final work, the scene of the presence and marriage supper of the Lamb, and of the new Jerusalem. Heaven plays an important role in the consummation of Salvation History and is closely associated with the eternal state.

Other than portraying the departed and resurrected righteous dead as being in heaven, there is little more that can be said about their eternal state. Along with the angels, theirs is the privilege of living eternally in and enjoying the presence of God. The broken relationship between God and his human creation is finally and completely mended. They are 'made perfect' in the fullest sense. Heaven is the place for rewards and benefits of the 'treasure' laid up there. Theirs is a joy and pleasure beyond comprehension.

Where shall it end? Either fully renewed in the glorious presence of his divine majesty or condemned and excluded from it.

The Millennium

The term *millennium* is literally the Latin word for one thousand; the Greek equivalent is *chilias*. With reference to eschatology it involves how one understands Revelation 20:1-6, the reference to Satan's being bound and the redeemed reigning with Christ 'a thousand years'.[42] The essence of the problem, in its most elementary

---

[42]Intertestamental Jewish sources suggest different lengths of time for an earthly messianic or kingdom reign: 2 Bar 40:3; (cf. 73:10) says that the Messiah shall reign 'until the world of corruption is at an end;' 2 Esdras 7:28 gives 400 years as the length of the Messianic period; Jub 23:27 (cf. Rev 20:2ff., 5, 7) mentions, but in a rather vague context, a period of 1000 years; the post-New Testament Jewish *Talmud*, Tractate 'Sanhedrin' 97a, mentions a period of 2000 years.

form, is whether the statement in Revelation 20 is to be interpreted *literally* or *figuratively*; does it refer to a specific *earthly* reign of Christ or to his more general *spiritual, heavenly* reign?

At deeper levels the issue involves such matters as whether *The End* will come as a result of a supernatural intervention by God or by naturalistic, developmental processes, and the question of the relation between the nation Israel and the church. The alleged difference between *Kingdom of God* and *Kingdom of Heaven* (sometimes assumed to be the millennial reign), might also be discussed in connection with *The Millennium*. It also contains a broad spectrum of questions relating to how the Bible is to be interpreted.

The millennial issue is often not only a matter of interpretation, but also an important element in the construction and/or conclusion of some theological systems; that is, it becomes a way of interpreting, rather than the results of interpretation. Furthermore, it is often closely associated with some attempts to uncover a chronological sequence of the end of history. That there is evidence of some chronology in New Testament eschatology is undeniable, but it is questionable that the data for a complete, detailed construction is available.

The major views of the millennium can simply be described; we leave a detailed description and discussion to others.[43] Here we will only look briefly at the three major views.

The *premillennial view* has a number of variants. The older, traditional view held by some in the ancient church, sometimes called chiliastic[44] view, held simply that Christ will come again, establish a thousand year reign on earth; at its conclusion there will be a final insurrection, Satan and his associates will be defeated, judged, and finally eliminated. Then will begin the eternal state of bliss.

Other premillennial views have added a number of features to this basic outline. They may include a rapture, Christ meeting his own in the air (cf. 1 Thess 4:15-17) before his later coming to earth,

---

[43]See Robert G. Clouse, ed. *The Meaning of the Millennium: Four Views* (Downers Grove, IL: InterVarsity Press, 1977) for a detailed description and discussion of the major views.

[44]The Greek word *chilias* means a thousand.

to establish the 'kingdom of heaven'. Additional discussion centers around whether this rapture will come before, during, or after a time of suffering, known as the Great Tribulation. Those holding this position usually assume there will be a plurality of judgments. The re-establishment of the nation Israel is an important part of their thought.

The so-called *amillennial view* interprets Revelation 20 as a symbol of God's spiritual reign between the ascension and second coming of Christ. Some proponents would prefer to call it a 'Heavenly (or Spiritual) Millennium', for by it they mean God's unseen, but real reign during this, the Final Age. Many of those holding this view believe that all privileges and promises to the nation Israel have now been transferred to the church and will be fulfilled by and for her.

The *postmillennial view* has at least two forms. The older, not radically different from the amillennial view, looks for the return of Christ after a 'millennium' which follows a world wide triumph of the preaching of the gospel. The postmillennial view also has a naturalistic form which expects no supernatural return of Christ; rather it looks for a utopian society on earth as a result of the culmination of the physical, intellectual, social, and other developmental forces at work within the natural order.

Belief in a distinctive and special place in the future for the nation Israel within God's redemptive work is usually associated with a premillennial view. Its adherents base their belief on a literal interpretation of Revelation 20. Without rejecting the possibility of a premillennial interpretation (personally, I use it in its chiliastic form as 'a working hypothesis'), I question whether belief in a future role for physical Israel is totally dependent upon a literal interpretation of all elements of Revelation 20.[45] Romans 11:11-32 provides strong support for such an expectation.

---

[45]Can Satan be bound with a literal chain? Is hell, or some form of it, shut and sealed with a lock requiring a literal key as might be implied from Revelation 20:1? Furthermore, 2 Peter 3:8 should warn against a too rigidly literalistic interpretation of the thousand years of Revelation 20.

Conclusion

Each generation has its own contemporary events and forces for which Biblical teachings about *The End* have implications. We cannot go into detail about all those of the late twentieth and early twenty-first centuries in the western world. Notice of a few of these and a comment or two about them might be a stimulus to thought. We have been told ours is a 'Post-Christian' era. I suspect the same could have been said for many periods of the past. Nevertheless the radical relativization of truth, the secularization of societies (particularly in the West), disavowal of universal moral and ethical standards, and the excessive emphasis upon the individual person and his or her need to find oneself, to experience 'self-actualization' by acts of personal decision, fit well with Biblical descriptions of conditions expected as the present age winds toward its conclusion. Whether the actual time for the Lord's coming be near or far, conditions make appropriate the reminder that the Christian is a minority in an alien environment. The Biblical writers' call for watching and constant preparedness and the reminder that it is God who defines truth needs to be clearly sounded, in spite of its probable unpopularity. The increasing popularity of religious pluralism, that one religious system is as good as another, is a blatant rejection of the opposite contention of Scripture. So too is the rejection, sometimes in the name of 'science,' of a supernatural end of the world and of history.

The denial of divine punishment, of hell, or of the permanence of such, stumbles over another point emphasized in Scripture, the justice of God. He loves, yes, but he is also just. The evaluation both of the ideas which press in upon us and of our own situation and environment needs to be made, and not only on the basis of reason, or science, or pragmatic concerns, or personal preference. For the Christian, the evaluation must be made on the basis of the person, character, and will of God as he has made himself known.

And so, we come to the only appropriate end of our survey of New Testament themes, of its basic teachings. The end, the climax toward which the entirety of the New Testament moves, raises our last question, 'What Does the New Testament Tell Us About God?' – especially about his person and being.

Chapter 12

What Does the New Testament
Tell Us About God?

Introduction

Too often the reader or student of the New Testament forgets that the ultimate purpose of any Biblical or theological study should be to know God better. Christianity is a 'relational' religion; it is concerned with *the* ultimate relation – the one between a person and God. Its goal is to know him and to live in ways pleasing to him. The Bible discloses God's actions to bring people into a right relationship with himself, the expected results of that relationship, and its implications for all of life – all so people may *know* him.

We read letters from our loved ones carefully. In doing so we seek information about their affairs. Even more, often subconsciously, we seek to know and understand them better and how they regard us. Such must be the ultimate purpose of reading, studying, and meditating upon the Bible. The coming together and work of the written word and the Holy Spirit within us is our major way of coming to know God better. With a deeper knowledge of God it is expected that the believer's love for him will grow. An increasing knowledge of God and love for him should result in worshiping him properly, in spirit and in truth, better understanding his will, and obeying him more completely.

The New Testament view of God assumes and is built upon that of the Old Testament. New Testament writers presume the reader is familiar with the revelation of the person and the acts of God given to Israel of old. However, the New Testament adds an important dimension to the Old Testament revelation of God. It declares that to know Jesus Christ is to know God; Jesus himself said, 'If you had known me, you would have known my Father also; henceforth you know him and have seen him' (John 14:7). Our initial question,

'Who is Jesus?' must be remembered as we consider this last one, 'Who is God?'

In the introduction to this book I gave a brief rationale for placing this chapter about God last, rather than first, which some consider the premier position. We are now, I believe, better equipped to understand the New Testament portrayal of God as the one revealed by and at work in Jesus, he whose work includes salvation, and the one with whom the Christian life is lived in a close, accepting relation. It is God, in Christ, who is the Lord and Head of the Church; the relation between the church and society is dominated by the church's relationship with and prior allegiance to God.

This whole study is about God, God revealing himself through his works and words in different ways, but always supremely through his beloved Son, Jesus Christ. To pause here to contemplate God must be, as we said earlier, the grand climax of our consideration of New Testament themes.

The Existence, Being, and Knowability of God

Like the Old Testament, the New Testament never tries to prove the existence of God. It simply asserts his existence as an article of faith and proceeds to show him at work. Hebrews 11:6 presents the starting point of Christianity, 'Without faith it is impossible to please him. For whoever would draw near to God must believe that he exists and that he rewards those who seek him.' Here the writer states two things that must be accepted by faith. First, the phrase 'that he is,' refers to the existence of God. To seek to 'please him . . , [to] draw near to God' one must have some confidence that he exists. It is futile to try to contact a non-existent being. Second, one must be convinced 'that he rewards those who seek him.' An approach to God must assume that he is knowable, that he will reward with success those who seek him (even if God exists, it is fruitless to seek him unless he is also knowable).

But from where does this evidence of an existing, knowable, eternal being come? Bible students speak of two different general types or classifications of sources for such information, General Revelation and Special Revelation.

General Revelation is that information about God available to all people, at all times, and in all places. It includes the revelation of God in nature. In Romans 1:19-20 Paul asserts, 'What can be known about God is plain . . . , because God has shown it. . . . Ever since the creation of the world his invisible nature, namely, his eternal power and deity, has been clearly perceived in the things that have been made.' The nature of God, the Creator, including his existence, as well as his knowability and power, is evidenced in the created order.

In Acts 17:24-27 Paul speaks of an even broader form of General Revelation, one which includes the origin and nature of human beings and the limits of human habitation (history).

> The God who made the world and everything in it, being Lord of heaven and earth, does not live in shrines made by man, nor is he served by human hands, as though he needed anything, since he himself gives to all men life and breath and everything. And he made from one every nation of men to live on all the face of the earth, having determined allotted periods and the boundaries of their habitation, that they should seek God, in the hope that they might feel after him and find him. Yet he is not far from each one of us.

The other form of information is *Special Revelation*, that knowledge about God available to only some people in some times and places. In the Old Testament God revealed himself in the history of Israel and through his words to 'the Fathers,' Abraham, Moses, and by the prophets. The supreme act of Special Revelation came through Jesus Christ, 'the Word.'

> The Word was God.... the Word became flesh and dwelt among us, full of grace and truth; we have beheld his glory, glory as of the only Son from the Father.... No one has ever seen God; the only Son, who is in the bosom of the Father, he has made him known (John 1:1, 14, 18).

We are, of course, speaking of the revelation of a person. There is a difference between *knowing about* a person and *knowing* the person. Nevertheless, information about a person is helpful, often essential, in moving into more personal knowledge. Adam, Enoch, Noah, Abraham, Moses, the prophets, and others entered into conversation with God; Israel saw and heard thunder and lightning, and a thick cloud as the voice of God came to her from Mount Sinai. God also made his person known through other actions and words and in the record of them. These were passed on from generation to generation. Israel was told that this same God lived in her midst.

In Jesus Christ, the same God appears, not in terrifying signs and booming voice, but in a form human beings could understand and relate, that of another human. Again, the record of the 'Jesus event,' including his words, were preserved and passed on. Again, the community of those who believed on him is expected to live, not only with knowledge of facts, but with the assurance that the same one remains and lives in their midst.

Thus the Bible primarily reveals God through his words and deeds. It is as if the Biblical writers record something about God and pause to ask, 'Now, what kind of being says or does this?' They then go on to recount other words and deeds, pausing each time to ask the same implied question. Then, the impact of all such accounts is intended to enable the reader to come to know about God and to be prepared to recognize evidence of his presence and continuing work among us.

They also believe that there is a subjective knowledge of God. Just as speech and actions led people in the past into personal awareness and knowledge of God, so too, that should and must continue to happen. The objective is to know God, to know him as he is.

Short Definitions of God

There are within the New Testament a few brief statements which tell something about God. They are important in gaining an answer to our question, 'What Does the New Testament Tell Us About God?'

The New Testament writers affirm several times that 'God is *One*' (Rom 3:30; Gal 3:20; Jas 2:19). They do so in such a way as to make clear that they are in complete agreement with the teaching of Deuteronomy 6:4, the heart of the Old Testament faith (the Shema). The Judeo-Christian religious tradition is united in the worship of only one God, the one who revealed himself and acted in the history of Israel in the past. This is not the contention of the writers of the epistles alone. In Mark 12:29-30, Jesus accepted the truth of the monotheistic nature of God. Even more pointed is his statement in the Gospel of John, 'The Father and I are one' (10:30).

To the Samaritan woman beside Jacob's well, Jesus made one of his more profound statements, 'God is *spirit*' (John 4:24).[1] The context was a discussion of the proper place for worship. Jesus rejected the notion of the priority of a particular place because God is not the sort of being who can be limited to one location nor is contact with him restricted to a particular place. 'Placeness' is appropriate in discussing human beings who, because of their material make-up, are bound to but a single location. God, on the other hand, is a very different type of being.

God is spirit, not material. One must not to try to think of him materially; to attempt material representation of God is one form of the sin of idolatry. It is wrong to try to restrict a spiritual being to a single material substance, or 'stuff.'

As spirit, God has presence, knowledge, power, and other characteristics and abilities far beyond the imagination of human beings. People who draw near to God must get used to the fact that he is spirit, that he is utterly different from anything or anyone we have previously encountered. From the human point of view, God's 'spirit-ness' is a part of his total difference from us.

In 1 John 1:5 it says 'God is *light* and in him is no darkness at all.' *Light* is a symbol frequently used of God in the Bible. Two ideas are usually associated with light, 1) revelation and salvation and 2) moral purity or holiness. In 1 Timothy 6:16 God is said to dwell 'in unapproachable light.' In the verses in 1 John which follow the declaration, 'God is light,' human sin as darkness is contrasted

---

[1]Note that the text says 'spirit', not 'a spirit' or ' the spirit'. The grammatical construction could be understood something like 'God = Spirit.'

with God's shining purity. Here, then, 'brightness' or 'light' seems to be a way of speaking of God's absolute purity and holiness, that he is separate from any kind of moral defilement or sin.

Light is either present or it is not. In the same way, one is either holy or is not; can we imagine speaking of someone as 'half' or 'partly holy'? This special statement about God says something about his moral nature. He is absolutely pure, without sin; God is holy.

This has important implications for those who would draw near to him. His very nature cannot tolerate that which is not holy. Left to our own devices, we could not gain acceptance before God. His holiness would prevent it.

The writer to the Hebrews says, "Let us offer to God acceptable worship with reverence and awe; Our God is a **consuming fire**" (12:28-29). This short definition of God comes from Deuteronomy 4:24. Jewish Christian readers of the letters would be transported back to the Plain of Moab during the latter days of Moses' life. He was giving his last words to the people. God had used him time and again to remind them of his covenant, his delivery from slavery, how he led them through the howling wilderness, gave the law, organized the nation, established worship, and more. Moses served as the prototype of those very human political and religious leaders whose presence had reminded Israel that God was in their midst. His person and the remembrances of him were a proclamation of God's grace to his people.

The quotation of Moses' words, "your God is a consuming fire" took the readers of the Epistle back to the moment their ancestors stood at the foot of Mount Sinai. There the Lord had appeared, so that, as he said, "they may learn to fear me" (Deut 4:10). As the Mount blazed with fire and smoke they shook with fear, both terror and awe. They heard the Lord's voice, but saw no form, as he declared his covenant (vss 11-13). As Moses had spoken of all this he reminded Israel that they were to both live and worship in ways in conformity to and appropriate for the nature of the Lord.

God's grace and care must never cause the ancient Hebrews to forget who he is. The writer of the Epistle had expounded in detail God's gracious redemptive acts in Jesus. It would be tempting for them to begin to take God for granted (some already had and the writer warned of the consequences for those who had 'fallen away' (Heb 6:4-6; 10:26-31). He used Moses' words to remind his readers of the nature of God, of what must be their response to him, and the consequences of failing to respond properly in both life and worship.

And, all of life should and must be an act of worship (cf. Rom 12:1); all of life must be lived with a proper attitude of reverence and respect for God. God, a Consuming Fire, is a judge who will punish all disobedience and sin.

Awareness of the Lord as a condemning, punishing judge would be intolerable were it not for our next statement about God. The same writer who announced the holiness of God by asserting that he is light, also affirmed, "God is love" (1 John 4:8). Is it possible to contemplate, to see, God as both a holy judge who burns with "consuming fire" against sin and who is also love? Yes, look at and contemplate the cross! See there the propitiatory sacrifice whom, in love, God put forward, to turn away his own wrath (Rom 3:25). There we see his mercy and kindness, extensions of his love and another demonstration of his essential being. It is his nature to love and that nature expresses itself in making forgiveness, salvation, acceptance, and fellowship available to those who deserve the consuming fire of his judgment. The God who is love is also present, compassionate, and provides support to his own in times of pain, sorrow, persecution, stress, and all other forms of distress and difficulty.

Finally, two verses – 2 Corinthians 1:3; 1 Peter 1:3 – refer to *The God and Father of our Lord Jesus Christ*. The New Testament frequently refers to the individual believer and the church as being 'in Christ'. These particular verses define God in terms of his special relation to Jesus Christ. In a few other places Peter and Paul build on this. God in Christ 'reconciles the world to himself' (2 Cor 5:19), 'blesses us ... with every spiritual blessing in the heavenly places' (Eph 1:3), 'shows the immeasurable riches of grace in kindness toward us' (Eph 2:7), reveals his will (1 Thess 5:18), and 'leads us in triumphal procession' (2 Cor 2:14).[2] In Christ, God issues 'the

---

[2]The imagery here is of a conquering general leading his troops into their capital city in a triumphant procession.

upward call' (Phil 3:14); 'saves us and called us with a holy calling .
. . in virtue of his own purpose and grace' (2 Tim 1:9), and calls us
'to his eternal glory' (1 Pet 5:10).

Reflecting the relationship in which Christ, as the Son, does the
Father's bidding, Paul says, 'Christ is God's' (1 Cor 3:23). God
reveals himself in and works through Jesus Christ. Who is God?
Look at Jesus Christ!

The Nature of God

A Summary of the Biblical Evidence
The statement 'God is spirit' could leave us with some vague notions of
an influence for good, or an ideal. Some forms of liberal Christianity
have come very close to holding such a view. Hence, it is important to
note that the Bible shows God as a *personal being*. He has a distinct
center of consciousness, can think, speak, feel, hear, and he displays
other characteristics of a 'person'. He is a spiritual person. Therefore
we should seek to relate to him on a person-to-person basis, although,
as we have previously said, certainly not as *equal* persons.

Not only is God a spiritual person, he is also an *eternal* person.
This is yet another truth about God carried over into the New
Testament from the Old. That God is eternal means that he is without
beginning or end. As the Old Testament opens, 'In the beginning
God...' (Gen 1:1), we find similar wording and ideas in the New
Testament, 'In the beginning was the Word and the Word was with
God and the Word was God' (John 1:1). Paul assumes as much
when, in Ephesians 1:4, he refers to actions of God taken 'before
the foundation of the world.' The voice from the throne in Revelation
declares, 'I am the Alpha and the Omega, the beginning and the
end' (21:6; cf. 22:13).

This spiritual, eternal being is the *one God*. Here we mean two
things. He is the only God. There is no other being who is truly God.
All other so-called gods are 'false gods' because they do not exist;
they are figments of human imagination.[3]

---

[3] Note Psalm 96:5, 'For all the gods of the peoples are idols; but the LORD
made the heavens.'

The other point is that God is a unity; he is one. Here the New Testament is in complete agreement with the Old. In Mark 12:29-30, Jesus accepts the monotheistic nature of God proclaimed in Deuteronomy 6:4. In John 10:30 he says, 'The Father and I are one,' in James 2:19, 'You believe that God is one; you do well.'

The difficulty arises when we begin to note that the New Testament writers imply that there are three 'distinctions' within this one God. In the baptism of Jesus[4] the Son is baptized, he is acknowledged from heaven by the voice of the Father, and the Holy Spirit descends in the form of a dove.

In his final conversation with his disciples before his death, Jesus develops a distinction between himself, the Father and the Holy Spirit (John 14–17). He says, 'I am in the Father and the Father is in me... I am going to the Father,... I will pray the Father, and he will give another Comforter (*paraklete*) to be with you for ever ... the Spirit of truth' (John 14:10, 12, 16-17), etc. Here the Son speaks, the Father and the Son send the Holy Spirit. Just before his ascension Jesus commissioned, 'Go therefore and make disciples of all nations, baptizing them in the name of the Father and of the Son and of the Holy Spirit' (Matt 28:19). There is one God, the word 'name' is singular, but there is also Father, Son, and Holy Spirit.

Peter addresses his epistle 'To the exiles of the Dispersion... who have been chosen and destined by God the Father and sanctified by the Spirit to be obedient to Jesus Christ and to be sprinkled with his blood' (1 Peter 1:2). Again, one God, but also reference to three distinctions.

A number of the apostolic benedictions toward the end of epistles also display awareness of this 'three distinctions within the one God.' 2 Corinthians 13:14 will serve as an example, 'The grace of the Lord Jesus Christ, the love of God, and the fellowship of the Holy Spirit be with all of you.'

The fact of the 'unity' and the 'diversity' of God has an important implication, God is a relational being. Relationship is inherent within the being of God himself. He also enters into relationship with his

---

[4]Mark 1:9-11; Matthew 3:13-17; Luke 3:21-11.

creation and especially with human beings within it. Within the being of God each of the distinctions are equal, theirs is a relationship of equals. When one 'person' assumes a subordinate role to accomplish the will of God there is no concept of inferiority of being or of a striving for power within the person of God. The relationships within the one God are characterized by perfect harmony.

God as 'Trinity'

In our discussion of the nature of God thus far we have not used the word *Trinity*; it is not a New Testament word. It came into use toward the end of the second and during the following centuries after Jesus' earthly sojourn in attempts to understand and express the types of evidence we have just surveyed, that which indicates the 'oneness,' the 'unity' of God along and also his 'three distinctions within the one God.' The early church believed the Bible, especially the New Testament teaches the existence, personality, full deity, and unity of the one God who is also Father, Son, and Holy Spirit. Within the context of Greek philosophy and thought-forms, early Christians sought to express this truth in clear, unambiguous terms. It did so most often as views about the nature of God were expressed which early Christians recognized as contrary to the teachings of Scripture; in reaction they were driven again and again to restudy what the Scriptures seem to assume and set forth on this subject.

The summaries of Biblical teachings, such as those in the ancient creeds of the church, are the results of centuries of study and debate. They employ the language and logic of the past. Some contemporary students of the New Testament argue for abandoning use of the term Trinity. Some of those who do so actually believe the Biblical teachings about the nature of God to be that contained in the traditional doctrine of the Trinity. I suggest what is needed is not relinquishing the term but rather providing clearer expositions of it and the Biblical truths it seeks to express.

This is not the place for such. Rather we repeat that the word is an attempt, a human attempt, to express the meaning and implications of the New Testament data we have just considered (*tri* means three; *unity* speaks of oneness; *trinity* designates the three in one).

The early Christian writers insisted that there is only one God, but within this one God there are three 'persons' who are distinct.

From the modern perspective *person* may not be the best term to use. The ancients employed it with some special senses into which we cannot now go. It is useful in that it refers to distinctions with their own centers of consciousness, feelings, expressions, and abilities to communicate. These 'persons' are not, however, independent, individuals. In thinking of the 'persons' we must remember that God is spirit and thereby divest ourselves of any concept of a person with a separate distinguishable material body.

One past attempt to explain the unity and diversity spoke of one person playing and relating in three different roles – such as, I am at the same time son, husband, and father, but function differently in each role. This, however, the church came to see is NOT what the New Testament teaches. Rather, it is helpful to think in terms of God being Father, Son, and Holy Spirit – hence the unity of the one God. At the same time the Father is not the Son and the Son is not the Father, the Holy Spirit is not the Father and the Father is not the Holy Spirit, The Son is not the Holy Spirit and the Holy Spirit is not the Son.

Is all this perplexing? Yes. It is beyond human ability to comprehend it in its fullest sense. It is both humbling and helpful to recall the observation of A. W. Tozer, 'Since we cannot understand the fall of the leaf by the roadside or the hatching of a robin's egg in the nest yonder, why should the Trinity be a problem to us?'[5]

Characteristics of God

In addition to the short definitions of God given above, the New Testament is filled with information about him. At least in its present order the New Testament begins with the story of 'Emmanuel', the word which means 'God with us'. That word by itself, when understood in the context of the whole of the Bible, is a mind-boggling

---

[5]A. W. Tozer, *The Knowledge of the Holy* (1961), 27. Note also the observation of the sixteenth century scholar Erasmus, 'The Holy Trinity is better pleased with adoration of it than speculation upon it.'

statement. The same Bible which affirms God's holiness and justice, and which contains shaming accounts of human rebellion, sin, and degradation, tells of the History of Salvation and says this kind of God is with that kind of people! But Emmanuel comes in the form of a human baby, into what seems to be a peasant family.

The New Testament ends with the Book of Revelation. To look at nothing in this book save its presentation of God is, immediately, almost stupefying and numbing. We glimpse the adoration of heavenly creatures around the throne who constantly sing, 'Holy, holy, holy, is the Lord God Almighty who was and is and is to come!' (Rev 4:8). 'To him who sits upon the throne and the Lamb be blessing and honor and glory and might for ever and ever' (5:13). And, he receives 'the prayers of the saints' (5:8).

In the Book of Revelation the all-controlling and determining power of God directs the drama of history, bringing it to its appointed end. His wrath goes forth upon his enemies. Centuries earlier Malachi said, 'Who can endure the day of his coming, and who can stand when he appears?' (Mal 3:2). Revelation records that as the sixth seal is opened, the peoples on the earth flee 'from the face of him who is seated on the throne and from the wrath of the Lamb; for the great day of their wrath has come, and who can stand before it?' (Rev 6:17). Heavenly bodies fall, seas turn red, mountains collapse, plagues rage forth. The earth is cast into tumult and agony. Beholding God's judgment upon the wicked, from heaven the multitude sings,

> Great and wonderful are your deeds,
> O Lord God the Almighty!
> Just and true are your ways,
> O King of the ages!
> Who shall not fear and glorify your name, O Lord?
> For you alone are holy.
> All nations shall come and worship you,
> For your judgments have been revealed (Rev 15:3-4).

> Just are you in these your judgments,
> you who are and were, O Holy One.

For men have shed the blood of saints and prophets,
and you have given them blood to drink.
It is their due (Rev 16:5-6).

Side by side with judgment is the comfort, and salvation, and reward of 'the saints'. Their cause is vindicated. It is their Savior, who is the Lamb, who conquers (Rev 17:14). As heavenly throngs sang of judgment, they also cry,

Hallelujah! Salvation and glory and power belong to our God,... He has avenged ... the blood of his saints.... Praise our God, all you his servants, you who fear him, small and great... Hallelujah! For the Lord our God the Almighty reigns (Rev 19:1-2, 5-6).

It is God who, from the throne, presides over 'a new heaven and a new earth'. It is he who, after the skies have rolled together as a scroll, the small and great resurrected to stand before his judgment seat, the saints dined at the marriage supper of the Lamb, and Satan and his hosts been cast into the lake of eternal fire, affirms, 'It is done! I am the Alpha and the Omega, the beginning and the end' (Rev 21:6). It is his glory which is the light of the new city (21:23) in which there is the 'water of life' and 'the tree of life', and from whence comes the healing of the nations (22:1-2). 'And his servants shall worship him; they shall see his face, and his name shall be on their foreheads . . . They shall reign forever and ever' (22:4-5).

What are some of the things we learn of God between the accounts of Emmanuel's birth and the vision of the new heaven and earth? He is *everywhere present, all powerful, all knowing*. He is *holy*. The holiness recognized and ascribed by the heavenly hosts of Revelation is both assumed and, as we have seen, set forth elsewhere. And, God is *good*. Jesus himself, speaking in the absolute sense, said, 'No one is good but God alone.'[6]

Closely associated with both God's holiness and goodness is the fact that he is *righteous*. When we spoke of righteousness and

---

[6]Mark 10:18 = Matthew 19:17; Luke 18:19.

justification we stressed that God demands and, in Christ, makes righteousness available because he is righteous. In Romans 3:25-26 the work of Christ was 'To show God's righteousness ... to prove at the present time that he is righteous.'

Pilate, the man of the Greco-Roman world where truth was assumed to be abstract, asked, 'What is truth?' (John 18:38). The New Testament witnesses to a person, that 'God is *true*' (John 3:33). That is his nature, consequently both his words and actions are true. Jesus, referring to God, insisted, 'He who sent me is true' (John 7:28; 8:26) and that he, Jesus, had come to make known 'the only true God' (John 17:3). In Revelation the Sovereign Lord is 'holy and true' (6:10) and 'is called Faithful and True' (19:11). The Christian message is summarized in 1 John 5:20: 'We know that the Son of God has come and has given us understanding, to know him who is true; and we are in him who is true, in his Son Jesus Christ. This is the true God and eternal life.'

God as 'true' assures us of his consistency. That is the point of referring to him as '*faithful*' in Revelation 19:11 (quoted above). Paul's affirmation, 'God is faithful' (2 Cor 1:18), is a given fact and the basis for the Christian's assurance in God's promises;[7] Hebrews 10:23 expresses the same confidence for the same reason. Because God is faithful we may be sure that we will not face inescapable temptation (1 Cor 10:13). John assures his readers that God will forgive confessed sins because 'he is faithful and just' (1 John 1:9). As 1 Peter 4:19 says, 'Let those who suffer according to God's will do right and entrust their souls to a faithful Creator.'

Consistency is also assured because God *never changes*. Speaking of Christ, the writer to the Hebrews insists that he is 'the same, yesterday, today, and forever' (13:8). The same epistle affirms, 'The Lord has sworn and will not change his mind' (7:21). James says of God, that he is 'the Father of lights with whom there is no variation or shadow due to change' (1:17).

In 2 Corinthians 1:3, God is referred to as '*the Father of mercies and the God of all comfort*.' Centuries earlier, when confronted

---

[7] 1 Corinthians 1:9; 1 Thessalonians 5:24; 1 Timothy 2:13.

with the destruction of home, nation, family, and the temple, the writer of Lamentations states,

> But this I call to mind, and therefore I have hope: The steadfast love of the LORD never ceases, his mercies never come to an end; they are new every morning; great is thy faithfulness (3:21-23).

The *mercy* of God is affirmed as sinners cry for it and prophets and apostles give assurance of it. Mary, after receiving word that she was to bear the Messiah, sings of God, 'His mercy is on those who fear him from generation to generation... He has helped his servant Israel, in remembrance of his mercy '(Luke 1:50, 54). Jesus instructed his disciples, 'Be merciful, even as your Father is merciful' (Luke 6:36). Paul speaks of 'God, who is rich in mercy, out of the great love with which he loved us' (Eph 2:4) and that 'He saved us, not because of deeds done by us in righteousness, but in virtue of his own mercy, by the washing of regeneration and renewal in the Holy Spirit' (Titus 3:5). James reminds those who suffer, 'You have heard of the steadfastness of Job, and you have seen the purpose of the Lord, how the Lord is compassionate and merciful (Jas 5:11). And Peter speaks of God's greatest act of mercy, 'Blessed be the God and Father of our Lord Jesus Christ! By his great mercy we have been born anew to a living hope through the resurrection of Jesus Christ from the dead' (1 Pet 1:3).

Comfort, as a characteristic and function of God, was well known in the Old Testament. The Psalmist acknowledges, 'Thy rod and thy staff, they comfort me' (Ps 23:4) and God himself cries, 'Comfort, comfort my people' (Isa 40:1). Paul enlarges upon his designation, the 'God of all comfort,' with the words, 'Who comforts us in all our affliction, so that we may be able to comfort those who are in any affliction, with the comfort with which we ourselves are comforted by God' (2 Cor 1:4). In 2 Thessalonians he speaks of the 'Lord Jesus Christ himself, and God our Father, who loved us and gave us eternal comfort and good hope through grace' (2:16).

Upon arriving in the home of the Gentile centurion (an army officer), Peter exclaimed, 'Truly I perceive that God is one who shows no partiality' (Acts 10:34). Behind this statement, addressed to a specific situation, is the understanding that God is *impartial*. This characteristic of God is first stated in Deuteronomy 10:17-19; in the Old Testament it is understood to be the basis for God's absolutely fair administration of justice; he does not favor one person above another and he cannot be bribed. This impartiality of God is the principle upon which Paul bases his assertion that God will judge Jews and Gentiles on the same basis (Rom. 2:11). Peter's statement to Cornelius and his friends is in the context of his coming to realize that God is impartial in determining candidates for salvation, both Jews and Gentiles are eligible. We have already noted that God's impartiality is cited in the New Testament as the basis for relationships among believers and within the church.

Earlier we noted that God is a being of appropriate *anger* and *wrath* and also had occasion to note his *glory* and *majesty*. We close this brief survey of some of the characteristics of God with two general statements from 1 Timothy.

> To the King of the ages, immortal, invisible, the only God, be honor and glory forever and ever (1 Tim 1:17).

> He who is the blessed and only Sovereign, the King of kings and Lord of lords. It is he alone who has immortality and dwells in unapproachable light, whom no one has ever seen or can see; to him be honor and eternal dominion (1 Tim 6:15-16).

Roles and Activities of God

Who is God? To enquire of God's nature is to ask who he is, what kind of being he is. We must also consider his roles and activities for the writers of Scripture assume that his nature is shown in his functions and works. We have already noted that God is a person who is spirit and, therefore, different from human beings. He is the absolute spirit, in that he is complete in himself, unlimited, and unrestricted by anything except his own nature. Hence, the Biblical writers assume he is The Supreme Being. He is, therefore supreme in all he is and does. We must comment on several of his roles and activities as seen or assumed in both the Old Testament and the New which help define him.

God is the supreme ruler, creator, sustainer, redeemer, and judge. As *King-Sovereign* he is in absolute control of all things. He is the Sovereign King of heaven, earth, and the whole universe. In keeping with a major emphasis of our study, let us note again that God is the King-Sovereign in the Kingdom of God.

Passages affirming this role and activity of God are too numerous to mention. We noted his kingly authority and control in the Book of Revelation. The verses quoted just above from 1 Timothy affirm his kingship and eternal dominion. Below we will cite the marvelous affirmation of his sovereignty in Romans 11:33-36. In 8:38-39 of the same epistle Paul expresses his confidence in the power and all-encompassing sovereignty of God and places it within the context of his love expressed in Jesus,

> For I am sure that neither death, nor life, nor angels, nor principalities, nor things present, nor things to come, nor powers, nor height, nor depth, nor anything else in all creation, will be able to separate us from the love of God in Christ Jesus our Lord.

Early in this chapter we reminded ourselves that the presentation of God as *Creator* in the Old Testament is equally strong in the New Testament. In the face of contemporary aspersions on the world and life in it as meaningless, purposeless, even evil, Paul, who also speaks of the eventual redemption of the created order, says that because God is good, 'everything created by God is good' (1 Tim 4:4). Thus, we hear an echo of Genesis 1, both that 'God created the heavens and the earth' (1:1) and that 'God saw everything that he had made, and behold, it was very good' (1:31). In 1 Peter 4:19 the creatorship of God is a practical doctrine. To those in distress as they live in the midst of a world that is hostile to Christians because of Satan's presence in it, he says, 'Let those suffering in accordance with God's will entrust themselves to a faithful Creator, while continuing to do good.'

Closely related to God's work as Creator, and an extension of it, is his continuing involvement in the created order in what Biblical

---

[8]But the idea is contained in the Greek words *pronoia, pronoeō*.

students call *providence*. It portrays God as sovereign over the universe, but also as the one who relates personally to people, especially those who acknowledge him. The word *providence* does not occur in most English translations[8] but conveys a Biblical concept, one sensed in the New Testament as well as in the Old. Like other themes, the New Testament sets forth God's work in providence as taking place in Christ, the Mediator, through whom he works out his purpose.

Paul affirmed both God's creatorship and providence in Christ, 'the image of the invisible God ... for in him all things were created ... and in him all things hold together' (Col 1:15-17). Jesus himself said, '[It is] your Father who is in heaven ... [who] ... makes his sun rise on the evil and on the good, and sends rain on the just and on the unjust' (Matt 5:45). Jesus' well-known admonition, 'do not be anxious,' is rooted in the providential care and activities of God (Matt 6:25-34). It is through the continuing evidence of God's handiwork in nature and his providential work in history that his existence, power, deity, and Lordship is evident to all peoples in all times, leaving them 'without excuse' (Acts 17:22-30; Rom 1:18-23). God's providence is seen also in his acts of judgment (Rom 12:19). So much is he involved in the daily affairs of life that failure to provide for one's family has spiritual ramifications (1 Tim 5:8). Confidence in God's providence assures the believer that, 'In everything God works for good with those who love him, who are called according to his purpose' (Rom 8:28).

The fourth role and activity of God is that of *Redeemer*. God's work of redemption is a major theme of the New Testament. We answered the question, 'What must I do to be saved?' with the subject of redemption. We mention God's redeeming activity here only because with so much attention to redemption, it might be easy to overlook the Redeemer. When 'Christ redeemed us' (Gal 3:13) he did so because he was doing the will and work of God.

God's role and activity as Redeemer put into perspective his fifth function and activities, that of *Judge*. God as judge, including the one who punishes, must be seen alongside his redeemership; he is the just redeeming judge and his is a just redemption.

Of course, there is much more that could be said about God in relation to the Christian. He is their *Savior* and *Lord*. We have also noted that he is *The God and Father of our Lord Jesus Christ*. He is *The God of the Covenant*, the framework within which he says, 'I will be your God and you will be my people.'

We have spoken also of that very special, intimate relationship between God and the believer within which the Christian may refer to the eternal, holy, righteous, majestic, glorious, all-powerful King of Kings and Lord of Lords as *Father*. And, even more intimately, he is the Christian's *Abba*, Daddy.

Conclusion

Who is God? The whole of the New Testament, as the Old, is focused upon answering this question. The New Testament does not contradict the Old, but adds new insights and new emphases. Let it speak for itself.

> No one has ever seen God; the only Son, who is in the bosom of the Father, he has made him known. (John 1:18)

> It is the God who said, 'Let light shine out of darkness,' who has shone in our hearts to give the light of the knowledge of the glory of God in the face of Christ. (2 Cor 4:6)

> O the depth of the riches and wisdom and knowledge of God! How unsearchable are his judgments and how inscrutable his ways! 'For who has known the mind of the Lord, or who has been his counselor?' 'Or who has given a gift to him that he might be repaid?' For from him and through him and to him are all things. To him be glory for ever. (Rom 11:33-36)

> [He] is able to keep you from falling and to present you without blemish before the presence of his glory with rejoicing, . . . the only God, our Savior through Jesus Christ our Lord, be glory, majesty, dominion, and authority, before all time and now and for ever. Amen. (Jude 1:24-25).

BIBLIOGRAPHY

WRITERS AND WORKS TO WHICH REFERENCES HAVE BEEN MADE

Alexander, Donald A. ed., *Christian Spirituality: Five Views of Sanctification* Downers Grove, IL: InterVarsity, 1988.

Bethge, Eberhard. *Dietrich Bonhoffer*. New York: Harper and Row, 1970.

Bray, Gerald. *Biblical Interpretation: Past and Present*. Downers Grove, IL: InterVarsity, 1996.

Bruce, F. F. "Women in the Church: A Biblical Survey," *A Mind for What Matters.* Grand Rapids, MI: Eerdmans, 1990.

Bruce, F. F. *The Epistle of Paul to the Romans* (TBC). Grand Rapids: Wm. B. Eerdmans Publishing Co., 1963; 2d ed, 1985.

Bruce, F. F. 1 and 2 Thessalonians. Word Biblical Commentary; Elwell, Walter A., ed. Waco, TX: Word Books 1982.

Bruce, F. F. "Eschatology," *Evangelical Dictionary of Theology*. Grand Rapids: Baker, 1984, 362-365.

Bruce, F. F. *The Time is Fulfilled: Five Aspects of the Fulfillment of the Old Testament in the New*. Grand Rapids, MI: Eerdmans, 1978.

Bruce, F. F. *The New Testament Development of Old Testament Themes*. Grand Rapids, MI: Eerdmans, 1968.

Bruce, F. F. "Christianity Under Claudius," *Bulletin of the John Rylands Library*, 44/2 (March 1962), 309-326.

Bultmann, Rudolf. *The New Testament and Mythology and Other Basic Writings*. Philadelphia: Fortress Press, 1984.

Bultmann, Rudolf. *Theology of the New Testament*. Translated by Kendrick Grobel. London: SCM, 2 vols, 1951, 1955.

Clouse, Robert G, *The Meaning of the Millennium: Four Views* (Downers Grove, IL: InterVarsity Press, 1977.

Coenen, Lothar. "Church, Synagogue," *The New International Dictionary of New Testament Theology*, English trans., Colin Brown, ed., (Grand Rapids, MI: Zondervan, 1975) Vol. I, 291-307.

Cullmann, Oscar. *The Christology of the New Testament*. Translated by Shirley C. Guthrie and Charles A. M. Hall. London: SCM Press, 1957.

Cullmann, Oscar. *Christ and Time: The Primitive Christian Conception of Time and History*. Trans. Floyd V. Wilson. 3rd ed., Eng. trans., 1964.

Cullmann, Oscar, "The Kingship of Christ and the Church in the New Testament," *The Early Church: Studies in Early Christian History and Theology* (A collection of essays). Edited by A. J. B. Higgins (Philadelphia: Westminster, 1956.

Cullmann, Oscar. *Jesus and the Revolutionaries*. New York: Harper, 1970.

Cullmann, Oscar. *The State in the New Testament*. London: SCM, 1956

Cullmann, Oscar. *The New Testament: An Introduction for the General Reader*. (Trans. by Dennis Pardee; Philadelphia: Westminster, 1968.

Cullmann, Oscar. AThe Relevance of Redemptive History," Soli Deo Gloria: *New Testament Studies in Honor of William Childs Robinson*. J. McDowell Richards, ed. Grand Rapids, Eerdmans, 1968, 9-22.

D'Aubinge, J. H. Merle. *History of the Reformation of the Sixteenth Century*. H. White, trans. New York: American Tract Society, 1847.

Dodd, C. H. *The Apostolic Preaching and its Developments*. 2nd ed. London: Hodder, 1936); reprint Grand Rapids: Baker, 1980).

Dodd, C. H. *According to the Scriptures: The Sub-Structure of New Testament Theology*. Welwyn, Hetts: James Nesbit and Co, 1952.

-----Dodd, C. H. *The Old Testament in the New* (Philadelphia: Fortress Press, 1952; reprinted 1963)

Ellis, Earl E. *Paul's Use of the Old Testament*. Grand Rapids: Wm. B. Eerdmans Publishing Co., 1957.

Fee, Gordon D. and Stuart, Douglas. *How to Read the Bible for All it Worth*. 3d ed. Grand Rapids: Zondervan, 2002.

Fee, Gordon D. *God's Empowering Presence: The Holy Spirit in the Letters of Paul*. Peabody, MA: Hendrickson, 1994

Foster, Richard J. *Money, Sex and Power: The Challenge of the Disciplined Life* (San Francisco: Harper and Rowe, 1985.

France, R. T. *Women in the Church's Ministry. A Test Case for Biblical Interpretation*. Grand Rapids, MI: Eerdmans, 1995.

Goppelt, Leonhardt. *Theology of the New Testament. Grand Rapids*: Eerdmans, 2 vols. 1976/1982.

Guthrie, Donald. *New Testament Theology*. Downers Grove, IL: Inter-Varsity

Henry, Carl F. H. *Aspects of Christian Social Ethics* (Grand Rapids, MI: Eerdmans, 1964.

Hunter, A. M. *Introducing New Testament Theology*. London: SCM Press, 1957.

Hunter, A. M. *Introducing the New Testament*, 2d ed. SC M Press, 1957.

Jeremias, Joachim. *The Central Message of the New Testament*. London: SCM Press, 1965.

Jeremias, Joachim .*The Sermon on the Mount,* Norman Perrin, trans. Philadelphia: Fortress Press, 1963.

Kümmel, G. E. *The Theology of the New Testament According to Its Major Witnesses: Jesus-Paul-John*. Nashville: Abingdon Press, 1973.

Kümmel, G. E. *Promise and Fulfillment. The Eschatological Message of Jesus.* Dorothea M. Barton, trans. London: SCM, 1957.

Ladd, George E. *A Theology of the New Testament*. Rev. ed, Donald A. Hagner; ed, Grand Rapids, MI: Eerdmans, 1974; Revised ed, 1993.

Luther, Martin. "Ninety Five Theses."

Lewis, C. S. *The Screwtape Letters*. London: Geoffrey Bles, 1942.

Mahedy, William and Bernardi, Janet. *A Generation Alone: Xers Making a Place in the World* (Downers Grove, IL: InterVarsity, 1994).

Marshall, I. Howard. *New Testament Theology. Many Witnesses, One Gospel.* Downers Grove, IL: InterVarsity, 2004.

McCartney, Dan and Clayton, Charles .*Let the Reader Understand: A Guide to Interpreting and Applying the Bible* (Grand Rapids, MI: Baker, 1994.

Minear, Paul S. *Images of the Church in the New Testament*. Philadelphia: Westminster, 1960.

Morris, Leon. *New Testament Theology*. Grand Rapids: Zondervan, 1986.

Morris, Leon. "Reconciliation," *New Bible Dictionary*, 2d ed= Doweners Grove, Inter Varsity Press, 1982.

Newman, Carey C. "Images of the Church in Acts," *The People of God*. Nashville: Broadman, 1991.

Phillips, Timothy and Okholm, Dennis *Family of Faith* (2d ed; Grands Rapids Baker, 2001

Scott, Jr., J. Julius. "Paul and Late-Jewish Eschatology S A Case Study, I Thess 4:13-18 and II Thess 2:1-12," *Journal of the Evangelical Theological Society* Vol XV, Part 3 (Summer 1972), pp. 133-143.

Scott, Jr., J. Julius . "Race Relations, Social Change, and the Church," *Presbuteron* 3 (Spring, 1977), 20-29.

Scott, Jr., J. Julius. "Stephen's Speech and the World Mission of the People of God," *Journal of the Evangelical Theological Society*, 21/2 (June 1978), 131-141.

Scott, Jr. J. Julius. "*Arch 'gos* in the Salvation History of the Epistle to the Hebrews," *Journal of the Evangelical Theological Society*, 29/1 (March, 1986), 47-54.

Scott, Jr., J. Julius."The Cornelius Incident in the Light of its Jewish Setting," *Journal of the Evangelical Theological Society*, 34/4 (December 1991), 475-484.

Scott, Jr., J. Julius. *Jewish Backgrounds of the New Testament*. Grand Rapids: Baker, 1995 (from 1995-2000 this volume was published under the title *Customs and Controversies: Intertestamental Jewish Backgrounds of the New Testament*).

Scott, Jr., J. Julius. "The Church's Progress to the Council of Jerusalem" *Bulletin for Biblical Research* 7 (1997), 1-20.

Scott, Jr., J. Julius. Acts 10:34, A Text for Racial and Cultural Reconciliation Among Christians,@ *The Gospel in Black and White. Theological Resources for Racial Reconciliation*, Dennis L. Okholm, ed. Downers Grove, IL: InterVarsity Press, 1997, 131-139.

Scott, Robert H. "A Broad View of Freedom and a Narrow View of Sin," (unpublished Poem-song, 1994).

Shakespeare, William. AHamlet@.

Sproul, R. C. *Knowing Scripture*. Downers Grove, IL: Inter Varsity Press, 1977.

Stauffer, Ethelbert, E. *New Testament Theology*. Trans. by J. Marsh. London, SCM, 1945.

Richards, Lawrence . *A Practical Theology of Spirituality*. Grand Rapids, MI: Zondervan, 1988.

Turner, Philip. *Sex, Money, and Power: An Essay in Christian Social Ethics*. Cambridge, MA: Cowel Publications, 1985

Taylor, Vincent. *The Names of Jesus.* London: Macmillan, 1953.

Thielman, Frank. *Theology of the New Testament: A Canonical and Synthetic Approach*. Grand Rapids: Zondervan, 2005.

Tozer, A. W. *The Knowledge of the Holy*. 1961

Virkler, Henry A. *Hermeneutics: Principles and Processes of Biblical Interpretation* (Grand Rapids, MI: Baker, 1981).

OTHER REFERENCES

For Further Study

Alexander, T. Desmond, et al, *New Dictionary of Biblical Theology*. Downers Grove, IL: InterVarsity, 2000.

Balla Peter, *Challenges to New Testament Theology*. Tübingen, Mohr Stiebeck, 1997.

Bromiley, Geoffrey W., ed. *Theological Dictionary of the New Testament — Abridged in One Volume*, ed. by G. Kittel and Gerhard Friedrich, 1985 = "Little Kittel."

Brown, Colin, ed. *New International Dictionary of New Testament Theology*. Grand Rapids: Zondervan, 1975-1985, 3 vols. plus index in vol. 4.

Bruce, F. F. *New Testament History*. Garden City, NY: Anchor, 1972.

Caird, G. B. *New Testament Theology. Completed and Edited by L. D. Hurst*. Oxford: Clarendon Press, 1994.

Childs, Brevard S. *The New Testament as Canon. An Introduction*. Philadelphia: Fortress, 1984/85.

Childs, Brevard S. *Biblical Theology of the Old and New Testaments. Theological Reflection on the Christian Bible*. Minneapolis: Fortress Press, 1992.

Danker, Frederick W. *A*. (Revisor and editor of 3rd ed =DBAG) of Bauer, Walter, translated and adapted by Arndt, William F., Gingrich, F. Danker, Frederick W. *A*. Wilbur, and *Greek-English Lexicon of the New Testament and Other Early Christian Literature*. 3rd ed; Chicago: The University of Chicago Press, 2000.

Dictionary of Jesus and the Gospels. Eds., Green, J. B., McKnight, S., Marshall, I. Howard. Downers Grove, IL, 1992.

Dictionary of Paul and His Letters. Eds., Hawthorne, Gerald F., Martin, Ralph P., Reid, Daniel. Downers Grove, IL, 1993.

Dictionary of the Later New Testament and Its Developments Eds., Martin, Ralph P. and Davids, Peter H. Downers Grove, IL, 1997.

Dictionary of New Testament Backgrounds. Evans, Craig A. and Porter, Stanley E. eds., Downers Grove, IL, 2000.

Elwell, W. A., ed. *Evangelical Dictionary of Theology* (Grand Rapids: Baker, 1984; 2d ed, 2001).

Elwell, Walter A., ed. *Evangelical Dictionary of Biblical Theology* (Grand Rapids: Baker, 1996)

Esler, Philip F. *New Testament Theology. Communion and Community.* Minneapolis: Fortress, 2005.

Fee, Gordon D. and Stuart, Douglas. *How to Read the Bible Book by Book.* Grand Rapids: Zondervan,

Ferguson, S. B.,Wright, D. F. Packer, J. I., eds. *New Dictionary of Theology.* Downers Grove, IL: IVP, 1988.

Gingrich, F. Wilber, *Shorter Lexicon of the Greek New Testament.* 2d ed, edited by Frederick W. Danker. Chicago: University of Chicago Press, 1983.

Hasel, Gerhard. *New Testament: Basic Issues in the Current Debate.* Grand Rapids: Eerdmans, 1978.

Marshall, I. Howard. *New Testament Theology. Many Witnesses, One Gospel.* Downers Grove, IL: InterVarsity, 2004.

Marshall, I. Howard. With essays by Kevin J. Vanhoozer and Stanley E. Porter. *Beyond the Bible. Moving from Scripture to Theology.* Grand Rapids: Baker, 2004.

Marshall, I. Howard. *Christian Beliefs: A Brief Introduction.* London: Inter-Varsity, 1963.

Morris, Leon. *The Apostolic Peaching of the Cross. A Study of the Significance of Some New Testament Terms.* 3rd ed, Grand Rapids: Eerdmans, 1965.

Morris, Leon. *The Cross in the New Testament.* Grand Rapids: Eerdmans, 1965.

Neil, Stephen. *Jesus Through Many Eyes. Introduction to the Theology of the New Testament.* Philadelphia: Fortress, 1976.

Stuhlmacher, Peter. *How to Do Biblical Theology.* Allison Park, PA, 1995.

Stuhlmacher, Peter. *Reconciliation, Law, and Righteousness. Essays in Biblical Theology.* Philadelphia: Fortress,1986.

Yarbrough, Robert W. *The Salvation Historical Fallacy? Reassessing the History of New Testament Theology. Leiden*: Deo Publishing, 2004.

SUBJECT INDEX

SCRIPTURE INDEX